School Leadership

School Leadership

A CONTEMPORARY READER

Edited by Joel L. Burdin

SPONSORED BY
THE UNIVERSITY COUNCIL ON EDUCATIONAL ADMINISTRATION

SAGE Publications
The Publishers of Professional Social Science
Newbury Park   London   New Delhi

For information address:

SAGE Publications, Inc.
2111 West Hillcrest Drive
Newbury Park, California 91320

SAGE Publications Ltd.
28 Banner Street
London EC1Y 8QE
England

SAGE Publications India Pvt. Ltd.
M-32 Market
Greater Kailash I
New Delhi 110 048 India

Printed in the United States of America

Library of Congress Cataloging-in-Publication Data

Main entry under title:

School leadership : a contemporary reader / edited by Joel L. Burdin ;
   sponsored by the University Council for Educational Administration.
      p. cm.
   Selected articles from recent issues of Educational administration
quarterly.
   Includes bibliographies.
   ISBN 0-8039-3362-2.   ISBN 0-8039-3363-0 (pbk.)
   1. School management and organization—United States. I. Burdin,
Joel L. II. University Council for Educational Administration.
III. Educational administration quarterly.
LB2805.S417   1988
371.2'00973—dc19   88-19104
                                         CIP

FIRST PRINTING 1989

Contents

Foreword

For over five years, SAGE Publications has published the journals of the University Council for Educational Administration, including *Educational Administration Quarterly (EAQ)*. Several years ago, Mitch Allen, SAGE's executive editor, and I decided that carefully selected collections of recent *EAQ* articles might serve the purpose of exposing especially useful writing to a broader administrator audience than is typically reached by a scholarly journal. *School Leadership: A Contemporary Reader* is the first collaborative fruit of this discussion.

Late in 1986, Professor Joel L. Burdin, on sabbatical leave, temporarily joined the staff of the University Council for Educational Administration. In view of his experience and skills as an editor of the *Journal of Teacher Education,* and his experience as a professor and practitioner of educational administration, I asked him to explore the development of several collections of articles based on the most recent volumes of *EAQ*. This book emerged as a collection of readings with potential interest and use for practicing administrators, graduate students, and professors of educational administration. It contains a wide variety of writing and research styles, organized around the concepts of society, organizations, action theories, and visions. Professor Burdin has done an exceptional job organizing and selecting the material for inclusion. We hope the book exposes the superior work of these contemporary scholars to a broad new audience.

PATRICK B. FORSYTH, *Executive Director*
University Council for
Educational Administration

7

Preface

The chapters in this book are extracted mostly from recent issues of *Educational Administration Quarterly,* articles that I hope will stimulate and challenge those who wish to be thoughtful, effective, and humane leaders, as well as technically proficient and productive administrators.

To become thoughtful and effective leaders, prospective and practicing leaders need to eliminate discrepancies between what they know and don't know. As society's education leaders, they should know about the intricacies of political substance, structures, and processes. They should learn to be effective politicians who can influence and direct policy development, decision making, and implementation. Political action is a critical role for the education leader. There are several political arenas in which society makes decisions about education. Those arenas may be formal units of government, special interest groups, or even blocks of inarticulate peoples who occasionally coalesce into pressure groups. There are many kinds of silent majorities. Increasingly they want to be heard—along with the traditional controlling elites. Administrators need to have a *knowledge* of politics that have become increasingly complex and fluid, and accept the fact that they are politicians as well as super teachers, that they should make a commitment to becoming chief politicians in their particular sphere.

Matching the increasing societal complexity of which the schools are a part is the growing complexity and diversity of education enterprises. To understand those enterprises leaders need to study organizational power, beliefs, values, climate, pluralism, economics, politics, and change. This list is a short one. A long one would include elements of all the "ways of knowing"—the many fields of scholarship. Leaders need to understand both the individual fields and their interrelationships, and then to integrate the knowledge into practice.

Traditionally, education leaders were principal teachers who could coordinate a school. Superintendents were principal teachers whose arena was the school system. Education leaders primarily were school-based leaders. Classical administrative theories in their rudimentary forms worked. As schools increased in size, diversity, and complexity, simple applications of classical theories became inadequate and inappropriate. Theories of *educational leadership* emerged in response to the requirements of large organizations. Theories of educational leadership were developed in recognition of the uniqueness of the education role

9

in society and of education institutions' uniqueness as organizational entities.

In his (Part III) statement, Robert Stout notes that school principals may engage in some 150 disparate and different activities in *one day*. Other kinds of education leaders probably equal that magnitude. No wonder that we call for undergirding theories to provide some integrating, facilitating sense to their individual daily decisions. An additional element in the leader's repertoire is knowledge and skill to develop images of alternative futures. What's expected is the creation of alternative images of what would be "good" for society and its diverse individuals, and leadership, which facilitates movement toward desired futures. At the same time the leader is supposed to maintain the best of past wisdom *and* experience and to maintain the most effective system for contemporary demands!

This book of readings provides an overview of the knowledge, perspectives, and skills of administration. Research and theories can become the basis for creating professional practice that responds, in an integrated and effective fashion, to an amazing array of expectations and to society's arenas in which administrators function or which affect the education arenas. The book's overview may challenge, inspire, and help the leader who wants to be responsive, responsible, and effective. The book's state-of-the-art knowledge base can be a prelude to learning that is helpful now and can start the process of life-long learning, a worthy goal for school leaders, their colleagues, and constituencies.

My hope is that the selections will stimulate and challenge readers to think through the *What*, the *Why*, the *Where*, the *When*, and the *Who* in educational leadership. These "W's" are policy elements in the organization of education. They can become the underpinning of the *Hows:* how administrators delineate tasks, get them done, and evaluate them in order to build in continuing improvement and renewal. My agenda is to encourage administrators to learn the important five "W's" and then do those "things" well for diverse constituents.

My review of *EAQ's* recent volumes has stimulated me. I am reminded that the editor, the writer, and the researcher learn much in the process of preparing to share with the reader. The selections that I have included are arbitrary in some ways, a kind of intuition in practice, and in other ways, there is a kind of applied rationality in that I used a rating instrument that forced me to be more thoughtful than arbitrary. The peer review process used by editors assured me that the intellectual and methodological criteria have been met by the writers.

The writers in turn have made decisions on what is important. Very importantly, they have selected the thoughts, the data, and the research of others to share with us. Theirs is not the last word. They have told us what they read, how they did their research, and what other kinds of scholarship they used. They made it possible for others to build on what they did through replicated research, new laboratorylike research, library research, and field research. The references at the end of the articles are a goldmine for scholars and practitioners! The readers have the last word through their own professionalism through their theory building, research, and practice.

There are some acceptable levels of unevenness in this book. The articles are drawn from several volumes of *EAQ,* and that means several editors and associate editors have determined what particular journals would look like and be like. Their wisdom and choices are reflected in this book. There are gaps and redundancies in content, a function of editors' decisions as well as mine. What the book suffers in style inconsistencies and substantive gaps/ redundancies, the stuff of readings books, it gains in needed freshness, convictions, and directions. This assertion makes me vulnerable to anyone who finds or punches holes in my assertion. Writing and editing make one visible and vulnerable. So be it, if this book attains its goals of contributing to education, to individual students in the vast and varied educational system, and to the emerging profession of education, especially its administrative leaders.

I end this preface with two invitations: (a) When reading this book creates cognitive dissonance (thanks to Leon Festinger for the concept), please take personal action to deal with it; (b) If you are not in the field of educational leadership, welcome and join with those who are building the best education possible for all the people.

A special thanks goes to Patrick B. Forsyth, UCEA executive director, who listened, who raised thoughtful questions, who shared, and who, with other UCEA staff people, facilitated the editor's work. I am grateful, too, to you who will join me in the continuing effort to build the strongest cadre of education leaders possible and thereby make a most vital contribution to the broader field of education and human services and thereby to society and world.

JOEL L. BURDIN

Acknowledgments

Three kinds of acknowledgments seem appropriate as I think of people whose direct assistance made this book possible.

The first, a professional one, acknowledges the professional support of Patrick B. Forsyth, UCEA Executive Director, who provided friendly and competent assistance during the life of this book's conceptualization and preparation. Other UCEA staff people made technical contributions; their warmth made the office a fine place in which to work.

The second acknowledgment is a personal one, to my sister and brother-in-law, Mr. And Mrs. James Nelson. They provided an attractive home setting for my sabbatical and a warm, loving demonstration of "family."

The third acknowledgment is for the host of individuals who make books possible. The contribution of authors is acknowledged in the contents page. Professional writing has its own rewards. I hope that they are very richly rewarded. There are hundreds of anonymous people who made this book possible: editors and editorial boards, colleagues, researchers and practitioners, crisis specialists, secretaries, administrators, spouses and friends, the staff of the publisher, and lots of unrecognized others who collectively and continuously are involved in profession building through knowledge production and utilization. UCEA and the varied education professions are richly blessed with the tens of thousands who work in the broad profession of education and additionally are builders of competence and are researchers and writers. I'm proud to be one of the host of people just noted. Having worked as an editor and publisher for many years, I particularly appreciate the size and diversity of that host.

—J.L.B.

Contributors

ALEXANDER, KERN, President, Western Kentucky University.

ASTUTO, TERRY A., Associate Professor, Teachers College, Columbia University.

BAPTISTE, H. PRENTICE, JR., Professor, University of Houston.

BOYD, WILLIAM LOWE, Professor, Pennsylvania State University.

BREDESON, PAUL V., Associate Professor, Pennsylvania State University.

CLARK, DAVID L., Professor, University of Virginia.

CONWAY, JAMES A., Associate Professor, State University of New York at Buffalo.

DEYOUNG, ALAN J., Associate Professor, University of Kentucky.

DUKE, DANIEL L., Professor, University of Virginia.

FERGUSON, JUDITH, Business Administrator, Princeton Public Schools.

FIRESTONE, WILLIAM A., Associate Professor and Senior Fellow, Center for Policy Research in Education, Rutgers University.

HAAS, JOHN D., Professor, University of Colorado, Boulder.

HOY, WAYNE K., Professor, Rutgers University.

JUNG, RICHARD, Principal, John Burroughs School, St. Louis.

KIMBROUGH, RALPH B., Professor, University of Florida.

KIRST, MICHAEL, Professor, Stanford University.

LOTTO, LINDA S., Associate Professor, University of Illinois, Champaign.

LYSAUGHT, JEROME P., Professor, University of Rochester.

MCGIVNEY, JOSEPH H., Associate Professor, Syracuse University.

MITCHELL, DOUGLAS E., Professor, University of California, Riverside.

MORRIS, G. BARRY, Associate Professor, University of Saskatchewan.

MUTH, RODNEY, Associate Professor, Fordham University.

POPPER, SAMUEL H., Professor Emeritus, University of Minnesota.

STOUT, ROBERT T., Professor, Arizona State University.

WILSON, BRUCE L., Senior Research Associate, Research for Better Schools, Inc.

PART ONE

The Society in Which Leaders Lead

In simpler times education leaders were "above" politics and other aspects of society. The chief administrator was called superintendent of schools. He (*now* he or she) was to run the schools to reflect the community power structure's values, goals, and ways of doing things.

Expectations for the schools were to be kept reasonable. The middle and upper middle class students were to be prepared for college. Poorer students were to be given some vocational training and a bit of basics like English and history. There was to be some entertainment for the community, in sports, music, and drama. People—usually the middle- and upper- middle-class parents— were invited to an occasional open house to hear what the school was doing and how parents could support the teachers. What the school was to do, how, for whom, and when were pretty clear.

Reasonable people understood and supported the schools. In turn, school people were reasonable about expectations: moderate support such as helping with homework, manageable taxes, and enough votes to elect a "good" school board. Everybody who was anybody was reasonable. There was stability and continuity.

Tranquility was shattered as the society underwent a major post-World War II metamorphosis. Now a world power, the United States no longer could proceed in its own ways at its own pace. Dominance was no longer assured by industrial might, mining, and agriculture. The new United States was one of exploding knowledge production and utilization, of expanding service industries, and of proliferating government at all levels. Reversing the exclusive pattern started in our founding years, white males adjusted to the emergence of very active power-seeking by people such as racial minorities, women, and the poor. The courts began to respond to human rights advocacy for all the people, the Congress set programs in motion more adequately to serve the poor, the bilingual, and the handicapped. The media portrayed in stark scenes the realities of inequities in the land of opportunities. The realities entered America's living rooms and ultimately affected the nation's leadership. Institutions, agencies, organizations, and enterprises were caught up in a significant evolution—felt by many to be revolution; by others to be only slightly speeded up reactionary times. The nation did change economically and politically. Its "skins" became darker. Its hair became grayer. Leaders adjusted and adapted. Some dreamed, analyzed, and led the nation to its new promise.

Education leaders found their "world" integrated into the total society. Politicians, judges, caucuses, pressure groups, and activist individuals provided laws, rulings, advice, and demands. Education, to mix metaphors, moved from the ivory tower into the mainstream.

Calls were heard for accountability and excellence. The schools were blamed for not keeping the United States competitive with other nations. An example was the widespread outcry about U.S. education when the Soviets launched Sputnik. They faced demands to catch up with other nations' math scores, match other nations' foreign language proficiency, work harder and longer, undo all of America's ills, and attain everyone's dreams and expectations. The time for action: *now.*

The following series of articles captures some of the essence of the changing society and of the necessary education leaders mandate to be responsibly responsive.

The annotations that follow often were originally printed with the articles.

CHAPTER ONE

Do Political Ideologies Influence Education in the United States?

RALPH B. KIMBROUGH

This article is a preliminary consideration of the influence of political ideologies on education. Following a review of existing research on the politics of education, left-of-center and right-of-center influences are analyzed. The need for expanded research activity on the influence of political ideologies is posited and avenues for inquiry are explored.

Research concerning the influence of political ideologies on education has been greatly neglected. To make matters worse, many educators view the society and politics as "ideologyless," as supported by Bell in his popular book *The End of Ideology.*[1] Most discussions of politics either avoid the motivation question, view political behavior as self-interest based, or simply describe participants as acting from personal preference or a predisposition to act in certain directions. Yet, a politician would seriously damage himself or herself if the only explanation given constituents was, "I had the predisposition to vote that way."

In view of the ideological political movements, past and present, in the United States, this neglected area of research is unfortunate. Our history texts chronicle social movements led by Know-Nothings, Greenbacks, Grangers, Caughlinites, McCarthyites, New Dealers, proponents of Great Societies, and great populists of the likes of Ben Tillman and Huey Long. One can feel the anarchism of Henry David Thoreau's, "If a man does not keep pace with his companions, perhaps it is because he hears a different drummer. Let him step to the music which he hears, however measured or far away." Moreover, politics in our nation has been joined by the ranks of socialists, communists, fascists, conservatives, liberals, and those of other ideologies stimulated by their European cousins. Explored in this article is a preliminary consideration of the question: Do political ideologies influence the nature of education in the United States?

SOURCE: Ralph B. Kimbrough, "Do Political Ideologies Influence Education in the United States?" *Educational Administration Quarterly,* Vol. 18, No. 2, pp. 22-38. Copyright © by The University Council for Educational Administration. Reprinted with permission.

Ideology is frequently defined as a systematic body of concepts in action. This definition differentiates it from idle, "ivory tower" thinking. Thus, extraneous babblings of beliefs that are unrelated to political action are not political ideologies. Ideologies guide people (and groups) in political activity and concern the nature of governance, economics, social systems, education, and other aspects of "what kind of town this should be."

Do ideologies shape political behavior, or are they rationalizations of personal interests? Concerning this question, Agger, Goldrich, and Swanson wrote, "We prefer to make the distinction between ideology and interests rather than between ideological and nonideological interests."[2] Persons may be motivated by personal interests in decisional preferences or by ideology or, when the two are convergent, by both. Moreover, persons who are part of any ideologically oriented political movement are not all motivated by its expressed values. There are various assortments of motives and ambitions.

Just as the abolition of slavery issue in America was attended by idealists, political opportunists, carpetbaggers, and scalawags, the more recent civil rights movement was peopled by altruistic idealists, political opportunists, pseudoliberals, and some self-interested thrill seekers with a variety of motivations. Many people made a lot of money by participating. Of course, there were rationalizations to cover political tracks—in fact, downright demagoguery. All movements are so peopled. Kaufman, for example, felt that the New Left was impaired by those who practiced what he called, "The Politics of Self-Indulgence."[3] These were described as the middle- and upper-class young having moral guilt but without the discipline of reasoned ideology for behavior. Therefore, one may mistakenly condemn an ideological movement as a rationalization for ulterior motives simply because some in the movement are motivated by self-interest.

AMERICAN POLITICS AND EDUCATION ARE INFLUENCED BY IDEOLOGIES

A persistent view that was given much visibility by New Left leaders during the 1960s was that there is no ideological difference between the two national political parties. The study of party ideologies by McClosky and associates demonstrated that this was an erroneous assumption. "Examination of the opinions of Democratic and Republican leaders shows them to be distinct communities of co-believers who diverge sharply on many important issues."[4] They further reported, "Democratic leaders typically display the stronger urge to elevate the lowborn, the uneducated, the deprived minorities, and the poor in general; they are also more disposed to employ the nation's collective power to advance humanitarian and social welfare goals." Republican leaders, however, subscribed "in greater measure to the symbols and practices of individualism, laissez-faire, and national independence" and believed that the human misfortunes of society could best be overcome through reliance on personal effort, private incentives, hard work, and personal responsibility.[5] As well, Field and Anderson demonstrated that national politics varied in ideological emphasis. For example, they found that people expressed greater ideological commitments in the 1964 presidential election (Goldwater vs. Johnson) than in the 1960 campaign (Kennedy vs. Nixon).[6]

Academicians differ concerning the extent to which the general public is motivated by ideologies. The elitists are persuaded that only the leaders hold internally consistent ideologies. The general public is much less discriminating in ideological positions, is more prone to express conflicting beliefs, and is somewhat random in the selection of expressed ideologies as bases of behavior. This view was supported, in part, by the data from the national study by McClosky and his associates who found that the party leaders differed strongly in ideologies, whereas the rank-and-file sample of party members differed only moderately.[7] Converse also expressed agreement with the elitist position.[8]

The populists, however, are persuaded that ideologically based expressions and behavior are characteristic of most of the general public. Brown, Litwak, and Luttbeg are among those who found the rank-and-file citizen thinking and acting from ideological positions.[9] The populists argue that many citizens have consistent views but do not express them in the forms expected by scholars.

Ideologies expressed by citizens indeed may not always fit into the academic mold. Based on their analysis of political behavior in four communities, Agger, Goldrich, and Swanson found eight ideologically oriented political groups that did not fit classical descriptions of political ideology. These groups were: Orthodox Conservatives, Progressive Conservatives, Community Conservationists, Jeffersonian Conservatives, Radical Rightists, Liberals, Radical Leftists, and Supremacists.[10] Ladd conducted in-depth studies of political ideologies in three Connecticut cities (Hartford, Bloomfield, and Putnam).[11] He specifically pointed to the fact that the ideologies did not fit traditional descriptions of political ideologies. Nevertheless, the ideological groups (e.g., conservative parochials, liberal parochials, conservative cosmopolitans, and liberal cosmopolitans) were significant factors in the educational politics of the three communities. The description of politics in Hartford and Bloomfield is of interest to educators because so much of the politics involved the racial integration issue in schools.

In 1962, Lane reported the results of an ambitious study of the ideologies of fifteen "common" men of fictitiously named Eastport, an eastern seaboard city. He concluded that "lest one be deceived by a phrase, there should be no doubt that in Eastport the common man *has* a set of emotionally charged political beliefs, a critique of alternative proposals, and some modest programs of reform. These beliefs embrace central values and institutions; they are rationalizations of interests (sometimes not his own); and they serve as moral justifications for daily acts and beliefs."[12] Also, the "common men" of Eastport had a deep and abiding faith in the process of education.

During the early 1950s some very intensive studies of a small school district were conducted by the central staff of the Southern States Cooperative Program in Educational Administration. One goal of these studies, primarily the responsibility of the author, was to discover the operational beliefs (ideologies) of eleven of the most influential political leaders in the school district.[13] The most powerful groups in the district were engaged in a bitter ideological power struggle to determine "what kind of town are we going to have."

Five of the leaders of the Banking and Legal Interest Group, the most powerful group in the political system, followed adaptations of the classical liberal ideology. They believed in very restricted concepts of government function; were fiscally conservative; held a very simplistic, "basics" concept of schooling; aided efforts to keep educational spending low; and placed emphasis upon individualism, self-reliance, responsibility, and hard work. The three most influential leaders studied in the Emerging Business Group were New Deal (or Fair Deal) liberals. They supported broadened social-welfare functions of government, school consolidation (a divisive issue at that time), increased school financing, broadened curricular offerings, and increased opportunities for education.

One of the most influential leaders was best described as behaving from unadulterated opportunism. Although some observers might describe him, John Barnes (pseudonym), as Machiavellian, this would be a disservice to Niccolo Machiavelli. John Barnes did not want to be the prince; in fact, he was almost completely devoid of social purpose. He used his political expertise (manipulating people, winning over friends, influencing votes) in exchange for a job. As such, he became the "tool" of other influential men in the structure who were the ideological clergy. He was a petty opportunistic politician.

This study was replicated in two school districts in Florida that differed more than one standard deviation in financial effort for education relative to an analysis of local taxes. The difference in civic "conservatism" and "liberalism" between the leaders of the two districts was statistically significant beyond the .001 level; the leaders of the low financial effort district were more conservative than were the leaders of the high effort district.[14] Major interest of the Florida research group for the 1964-70 period focused on the use of the Florida Scale of Civic Beliefs (FSCB)—a 60-item instrument that measures liberalism and conservatism on a single dimension.[15] Use of the FSCB demonstrated that a statistically significant difference in civic beliefs was found between the leaders (and citizens) of the two districts differing one standard deviation in financial effort. In this study it was found that the low effort district had the more conservative beliefs. However, the instrument has not proved to be sensitive enough to differentiate among the specific ideologies held by multiple competing political groups. An instrument developed by Levine has also been used in a number of related studies.[16]

Studies of the influence of "educational ideology" on the nature of schooling are legion. The study by Lee is illustrative[17] He found that "progressive education" and "basic education" were the basis of ideological conflict in the San Francisco school system for a period of several years. Iannaccone and Lutz also reported studies of school district politics and postulated a sacred-secular continuum.[18] The sacred community is characterized by a high degree of consensus and closedness to inputs for change, whereas secular communities have cosmopolitan attitudes with a high degree of openness and momentum toward change.

Some research has been reported in which the historical method was employed. The political history of the New York City schools (1805-1973) by Ravitch is illustrative; however, her analysis did not concentrate on the impact of political ideologies.[19] Bilski traced the great educational struggles between the major parties in England and found that party ideologies rather than the education ideologies of educators were the decisive belief systems in the struggles.[20] In 1964, Goldhammer and Farner reported a political history of Jackson County, a fictitiously named school district of 300,000 population.[21] They described a political system that appeared to grow increasingly into an ideologically based competitive system from 1922 to 1964.

That political ideology is one of the variables influencing the political system in general is supported by the results of empirical and historical research. These studies also suggest that ideologies are changing and that innovative views are emerging; the eighteenth and nineteenth century ideologies (e.g., communism, fascism, socialism) may not be very relevant in understanding the current political struggles about the nature of schooling in the United States.

To say that political ideologies influence society is, of course, to contend that groups influence education within a complex system that is influenced by multiple variables. Power, leadership resources, political structure, personal interests, control of governance, and other circumstances are additionally important variables influencing the nature of schooling.

The visibility of political ideology in school districts is dependent on the extent to which school districts are torn by the regime conflicts concerning "what kind of town this should be." However, in a four-state study, noncompetitive political structures (usually characterized by much ideological consensus) were the most frequently found structures among the twenty-four districts studied.[22] Ladd also found this to be characteristic of Putnam, the small town in his study.[23] In districts marked by a high degree of ideological consensus, political competition primarily involves personality contests for office and competition restricted to economic advantage. Yet, support of the consensus is still necessary for legitimization as a candidate. In still other school districts, an imposed consensus exists in the form of a monopolistic power structure—that is, a singularly led group or coalition (e.g., a ruling political machine, an economic domination, or a ruling coalition) has enough influence with the people to control the ideological basis for local government, including public education.

When any singular political ruling group wins control of the legislative process in a nation, an attempt is usually made to restructure schooling in conformity with the tenets of the ruling system. The Castro regime has achieved much restructuring of the educational programs in Cuba.[24] The Nazi regime restructured German education as did the Bolsheviks following the Russian revolution. The controlling groups of the President and Congress of the United States are no exception to the inevitable attempt of politicians to structure educational legislation in conformity with the prevailing political ideology. After many decades of new liberal ascendancy in Washington, the Reagan administration has astounded observers by its initial success in implanting strong footholds of change toward a classical liberal ideology. This analysis can turn now to a discussion of some illustrative examples of ideological influence upon education.

LEFT-OF-CENTER IDEOLOGIES INFLUENCE EDUCATION

This section consists of a discussion of some left-of-center political ideologies that have influenced the development of education in the United States. The author emphasizes that this is illustrative only and is not intended as a comprehensive coverage of all of these ideologies. A comprehensive discussion of all left-of-center adaptations would be prohibitive in length and, because of limited field research, impossible.

New Liberalism and National
Legislation for Education

As a general ideological movement, "liberalism" in America is a broad, mercurial stream with numerous tributaries. Among these are mainstream new liberals, so-called knee-jerk liberals, democratic socialists, new leftists, and others. Liberalism is a circuslike tent of groups with conflicting ideologies which are forced into coalescence only by the disliked ideologies to the right-of-center.

Mainstream new liberals, unlike classical liberals, reject the concept of a natural law as truth for the society and place faith in the superiority of intelligence as the basis for the good life. Contrary to popularly expressed opinion, mainstream new liberals believe in a capitalistic democracy; however, unlike the Darwinism of classical liberalism, they believe that a person achieves full humanity through a society and government that provide a floor of support for a person's fundamental and derived needs. Consequently, new liberals have supported a broad range of governmentally sponsored social welfare and educational programs to help the poor and disadvantaged enjoy the full fruits of the system, provide the full civil rights guaranteed in the Constitution, and advance humanitarian and social welfare goals. As will be discussed subsequently, mainstream classical liberals will have none of this governmental interference, relying instead on personal self-reliance, hard work, and voluntary organizations to lift up the poor and downtrodden.

During the administration of Franklin D. Roosevelt the New Deal emerged as an expression of new liberal ideology. The New Deal was followed after World War II by the Fair Deal, New Frontier, and Great Society. Although these represented certain continuities of new liberal thought, their political bases included conflicting forces (e.g., pro-war liberals and antiwar protesters in the Johnson administration).

The Johnson administration illustrates perhaps the clearest example of how new liberal ideology heavily flavored by populism influenced the nature of federal legislation for education. In *The Transformation of Southern Politics,* Bass and DeVries wrote that populist ideology held an important influence on President Johnson:

> If Lyndon Johnson was a wheeler-dealer senator who looked out for the moneyed interests in Texas and made a personal fortune of his own, he was also a man who had grown up poor and absorbed from his father the legacy of the populist movement that had its roots in Texas. As a young congressional aide in the 1930s, he had made a point of going to the Senate galleries to listen to the economic radicalism of Huey Long's speeches. His natural instincts for the underdog coincided with his national ambitions as Senate majority leader in the 1950s.[25]

The writer believes that an analysis of political ideologies of leaders in the Johnson and Reagan administrations would reveal decided differences of ideology between the two groups. President Johnson was an early New Deal ideologue who highly revered Franklin D. Roosevelt and is said to have "worshiped" FDR. Key decision makers in the Reagan administration express classical liberal views. Johnson's key economic advisors, for example, were of the post-Keynesian persuasion; whereas Reagan's advisors, for the most part, express a variation of the classical economic view (e.g., supply-side economics). If one could have obtained an operational measure of the ideological beliefs of the most influential executives in the Johnson administration and could compare this with the leaders of the Reagan administration, the difference in political ideology would probably be statistically significant beyond the .001 level. Of course, this is pure speculative opinion. We simply do not have the data. In any event, the passage of massive amounts of educational legislation during the Johnson administration cannot be explained simply as a response to the demanding power of educators or to chance.

Describing ideology as one variable in legislation does not discount the existence of special interests, Machiavellian political techniques, and political compromise involved in educational legislation. In assuming a conspiratorial view, one might attribute the passage of the Elementary and Secondary Education Act of 1965 to business interests desiring profits on education. Business interest in education was obviously at a high point during the early 1960s, and a flurry of purchasing of publishing houses, of performance contracting, and of other "free enterprise" activities was present to "cash-in" on the anticipated legislation. However, basing this explanation entirely on political bossism and greedy businessmen would be erroneous and unfair. The writer is persuaded that the political ideology of President Johnson and of those key leaders in his administration was a powerful motivation.

New Liberalism and School District Politics

Mainstream new liberalism has been a powerful factor influencing the nature of schooling in school districts. This ideology may have been a bulwark of support for the progressive transformation documented by Cremin.[26] The results of the Southern States Cooperative Program in Educational Administration research in the Cheatham County Studies, discussed previously, describe a political system embroiled in an ideological power struggle in which the entrenched "conservative" leaders were challenged by leaders with a new liberal persuasion. The "liberal" leaders strongly supported schools with broadly based programs oriented toward teaching social interdependence and increased opportunities for the less fortunate. They also demanded stronger financial support for education, governmentally sponsored health services, extensive social welfare programs, and numerous other "progressive" changes.

So-called liberal vs. conservative political struggles in school districts frequently result in significant transformations in the nature of politics and education. As an example of this, the rise of a coalition with new liberal leanings successfully challenged the ruling elite of classical liberals of a Florida school district by the writer. This new liberal challenge was a broadsided one and eventually transformed the total way of life in the district. For example, a meaningful planning and zoning ordinance was instituted, public housing for the poor was initiated, parks and playgrounds were greatly expanded, civil rights were supported, and other progressive changes initiated. The provincially oriented educational policies of the old order were "liberalized," a reform model of school governance adopted, "progressive" changes in school programs established, and enlightened programs for racial integration instituted. Analysis of the political ideologies of the leaders of the two political groups competing in this struggle revealed a difference statistically significant beyond the .001 level.

Zeigler and Jennings found in their national sample that school board members were lobbied more frequently by left-wing than by right-wing ideological groups.[27] Liberal groups were actively engaged in the decision making process for some communities included in the study by Agger, Goldrich, and Swanson.[28] In Ladd's study of Bloomfield, Connecticut, the liberal-cosmopolitans failed in their efforts to influence restructuring education for the racial integration of schools. However, their pressure forced the established (more conservative) leaders to make a decision they would not have made without the ideological competition.[29]

In summary, new liberal ideological groups have been actively influencing educational policies in many school districts. Mainstream new liberal groups have favored broad educational curricula consistent with social welfare capitalism and have pressed for compensatory school programs to increase educational opportunities for the less fortunate. New liberals provided very strong support for the broad range of civil rights legislation and litigation that infused massive change in the way colleges and schools are administered. The dual school systems of the South were restructured, women's rights were supported, federal influence on the process of education was greatly strengthened, textbooks were rewritten, crash programs in higher education were initiated to assist minorities and women, and some rather significant changes were made in administrative responsibility, style, and flexibility. Although many leaders on the right supported most of these changes, they were less inclined to use governmental powers in the process.

The New Left Influenced Education

The political pot in America became overheated to the boiling point by the emergence of many ideological groups during the 1960s. One of the political forces that emerged during the 1960s was the New Left. Although the term, New Left, is often applied to any radically left or far left-of-center group, the core of the movement was on university campuses—in particular, the Students for a Democratic Society (SDS). Leaders in the mainstream New Left movement were heavily influenced by existentialism and by feelings of alienation and revolt against the existing social order. Among the tenets of the ideology was emphasis upon participatory democracy and community participation, the use of violence to eliminate enslavement by "the system" and emphasis upon each person making his or her own decisions for self-fulfillment.

Because so little documentation exists, an overall assessment of the influence of the New Left on education is speculative, to say the least. However, radical expressions of the New Left were a challenge that could not be ignored, and this enhanced the power of the less radical left-of-center groups in supporting their programs. For example, environmentalist groups have demonstrated throughout the United States that they are a force to be considered in national, state, and local politics. New Left ideology was noticeable in the alternative school movement during the late 1960s—particularly in the "free school" movement. The movement had a profound influence on the administration of many colleges and universities. Moreover, pressure from the New Left aided those who advocated increased teacher and student rights and conceivably was a factor in court decisions favorable to these objectives.

Most radical social movements, such as the New Left, have some initial political successes followed by a counteraction. By the late 1960s, many legislative sessions were heavily laden with bills to stifle the New Left movement. There is widespread opinion that, in the 1970s, the universities felt a strong backlash in the form of oppressive legislation and lowered financial resources because the New Left activities were centered on their campuses and many professors joined in the movement.

RIGHT-OF-CENTER INFLUENCES ON EDUCATION

Currently, there are several influential ideologies to the right-of-center. One stream of limited influence is consistent with Burkean ideology. According to Auerbach, this ideology figured prominently in Southern politics prior to the Civil War and had some foothold throughout America during that period.[30] Classical liberalism, however, is the predominant ideology to the right-of-center. A third stream is that of those championing classical liberalism who accept, with restraints on desired extensiveness, some of the programs of new liberalism. They are sometimes referred to as "reconstructed conservatives." Currently the new right is a political movement popularly referred to as conservatism with a difference. Although limited in influence in comparison to other right wing groups, the Libertarian party is actively pursuing goals far right of center. Reporting on the loose coalition of groups supporting the Reagan administration, *Newsweek* named the following groups: neoconservatives, GOP establishment, old right, new right, and religious right.[31] Again, space requires that the discussion of right-of-center ideologies be illustrative only.

Modern Conservatism: A Weak but Troubling Influence

In the Burkean modern conservative credo, men are believed to be unequal in mind, body, and spirit, and are creatures of appetite—governed more by emotion than reason—needing a Higher Law administered by an elite. Those things that have stood the "test of time" (the ordeal of history) become the accumulated wisdom of the society; change in this body of wisdom is not sensible. Providence, not reason, should be the source of truth undergirding society. Orders and classes of society are inevitable and, in fact, necessary to give people aspirations. Order and authority are essential defenses against the impulse of mankind to violence.

The tenets of new conservative ideology are evident in varying degrees in groups often identified as "John Birchers," the radical right, or the far right. Wolfinger and associates, who reported the results of a study of these groups, wrote: "For the most part, their influence has not been enduring at the national level. They seem to have their greatest success in local communities, chiefly in intimidating educators and librarians."[32] However, some of the leaders were found to hold key places of influence in party conventions. Wolfinger and his associates reported that the membership of one of these groups was almost unanimously registered Republicans. Not to be overlooked is the probability that the intimidating influence of far right groups prevents educators from making progressive moves in school systems and colleges. Research is needed to determine whether persons of the new conservative persuasion are leaders in entangling sex education, library book, textbook, and other emotionally charged educational issues.

Classical Liberalism (or Liberal Conservatism)

The United States was born in the tenets of classical liberalism, which is popularly known by many labels, such as "free enterprise." The movement was heavily influenced by the social contract theorists (e.g., John Locke). With the persuasive economic views of Adam Smith fitting like a glove, classical liberalism soon enveloped most societal institutions during the nineteenth century. Although somewhat blunted by its chief adversary, new liberalism, classical liberalism is a very influential ideology today. Classical liberalism is a naturalistic-oriented view. Natural man is a sort of Robinson Crusoe beset by the necessity of jungle struggle—inherently individualistic. Being an atomistic collection of individuals, the important relations in the society are contractual, such as those between employer and labor. Government is a social contract and should be governed by the natural law—not Providence. As a reasoning being, man can discover the natural law.

Classical liberalism is a widely entrenched view in the economic (business) sector, and literature is pervasive concerning the influence of business ideology on the structure of education. Fairly exemplary of this literature is Callahan's documentation of how business ideology pervaded the management, organization, and instructional processes of American schools during the first half of this century."[33] During the 1960s, educators experienced a resurgence of the efficiency movement. Such administrative systems as PPBS (Planning, Programming, Budgeting System), PERT (Program Evaluation Review Technique), and MBO (Management by Objectives) were forced upon school systems through legislation, federal guidelines, and school board policies. Gubser described how groups in Arizona with right-of-center ideologies were able to influence the legislature, the state board of education, the state curriculum commission, and the state department of education.[34] For example, high school graduates were required to complete a course in "the essentials and benefits of the free enterprise system." According to Gubser, curricular offerings, textbooks, and instructional processes were controlled and monitored through the state structure.

The Jarvis-Gann Amendment in California, better known as Proposition 13, shows very clearly that right-of-center ideologies can be instrumental in moving people at the state level. From all popularly written accounts, the Jarvis-Gann Amendment was initiated by leaders whose expressed ideologies were to the right-of-center. The specter of a tax revolt has influenced educational legislation in all of the states and has had devastating results in some.

Right-of-center ideologies were visibly reflected in the passage of numerous "accountability related" laws during the 1960s and 1970s. Conservative political leaders supported legislation for such schemes as performance objectives, uniform evaluation, state prescribed courses of study, minimum competency testing, and performance-based certification of teachers. This is not to contend that some self-proclaimed liberals were not involved in passage of these measures.

Some rather influential leaders of the classical liberal orientation favor the freedom of choice movement. One important aspect of this movement is, of course, parental freedom to choose the school for their children. Milton Friedman is among those economists who are providing ideological bases of support for private schools, tuition tax credits, and educational vouchers.[35] However, to contend that all classical liberals support a private school system would be a disservice to many. Many of the strongest advocates of the public school system are reconstructed classical liberals. On the other hand, most classical liberals advocate an efficiently operated school concentrating on a narrowly conceived curriculum of basics as opposed to the rather comprehensive program championed by new liberals.

INFLUENCE OF POLITICAL IDEOLOGIES ON EDUCATION: AN AREA OF NEEDED RESEARCH

This discussion of research about political ideologies leads to two propositions. First, political ideology is an element (among other elements) influencing political behavior and this influences the nature of education at the local, state, and federal levels. Second, there is need for expanded research effort concerning the influence of political ideologies on education. This latter proposition, the needed research of ideologies, forms the concluding comments of this article.

What kinds of political ideologies are found among the states and local school districts? Are these expressed in federal policies affecting education? An important finding from studies conducted to date is that ideologies expressed as bases of political behavior may be different from logically derived, textbook descriptions of ideologies. Moreover, there is evidence of considerable variation of ideology among the states and among local school districts within the states. Additional field research is needed to document and describe the ideologies expressed by community and state leaders that are relevant to the political behavior of these leaders. That is, what are the expressed ideologies that become critical in the pressing public policy issues, including educational policy questions? Finally, there is need to document whether political ideologies influence the formulation and passage of federal legislation.

Educational administrators and other educational leaders are frequently faced with the task of influencing the people to accept educational

policies and practices. Do these leaders use knowledge of political ideologies in the development of strategies to move political systems? Or, is
the tendency to promote leadership strategies designed to outmaneuver
rather than to influence what people believe? One finds in the educational
literature numerous accounts of how pressure groups become entangled
in issues involving financial support, curriculum, and other educational
issues. Yet, much of this literature does not really delve into a full analysis
of differences in political ideology among the groups involved. Emphasis
is, instead, on altruistic slogans concerning how education is good for boys
and girls or how the adversaries are "reactionary" villains opposed to
good, progressive schools. Yet, these descriptions frequently indicate the
possibility of rather deep divisions of political ideology among the political
groups (including educators) of school districts.

How do political leaders decide whether to support, not support, or
remain neutral concerning proposed educational policies and programs?
Are their actions influenced on a compartmentalized set of beliefs about
education? Based on his study of political leaders, the author advances
the hypothesis that, in deciding what is best for educational systems,
leaders are influenced as frequently by their political ideologies as by
their isolated beliefs about the process of education. In a leader's "ideological eye" is a vision of economics, finance, function of government, nature
of the society, and other aspects of what a community, state, and nation
should be (including education). Consequently, when a powerful leader
considers educational policy proposals, he or she may be persuaded more
by how such educational programs will benefit the economy in a perceived
"kind of town this should be" than by altruistic notions about giving boys
and girls a good education. Some research suggests that most community
leaders have given very serious thought to "what kind of town this should
be." How frequently does formal schooling fit into these leaders' perception of the "good town?"

The interaction of personal interest and ideology in the motivation of
leaders should be the basis of further research. Are the expressions of
ideologies a convenient means of concealing selfish interests as some
writers who hold a conspiratorial view of politics have expressed? As
discussed previously, some political leaders are very opportunistic or
otherwise eclectic in their ideological expressions. Some scholars feel,
however, that consistency of expressed ideology is more characteristic of
the elite leadership classes than of the followers. Is the ability to express
well a popularly held political ideology a factor giving rise to leadership?
Are leaders better informed about and more consistent in their ideologies
than followers? This might also be extended to the examination of
hypotheses concerning the relationship of the personally held ideologies
of school administrators to successful performance, tenure, community
leadership, and so on. For example, one might hypothesize that educa-

tional administrators with the highest power rank would express ideologies consistent with the dominantly held ideologies of community leaders. On the other hand, the hypothesis might be that the most highly ranked educational administrators would take an eclectic (or opportunistic) ideological position.

Finally, is the future support of the liberal, progressive tradition in education in a steep decline? Leaders of the new liberal persuasion have for many years been a bulwark of support and defense of a well-financed, broad, and vibrant public education system. They are presently in considerable disarray. Moreover, Owen has written that new liberals may have lost the hope they once expressed that education is a primary resource for uplifting the poor and unfortunate.[36] Although it is too early to predict a long-range trend, there is evidence from Washington to the courthouses of the United States that broad-based, right-of-center ideological viewpoints have taken a new foothold. If so, will educators experience radical changes that will be rather torturous to many of them? Many educators, for example, greatly fear the consequences of legislation to support private schools and colleges through tuition tax credits and other schemes, such as vouchers. Federal programs may be either eliminated completely or drastically restructured. One consolation of these educators, however, is that there is an ebb and flow in the predominance of ideological influence in school districts and the nation. Studies of transformations in power structure show that changes in community politics have been characteristic of many school districts. Thus, educators who fear these impending changes may mount community, state, and national campaigns to further the political ideology of their choice.

NOTES

1. D. Bell, *The End of Ideology* (New York: Free Press, 1962), pp. 399-400.

2. R. E. Agger, D. Goldrich, and B. E. Swanson, *The Rulers and the Ruled* (New York: John Wiley, 1964), p. 16.

3. A. S. Kaufman, *The Radical Liberal: New Man in American Politics* (New York: Atherton Press, 1968), pp. 46-55.

4. H. McClosky, P. Hoffman, and R. O'Hara, "Issues, Conflict and Consensus Among Party Leaders and Followers," *American Political Science Review* 54, 2 (June 1960): 426.

5. *Ibid.*

6. J. O. Field and R. E. Anderson, "Ideology in the Public's Conception of the 1964 Election," *Public Opinion Quarterly* 33, 3 (Fall 1969): 380-389.

7. McClosky, Hoffman, and O'Hara, "Issues, Conflict and Consensus," pp. 406-427.

8. P. E. Converse, "The Nature of Belief Systems in Mass Publics," in *Ideology and Discontent*, D. Apter, ed. (New York: Free Press, 1964), pp. 206-261.

9. S. R. Brown, "Consistency and the Persistence of Ideology: Some Experimental Results," *The Public Opinion Quarterly* 34, 1 (Spring 1970): 60-68; E. Litwak, N. Hooyman, and D. Warren, "Ideological Complexity and Middle-American Rationality," *Public Opinion Quarterly* 37, 3 (Fall 1973): 317-332; and N. R. Luttbeg, "The Structure of Beliefs among Leaders and the Public," *Public Opinion Quarterly*, 32, 3 (Fall 1968): 406.

10. Agger, Goldrich, and Swanson, *The Rulers and the Ruled*, pp. 1-32.

11. E. C. Ladd, Jr., *Ideology in America* (Ithaca, NY: Cornell University Press, 1969), pp. 1-350.

12. R. E. Lane, *Political Ideology: Why the American Common Man Believes What He Does* (New York: Free Press, 1962), pp. 15-16.

13. Reported in R. B. Kimbrough, *Political Power and Education Decision-Making* (Chicago: Rand McNally, 1964), pp. 109-112.

14. R. B. Kimbrough, *Informal County Leadership Structure and Controls Affecting Education Policy Decision-Making*, Final Report, Cooperative Research Project No. 1324 (Washington, DC: Department of Health, Education and Welfare, Office of Education, 1964), pp. 105-112.

15. M. E. Shaw and J. M. Wright, *Scales for the Measurement of Attitudes* (New York: McGraw-Hill, 1967), pp. 307-311.

16. D. B. Levine, "The Relation Between Attitudes Concerning Education and Attitudes Concerning Government and Society" (Doctoral dissertation, University of Chicago, 1963); and D. B. Hubbard, "School Board Member Recruitment, Political Ideology and Voting Behavior: Methodology for Testing Pluralist and Elitist Assumptions" (Doctoral dissertation, Clarement Graduate School, 1970).

17. R. D. Lee, "Education Ideology and Decision-Making in the San Francisco Public Schools, 1956-66" (Doctoral dissertation, Syracuse University, 1967).

18. L. Iannaccone and F. W. Lutz, *Politics, Power and Policy* (Columbus, OH: Charles E. Merrill, 1979).

19. D. Ravitch, *The Great School Wars* (New York: Basic Books, 1974).

20. R. Bilski, "Ideology and the Comprehensive Schools," *The Political Quarterly* 44, 2 (April-June 1973): 197-211.

21. K. Goldhammer and F. Farner, *The Jackson County Story* (Eugene, OR: Center for the Advanced Study of Education Administration, 1964), pp. 1-52.

22. R. L. Johns and R. B. Kimbrough, *The Relationship of Socioeconomic Factors, Educational Leadership Patterns and Elements of Community Power Structure to Local Fiscal Policy*, Final Report, Cooperative Research Project No. 2842 (Washington, DC: Department of Health, Education, and Welfare, Office of Education, Bureau of Research, 1968), pp. 110-113.

23. Ladd, *Ideology in America*, p. 347.

24. M. Carnoy and J. Wertheim, "Socialist Ideology and the Transformation of Cuban Education," in *Power and Ideology in Education*, J. Krabel and H. H. Halsey, eds. (New York: Oxford University Press, 1977), pp. 573-589.

25. J. Bass and W. DeVries, *The Transformation of Southern Politics* (New York: Basic Books, 1976), pp. 8-9.

26. L. A. Cremin, *The Transformation of the School* (New York: Alfred A. Knopf, 1961).

27. L. H. Zeigler and M. K. Jennings, *Governing American Schools* (North Scituate: Doxbury Press, 1974), pp. 99-100.

28. Agger, Goldrich, and Swanson, *The Rulers and the Ruled.*

29. Ladd, *Ideology in America.*

30. M. M. Auerbach, *The Conservative Illusion* (New York: Columbia University Press, 1959).

31. "The Right: A House Divided," *Newsweek* (February 2, 1981): 59-63.

32. R. E. Wolfinger et al., "America's Radical Right: Politics and Ideology," in Apter, *Ideology and Discontent,* p. 262.

33. R. E. Callahan, *Education and the Cult of Efficiency* (Chicago: University of Chicago Press, 1962).

34. M. M. Gubser, "Accountability as a Smoke Screen for Political Indoctrination in Arizona," *Phi Delta Kappan,* 55 (September 1973): 64-65.

35. M. Friedman, *Free to Choose: A Personal Statement* (New York: Harcourt Brace Jovanovich, 1980).

36. J. D. Owen, *School Inequality and the Welfare State* (Baltimore: The Johns Hopkins University Press, 1974), p. 157.

CHAPTER TWO

Excellence in Education: The Opportunity for School Superintendents to Become Ambitious?

ALAN J. DeYOUNG

This article briefly discusses the nature of the recent calls for educational reform and highlights difficulties researchers have had in explaining why earlier educational innovation strategies have not gone as expected. Subsequently, the argument is made that a crucial understanding of the historical development of the public school movement and its current situation is needed better to understand educational functioning and school reform in the United States. In particular, it is suggested that the historical role of the school superintendent is pivotal in predicting the direction of school policy in the "era of excellence." A case study is provided in an attempt to show how current calls for school reform have been utilized by one metropolitan school superintendent to facilitate educational innovation and to solidify his own organizational power within his district. The argument is made that the current context for educational reform provides a historical setting both as a significant alteration of school policy in the coming decade and as a renewed opportunity for many local school superintendents to become ambitious.

Public education in the United States is currently the target for numerous reform strategies, most of which are couched in the language of educational "excellence." Given the various critical reviews the schools have received since 1983, it is sure that attempts at serious reform will be present for at least the next decade. Importantly, while national and state commissions and agencies increasingly make proposals and recommendations for educational change, the governance and administration of educational programs are still the prerogative of the local school district and its administrative head, the superintendent.

SOURCE: Alan J. DeYoung, "Excellence in Education: The Opportunity for School Superintendents to Become Ambitious?" *Educational Administration Quarterly*, Vol. 22, No. 2, pp. 91-113. Copyright © by The University Council for Educational Administration. Reprinted with permission.

Those seeking to investigate and understand how school reform may come about during the rest of this decade can either focus on the political forces external to the school which influence important policy implementation or they can attempt to observe and understand the meaning of the educational excellence reports as interpreted and operationalized at the school building and/or district level. While either of these interrelated topics seems worthy of important considerations, so far the former seems to have gathered most of the academic attention. A number of historians and sociologists for example have studied and written about the social and political origins of the current public interest in restoring educational "excellence" to the schools. For the most part, such appraisals agree that emphasis on science and math in the public school has diminished somewhat during the past two decades. However, rather than suggesting that the public school has been "disarmed," most of these assessments suggest that the goal of providing equality of educational opportunity through the introduction of diverse curricula has inadvertently diluted some more academic offerings.[2] Some scholars go on to identify the noneducational forces responsible for most recent school reform movements in the United States. Several authors argue, for example, that public concerns over high unemployment levels and concern other countries (e.g., Japan) have more productive economies are responsible for the current "scapegoating" of the school in the United States.[3] Such assessments typically note that significant school reform comes about only after the external crisis situation which triggered it has subsided, and that this "boom and bust" pattern of school reform has been visible at least three times during the past 30 years.[4]

The possibility that public education does not deserve the criticism it has received during the past few years should not imply that current calls for school reform will not have real consequences for students, teachers, and administrators in thousands of local school districts. Yet, investigations into the external social and political causes of current educational reform efforts do not easily inform concerning the ways particular school reforms may become interpreted, ignored, or utilized at the district level. Instead, some understanding of the historical antecedents of current reform strategies and their leaders may give us a better viewpoint on the potential success of current calls for educational excellence.

THE POLITICS OF EDUCATIONAL INNOVATION

It is important to realize that local school districts and their leadership have long and distinguished histories of their own in this country and that major national and/or state initiatives in school reform must take place within both current and historical political contexts. The investigation and understanding of how particular school districts may respond to calls for educational excellence may well depend upon the analysis of such factors. What follows will briefly review and attempt to expand theoretically upon much of the recent work accomplished under the framework of educational evaluation and will attempt to illustrate the pivotal role of the school superintendent in current possibilities for significant school reform. The case study then presented will attempt to show the ways much of the current rhetoric on "making schools excellent" has been utilized within one metropolitan school district, both to attempt serious programmatic reform and to enhance the political status of the person most responsible for attempting to facilitate them: the local school superintendent.

Attempts at measuring and understanding the processes of accommodation and resistance to school reform measures prior to current interest in educational excellence have led to a host of significant evaluation studies. These are perhaps responsible for the creation of a whole new subdiscipline within the educational research establishment: that of educational evaluation. Studies done on the factors associated with program implementation during the past two decades have typically focused on successful or unsuccessful methods utilized by local districts to facilitate a variety of mandated federal and state programs including Head Start, PL 94-142, and various school desegregation strategies, among others.[5] Many researchers and reviewers of research now agree that the imposition of many "top-down" educational reforms upon particular school districts has often been less than enthusiastically received and/or implemented.[6] Such studies seem to suggest that local school and community political factors can clearly influence program use and effectiveness, although not always in the way that community, state, or federal agencies typically envision.

The finding that local school districts are resistant to *mandated* program changes or innovations is of course predicted by classical organization theory. That is, school bureaucracies should resist and/or reformulate external efforts at such reforms in an effort to maintain boundaries.[7] On the other hand, recent studies of *voluntary* staffing and curriculum innovation in many public schools have demonstrated that schools can be innovative when they so choose.[8] Schools can and have been innovative when the terms of such innovation have been under their control. In fact, the failure of externally applied rational systems theory to adequately and accurately predict and control mandated school reforms, together with the observation that schools can and do change, seemingly led to the currently popular "organizational decoupling" paradigm used in the analysis of school organization.[9]

The school's ability to minimize, distort, alter, ignore, or circumvent external policy requirements has become almost legendary among educational sociologists and political scientists. The public school has become enviously adept at satisfying or at least appearing to satisfy almost any educational demand presented to it by local communities or the state. As Meyer and Rowan argue:

> Educational organizations have enjoyed enormous success and have managed to satisfy an extraordinary range of external and internal constituents. The standardized categories of American society and its stratification system are maintained, while the practical desires of local community constituents and the wishes of teachers, who are highly satisfied with their jobs, are also catered to. As new constituents rise up and make new demands, these pressures can be accommodated within certain parts of the system with minimal impact on other parts. A great deal of adaptation and change can occur without disrupting actual activity; and, conversely, the activities of teachers and pupils can change a good deal, even though the actual categories have remained constant.[10]

SCHOOL REFORM PROPOSALS IN THE ERA OF EXCELLENCE

The current crusade for educational excellence then suggests a paradox. It is known that schools can change, but that they are often resistant to external policy demands. It is known that educational leaders who create a climate of excellence can affect program effectiveness,[11] yet it is recognized that many school administrators view their role not only as instructional leaders, but also as political agents with an interest in shielding and controlling educational change proposals from destabilizing their institutions.[12]

Perhaps then school reform measures being developed now should be viewed as yet another series of attempts to force unwilling educators to adopt measures about which they are skeptical. Perhaps educational evaluators should continue to look for particular strategies useful in particular schools to institute changes in relatively hostile environments. On the other hand, it is possible that the conventional ways in which social scientists view educational innovations may overlook an important distinction between former program specific mandates for school change and current sentiment for educational reform. What may distinguish these calls is that they are frequently rather diffuse instead of program specific.

Many calls for strengthening public education in the United States today are still at the rhetorical stage, particularly at the local district level. What is seen in many states is the development of an educa-

tional climate conducive to the facilitating of local excellence, in addition
to the strengthening of some existing state control guidelines (e.g.,
teacher certification requirements). While important curricular and staffing changes may be proposed and adopted in many of these local districts,
of crucial importance is that local school administrators in many cases
are involved in making recommendations about programs of excellence
before they become adopted. Such a climate of educational reform, in
which school leaders may be able to lead (rather than respond to)
programmatic mandates, has not been present since perhaps the decline
of "Progressive Education" in the 1940s.[13] Focusing upon how school
leaders do (or don't) become involved in current reform efforts may be the
key to understanding local district success at achieving educational
excellence, as well as the key to predicting the future leadership role(s)
of school superintendents.

ONE HUNDRED YEARS OF THE SCHOOL SUPERINTENDENCY

In a number of ways, the success and importance of American public
education have been integrally linked to the prestige and influence of its
superintendents. Like the public perception of the school's performance,
the past hundred years have seen dramatic reversals in the fortunes of
America's school superintendents. Some have argued that the American
common school movement, which originated in an industrializing and
urbanizing America from the mid-nineteenth century, is perhaps the
singularly most important contribution of the United States to Western
civilization.[14] Those credited (or blamed) for the introduction and implementation of the common school into the lives of most of America's
children were the direct ancestors of the modern school superintendent.
The likes of Elwood Cubberly, George Strayer, and Frank Spaulding are
typically credited with altering what had been primarily a collection of
local, democratic, and voluntarily attended schools into a series of compulsory, age graded, efficient, and professionally managed institutions by
the beginning of the twentieth century.[15]

Inheritors of the millennial movements of the early nineteenth century, leaders of the common school movement to help "Americanize"
immigrants later in the century, and proponents of bringing rational and
efficient school reforms to a country where business values and organization were seen in almost sacred terms by a still Protestant-dominated
America, the "Administrative Progressives" have even been characterized recently as American "Managers of Virtue."[16]

As the "science" of educational administration became well accepted
in the early twentieth century, the professional educators who directed

the public school also became very prominent and important civic leaders during this period. The routes into the superintendency across the nation typically came through a sponsorship network of the "founding fathers" of the public school, individuals who by now moved freely between the world of the university and the world of public education.[17] School administrators were also extremely important in the growth and prominence of "Progressive Education" from the twenties until at least the end of World War II. Public school superintendents were on the cutting edge in proposing and elaborating upon what "modern education" should look like during this period, playing leadership roles in curriculum planning, teacher preparation, and staff development.[18]

Moves to solidify and advertise the professional nature of the public school enterprise and the school superintendency have been important elements in the success of both since the nineteenth century, and this trend has clearly continued during the past three decades. The image of the school superintendent as an instructional leader, popular among many superintendents today, seems clearly reflected in current educational administration preparation programs typically entitled programs in "Educational Leadership," as opposed to earlier programs in "Educational *Administration*." The academic journals read by future educational administrators are full of references to the leadership roles which such professionals must continue to undertake in their organizational lives.[19]

The life histories of the school and its chief officers have not been without significant difficulties. In the early twentieth century, critics of the school were fond of organizing and publishing "school surveys" to embarrass school officials. As some authors point out, however, school administrators and their allies in prestigious colleges of education soon learned to establish their own surveys and to utilize them successfully to argue for more public support to centralize and professionalize local school districts.[20] Since the demise of progressive education, however, escaping public criticism of the purpose and operation of the public school has not been so easy to accomplish. Public schools were heavily criticized during the late 1950s for being "too soft" on students. Educators, it seems, had not pushed hard enough on academic subjects, particularly math and science. After a decade of systematic attention to this "shortcoming," a new wave of student and parent protests emerged, this time claiming that schools had become irrelevant to the real lives and interests of students. During this same period, the demands of numerous minority groups for fuller participation in educational and economic life were keenly felt by public school leaders. Now educators are faced with the task of making schools "excellent."

THE SCHOOL SUPERINTENDENCY IN THE ERA OF EXCELLENCE

As one might expect, three decades of public concern and external intervention into the functioning of local district school operation has dramatically influenced and frequently minimized the superintendent's ability to direct public school policy.

> The Superintendents of the early 1950s guided public education in an era when familiar goals, systems of governance, programs, and professional norms seemed to work. Their code of ethics stressed principles that Cubberly would have applauded: keeping schools out of politics, especially resisting pressure groups; impartially administering the rules; preserving the integrity and dignity of the profession; and keeping the faith that "what happens in and to the public schools of America happens to America" . . . (but) by the late 1960s local school administrators found themselves in an environment both inside the schools and in their communities that was often far different from what they had known. . . . Growing up in a different ethos of professionalism, many had trouble sharing decision making with new and often angry groups that had only recently found a collective voice and preferred confrontation to genteel lobbying.[21]

The "angry groups" referred to above managed to alter school policy-making in America, typically via the imposition of categorical programs directed from outside local school districts. Such programs, coupled with successful demands made by professional and citizen special interest groups, have combined over the past two decades to limit seriously many programmatic leadership interests of the current generation of school superintendents. While the educational opportunities for individual children may have been improved during this period, control and direction of school organizations have become much more problematic for local school districts and school superintendents. Several reviewers of school leadership between 1960 and 1980 in fact describe this period as "The Era of Nobody in Charge."[22]

While generations of school superintendents had earlier been schooled that the public school and its policies were beyond the pale of politics, rarely are such positions visible in the literature of the superintendency today. To be sure, the dynamics of school board and superintendency interactions have been described by academics as "political" for years.[23] But not until the last two decades have inheritors of the legacy of the "great men" in education begun to publicly acknowledge and train for the political life of school leadership. The new "conventional wisdom" seen in the training of school superintendents suggests both the political nature of policy implementation in the public schools and how difficult the role of educational leadership is today. With regard to the former, Rubin argues:

> The policy crisis now confronting the schools is virtually without precedent. Confusion rages over what policies are essential and over the best means of their accomplishment. The unfolding drama is extraordinary because of several remarkable circumstances: the media has mounted a blistering attack on educational ineptness; political candidates at all levels have made education a major issue; the rising clout of teacher organizations has enabled them to exercise unparalleled power; and policymaking itself, once arrived at by consensus, has become a free-for-all.[24]

Perspectives on just how future superintendents should view their prospective roles within such a politicized environment are underscored in the testimony of current superintendents surveyed by Blumberg:

> A seemingly absolute condition of the superintendents (today) is that there are only rarely days when the superintendent is not called upon to make a decision that will create some conflict, or is not involved somehow in conflicts not of his own making. All of this seems to occur irrespective of the person involved. "It comes with the territory." . . . the superintendency today, if it is to be an effective office, must be conceived in political terms, if by that we mean the ability of the incumbent to work with a wide array of conflicting forces so as to maintain the delicate balance upon which the vitality of the school depends.[25]

On the other hand, some educational historians and political scientists suggest that the time may be ripe for a reversal of the poor fortunes of the school and its leadership during the past thirty years. As Tyack and Hansot argue:

> The great irony is that the present could potentially be a favorable time in American history to concentrate on improving the quality of schooling, for after a century of struggling to find enough teachers and build enough classrooms to keep up with the rapidly expanding number of new students, now most communities have surplus space and plenty of trained teachers. . . . The local superintendent, standing at the juncture of outside forces—court mandates, federal and state governments, new professional outlooks—and the local community, can be a critical mediator between the small town and the broader society . . . [and] educational leaders in affluent communities must not only convince parents that public schools are best for their children, but must also persuade taxpayers without children of school age that public schools deserve their support and concern.[26]

Should in fact the time be right for a new consensus on the direction of public schools, leaders seem near at hand. Lingering visions of a glorious past ready for rebirth still appear to be an important component of the legacy of school administrators. The work of Cuban[27] and Pitner and Ogawa,[28] for example, both suggest that images of school superintendents as "interpreters of organization history, interpreters of contemporary events, managers of meaning, and managers of organizational myths and sagas" are important perspectives shared and communicated among such educational professionals.[29] The primary question addressed by those discussing future roles of school superintendents is not *whether* school administrators will ever have important leadership duties in public education, but rather *under what* community *circumstances* is aggressive school leadership possible? Such studies clearly indicate that leadership interests of school superintendents are alive and well and that under certain circumstances can be accomplished.[30]

EXCELLENCE IN EDUCATION:
THE CASE OF BLUEGRASS COUNTY

While speculation concerning the ways local school districts may interpret and utilize (or ignore) the educational excellence reports is visible in national media, very few attempts to document "grass roots" school excellence activities have been published. In the school district under discussion here, the implications and possibilities for significant educational reform are clearly visible.[31]

Bluegrass County lies in the middle of one Southeastern state in the United States, and has a population of approximately 200,000. Of these, about 30,000 are children in the public school system. The economy of this region is primarily based on white collar and service industries, agriculture, and tourism. In addition to a large state university there are a number of smaller private colleges, although interestingly enough, few private elementary and secondary schools in competition with the public system. Compared to the rest of the state, Bluegrass County is rather prosperous, with low unemployment, high per capita income, and a good reputation for scenic beauty.

The school system for the most part shares in the positive economic aspects of the county. While the average state per pupil expenditure in 1983 was $1,880, for Bluegrass County this figure was $2,315. The average percentage of students defined as "economically disadvantaged" in the state for the same year was 36%, but for Bluegrass County, 24%. Average teacher salaries exceeded the state average in 1983 by almost 8%.

Student performance figures for Bluegrass County are also among the region's best. In 1983, over 75% of ninth graders three years earlier graduated from high school, compared to the state average of 66%. Approximately 58% of its high school graduates went on to college, compared to a state average of 44%. While these figures may all be somewhat marginal compared to some metropolitan school districts, local and state political leaders typically cite them as being impressive for a primarily rural state without many large population centers or an extensive industrial base.

Controversies over goals and processes in education recently seen in Bluegrass County have been similar to those observed in many other school districts around the country. In the mid-seventies for example, a number of local teachers, through their NEA affiliate, lobbied for collective bargaining with the school board. Local citizens, headed primarily by the business community, organized to defeat this attempt by helping to elect several new school board members publicly opposed to such a prospect. Another educational controversy in the county revolved around the possible introduction of scientific creationism in the school curriculum. School board elections since 1980 have all dealt in one way or another with this issue.

As in other metropolitan school districts in the United States, redistricting issues occasionally become problematic and Bluegrass County saw much dissent among middle-class parents several years ago. Faced with overcrowding in one of the county's more elite junior high schools, local school officials proposed to bus approximately 100 13- and 14-year-olds into an inner-city school with a high concentration of minority students. For several months predictable arguments over neighborhood property values and lack of cultural events and academic programs of the inner-city school were highlighted in local papers and on television. Although this issue generated much anguish, school district lines were redrawn as proposed.

The most recent educational issue in Bluegrass County concerned the process utilized by the school board in 1984 to hire the current school superintendent. The outgoing superintendent had been in charge of the district's schools for several decades and one indicator of his power and prestige in the community was manifested when the renovated central administration building for the county was named in his honor—long before he was to retire. To suggest that his status in the community was unassailable would be an overstatement. But his ability to influence school policy and deflect serious criticism of his policies in the district was well attested to by both supporters and critics of his administration.

The ability of the previous school superintendent to resist special-interest citizen and teacher groups may have generated the intense concern seen in the selection of the current superintendent. With the announcement of retirement by the former superintendent, a number of citizen groups placed their separate hopes for the introduction of particular school programs in the policies of the new one; at least if they could help hire one whose views was consistent with theirs.

As in other districts around the country, these various special interest groups had a litany of needs which each felt was being ignored within the district. Frustrated in attempts to fund special programs for the gifted, "Citizens for Talented Education" sought an ally in the new superintendent to provide an enriched curriculum for such students. Concerned over "leftist subversion" in the school, the "Falcon Forum" sought a school administrator who would reintroduce the "correct" history of the United States into the school curriculum. Advocates of voluntary prayer in the school hoped for some intervention in school programs and those seeking more funds and programs in computer sciences also expressed interest in such a focus from the soon to be chosen superintendent. Teachers in Bluegrass County had for almost a decade been on the receiving end of school budget cutbacks such as experiencing cuts in their professional leave days made to compensate for declining school revenues. Thus district teachers also expressed great interest in who the new superintendent would be and articulated clearly their desires for a new school leader sympathetic to their ostensibly declining professional status.

The controversy which erupted over the hiring of the present school superintendent however centered not on how he addressed each of the needs of the multiple special interest groups vying for influence in his appointment, but upon the fact that they were excluded from the selection process itself. The school board would not agree to open meetings on the selection of the new superintendent as desired by the several groups just mentioned and many "nonaligned" citizens. Instead the school board contended that an open selection process would make the process too long, would make applicants vulnerable to criticism in jobs they currently held, and would allow only the most vocal of citizen groups in the county to be heard. Besides, argued the head of the school board, as duly elected representatives of the county, it was the duty of the school board to proceed as a group in just such matters as these rather than to have the community as a whole deal with such a labor-intensive process.

In addition to these heated political disputes over educational policy at the local level, Bluegrass County and the rest of the state had been caught up during the previous two years in the educational excellence movement. Both the governor of the state and the state Superintendent of Public Instruction had put together advisory groups to recommend ways and means for improving state educational conditions. The Governor's Council on Educational Reform helped to sponsor several public discussions on how to improve education in the state and the governor urged local citizen groups to pressure state political leaders to provide resources in the legislature for the improvement of public instruction. Also, claiming that the improvement of public education should be a primary goal as well for institutions of higher learning, a state Council on Higher Education committee sponsored numerous citizen forums for suggestions on ways to upgrade education in the public schools.

One method utilized by the governor's task force to stimulate critical discussion of ways to improve state educational efforts was publicly to release educational statistics comparing state educational performance with the rest of the country. For example, this group published 1984 data showing the state had the lowest percentage of its citizens with a high school diploma in the country; ranked 48th among the states in the percentage of its population who were college graduates; ranked 44th among the states in the ratio of pupils to teachers; ranked 31st among the states in average teacher salaries; and ranked 46.5 among the states in expenditures per pupil. Such figures, which might ordinarily be withheld from public view, were utilized by the governor and her staff to support local district efforts at making schools excellent. The governor went on record several times in 1984 and 1985 suggesting that "inferior" local school performance had hindered her efforts at bringing business and industry investments into the state, which she frequently argued was her number one administrative priority.

The new superintendent of schools in Bluegrass County thus came into his new position with local citizens up in arms over the manner in which he was selected, followed a retiring incumbent of legendary status, faced classroom teachers who were at best disgruntled with the school board over their treatment, and was assuming his duties at a time of intense statewide concern and interest in educational excellence. Under "normal" circumstances perhaps such a situation would suggest monumental political problems for the new superintendent, Dr. Winthrup. He was clearly aware of the nature of school political pressures when he came to Bluegrass County. As he put it:

> School superintendents in this country turn over rather quickly. This is especially true with large urban areas. Thus, these types of jobs are available regularly. The average tenure of a superintendent on a national basis is now about five years, I believe. I don't consider that a long time.

However, these potential political pressures surrounding the superintendency had not been apparent to date in Bluegrass County. It is the suggestion contained here that the educational excellence movement has been a key factor in the current situation.

EDUCATIONAL EXCELLENCE AND THE SUPERINTENDENT

Profiling the new superintendent of Bluegrass County is not difficult since his characteristics may be seen as similar to those of many others in the field. Coming from an especially rural, midwest background, Dr. Winthrup is a white, middle-aged, family man with a career history as a classroom teacher, school principal, and superintendent in three smaller school districts. He has an Ed.D., has lectured in educational administration at the university level, is a member of several professional educational administration organizations, and states, concerning the relationship of the superintendent and the school board:

> The Board employs a superintendent to run the school system as per policy direction provided by the Board. I have felt that the Board here understands that relationship very well. I'm not sure that all Board members in (his previous district) understood it as well. By law, the Board has the final authority on all major issues. This would include curriculum, special services, administrative structure, or organizational patterns, etc. However, most boards defer to the judgment of the professional staff in areas where they might lack training or expertise.

When asked to account for the reasons he felt he was chosen as the superintendent of Bluegrass County, Dr. Winthrup responded that perhaps it was due to his interest in developing quality instructional programs. As he put it:

> [The development of instructional programs] should be our primary mission. Too often superintendents get too involved with the minutiae of administration and lose sight of their role as instructional leaders. . . . I've also tried to state publicly on many occasions that my main goal is to provide a comprehensive instructional program of high quality.

Thus, the new school superintendent was able to articulate both politically wise sentiments concerning the nature of school control, while at the same time indicating he had particular instructional objectives he would like to see in place. But Dr. Winthrup's manifest ability to defer to the local school board on matters of policy while at the same time emphasizing his "leadership role" in the school could not have been expected to be enough to appease many local citizens who vigorously opposed the way in which he was chosen. But it can be seen that in his favor politically was the local and statewide efforts to improve public education, since the superintendent was able to turn these to his advantage.

One major citizen group which had increasingly turned its attention to public education was the local business community. Echoing the sentiments of the governor, the Bluegrass County Chamber of Commerce took a keen interest in the new superintendent's role in bringing about educational improvement. On one occasion, leading members of that group went on record in support of local tax increases "if we get what we want out of it." Many local business leaders thus made arguments similar to those of the governor of the state. That is, "quality" educational opportunities must be supported and/or added to the local school district in order to provide better trained employees for local business and to attract future industries to the area. Early on in the superintendent's tenure, the Chamber of Commerce flew Dr. Winthrup to North Carolina. He was sent because it was there in a noted "research triangle" that the collaboration between business and education had been shown to pay off. Importantly then, unlike many earlier efforts to increase revenues for local education, the movement toward educational excellence in Bluegrass County and the rest of the state brought back a champion of the schools perhaps not seen since the early twentieth century: the business community.

According to Dr. Winthrup the keen interest by the local Chamber of Commerce was welcomed. But he argued that their attention did not dictate programmatic changes he would not ordinarily entertain. According to him, if a closer working relationship between business and education would generate support for the educational improvements he desires, then he favors their attention. "When support for educational programs has been low, you take (it) from anywhere you can."

Just as local Chambers of Commerce have been exhorted by their national affiliations to become involved in educational excellence movements during the past two years, professional school leadership organizations have encouraged their members to involve more citizen groups in the educational process. The newly appointed superintendent of Bluegrass County Public Education did just that. According to the superintendent, "The potential for education in this community is unlimited. I believe the time is right for building a new coalition of teachers-parents-community for the improvement of education." To facilitate school reform in his district, the superintendent instituted a number of particular strategies he saw useful in building community support, which he argued were essential for instituting the instructional programs he favored. But the particular form of citizen input put into motion by the superintendent carefully employed national and local calls for educational excellence without dealing directly with groups already demanding particular kinds of educational reforms.

THE BLUEGRASS COUNTY PUBLIC SCHOOLS'
TASK FORCE ON EXCELLENCE

Taking his lead from "an article I read in a professional journal," Dr. Winthrup organized the Bluegrass County Public Schools' Task Force on Excellence. The purpose of this task force, as he saw it, was to involve "all segments" of the community in helping to decide the future of public education in the district for the next "three to five years." The 16 members of the task force came from the business community, from the University, and from the "community at large." The chairman of the task force was very active in the Chamber of Commerce. The goal of the task force was to suggest future policy directly to the Board of Education.

The real field work of the task force however was to be accomplished by six large "task committees." The composition of these committees included representation from parents, students, the school "professional staff," classroom teachers, and other community members. Each of the six task committees was to include approximately 50 members, whose charge it was to break down into smaller groups for discussion of particular issues within the broad categories assigned. These six areas included the committees on: Goals and Curriculum Priorities; Standards and Expectations; School Organization and Special Programs; Personnel; Finance and Physical Plant; and Community Involvement. Topics for policy discussion within each of these areas included those decided upon by each task committee, but more importantly those topics in need of quick attention as demanded by impending state requirements and concerns of the superintendent. For example, the Committee on Personnel[32] was charged with suggesting policy recommendations on inservice education, compensation plans, and evaluation. These were matters the task force felt were "high priorities." In addition, the Personnel Task Committee chose to form subcommittees on the topics of teacher transfer policy, selection, and the use of teacher aides.

Selection and operation procedures for each of the task committees were not left to chance. Early in the school year (1984-1985), those identified by the school superintendent as possibly interested in the mission of the larger task force were contacted and asked to attend a "kick-off" dinner meeting. In addition to those individuals suggested to the superintendent by his staff and members of the task force, the superintendent sent invitations to prominent members of most of the special interest groups alluded to earlier. According to the superintendent, almost half a dozen such groups appeared at his door soon after his arrival in July, each with their list of requests for immediate attention. This dinner meeting was presided over by the task force. Handouts on the mission of the committees, speeches about the importance of the job ahead from two business leaders on the task force, and encouragement from the president of the local school board were included in the agenda. A timeline was also presented to the task committee volunteers at this meeting. This specified the procedures to be used and when these would have to be accomplished in order for committee reports to be useful to the task force. These task committees were to meet quickly to divide into subcommittees; would meet several times each month for approximately five months; would then meet again as a Committee of the Whole to review, revise, and prioritize recommendations; and would then report to the task force at a specified time in the early spring of the current school year. After this presentation of the individual task committee reports, the task force was then to discuss each of them and to make recommendations to the school board based on their deliberations. Of prime importance to the task force were any financial implications of committee recommendations.

In addition to the structuring of task committee assignments and time schedules, the leadership of each task committee and the subcommittees within them was arranged by the staff of the superintendent. In the subcommittee of the Personnel Committee to which this author was assigned, a local school teacher with previous administrative experience on the issue in question was selected to organize and run the meetings. For the most part, an "insider" was responsible for the coordination of each of the other subcommittees of the Personnel Committee as well. In addition, school administrative staff members were assigned by the superintendent's office to provide expertise and/or information to each subcommittee if requested. These members were also consulted near the end of the deliberations regarding the financial impact of the proposals that were about to be made.

The agenda of the early spring meeting of the entire Personnel Committee took several nights to be completed. While some of the subcommittee reports were rather noncontroversial, those dealing with teacher evaluation and compensation were more hotly debated. The teacher compensation subcommittee, represented at the meeting of the Committee of the Whole by several persons from the business community, presented a substantial merit pay program as one of their recommendations. Many committee members identifying themselves as teachers spoke heatedly against merit pay in general and against this proposal specifically. In the committee's final vote, the merit pay component of the teacher salary package was voted down, and in fact was the only subcommittee proposal to be turned back by the Committee of the Whole. Apparently dismayed by the vote, subcommittee members from the teacher compensation group then voted against the rest of their own proposals, arguing that they could not in good conscience recommend to the Board of Education and the taxpayers of the county a program that would raise teacher salaries across the board without some competitive mechanism to instill higher achievement levels within the teaching profession.

According to one member of the task force, the complexity and comprehensiveness of the task committee reports were virtually overwhelming when they were finally presented to that body in April of 1985. In order to summarize and distribute task committee recommendations to the board and to the public, a technical writer was "loaned" to the task force by the state Council on Higher Education in consultation with the superintendent's office. In June, a glossy covered 34-page document was distributed by the task force to the public and the school board which contained goals, priorities, and recommendations of the task force. Attractively fashioned, widely distributed, and appealingly entitled "Forging the Future," this document became the capstone of local citizen and school administration efforts to present to the public the ways Bluegrass County could and should meet local, state, and federal calls for educational excellence.

Among the specific proposals recommended in that document were the introduction of middle schools in the county, the raising of teacher salaries across the board by 5%, the creation of magnet schools within the district, and the immediate purchase of over one million dollars of new computers for the school system. To fund these programs and new equipment purchases, the task force recommended a significant school property tax increase. And even though such an increase was far from assured, task force members interviewed felt quite confident that "what we heard very strongly is that the people of [Bluegrass] County wanted a superior school system and were willing to pay for it."

In the meantime, the superintendent of Bluegrass County enjoyed a relatively trouble free and noncontroversial first year in a school district that, given its history, might well have been difficult to operate. One local newspaper columnist, when queried about a possible feature story on the superintendent, replied that his first year in office did not deserve one. This was because, in her words, he "hadn't pissed anyone off yet." The implication being that the first year of Dr. Winthrup's tenure was not interesting enough to attract the attention of readers looking for a good story.[33]

DISCUSSION

Were the preceding just an ethnographic portrayal of the life and circumstances of a particular school superintendent in the United States, attempting to generalize this case study to national trends in education might be suspect. That is, the most ethnographically responsible discussion at this point would concern itself primarily with internal consistencies and inconsistencies and other points of information/observation of interest to school officials in the study itself. On the other hand, some readers of this case study might be more interested in how the experiences of Dr. Winthrup do or don't coincide with the particular experiences, leadership strategies, and/or innovative mechanisms typically employed by incoming school superintendents.[34] While it is certainly hoped that the Bluegrass County case might contribute to the established literature on school superintendent styles and situations, the analytical interests of this work have been somewhat more ambitious. It is suggested that the case of Bluegrass County may illustrate the particular options available to school superintendents to regain new leadership initiatives in public education in this era of excellence. While the linking of this case study to a still evolving educational movement may seem tenuous, it also seems quite plausible. Obviously, only further observation and analysis can gauge its adequacy and accuracy.

To this point, the case presented here argues that Dr. Winthrup's success in Bluegrass County stems from several sources. Clearly he is aware of the political nature of the school superintendency and its complexity, the characteristics emanating from the history of school/community relationships during the past thirty years, and the search for excellence as a phenomenon visible in his own school district. In addition, his identification with professional school leadership organizations, and his belief in the programmatic leadership mission of the superintendency clearly suggest his location within the historical traditions of nineteenth- and early twentieth-century schoolmen. The success to date of Dr. Winthrup, however, stems from the particular historical opportunities offered and taken during the late 1980s in the educational excellence movement.

One factor in favor of Dr. Winthrup's efforts was that the public was willing to raise, or at least willing to consider raising, taxes to fund educational improvement. Such publicly visible sentiments have rarely been seen in most of the United States for at least a decade. This has certainly been the case in Bluegrass County. Importantly, Dr. Winthrup managed to use the renewed interest of the business community and the public in general to defuse the demands of previously vocal special interest groups by visibly pursuing educational agenda items identified as most pressing, according to the national excellence reports. Dr. Winthrup publicly acknowledged the relationship between economic development and education, and visibly was supported by local business elites.

Not only did the new school superintendent manage comfortably to ride out potentially disruptive community influences during his first year of office, but through the task force Dr. Winthrup was able to spearhead a concerted effort at educational reform. Virtually every curricular and staffing innovation which the superintendent desired was put forward by the citizen task force—in which he had such a strong influence. Significant movement in directions favored by the superintendent were also accomplished in the only two programmatic policy areas pursued independently of the task force. These were in the areas of computers in the school (subsequently merged back into one task force committee), and developing more formal partnerships between businesses and particular schools.

By effectively and silently helping to introduce significant proposals for school reform under the auspices of the task force the superintendent was not only able to distance himself technically from policy proposals which he favored, but also was able to minimize those strident voices earlier calling for particular changes. His office supplied the "hard facts" and administrative advice to community members as they went about their discussions, yet he continually couched his participation in the proceedings of these groups as advisory and administrative in nature. Thus, although the handiwork of his administration was continuously visible in the affairs of each task committee, when the final report was handed to the school board, he was not to be held primarily accountable for its recommendations. Rather, he was able to argue, its contents came from citizen deliberation. Whenever the hard decisions were eventually to be made by the school board concerning future curricular and staffing needs, he would not officially be in a position to take the responsibility for them, although there seems little doubt he would be credited with helping to bring about whatever educationally excellent programs were to be adopted.

It was attempted early in this article to suggest the organizational and contextual forces which have operated historically to influence school policy in the United States. Similarly, an argument has been fashioned that contemporary climates for educational change and innovation must be seen in the light of the institutional and organizational histories where such changes are expected to occur. Although it is quite possible that the dynamics of education in Bluegrass County are idiosyncratic, this article proposes a more theoretical approach to viewing the relationship between the history of public school organizations and their leadership. This stance places the case study presented here in a comprehensible and valuable position for those seeking to understand and evaluate local educational policy.

In the title of this article, the question raised was, "Is the time right for school superintendents to become ambitious?" Clearly in some states and some local districts, preexisting political and contextual factors may militate against the ability of even the most politically adept superintendent to bring about new leadership initiatives during the era of excellence. Where states have taken the upper hand, where local superintendents have already worn their welcome thin, or where politically powerful superintendents may be able to wait out current calls for excellence, perhaps little initiative at the local level can be expected in the coming years. As well, should state and local governments continue to be called upon to replace lost federal social service dollars, tax revenues needed to help fuel the cost of new educational innovations may be harder to come by even if accompanied by a national mood to improve public education. However, given the public climate for educational improvement, and recognizing that many school superintendents believe seriously in reestablishing their leadership roles in the public school, the current movement to once again make American education excellent may in fact provide many of them with the opportunity to become ambitious.

NOTES

1. The title of this manuscript is respectfully adapted from one published by Elizabeth Cohen entitled "Open-Space School: The Opportunity to Become Ambitious," which appeared in *Sociology of Education* 46 (Spring 1973): 143-161. Special thanks are extended to Richard Angelo who made several substantive recommendations which hopefully improved this manuscript.

2. M. Kirst, *Who Controls our Schools?* (New York: Freeman, 1984).

3. M. Raywid, C. Tesconi, and D. Warren, *Pride and Promise: Schools for All the People* (Westbury, NY: American Educational Studies Association, 1984); and H. Shapiro, "Capitalism at Risk: The Political Economy of the Educational Reports of 1983," *Educational Theory* 35 (1985): 57-22.

4. F. Keesbury, "Who Wrecked the Schools? Thirty Years of Criticism in Perspective," *Educational Theory* 34 (1984): 209-217.

5. A. Lantz, "Effectiveness of Strategies to Encourage an Innovative Education Program," *Educational Evaluation and Policy Analysis* 6 (1984): 53-61; and A. Davis and M. Smith, "The History and Politics of an Evaluation: The Colorado Learning Disabilities Studies," *Educational Evaluation and Policy Analysis* 6 (1984): 27-37.

6. D. Cohen and M. Garet, "Reforming Educational Policy with Applied Social Research," *Harvard Educational Review* 45 (1975): 17-43; G. Papiagiannis, S. Klees, and R. Bickel, "Toward a Political Economy of Educational Innovation," *Review of Educational Research* 52 (1982): 245-260; and J. Murphy and P. Hallinger, "Policy Analysis at the Local Level: A Framework for Expanded Investigation," *Educational Evaluation and Policy Analysis* 6 (1984): 5-13.

7. R. Corwin, "Education and the Sociology of Complex Organizations," in *On Education: Sociological Perspectives*, D. Hanson and J. Gerstle, eds. (New York: John Wiley, 1967); and C. Bidwell, "The School as a Formal Organization," in *Handbook of Organizations*, J. G. March, ed. (Chicago: Rand McNally, 1965).

8. D. Messerschmidt, "Federal Bucks for Local Change: On the Ethnography of Experimental Schools," in *Ethnography in Educational Evaluation*, D. Fetterman, ed. (Beverly Hills, CA: Sage, 1984).

9. W. Seidman, "Goal Ambiguity and Organizational Decoupling: The Failure of 'Rational Systems' Program Implementation," *Educational Evaluation and Pol-*

icy Analysis 5 (1983): 399-413; and J. Meyer, W. R. Scott, and T. Deal, "Institutional and Technical Sources of Organizational Structure: Explaining the Structure of Educational Organizations," in *Organizational Environments*, J. Meyer and W. R. Scott, eds. (Beverly Hills, CA: Sage, 1983).

10. J. Meyer and R. Rowan, "The Structure of Educational Organizations," in Meyer and Scott, *Organizational Environments*, p. 92.

11. R. Edmonds, "Some Schools Work and More Can," *Social Policy* 9 (1979): 28-23; and M. Rutter, P. Maughan, J. Mortimer, and A. Smith, *Fifteen Thousand Hours: Secondary Schools and Their Effect on Children* (Cambridge, MA: Harvard University Press, 1979), p. 7.

12. F. Wirt and M. Kirst, *The Political Web of American Schools* (Boston: Little, Brown, 1972).

13. D. Ravitz, *The Troubled Crusade: American Education 1945-1980* (New York: Basic Books, 1983).

14. L. Cremin, *The Genius of American Education* (New York: Random House, 1966).

15. M. Katz, *Class, Bureaucracy and Schools* (New York: Praeger, 1971); and D. Tyack, *The One Best System* (Cambridge, MA: Harvard University Press, 1984).

16. D. Tyack and E. Hansot, *Managers of Virtue* (New York: Basic Books, 1982).

17. R. Rose, "Career Sponsorship in the School Superintendency" (Doctoral dissertation, University of Oregon, 1969).

18. Ravitz, *The Troubled Crusade*.

19. R. Campbell, L. Cunningham, R. Nystrand, and M. Usdan, *The Organization and Control of American Schools*, 5th ed. (Columbus, OH: Charles E. Merrill, 1985).

20. Tyack and Hansot, *Managers of Virtue*.

21. *Ibid.*, p. 232.

22. F. Wirt and M. Kirst, *Schools in Conflict* (Berkeley, CA: McCutchan, 1982).

23. G. Counts, *The Social Composition of Boards of Education* (Chicago: University of Chicago Press, 1927); and D. Easton, *Frameworks for Political Analysis* (Englewood Cliffs, NJ: Prentice-Hall, 1965).

24. L. Rubin, "Formulating Educational Policy in the Aftermath of the Reports," *Educational Leadership* 42 (October 1984): 7-10, p. 7.

25. A. Blumberg, *The School Superintendent: Living with Conflict* (New York: Teachers College Press, 1984).

26. Tyack and Hansot, *Managers of Virtue*, pp. 251, 252.

27. L. Cuban, *Urban School Chiefs Under Fire* (Chicago: University of Chicago Press, 1976).

28. N. Pitner and R. Ogawa, "Organizational Leadership: The Case of the School Superintendent," *Educational Administration Quarterly* 17, 2 (1981): 45-65.

29. Campbell et al., *The Organization and Control of American Schools*, p. 210.

30. R. Campbell, "Time for Vigorous Leadership," in *Bad Times, Good Schools*, J. Frymier, ed. (Kappa Delta Pi, 1983), mimeo.

31. Ethnographic data for this study came primarily from the author's involvement as participant-observer for a citizen task force on educational excellence, put together by the local school superintendent. In addition, information utilized to describe the context for educational policy here came from newspaper accounts, interviews with key informants, official school board records, school documents,

and testimonials given at public meetings. As is typically the case in ethnographic work, entering conceptualizations of what would be found did not correspond with later analyses. In retrospect, the case study presented here, and its interpretation, are vastly different than what the author expected to observe and describe. In order to protect several sources who chose not to be identified, all names and locations presented in this discussion are fictitious.

32. The author of this article was a member of the Committee on Personnel.

33. Questions of validity and reliability are typically the first ones raised in any ethnographic account, including case studies. Because most of the data for the preceding account came from participant observation and interviews, there are no "official" sources for much of the preceding, except what I have in my field notes. One typical method of "reality checking" in ethnographic work is to submit written accounts or manuscripts based on participant observation to those whose actions have been described and discussed. In order to help improve the description and analysis provided here, this study was read and critiqued by two different members of the "Bluegrass County Task Force on Excellence," including the school superintendent himself. As well, several key community members instrumental in the bringing of Dr. Winthrup to Bluegrass County also read the preceding account of factors instrumental in his hiring. Comments and corrections to factual details in the preceding were all included in the final version of this manuscript.

34. Blumberg, *The School Superintendent,* p. 57; C. Miskel and D. Cosgrove, "Leader Succession in School Settings," *Review of Educational Research* 55 (1985): 87-105; and R. Carlson, *School Superintendents: Careers and Performance* (Columbus, OH: Charles E. Merrill, 1972).

CHAPTER THREE

State Educational Governance Patterns

JOSEPH H. McGIVNEY

Several attempts to present a theory of the state politics of education have led to mixed results. These past attempts at theorizing about or modeling in the literature are reviewed and synthesized in a reconstructed framework based on the theoretical underpinnings of Tonnies and Weber. The developed framework also integrates and explains several studies that have heretofore been viewed as in conflict.

To continue the process of developing a theory of the state politics of education—a theory that describes, explains, and predicts educational governance change—a model embracing and explaining a number of conceptual relationships needs to be elaborated. This article continues in that vein of theory development and contains three major sections: (1) a general review of the current state of the art, (2) the development of a model along with the consideration of the efforts of others who have worked toward this goal, and (3) the application of extant data to the model.

THE STATE OF THE ART

The link between politics and education has long been recognized. The Greeks placed education in a role instrumental to the political order. Plato in *The Republic* spoke of the relationship between the educational system and the political order in observing that education was a means to a harmonious state. Modern philosophers, too, like Chairman Mao, have reviewed the relationship of education and politics in a similar vein. The link between politics and education has long been noted from a variety of perspectives.

However, in the United States, a successful attempt to sever the connection between education and the political arena was a part of the reform era (1880-1920). The educational progressives were in large part

SOURCE: Joseph H. McGivney, "State Educational Governance Patterns," *Educational Administration Quarterly*, Vol. 20, No. 2, pp. 43-63. Copyright © by The University Council for Educational Administration. Reprinted with permission.

responsible for promulgating the myth that politics and education should be separate. They exerted efforts to divorce or separate education from politics and did so with considerable success. These reformers elevated education to a higher position than politics; in their view, education was too important to be left to or be affected by the politicians. In the stream of reform that led to the city manager, merit systems, and the other reforms, the education reformers developed a notion of the professional model of schooling that was to put an end to the political control of schools. This reform was focused on and had its legal ties to the state level of government. Indeed, in the crucial policy areas of school finance, school district organization, and the certification of professionals, the state's role was to grow from this important reform base in education.

By the late 1920s, many educational reforms were well under way under the guise of the professional model of education. It was not until 1959 that Thomas Eliot published an essay about the need for the study of education from the vantage point of political science. His essay marked the beginning of research into the politics of education. Considerable work has been accomplished along these lines in the last 25 years, but much more effort on the state politics of education is needed.

For many reasons, the study of the state politics of education, in particular, is critical to the field of the politics of education. Most important is the fact that the United States Constitution reserves to the states and the people those powers not expressly or implicitly conferred on the federal government. Since education is not mentioned in the Federal Constitution, education is legally a state function, and local school districts as such are creatures of the state. The local school districts receive much financial and in-kind support. Because the states receive aid from the federal government, the politics of education at the state level should be examined from a perspective that recognizes that the state is not only a regulator but also a regulatee—it is controlled by other factors in its environment including the local and national levels of government.

Indeed, state-level educational structures and processes have been subjected to heavy influence from the federal government over the last three decades. The 1950s, 1960s, and 1970s reflected increasing national influence on education. This is clearly illustrated by the NDEA legislation of 1957, the ESEA legislation of 1965, and the Handicapped Legislation of 1975. These acts illustrate the recent past growth of the national government's involvement in education. Although several studies of the impact of these federal thrusts have been undertaken, Berke and Kirst[1] were among the first to pay attention to the vertical aspects of the educational finance structure (in viewing the states as their units of analysis) and to show the vast inequities in allocations of federal monies to the states and, in turn, to localities. Recent federal-level policies and decisions under the Reagan Administration portend to add even greater pressure on state governments to decide what educational policies to follow.

The literature on the state politics of education can be divided into two major categories: (1) that describing the political structures, processes, and environments of states; and (2) that dealing with theory building.

Descriptive Studies. Most of the research undertaken to date has been in the form of case studies. Bailey,[2] Usdan,[3] and Masters[4] all contributed important case analyses of the state politics of education. These researchers reported on the six states of New England and the states of New Jersey, New York, Illinois, Michigan, and Missouri. In addition, Wiley[5] described New Mexico's system for state educational decision making. He examined the power of educational interest groups at the state level and also investigated the structure of educational organizations and the formation and means of coalitions. Only in a very limited way, however, did Wiley and others mentioned above examine the process of policymaking within the broader formal structure of government. Wahlke[6] and Ferguson[7] have considered the process of policymaking within the formal structure of government but did so within a more inclusive context than education. In like fashion, Donnelly,[8] Fenton,[9] Key,[10] Jonas,[11] Lockard,[12] and Munger[13] all have discussed general policymaking for several states, but they, too, have provided little elaboration on educational policymaking.

Milstein and Jennings' work[14] added depth to earlier studies investigating educational policymaking at the state level of government. They studied a single state, New York, and their results have limited generalizability. They did, however, provide an important lead to other investigators with their finding that the legislation in New York State tended to play a central role in educational policymaking. This result helped verify similar findings of Fahey in California.[15] In 1974, Iannaccone and Cistone[16] summarized the literature on the politics of education and devoted 11 pages to the state educational politics. Campbell and Mazzoni's Educational Governance Project[17] contributed several cases that described policymaking at the state level for the public schools. The states in this project included California, Colorado, Florida, Georgia, Massachusetts, Michigan, Minnesota, Nebraska, New York, Tennessee, Texas, and Wisconsin. Beyond the case studies, Campbell and Mazzoni's work also included two other volumes[18] that reported their comparative analysis of state policymaking for the public schools and set forth several state governance models for the public schools. A study of New Jersey's educational finance changes[19] has provided a rich description of New Jersey's state politics of education and updated the prior work of Bailey on that state.

Two voluminous but somewhat esoteric compilations replete with data on education in the states were published by the National Education Association in 1969. The first volume[20] traced the development of each of the 50 state departments of education and the central school agencies of Puerto Rico, American Samoa, Guam, the Panama Canal Zone, and the Virgin Islands since 1900. The second volume[21] dealt on a nationwide basis with 16 areas of concern to all state departments of education. Both volumes helped fill a vast void in the availability of data on the state politics of education. Unfortunately, however, no study or analysis has yet been found that ties those data together in a workable framework. Thus, the potential of these two volumes remains unexploited.

Wirt[22] annotated most of the previously published literature on the state politics of education. He also provided new data showing how the legal outputs of the political process varied by state.[23] He provided not only more refined legal data,[24] but also presented his school centralization scale. Other studies providing additional descriptive analyses will be elaborated in the next section because of their relevance to theory development.

Conceptual Models. Considerable effort has been expended thus far in conceptualizing the area of state politics of education, and many writers have cited the need for analyses of the study of the politics of education. Some of these have also noted the heuristic value of Easton's systems model, for example, that provides a model for asking appropriate questions and for finding appropriate ways of seeking answers about political activity. This model provides a framework for viewing policymaking as an interactive process. Milstein and Jennings, and Campbell and Mazzoni have utilized systems models to describe their data, but since systems models are not strong in explanatory power, their theoretical contribution has been limited.

Another type of model was developed by Ziegler and Johnson.[25] Inspired by the work of Dye,[26] they presented a systematic, comprehensive, and well researched quantitative analysis of educational policymaking in four American states. Their study incorporated systems theory, economic analysis, group theory, legislative process research, and attitudinal and behavioral studies in exploring two basic models: the economic and the legislative. They found, unlike Dye, that the economic model was inadequate in explaining changes in educational expenditures from previous levels; instead, the changes from their analysis were a joint product of social, political, and economic variables. They also developed a legislative model that included the variables of per capita income, state level revenues per capita, and a number of structural variables including urban percentage of the total population, Hofferbert's cultural enrichment factor, a Gini index, and the federal percentage of total welfare expenditure. Moreover, individual legislator behavior was related to several types of variables (personal, structural, and environmental). Unfortunately, however, although their data base included four states, they were able to get legislative roll call data in only one state. In addition, this effort was further limited in that it was not longitudinal.

Iannaccone[27] published his provocative conceptual framework in the volume *Politics in Education.* He built upon the work of Bailey, Usdan, and Masters, and used their studies of eleven states in formulating a four-stage typology of linkage structures for studying the state politics of education. The typology included the following categories of linkages: Type I—disparate, with a locally based linkage structure; Type II—monolithic, with a statewide linkage structure; Type III—fragmented, with a statewide linkage structure; and Type IV—syndical, with a statewide linkage structure. Iannaccone noted that the politics of education in states appears to develop over time along a continuum from Type I to Type IV, and he also noted that movement from stage to stage in the educational arena accompanied changes in the larger political system of state government. However, because he described two different typologies in which the sequence of stages III and IV were reversed, the user of his model is left with the problem of two different conceptualizations of the long-term secular trends in society. In the first instance, Iannaccone cited Tonnies's *gemeinschaft* (community)-*gesellschaft* (larger society) continuum and placed Type III at the most advanced end *(gesellschaft)* following Type IV. But when he further discussed the four-stage typology, he made no mention of *gesellschaft* and Type IV was considered to be the most advanced secular stage, in this case following Type III. This contradiction may well be related to problems other researchers have encountered with Iannaccone's conception of the fourth stage of his typology.

In an article, McGivney[28] provided more graphic and explicit descriptions of the stages in Iannaccone's typology, and further conceptualized the stages as influence structures. More importantly, he included an integrated set of decision-making concepts—initiation, information, accommodation, and legalization—along with his treatment of the typology. McGivney explained each of the decision-making concepts and then related them to the influence structure concepts which were derived from empirical studies of states at each of the stages. Each stage in the Iannaccone typology was, thus, extended to include a corresponding influence structure and decision-making process.

This treatment of the notion of legalization in the state politics of education fits well with the efforts of Wirt, whose work was based on the analysis of massive numbers of laws pertaining to education in each state. Wirt[29] constructed a School Centralization Scale that was based on the laws of each of the 50 states (circa 1970). He set up his index for classifying states on a seven-point scale using 36 areas of school policy gathered from statutes, constitutions, and court opinions of the states as a basis for his examination. In a sense, Wirt has provided a scaled measure of McGivney's concept of legalization. What the state laws revealed about state versus local control as indicated in the Wirt study seems to verify the available case-study findings on state and local control.

Kirst and Somers[30] used data associated with the politics of Proposition 13 in California to apply and refine Olson's[31] interest group theory and Riker's[32] coalition theory. They noted that California did not and may never fit Iannaccone's fourth stage. They suggested that a fifth stage be added to Iannaccone's construct that they labeled a "collective" stage. In a similar vein, Mazzoni[33] observed that Minnesota had also not yet and may never pass through Iannaccone's fourth stage. He further saw Minnesota following California's pattern as a state aid collective.

Conclusion. The study of the state politics of education has clearly begun to emerge and be recognized as a serious and important field of study. The set of case studies and conceptual models presented here form a base from which research yet to be accomplished in the state politics of education can begin.

The available data and conceptual models have yet to be completely integrated into a clearly articulated and theoretically based conceptual framework. But with such a conceptual base of the state politics of education, scholars may be better able to study as well as predict and plan for change and continuity in educational governance in the future. Hopefully, work in this direction will characterize future efforts in studying the state politics of education.

In the next section, a developmental model of the state politics of education that attempts to integrate and synthesize the work that has been done to date and to reconceptualize the latter stages of Iannaccone's typology will be set forth. The model was explicitly developed from the theoretical insights of earlier scholars whose work has proven to be enlightening to more recent efforts in the state politics of education.

MODEL DEVELOPMENT

In this section, the reconstruction of a developmental model of the state politics of education will be undertaken. The notions of Tonnies and Weber, herein referred to as "the centralization imperative," will serve as a foundation for the revised typology.

The Centralization Imperative. The centralization imperative appears to be driving most private and public organizations toward an increasingly bureaucratic character in their structures. Consequently, educational policymaking systems and organizational structures over the long term are becoming more bureaucratic, specialized, and centralized. Because of the legal and historical significance of educational policymaking at the state level, the centralization imperative has and will probably continue to impact structurally at that level. For example, the rapid decrease in the number of local school districts and the growing percentage of state-level funds for the support of education over the last several decades are two prominent reflections of the impact of the centralization imperative on the public school system in the United States. The centralization imperative is not a new conception. Tonnies and Weber are but two of the earlier scholars who foresaw the development of this imperative.[34] They believed that society was set on an undirectional course that would ultimately lead to an urbanized, industrialized, bureaucratized, and governmentally centralized order.

Tonnies' thesis was that great cultural systems of the world have a life cycle that emerges with *gemeinschaft* and ends with a period of *gesell-schaft*.[35] The *gemeinschaft* period is typified by family and rural village life, and the *gesellschaft* period is characterized by city, national, and cosmopolitan life. In the earlier period, family life and a home-based economy are the essential elements. There is a feeling of sentiment and respect toward past generations or *gemeinschaft*. In the period of *gesell-schaft*, this close attachment to time and land becomes disconnected, and the growth of commerce and industry lead to the development of the city and cosmopolitan and national orientations. It is the continuous development in this direction that Tonnies considers to be the process of urbanization.

The main features of the move to urbanization-centralization are as follows. The anonymous mass of people represent the original and dominating power which creates the places where they are found: the houses, the villages, and the towns of the countryside. From this, the powerful and self-determined individuals of priests, artists, scholars, and merchants arise. It is through the merchants that the technical conditions for the associations of independent individuals and for capitalistic production are created. The merchant class is by nature, and mostly also by origin, urban and national as well as international—it is more cosmopolitan and not local or placebound in its orientation. Later, all social groups and, at least in tendency, the whole populace acquire the characteristics of *gesellschaft*.

Persons alter their outlooks as the locus and focus of significance in their daily life changes through restless striving. Concomitantly, along with this metamorphosis in the social order, a gradual change of the law takes place in meaning as well as in form. The rational will of *gesellschaft* or contractual relationship becomes the basis of the entire system. The rational will of persons and collectives combine with the authoritative will of the state to create, maintain, and change the legal system. Thus, (1) the forms of law change from a product of folkways and mores or the law of custom into a purely legalistic law, a product of policy; (2) the state and its departments, large aggregate associations, become the only agents of the law; and (3) the people at large are subjected to changes in adapting to new and national legal constructions.

In Weber's view,[36] military, religious, political, and judicial institutional systems are functionally related to the economic order in a variety of ways. For Weber, modern capitalism's institutions appear to be the very embodiment of rationality in the form of bureaucracy. The large corporation is rivaled only by the state bureaucracy in promoting rational efficiency, continuity of operation, speed, precision, and calculated results. And, all this goes on within institutions that are rationally managed and in which combined and specialized functions occupy the center of attention. Yet, the whole structure is dynamic and anonymously compels people to become specialized experts or professionals with the need to have special training for a career in specialized channels. Persons are thereby prepared for absorption in the socializing and working processes of the bureaucratic machinery.

Weber explained the trend toward bureaucratization that gained momentum in Europe at the beginning of the modern period when those royal leaders who most relentlessly took the course of administrative bureaucratization tried to consolidate their power. But significantly, he stated that the decisive reason for the advance of the bureaucratic form of organization had always been its purely technical superiority over other forms of organization. As compared with collegial, honorific, and avocational forms of administration, trained bureaucracy was clearly superior. And, as far as complicated tasks were concerned, paid bureaucratic work was not only more precise but, in the last analysis, it was often more economical than even formally unremunerated honorific forms of service. This was so according to Weber because bureaucratization offered, above all, the possibility for carrying through the principle of specializing administrative functions according to purely objective considerations. Individual performances are allocated to functionaries who have specialized training and who by constant practice obtain more and more skill.

The second important element set forth by Weber was society's need for predictability or certitude of behavior. This need could best be met by modern bureaucracy. The peculiarity of modern culture, and specifically of its technical and economic basis, demands a high level of calculability of results. The more complicated and specialized modern culture becomes, the more its external supporting apparatus demands the personally detached and strictly objective expert. Weber concluded that these trends were pervasive throughout society and were not limited to the state organization alone—they permeated all social institutions. In sum, Weber made a strong case for viewing bureaucratization as the general process by which the modern world was becoming ever more centralized.

Tonnies and Weber both concluded that society will continue to emerge along the lines of urbanization, centralization, and bureaucratization. Therefore, any developmental typology of the state politics of education must reflect the impact of ongoing and long-term trends. The revised typology or model that follows takes into account Tonnies' and Weber's notions as sketched above.[37]

The Revised Model.   At the outset, it should be understood that the first three stages in the revised model have all been verified or validated by studies undertaken after the original Iannaccone framework was developed.[38] However, the fourth stage of the Iannaccone typology, which was derived from the organization and functioning of the Illinois School Problems Commission, appeared functionally only for a short period of time, and it has never been verified or tested in subsequent inquiry. Indeed, observers of the scene in Illinois have described other organizational arrangements and procedures for developing educational policy in Illinois which seem more appropriately to fit the second or third stage in the model.[39] Moreover, recent studies (e.g., Kirst and Somers, and Mazzoni) have revealed that Stage IV, which was based on the Illinois School Problems Commission data, was not useful in explaining recent shifts in either California's and Minnesota's influence structures or decision-making processes. Thus, there is a need for major reconceptualization after the third stage. Before that task is begun, the structure and processes of the first three stages of the typology—those that have been empirically validated—will be reviewed.[40]

In the disparate structure (or Stage I), educators represent their own district first of all. Thus, the major distinction in the boundaries of the political subsystem is a geographic one. Moreover, customary behavioral patterns reflect a high preference for localism. Interaction with legislators is maintained in the pursuit of activities which increase (or at least do not decrease) the local school district's perception that the results of the decision-making processes of the state agencies are consistent with local control. Indeed the legislators themselves are very localistic, tending toward *gemeinschaft* relationships that are extant in the constituencies that elected them.

In the monolithic structure (or stage II), educators represent the interests of education on a statewide basis. Thus, the fundamental boundary distinction of the educational political subsystem is based on a closely knit set of interest groups and not on geography. Customary patterns of behavior reflect a high preference for professional educational leadership on a statewide basis. High interaction among the leaders of the monolithic structure (which is composed of a set of associations usually including the statewide NEA affiliate, the state school boards association, one or more state associations of school administrators, and one or more voluntary citizens groups such as the PTA) and high interaction between the leaders of the monolithic set of interest groups and the leaders of key committees in the state legislature take place in pursuit of activities which increase, or at least do not decrease, the monolith's perception that the results of the decision-making process are consistent with those of the monolith. Clearly, this political system of the state has evolved away from a purely *gemeinschaft* orientation, but it maintains many of its values such as local control. The state agencies are seen as mechanisms for coordinating policies which remain biased in favor of local (rural-village) interests in spite of some shift away from the *gemeinschaft* relationship of Stage I.

In the competitive structure (or Stage III), school board groups, one or more teacher groups, school administrators, parent groups, and other groups represent their own interests, some of which are always competitive, on a statewide basis. The basic boundaries of the educational political subsystems retain a distinction along educational interest group lines, but the consensus among the component lobby groups has evaporated. Moreover, new and/or formerly latent groups tend to become active, such as parochial school interests. Thus, customary patterns of behavior reflect different sets of preferences (teacher welfare vs. reorganization and property tax relief although most of the educational interest groups continue to couch their demands in the rhetoric of increased pupil payoff). In addition, interaction among the leaders of the different interest groups sharply decreases while the interaction between the leaders of the educational interest groups and the leaders of the legalizing agencies of government increases. All are in pursuit of activities that increase (or at least do not decrease) each interest group's own perception that the results of the decision-making process are consistent with those of its own interest group. Interpersonal trust between groups is low, and the need for law and contractual relationships is high even though much freedom of choice and interpersonal relations are shared within groups. This stage is moving even closer toward *gesellschaft*.

With increasing bureaucratization, the formerly competitive educational interest groups will still represent their own interests, but the linkage to legalizing agencies will change first to a loose collective of public educational interest groups. In some states this could be a loose coalition of public and private groups. It is also possible that an interim governmentally enacted policy development agency—in which both public and private educational interest groups would be given representation—

could be created, and such an agency would also have representation from governmental officials of both the executive and legislative branches. This "Blue Ribbon Commission" approach has been used with great success in the United Kingdom, Canada, and the United States as a mechanism for gaining support for new policies or forms of governance. Most important, however, would be the lobbies represented at the state, regional, and local levels. In the beginning of this revised conceptualization of Stage IV, interaction would be high among the members of the education lobby in concert with legislators and the representatives of the chief executive—similar to that described by Kirst and Somers in California and by Mazzoni in Minnesota. Over time, however, increasing influence is gained by or is delegated to the bureaucracy as the former lobby becomes more and more the bureaucracy. The bureaucracy then pursues activities which increase (or at least do not decrease) the members' perceptions that the results of the decision-making process are consistent with those of the bureaucracy. In short, conflict is accommodated through an impersonal, rational, and legalistic process which process becomes increasingly dominated by the bureaucracy. *Gesellschaft* has arrived and with it bureaucracy itself has taken control over policy and programs.

Most students of the politics of education would agree that these structural stages or types appear to evolve sequentially over time. That is, in the nineteenth century almost all state level public education policy decisions were made within the disparate structure. Even today, the educational policy decisions of some states are make within a disparate type structure. Moreover, state-level decisions for most big cities are made in this type of political-geographic framework. This is because the political processes of highly populated urban cities such as New York City or Chicago contain holistic, rational bureaucracies which require coordination by local political leaders who assert jurisdiction in general overall policy areas including educational programs, even while being increasingly dependent on the state for funding.

However, as the long-term trends continue their movement toward centralization, many states develop educational political structures that go beyond the disparate structure to the monolithic structure and some states have, in fact, advanced to the competitive stage or structure. Beyond this, at least one state (Hawaii) operates in the centralized, bureaucratized fourth stage as outlined above, and others may soon follow. If not immediately into the fourth stage, then states may well move to a temporary, instrumental structure similar to Kirst and Somer's "collective" (or what they called Stage V) prior to moving to the fourth stage. California with Proposition 13 and Minnesota, too, may be entering such a temporary structure or the early phases of the Stage IV. The recent U.S. Supreme Court decision on the tax deductibility of certain private school expenses for Minnesotans may well prompt efforts by all elements of the educational arena to coordinate their educational policy demands. Eventually, when a policy development mechanism bridging educational and political groups emerges, the revised model predicts that bureaucratization will follow.

THE REVISED MODEL IN THE LIGHT OF EXISTING DATA

In this section, the studies culled from the literature are used as data to validate the model. Twenty-one states have been described in existing studies and Hawaii's structure is sufficiently known to include it as the archetypic example of Stage IV. Some states, such as Massachusetts and New York, have been studied at least twice, each during different time periods, and thereby provide data to test the framework at two or more stages. In addition, there are available longitudinal data for New York, California, and Wisconsin.[41] In this section, 22 states are classified by stage (some more than once), based on the time when the data were published. After this classification, the states are also cross-classified by Wirt's School Centralization Scale (SCS) to show the close relationship between the revised typology or model and Wirt's measure of centralization of school governance.

Case Studies Classified by Stage.   In Figures 3.1 and 3.2 are reported the 21 states classified in terms of the revised model (Figure 3.1) and in terms of Wirt's SCS (Figure 3.2). Five New England states are included in Stage I, as is Florida. Florida, however, was classified both as Stage I and Stage III by Campbell and Mazzoni. However, the available data indicate that Florida is more likely to be at Stage III than at Stage I.

The states of New York, New Jersey, Rhode Island, Missouri, Tennessee, and Texas clearly fall in the second stage. Georgia is shown to be straddling Stages I and II, but since most of the educational issues reported in the Georgia study were in Stage II, Georgia more appropriately falls in that category as well.

In Stage III, there are 10 states—Michigan, New Mexico, New Jersey, California, Minnesota, New York, Wisconsin, Florida, Nebraska, and Massachusetts. Michigan was first described by Masters and then by Campbell and Mazzoni. In both cases, it was found to be at the third stage. New York and New Jersey were originally found to be in Stage II based on Bailey's description. New York was later assigned to Stage III by Campbell and Mazzoni and New Jersey was revealed to be at Stage III in Richard Campbell's study. The Florida case has already been discussed above, and Florida should be included in Stage III. Colorado was jointly classified as at Stages II and III by Campbell and Mazzoni. In this case,

	Stage I	Stage II	Stage III	Stage IV
Type of Influence Structure	Localistic Decentralized	Statewide Monolithic	Statewide Fragmented	Statewide Bureaucratized
Decision-Making Process Loci of Accommodation	Each Local Unit and Legislature	Informal Statewide Coalition	Governor Legislature Courts	Bureaucracy
Case Studies Bailey et al.	Ma, Vt, NH, Me, Ct	NY, NJ, RI		
Masters et al.		Mo	Mi	Il
Wiley			NM	
Campbell & Mazzoni	Fl	Tn, Tx Ga	Ca, Mi, Mn, NY Co Wi, Ne, Fl, Ma	
Kirst & Somers Mazzoni				Ca, Mn

Figure 3.1: The Stage of Evolution for 21 States as Classified by Iannaccone, Campbell et al., and McGivney

the researchers may have examined Colorado at a time of transition with
some issues at Stage II and others at Stage III. Massachusetts was
classified to be at Stage III by Campbell and Mazzoni, but one wonders
what criteria were used to make that judgment in that much other
evidence in the Bailey and Siegel studies suggests that Massachusetts'
decision making remains highly responsive to the local (or a disparate)
orientation. Hence, Massachusetts should be considered in Stage I on the
weight of evidence. Nebraska is classified in Stage III although the extent
to which the more than 1300 local districts remain viable units for
educational decision making can be questioned. Clearly, more data on
this state is called for, but because there is only one study on Nebraska,
it will be classified in Stage III until other significant data or case studies
show it to be otherwise.

    Illinois is shown to be in Stage IV. That was Iannaccone's classification
based on his reading of Master's description of the Illinois School Problem's Commission (SPC) as a locus of conflict resolution. Subsequent data
have revealed that the SPC has not continued to function as the locus of
accommodation. Thus, Illinois should probably be reclassified at Stage II
based on other data relevant to the state.[42] Also shown at the beginning
edge of Stage IV in Figure 3.1 are California and Minnesota. Kirst and
Somers, and Mazzoni, respectively, have described recent issues in these
states and have suggested a "collective" type of behavior on the part of
educational groups. This may connote a transitional type prior to bureaucratization or the early phases of Stage IV.

McGivney		WIRT'S SCS						
Iannaccone		0	1	2	3	4	5	6
Stage One								
Connecticut	2.68			x				
Massachusetts	2.73			x				
Maine	3.09				x			
New Hampshire	3.13				x			
Vermont	3.17				x			
Stage Two								
Missouri	2.84			x				
Texas	2.88			x				
Rhode Island	3.21			x				
Georgia	3.24			x				
Illinois	3.32				x			
Tennessee	3.48				x			
Stage Three								
Wisconsin	3.62				x			
New York	3.63				x			
California	3.65					x		
Colorado	3.79					x		
New Mexico	3.79					x		
Nebraska	3.81					x		
Michigan	3.85					x		
New Jersey	3.87					x		
Minnesota	4.10						x	
Florida	4.19						x	
Stage Four								
Hawaii	6.0							x

Figure 3.2: Revised Classification Using Wirt's School Centralization
Score for each of 21 States for Which a Case Study Has Been
Found plus Hawaii

The reconceptualized fourth stage in the state politics of education
typology appears to be a viable and useful substitute for Iannaccone's
earlier conceptualized Type IV. It fits well in considering Switzerland,
West Germany, and Australia, all of which function as highly bureaucratized political systems in terms of education. Canada seems to tend
more strongly toward state-level activity than does the United States,
although not quite to the degree of the other three countries just noted.[43]
In summary then, the framework outlined above seems to possess
explanatory value in terms of most extant case study data. To be sure,
Florida, Massachusetts, Illinois, and Nebraska are problematic cases for
classification purposes, but the revised model seems to clarify placement
of even these states.

The Revised Model, Case Studies, and SCS. Figure 3.2 reports the analysis of the classification of 21 states and Hawaii by the revised model and

with SCS scores. In the figure, California and Minnesota are grouped with the Stage III states because that was their classification at the time Wirt's data were collected. If Wirt's scale analysis was updated, it would more likely show a shift toward greater centralization at the state level due to great changes in these states' educational laws in the 1970s. Hawaii, by definition, is the only present example of a clear-cut Stage IV state. Although no case study data describing its educational politics has been found, common knowledge of its educational governance system justifies its inclusion in the fourth stage as an example of that level of development.

In Figure 3.2, 20 out of the 22 states classified were found to correspond with the results of Wirt's School Centralization Score (SCS) analysis. That is, with the exception of Missouri and Texas, as the states appear from Stage I through Stages II and III, their SCS scores increase accordingly. But the association should not be firmly ascertained from this analysis. One must remember that many states have undergone major political change in the 1970s and early 1980s. Case data and Wirt's scale analysis need to be updated at least every decade in order to keep current with critical changes in the decision-making structures for educational governance in the states. In California, Massachusetts and New Jersey, there are recent examples of extremely important changes in the educational governance sector that reflect a further shift away from local control to greater state control and greater involvement of the professional educational bureaucracies in educational decision making. Such developments should be monitored and included in further tests of the revised model of the stages of development in the state politics of education.

CONCLUSIONS

That the revised framework proposed in this article possessed explanatory power was indicated in the analysis of the case study and quantitative data discussed above. Its predictive value is less certain. Although the first three stages have been verified, the fourth stage (the bureaucratized, rational, legalistically structured stage) has only one state (a former monarchy) to exemplify it. California and Minnesota seem to be moving in the direction of the fourth stage or to be entering a preliminary phase of it. Operationally, Minnesota's Educational Consortium has shown the state's ability to cooperate and share expertise, at least in some areas. It bears watching for signs of further consolidation of school districts and for the further integration of private schools into the decision-making arena of education. In California, San Jose's recent bankruptcy suit may portend further consolidation or a state takeover of schools in that state. The pressures for state-level financing and school reorganization flowing from Proposition 13 will continue to force policy makers to seek solutions along the lines of regionalization, greater state financing and control, and even possibly state takeover. The Australian model might serve to tease out some of the structural-political options available to California. In any case, a return to an earlier stage of development seems to be clearly out of the question in that state.

The revised model presented above should be tested in a number of other ways. First, fresh case studies examining critical issues should be conducted. These issues should be researched from an historical perspective to insure the capturing of data on a state's development (or lack thereof) over time. Second, comparative, quantitative, and longitudinal studies focusing on variables that measure the secular, centralizing trends—including certain variables that reflect unique aspects of educational organization and finance—should be considered. These variables should provide measures of change on a statewide basis in the areas of governmental centralization, economic growth, urbanization, bureaucracy, and political culture. Also, studies of the joint functioning of public and private educational systems should be undertaken. Ireland, Australia, Canada, and Switzerland are examples of countries where various public-private mixes are operating.

The locus of decision making for education is shifting increasingly toward the state level. It is important to learn more about the environment, structures, and mixes of political power appropriate to educational policy development and implementation in the future. A refined typology of the state politics of education is an important part of that quest for knowledge.

NOTES

1. J. S. Berke and M. W. Kirst, *Federal Aid to Education* (Lexington, MA: Lexington, 1972).

2. S. K. Bailey et al., *Schoolmen and Politics: A Study of State Aid to Education in the Northeast,* The Economics and Politics of Education Series, Vol. 1 (Syracuse, NY: Syracuse University Press, 1962).

3. M. D. Usdan, *The Political Power of Education in New York State* (New York: Institute of Administrative Research, Columbia University, 1963).

4. N. A. Masters, R. H. Salisbury, and T. H. Eliot, *State Politics and the Public Schools: An Explanatory Analysis* (New York: Alfred A. Knopf, 1964).

5. T. Wiley, *Public School Education in New Mexico* (Albuquerque: Division of Government Research, University of New Mexico, 1965).

6. J. C. Wahlke et al., *The Legislative System: Explorations in Legislative Behavior* (New York: John Wiley, 1962).

7. L. C. Ferguson, *How State Legislators View the Problem of School Needs* (USOE, DHEW, Cooperative Research Project No. 532-8166, 1960).

8. T. C. Donnelly, *Rocky Mountain Politics* (Albuquerque: University of New Mexico Press, 1960).

9. J. H. Fenton, *Midwest Politics* (New York: Holt, Rinehart and Winston, 1966).

10. V. O. Key, *Southern Politics: In State and Nation* (New York: Alfred A. Knopf, 1949).

11. F. Jonas, *Western Politics* (Salt Lake City: University of Utah Press, 1961).

12. D. Lockhard, *New England State Politics* (Princeton, NJ: Princeton University Press, 1959).

13. F. Munger, *American State Politics* (New York: Thomas Y. Crowell, 1966).

14. M. M. Milstein and R. E. Jennings, *Educational Policy-Making and the State Legislature: The New York Experience* (New York: Praeger, 1973).

15. L. J. Fahey, "The California Legislature and Educational Decision Making" (Unpublished Ph.D. dissertation, Claremont Graduate School, 1968).

16. L. Iannaccone and P. J. Cistone, *The Politics of Education*, State-of-the-Knowledge Series, 10 (Eugene, OR: ERIC Clearinghouse for Educational Management, 1974).

17. For the *Educational Governance Project* Ohio State University, 1974, see: (general) R. Campbell, *State Policy Making for the Public Schools: A Comparative Analysis* (1974), 423 pages; (general) R. Campbell, *State Governance Models for the Public Schools* (1974), 228 pages; (California) J. A. Aufderheide, *State Policy Making for the Public Schools of California* (1974), 113 pages; (Colorado) L. C. Moffatt, *State Policy Making for the Public Schools of Colorado* (1974), 80 pages; (Florida) F. DePalma, *State Policy Making for the Public Schools of Florida* (1974), 112 pages; (Georgia) G. V. Branson, *State Policy Making for the Public Schools of Georgia* (1974), 112 pages; (Massachusetts) P. M. Siegel, *State Policy Making for the Public Schools of Massachusetts* (1974), 198 pages; (Michigan) E. Hines, *State Policy Making for the Public Schools of Michigan* (1974), 176 pages; (Minnesota) T. L. Mazzoni, *State Policy Making for the Public Schools of Minnesota* (1974), 218 pages; (Nebraska) R. Farrar, *State Policy Making for the Public Schools of Nebraska* (1974), 84 pages; (New York) E. R. Hines, *State Policy Making for the Public Schools of New York* (1974), 173 pages; (Tennessee) G. Branson, *State Policy Making for the Public Schools of Tennessee* (1974), 109 pages; (Texas) G. Branson, *State Policy Making for the Public Schools of Texas* (1974), 106 pages; and (Wisconsin) D. Brown, *State Policy Making for the Public Schools of Wisconsin* (1974), 103 pages.

18. R. Campbell and T. Mazzoni, *State Policy Making for the Public Schools* (San Francisco: McCutchan, 1976).

19. R. W. Campbell, "School Finance Reform in New Jersey" (Unpublished Ph.D. dissertation, Syracuse University, 1978).

20. J. B. Pearson and E. Fuller, eds., *Education in the States: Nationwide Development Outlook* (Washington, DC: NEA, 1969).

21. E. Fuller and J. B. Pearson, eds., *Education in the States: Nationwide Development since 1900* (Washington, DC: NEA, 1969).

22 F. M. Wirt, "Education Politics and Policies," in *Politics in the American States*, H. Jacobs and K. N. Vines, eds. (Boston: Little Brown, 1976), pp. 284-348.

23. F. Wirt, "Policy as Value, Region and History, in American States" (Paper prepared for Midwest Political Science Association, Chicago, April, 1978).

24. F. N. Wirt, "What State Laws Say About Local Control," *Phi Delta Kappan* (April 1978): 517-520.

25. H. Zeigler and K. F. Johnson, *The Politics of Education in the States* (New York: Bobbs-Merrill, 1972).

26. T. R. Dye, *Politics, Economics, and the Public: Policy Outcomes in the American States* (Chicago: Rand McNally, 1966).

27. L. Iannaccone, *Politics in Education* (New York: Center for Applied Research in Education, Inc., 1967).

28. J. H. McGivney, "The State Politics of Education: Toward an Emerging Theory," *Planning and Changing* 8, 2 (Summer 1977): 66-84.

29. See Wirt, "What State Laws."

30. M. W. Kirst and S. A. Somers, "Collective Action Among California Educational Interest Groups," *Education and Urban Society* (Summer, 1982).

31. M. Olson, Jr., *Logic of Collective Action* (New York: Schacken Books, 1965).

32. W. H. Riker, *The Theory of Political Coalition* (New Haven, CT: Yale University Press, 1962).

33. T. L. Mazzoni, "State Government and School Policy Making in Minnesota" (Paper presented at the annual meeting of the American Educational Research Association, Los Angeles, California, 1981).

34. Several other social scientists such as Tocqueville, Marx, Durkheim, and novelists such as Kafka in Europe and Steinbeck in America noted and decried this inexorable societal transformation.

35. F. Tonnies, *Community and Society (Gemeinschaft und Gesellschaft),* C. P. Loomis, trans. (New York: Harper and Row, 1967). I borrow quite liberally from Loomis; some words and phrases are verbatim.

36. M. Weber, *From Max Weber: Essays in Sociology,* Gerth and Mills, trans. (Princeton, NJ: Princeton University Press, 1958). Once again I rely on and borrow from the translation of Gerth and Mills, including words and phrases.

37. The centralization imperative has been challenged by modern writers such as Toffler, *Future Shock* and *Third Wave,* and Naisbitt, *Megatrends,* who see "trends" toward other forms of organization and/or more decentralization a la cottage industries. But they are not saying that hierarchy and bureaucracy will disappear; rather the shift is away from overtowering, pyramidal forms toward more regional and state level clusters of power and authority. But even so, other data contravene their assertions. For example, the continuation of the growth of conglomerates assures the persistence of control over strategic decisions by these large transnational corporations. Thus, Tonnies's and Weber's views remain extremely relevant as organizational and policymaking guides, especially in the field of education which has historic ties to the state level.

38. See, for example, J. McGivney, "The State Politics of Vocational Education in Wisconsin: 1910-1965" (Unpublished Ph.D. dissertation, University of Wisconsin, 1967); B. D. Bowles, "Educational Pressure Groups and the Legislative Process in California" (Unpublished Ph.D. dissertation, Claremont Graduate School, 1967); and C. G. Benenati, "The State Politics of Educational Decision Making for K-12 Education in New York State: 1920-1970" (Unpublished Ph.D. dissertation, Syracuse University, 1971).

39. See, for example, M. Burlingame, "Politics and Policies of Elementary and Secondary Education," in *Illinois: Political Process and Governmental Performance*, E. G. Crane, ed. (Dubuque, IA: Kendall Hunt, 1980).

40. Stages I through III are based on McGivney's reconceptualizations of the stages which include the operational concepts of influence structure and decision-making processes. The reader is referred to McGivney's graphic illustrations of these concepts. See McGivney, "The State Politics."

41. See Note 38, above.

42. See M. Burlingame, "Politics and Policies."

43. See *Educational Administration: A Comparative View*, D. Friesen, A. Farine, and J. Meek, eds. (Alberta, Canada: University of Alberta, 1978), for an excellent description of educational decision making in these and other countries.

CHAPTER FOUR

Beyond Mutual Adaptation, into the Bully Pulpit: Recent Research on the Federal Role in Education[1]

RICHARD JUNG and MICHAEL KIRST

The authors note that the federal government has traditionally been a "junior partner" in U.S. education. Beginning in the 1960s and the 1970s the federal government became actively involved in providing special services for underserved students (e.g., minorities, the poor, and special education students).

The federal government has always been a junior partner to state and local agencies in financing and operating American schools. The impacts of federal policies on the nation's classrooms, however, continue to fascinate researchers, policymakers, and the public. Interest and concern about this role intensified during the 1960s and 1970s, motivated in part by expanding expenditures as well as by the increasing directiveness of most new federal policies. Through the 1970s, the federal role emphasized securing extra services for traditionally underserved students, promoting innovation, and supporting research.

In the 1980s, the federal government's spending for elementary and secondary education has not kept pace with inflation. Nor has it kept pace with state and local support of schools. Relative to state and local levels, the U.S. Department of Education's share of elementary/secondary school expenditures dipped to 6.1% by the 1984-1985 school year, its lowest share in almost 20 years.[2] Also, the regulatory pressures from the federal government in education during the 1980s have subsided. Nonetheless, this decade has witnessed an unparalleled outpouring of research and commentary on a federal role that has exerted a substantial influence on elementary and secondary education.

This present article takes stock of the rapidly expanding literature on federal involvement in elementary and secondary education with three central purposes in mind: (1) to introduce several research resources to a broader audience; (2) to summarize the major findings, commonalities, and discrepancies in the pre-1980 literature; and (3) to present and assess

SOURCE: Richard Jung and Michael Kirst, "Beyond Mutual Adaptation, into the Bully Pulpit: Recent Research on the Federal Role in Education," *Educational Administration Quarterly*, Vol. 22, No. 3, pp. 80-109. Copyright © by The University Council for Educational Administration. Reprinted with permission.

literature on the federal role in elementary/secondary education subsequent to the publication of the most recent research anthologies.
Accordingly, this review identifies trends and themes that surface from
a rapidly expanding but dispersed literature on precollegiate education
in the 1980s, encompassing both empirical research and normative
commentaries.

The scope of this article was determined after reviewing abstracts from
two literature searches: (1) an automated search of ERIC and (2) a
manual review of a bibliography file on federalism in elementary and
secondary education prepared and maintained for the conduct of a
national study of Chapter 1 of the Education Consolidation and Improvement Act (ECIA), which became law in 1981.

The ERIC literature review encompassed the years 1981 through
1985, and used the following major descriptors: (1) federal government,
or (2) federal programs, or (3) federal legislation, and (4) education policy,
or (5) government role. The search also automatically filtered out articles
that pertained to countries other than the United States. The search
yielded 187 entries. A preliminary review of these abstracts revealed
serious limitations in using generic bibliographic searches such as ERIC
for the purposes of this review. The most limiting aspect of the research
reported in these abstracts was that it included only empirical work
completed *prior* to implementation of ECIA. This legislation enacted
important changes in federal education programs for school-aged children including streamlining the legal requirements of the largest federal
education program for local school districts, the consolidation of 28
smaller elementary and secondary programs into a single block grant,
and the curtailment of federal regulatory and monitoring authority. The
limitations of this search procedure stem largely from the extended lag
time between the fielding of empirical investigation in this area and the
reporting of findings from these studies in professional publications.

For coverage of more recent developments, the review relied on a
collection of reports and articles accumulated for a study of Chapter 1,
ECIA, conducted by the U.S. Department of Education's Office of Educational Research and Improvement. Included in this collection are over
350 entries contributed by individual researchers and scholars, as well
as by professional associations, advocacy groups, government agencies,
and other research organizations, among these holdings were three
bibliographic resources of particular utility for studying the modern
federal role: (1) *The Directory of Researchers in Educational Finance and
Governance*,[3] published annually since 1982 by Stanford University's
Institute for Finance and Governance; (2) the past four editions of the
U.S. Department of Education's *Annual Evaluation Report;*[4] and (3) *Data
Bases Related to Federal Elementary and Secondary Education Programs,*[5] a compendium of descriptive summaries for approximately 50

data bases on federal education programs contained on machine-readable tapes.

This review will focus primarily on a broad and largely uncharted literature that has evolved since the completion of the most recent research syntheses published in the early 1980s. It should be noted that federal policies established by the judicial system (e.g., desegregation and sex discrimination cases) were judged to deserve a full, separate study and, therefore, were not included in this review.

In the next section of this article, the stage is set for mapping this disparate body of research and commentary by first identifying the primary strategies available to federal education policymakers and then by summarizing a number of theoretical approaches that have been used to examine the most frequently employed of these policy levers. Next reviewed will be four interpretive research syntheses that summarized most of the significant empirical research on federal elementary/secondary policy through the late 1970s.[6] The remainder of this work picks up where these anthologies left off. A number of national studies conducted in the early 1980s are reviewed to characterize the advanced stage of intergovernmental relations in federally sponsored programs prior to ECIA, and the major early empirical research on state and local responses to ECIA is examined. The ascendancy of the federal leadership or bully pulpit role, especially under the Reagan administration, is documented, and the implications of this shift in policy strategies for educational researchers is assessed. After this review of recent empirical research and the gaps in this literature, perspective pieces on the proper and probable federal role in the 1980s are analyzed. The concluding section of the article suggests directions for research in this area during the remainder of this decade.

STRATEGY OPTIONS AND THEORETICAL DEVELOPMENTS

Catalogs of possible policy strategies are the most basic contributions theory can make to an improved understanding of the federal role in elementary and secondary education. Kirst,[7] for example, identified six strategies the federal government has used to address national education concerns: (1) general aid; (2) stimulation through differential funding; (3) regulation; (4) discovery and dissemination of knowledge; (5) provision of services; and (6) exertion of moral suasion.

Prior to the 1980s, the most highly visible forms of federal involvement in education were general aid-type programs; differential funding through an array of categorical programs and programs to stimulate educational innovation; and regulations that accompanied these two types of grants-in-aid programs or cut across such programs (e.g., civil rights mandates). Accordingly, theoretical advances have been most pronounced for these three federal policy strategies.

Peterson and Wong[8] have identified two stages of theory development across these federal strategies in the federal domestic arenas of education and housing. The so-called "marble-cake" theory of federalism (e.g., Grodzins and Elazar)[9] dominated conceptualizations of the federal role during the enactment stage of modern federal involvement in education. Similar to most Great Society initiatives, most federal education programs were "marbled," that is, formulated and financed at the federal level, but primarily administered and executed by state and local governments. Policymakers generally construed this theory of federalism to mean that reform could be accomplished rather simply through substantive infusions of federal dollars.[10] When early evaluations of federal domestic policy generally discredited the self-executing assumptions of the marble-cake conceptualization of federalism, a second theoretical framework evolved. These implementation theorists (e.g., Derthick; Pressman and Wildavsky)[11] argued that three factors led almost inextricably to programmatic dysfunctions: bureaucratic isolation, organizational complexity, and constituency influence.

Peterson and Wong found a number of deficiencies in the application of implementation theory to current federal involvement in education and housing.[12] Proponents of implementation theory, for instance, typically failed to take into account that federal programs sometimes generate a group of professionals who internalize and act to protect the objectives of the program. For example, Chubb[13] documented the ascendancy of advocacy groups for federally sponsored vocational and compensatory education programs in later years at the federal level; and Orland and Goettel traced the evolution of how state bureaucracies reacted to federal program goals during the later years of Title I of the Elementary and Secondary Education Act (ESEA).[14] However, most earlier implementation theorists, who typically studied only the early years of program operations, often assumed that solutions to intergovernmental resistance and conflict did not exist. These implementation theorists also tended not to differentiate between the various types of federal strategies.

To remedy the deficiencies of earlier conceptualizations, Peterson and Wong have proposed a differentiated theory of federalism that hypothesizes that successful local implementation of federal education policy is a function of the nature of the policy and the administrative units through which the program is operated. Using this framework, most federal categorical programs are more redistributional than developmental.[15] One can, therefore, expect high levels of conflict and less than complete compliance until autonomous government agencies develop to protect and promote the goals of the program during later stages of implementation. Most of the empirical research, summarized in even the most recently published reviews, however, focuses on the early and middle years of federal program implementation. Therefore, this review will first characterize the early and middle phases of federal program implementation through a review of existing research syntheses and then examine the later operation of these programs through a presentation of findings from a disperse and largely unpublished set of government reports.

Recent Research Syntheses

Among recent writings on the federal role in elementary and secondary education are several research reviews that synthesize a broad body of empirical findings on the evolution and implementation of federal policy for precollegiate education. Four of these syntheses, as a corpus, form an anthology of the most significant research on elementary and secondary education federal policy through the mid- to late 1970s. Each was published in the 1980s. The earliest (ACIR, 1981) was written prior to the Republican presidential victory in 1980. The second (Birman and Ginsburg, 1982) was completed after the initial formulation of the Reagan administration's education policy but prior to the passage of the landmark ECIA legislation. The latter two (Kaestle and Smith, 1982; Peterson, 1983) were written after enactment of ECIA but prior to its first year of implementation.

There was broad-based agreement among these and other recent research reviews[16] that passage of ESEA marked the beginning of the modern era for an activist federal role in precollegiate education. All four also treated in some detail the expansion of the federal role in the late 1960s and through the 1970s, including proliferation of federal categorical programs and the overlay of enforcement obligations or cross-cutting regulations such as those to eliminate sex discrimination (Title IX of the 1972 Education Amendments) and to ensure the rights of the handicapped (Section 504 of the Rehabilitation Act, 1973).

Each assessed modern federal involvement in American education in light of broad social and political patterns. Kaestle and Smith viewed the federal role since 1940 as an extension of the same historical process that led to the creation of state school systems and argued that such involvement "is continuous with general trends in American history."[17] Peterson saw the modern expansion of federal categorical programs and mandates as contributing toward, but also emblematic of, "a broad social trend toward increasing functional specialization in American education."[18] ACIR's major premise was that fundamental issues at the center of the federal role debate have "remained remarkably the same"—race, religion, and federal control.[19] Birman and Ginsburg wrote at a time when the

Reagan administration's policies on education were still neither widely known nor understood. In examining these nascent policies, they demonstrated that the administration's education policies were a reflection of Reagan's overall economic and domestic policy goals.[20]

A persistent theme of these research syntheses is that by the 1970s, the "patchwork quilt" of federal programs and regulations had resulted in an ever-more directive yet fragmented federal role.[21] ACIR, for example, concluded that the early and mid-1970s were "marked by the extension of the federal aid rationale to . . . [a number of] classes of educationally disadvantaged students, and the subsequent proliferation and fragmentation of interest groups, responding to the growth of new programs."[22] Birman and Ginsburg were critical of the multiplicity of federal programs and enforcement requirements, which "often pull[ed] state and local officials in different directions" and "sent conflicting signals to those who must deliver services from multiple sources."[23]

Kaestle and Smith also emphasized the proliferation and fragmentation of federal programs and enforcement obligations during the 1970s. They further noted that except in the area of court-mandated desegregation, federal programs were basically peripheral to the main business of schools, and "were often seen as interfering with the real business of the schools."[24]

Peterson, on the one hand, concurred that by the late 1970s, "the federal government may have gone too far in seeking detailed compliance with its numerous regulations." On the other hand, he cautioned that it was incorrect to blame the federal government for broad-based trends toward specialization, which had resulted in fragmentation of the self-contained classroom concept and erosion of the school administrators' authority.[25]

Peterson's analysis, as well as Kaestle and Smith's, indicated that policy contradictions documented during the early years of categorical programs had, to some degree, been ameliorated. Nonetheless, complaints and conflict about paperwork, lack of trust, and burdensome regulations persisted. Peterson credited the somewhat improved consistency of federal policy signals to "incremental modifications of federal law and regulations,"[26] while Kaestle and Smith cited accommodations on the part of school officials as contributing to "adequately implemented" federal programs.[27] Both sets of analyses portrayed persistent conflict.[28]

McLaughlin and others have characterized this stage of federal policy implementation as a period of "mutual adaptation."[29] During the mutual adaptation stage of implementation, the federal "project and institutional setting adapted to each other."[30] Through an extended examination of four federal change agent programs between 1973 and 1977, a number of changes were observed for those innovations that followed the mutual adaptation process. Changes in the projects included goal and expectation modification (usually reduction) and attempts to simplify administrative requirements. Changes observed in the institutional setting included both behavioral and attitudinal adjustments needed for integration of the project strategies into the classroom. The change-agent researches noted that the mutual adaptation stage "seldom meant smooth or trouble-free implementation."[31]

Despite the contributions made by these recent syntheses of theoretical empirical research on the federal role in education, they have at least four important limitations. First, these research reviews predated the availability of several significant bodies of literature on the implementation of federal education policy prior to passage of ECIA. Second, these syntheses were published prior to the first wave of empirical studies examining early state and district implementation of the New Federalism program reforms, such as ECIA Chapter 1's regulatory streamlining and the first major federally funded block grant, ECIA Chapter 2. Third, these collections antedated a notable shift in the relative emphasis on the federal strategy, which had earlier been labeled a leadership role or exertion of moral suasion,[32] but that more recently has been dubbed the federal bully pulpit strategy. Finally, these research reviews preceded the more recent outpouring of perspective pieces containing proposed prescriptions for remedying what many commentators diagnose to be a misaligned (e.g., Levin)[33] and, at worst, divisive (e.g., Walberg)[34] set of federal education policies and programs for school-aged children.

Beyond Mutual Adaptation

The findings from several national assessments of federal elementary and secondary policies published since the aforementioned research reviews suggest that implementation of the more mature federal categorical programs had progressed to an advanced stage, beyond that of mutual adaptation. This later stage of implementation is characterized by more limited or circumscribed intergovernmental conflict, highly customized applications of federal requirements and options to local circumstances, and broadly based, although not autonomous, support of the equity goals of federal programs.

A congressionally mandated School Finance Project commissioned two field-based studies to examine how school officials responded to and were affected by the combination of federal education programs operating during the 1981-1982 school year. This was a transition year. It was the first year of the funding cuts authorized by the Reagan-sponsored Omnibus Budget Reconciliation Act. It also marked the last year of operating federal compensatory education programs under the elaborate legal requirements of the 1978 ESEA Amendments. One of these studies examined federal policy implementation at the state level; the other at the local level.

The state-level study, conducted by the Education Policy Research Institute, examined the state administration of most major federal education programs and requirements for school-aged children as well as the federal and state relationships involved in serving special-need students. Characteristic of advanced stages of mutual adaptation, the study found that "state forces actively shaped federal programs and policies[and] . . . federal program and policy signals heavily influence[d] the course followed by the state."[35] The researchers also concluded that administrative problems frequently associated with federal programs—including lack of coordination, excessive paperwork burden, and federal intrusiveness—varied across states and programs, but observed that these administrative problems were overstated and inaccurately ascribed to federal programs as their singular source. Regarding intergovernmental relations, the researchers observed that "state conflicts with federal programs did not exhibit the intensity we had expected from popular accounts."[36] Areas of remaining conflict were largely related to newer requirements. For example, state officials generally resented the more recent planning, data collection, and special set-asides of the vocational education program as well as the due process procedures and related services requirements of the special education program.

The study also found that states tailored federal programs to suit state environments. The states' political traditions, educational priorities, and differential technical capacities especially affected the translation of federal education policies. Even though the study found that many states had developed sophisticated implementation capacities, it cautioned that "policymakers have little reason to expect that most states at this point will assume the equity agenda that defines much of the current federal role in education."[37]

The companion field study conducted by SRI International of the school district level also characterized local implementation as having moved beyond the mutual adaptation stage in many districts. The investigation examined the cumulative effects of a number of federal categorical programs and related civil rights mandates on schools and districts.

The three general findings of the study were:

(1) Collectively, federal and state policies for special populations have substantively improved and expanded the array of educational services for the intended target students.

(2) The policies have increased the structural complexity of schools and districts, which appears to represent a necessary consequence of providing targeted services.

(3) Over time, local problem solving, federal and state adjustments, and gradual local accommodation have generally reduced to a manageable level the cost associated with special services.[38]

In expanding upon these major findings, the study emphasized that federal funds, requirements, and signals were probably needed for these special services to reach needy students.

The follow-up examination to the Rand Change Agent Study, known as the Study of Dissemination Efforts Supporting School Improvement, also found that during the later years of implementing federal and state supported dissemination strategies, some states and districts had graduated from the conflictual negotiations characteristic of the mutual adaptation stage.[39] In summarizing the findings of this multiyear examination of school improvement efforts, study directory Crandall pointed out that the "most powerful and successful strategy that we saw was one that coupled high quality practices, conveyed by creditable facilitators external to the local schools, with strong central office leadership and follow through." The main message from the study, according to Crandall, was that regardless of the source of external assistance—state or federal programs, foundation initiatives, or private sector partnerships—it must "be around over the long haul."[40]

Thus, local implementation of categorical programs as well as externally supported school improvement efforts have moved beyond the stage portrayed in earlier research reviews—that is, beyond mutual adaptation. School officials, nonetheless, are not typically equipped to support, by themselves, the equity objectives of federal categorical grants or initiate, on their own, comprehensive school improvement without sustained external assistance. Overall, then, implementation of the more mature federal program and mandates stands somewhere between the stages of mutual adaptation and institutionalization posited in the Rand Change Agent Study.

At least two related features characterize this advanced stage of implementation in mature federal education programs. First, over time and often through iterative negotiations, school officials have become accustomed to the overall purposes and specific requirements of the program. During this stage, conflict is reduced or is relegated to certain requirements under certain circumstances. Second, over time, state and district officials have actively customized more mature federal programs to fit the specialized contexts and cultures of the institutions in which they operate. This customization was often made possible as federal policymakers adjusted expectations and shifted strategies, typically through extended negotiations with state/local implementers. These strategy shifts permitted local adjustments while also attempting to ensure realization of basic categorical policy objectives. The combined process of *accustomed* relationships and the *customization* of program requirements to fit the contours of local context have led to a characterization of this stage as a period of "accustomization." Compared to the stage of mutual adaptation, the accustomization stage is a time of reduced or more circumscribed conflict, of accustomed rather than new and adjusting relations, and of programs that are even more highly tailored to state/local contours as well as generally responsive to refined policy objectives.

The accustomization stage in mature federal education programs is more closely examined in two other national studies. Similar to the field examinations of the School Finance Study, these two studies were conducted during the 1981-1982 school year, and thus present companion state/local perspectives on federal policy implementation during the later years of the Title I, ESEA program.

The State Management Practices Study concluded that by the early 1980s, states had matured in their operation of the Title I program so that the elaborate legal structure of the program contained in the 1978 ESEA Amendments might not be necessary for some states. The researchers at the American Institutes for Research assessed that while "strict compliance measures were undoubtedly correct for a 'young' program in which states simply carried out federal policy, it was not clear that such prescriptive measures were appropriate for a 'mature' program, such as Title I in its later years."[41] The study found that some states were still primarily motivated in their administrative actions to minimize audit citations from federal oversight teams. Other states had moved beyond this compliance orientation. In what the study identified as "quality-oriented states," program administrators had moved beyond mere adherence to federal program regulations. During this accustomization stage, the study noted that "quality-oriented states often break new ground, and they extend themselves by making rules to further program goals—all of which can lead to problems and uncertainties as to whether their actions are in compliance with the law."[42]

Results from the Title I District Practices Study, a national study of the program just prior to Chapter 1's implementation, also documented the highly customized and diversified projects developed by districts over the years.[43] One example of districts' sophistication in customizing the program to fit their particular circumstances is in the area of selecting schools to receive program services. The rules for selecting schools to receive Title I services in the 1965 legislation were ambiguous and brief. They required that Title I projects be located only in schools or attendance areas with "high concentrations of children from low-income families" (Sec. 205(a)(1), P.L. 89-10). By 1978, federal direction was much more prescriptive, but it also permitted a number of exceptions. For instance, districts could decide which grade spans would be served and rank only those schools with these grade spans. Or, in districts where there was "no wide variance" in poverty, all schools in a district could be served, including those with below-average poverty. Over time, more than a handful of other exceptions or options to the general school selection rules for the program evolved. By the 1980s, districts were making extensive use of these options. Almost half the districts, for instance, used the grade span grouping option and almost 30% employed the "no wide variance" option when it applied.[44]

Overall, the program had become immensely popular with local school officials by the 1980s, even though its effectiveness in improving students' achievement in school continues to be debated.[45] By the late 1970s, complaints about the program were largely relegated to one or two aspects of its requirements, particularly, those pertaining to parent advisory councils and comparability.[46] Both of these areas were simplified by Chapter 1, ECIA.

THE UNFOLDING STORY: STATE AND LOCAL RESPONSE TO ECIA

Federal policy for elementary and secondary education under the Reagan administration has four notable features: (1) generally stable expenditures, with reduced purchasing power due to inflation; (2) programmatic reforms resulting primarily from enactment and implementation of ECIA; (3) less activist posture in enforcing civil rights regulations; and (4) expansion of the leadership or bully pulpit function.

While the U.S. Department of Education's budget for education increased by about 10% from approximately $14 billion to $15.4 billion between FY 1980 and FY 1984, the funding level in FY 1984 for elementary and secondary education of $6.9 billion was identical to the budget authority four years earlier. In the intervening years, the Education Department's budget for federal elementary and secondary programs had actually dropped to $6.1 billion in FY 1982. Another recent change in the Department of Education's budget has been the shift in support between elementary/secondary and postsecondary education, with expenditures for federal student aid and other college programs outpacing precollegiate federal funding beginning in 1981.[47]

The first substantive funding cuts for elementary and secondary education under the Reagan administration were contained in the Omnibus Budget Reconciliation Act of 1981, which reduced funding across most domestic functional areas. This budget act also made structural changes in a number of social programs. For elementary and secondary education, these structural changes were achieved through the com-

ponent of the 1981 Reconciliation Act entitled the Education Consolidation and Improvement Act of 1981 (ECIA).

The Act contained three sections or chapters. Chapter 1 was a major
rewrite and streamlining of provisions for the largest federally sponsored
program that was and still is targeted to low-achieving students in
poverty areas, the former ESEA Title I program. Chapter 2 of ECIA
consolidated 28 federally funded categorical grants into a single block
grant. Along with promises to reduce paperwork, the block grant reduced
funding by approximately 12% in its first year. Chapter 3, ECIA, placed
new restrictions on the U.S. Department of Education and state agencies
to regulate the use of federal funds by local schools.

Most currently available research on these programmatic and funding
changes are based on only the first or second transition years of ECIA's
implementation. In fact, a number of researchers jumped the gun by
asking school officials about the *expected* effects of ECIA.[48] Past research
on federal program implementation consistently has demonstrated that
such early assessments typically relied too extensively on the inflated
stated intent of legislative language as evaluation standards and overstated temporary start-up programs.[49]

The first wave of studies examining Chapter 1's initial implementation
tended to be either (1) exploratory case studies in a limited number of
districts or states examining select issues[50] or (2) larger scale investigations undertaken by interest groups that over the years had fought for
many of the provisions excised or streamlined by the Chapter 1 legislation
(e.g., parent advisory councils and quantitative indicators of supplemental use of federal funds). The two organizations, for instance, with the
most activist posture for an expanded federal oversight role during the
Title I years, the Children's Defense Law, produced the first two major
reports of Chapter 1's operation. Representative Hawkins (Democrat-
California), Chairman of the House Committee on Education and Labor,
also sponsored a study of administrative changes under Chapter 1. These
three reports concurred that (1) reduced funding, more than regulatory
changes, affected local implementation of the program; (2) the U.S.
Department of Education provided insufficient guidance to state and local
officials about their new roles under Chapter 1; (3) federal and state
monitoring had notably decreased; and (4) the number of parent councils,
previously mandated under Title I, had significantly declined.[51]

A more theoretically oriented assessment of Chapter 1's early implementation documented continuation of the accustomization phase
after the streamlining of the Title I requirements. The study, directed by
Milbrey McLaughlin, found that "Title I, without a question, stimulated
local activities that have persisted under Chapter 1." However, in such
areas as state oversight and parent councils, where most of Title I's
detailed requirements had been removed, state and local officials evi-

denced diminished attention to these activities.[52] The study concluded that despite more than 20 years of building the commitment and expertise of state and local staff, the categorical structures established under Title I could not be expected to remain if there were a substantial retreat in federal funds or direction.

Chapter 1's evaluation is complicated by the fact that Congress passed technical amendments to ECIA in December of 1983 that restored, in modified form, some of Title I's previous reporting and targeting requirements. These technical amendments also required the Secretary of Education to conduct a national assessment of compensatory education programs under Chapter 1 through the National Institute of Education (now the Office of Educational Research and Improvement). The study will examine issues of effectiveness, targeting, program design, services, and administration through national surveys and case studies, and report findings to Congress in time for the 1987 reauthorization of the program.[53]

The Chapter 2, ECIA block grant is the only major new programmatic initiative of the Reagan administration for elementary/secondary schools. Examination of its initial implementation, therefore, has been even more intensive. After less than two years of operation, at least 21 major empirical studies had been initiated or completed.[54] More than half of these were also designed or conducted by advocacy groups that were directly affected by the reduced funding or more redistributive nature of the block grant formula, including the Council of Great City Schools (CGCS), the National Citizens Committee for Education, the American Association of School Administrators (AASA), the Education Commission of the States, and the U.S. Catholic Conference.

Despite the fragmentary nature of these recent or ongoing studies of Chapter 2, they offer intriguing glimpses into early responses to this reform. In the first years, many districts tended to use Chapter 2 funds for computer purchases,[55] although there was no clear indication that these purchases were part of an articulated school improvement effort.[56] Preliminary indications were that the block grant had been successful in reducing administrative burden;[57] however, yet to be known is "if snipping the strings works for or against the development of well-planned and innovative solutions to local education problems."[58] Evidence regarding local participation was also mixed. While private school officials appeared more involved, local parents seemed to have less say in how Chapter 2 funds were spent than they did under the antecedent programs.[59]

It is also apparent that large, urban districts lost considerable funding not only as a result of the redistributional nature of the Chapter 2 allocation formula, but also due to the erosion of political support for the antecedent programs in the years prior to the block grant.[60] Also, while no exact figures are available for private school student participation under the antecedent programs, it appears that private school students are receiving proportionally more services under the block grant than they did under the earlier configuration of categorical programs.[61] Less, however, is known about how intradistrict resource allocations have been affected by Chapter 2 or how or whether the more than 85% of the districts that gained modest funding increments under Chapter 2 use these funds with long-range goals in mind. A national study being conducted by SRI International is currently examining these and other issues based on three years of data on state and local implementation experiences.[62]

CENTRALITY OF THE BULLY PULPIT ROLE

Previous administrations have used moral suasion or the bully pulpit to reinforce more direct regulatory, funding, and service efforts. For example, Commissioner of Education Sidney Marland's 1970 advocacy of career education was backed by a new grant program. However, the Reagan administration has featured this tactic of speeches, commissions, and advocacy by the secretary and president as a primary mode of action. Although a relatively inexpensive strategy, significant personnel and financial resources have been targeted toward influencing public opinion and thereby affecting policy.[63] In a self-assessment of his first term, President Reagan wrote:

> If I were asked to single out the proudest achievement of my administration's first three and one-half years in office, what we've done to define the issues and promote the great national debate in education would rank right up near the top of the list.[64]

The Reagan administration's use of the bully pulpit in education is consistent with its New Federalism philosophy that the state and local authorities and citizens are the proper and most effective means of action and change. This education strategy has similarities with the Reagan economic policy. A major premise of "supply-side" economics was that bold and dramatic action and rhetoric on the part of the national administration would signal investors that a new era was coming, thereby indirectly stimulating the economy. As David Stockman stated, in his infamous *Atlantic* interviews, "The whole thing is premised on faith."[65] Mr. Reagan has deliberately rerouted much of the responsibility for governing away from Washington. In that process, his use of the bully pulpit has been integral not only to promote devolution of authority but also to advocate "excellence" including discipline, merit pay, and prayer in the classroom.

In accord with the New Federalism philosophy, a major goal of the administration has been to deregulate the myriad categorical programs that began in 1965.[66] Reagan campaigned on a promise to dismantle the Department of Education in an effort to symbolize this decentralization of power. Likewise, in an interview with *Educational Record,* former Secretary of the Department of Education, Terrell Bell, stated that he hoped, if nothing else, to be remembered as one who reversed the relentless trend toward federal education control.[67]

Ironically, it was the Democratic administration that enlarged the national education pulpit from which Secretaries Bell and Bennett have spoken. Shortly after the creation of the U.S. Department of Education, an optimistic former Commissioner Howe stated: "A Cabinet-level department lends importance to the Secretary's voice, which will influence the thinking of many persons about education's goals, practices, results, governance, and costs."[68] However, there is still no overall federal education policy spokesperson because education programs remain scattered throughout the government. For instance, there are major education initiatives in the National Science Foundation, the National Institute of Health, the Veterans Administration, and the Educational Programs for Youth in the Department of Labor.

Certainly the most graphic example of this bully pulpit strategy has been the report of the National Commission on Excellence in Education (NCEE) and subsequent follow-up activities. The commission's report, *A Nation at Risk,* sold 70,000 copies during its first year. The Department of Education estimates that approximately seven times that number, 500,000, were copied and distributed within a year of the report's release. Extensive excerpts in national and regional periodicals, such as the *New York Times,* the *Washington Post,* and *The Oregonian* provided millions direct access to the report.[69]

The NCEE findings, as well as those of similar task forces and individuals, clearly captured the attention of Americans concerned about education. Whether the administration realized the potential of the commission's work at its inception is unclear. However, once NCEE had established the tone, the president and the secretary took full advantage of this rhetorical opportunity to advance their agenda. While at an obvious level the issue was one of return to quality, the "excellence movement" also has provided a vehicle for the administration to push the onus of responsibility for education back to the state, local, and parental levels.

President Reagan had a high level of involvement with the introduction of the report and subsequent activities. Among other things, the president visited schools around the country, participated in two regional forums, and addressed a plenary session of the National Forum on

Excellence in Education, with consistent themes stressing quality, discipline, merit pay, and the virtues of homework.

The Department of Education scheduled various activities to maintain the momentum fostered by the reports and to encourage action at the state and local levels. The department sponsored twelve regional forums and a National Forum on Excellence in Education. Secretary Bell designated most of his discretionary fund toward that effort and stated that a major portion of the budget was to be spent on the problems and priorities addressed by the commission report.[70]

Upon the first anniversary of the release of *A Nation at Risk*, the department disseminated a follow-up, *The Nation Responds: Recent Efforts to Improve Education*. The publication was at once an assessment and another push for continued action at the state and local levels. The report cited glowing stories and statistics about the "tidal wave of school reform."[71] After only a year, researchers were aware of 275 state-level task forces on education, stimulated in part by NCEE. Of 51 states and jurisdictions, 48 had adopted or were considering new high school graduations requirements. At that point, 35 states had approved new requirements.

The prevalence of the bully pulpit strategy is evident from a review of speeches, operational statements, and budgetary considerations.[72] Other efforts have included the very visible "Wall Chart" (comparing resources and college entrance scores across states), *Indicators of Education Status and Trends*, and *Becoming a Nation of Readers*. Secretary Bennett described the role of the bully pulpit in promoting the work of American education as follows:

> The work is principally the American people's work, not the federal government's. We, in Washington, can talk about these matters, comment on them, provide intellectual resources, and, when appropriate, limited fiscal resources, but the responsibility is the people's.[73]

Issuance of the Wall Chart that compared state education outcomes exemplifies the Reagan administration's use of the bully pulpit strategy. "The publication of the 'wall chart' brought to the forefront the issue of state-to-state comparisons," wrote the report's authors. "On a political level, the attention given to the Secretary's wall chart makes inevitable future state-to-state comparisons on outcome measures."[74] In a dramatic policy reversal, the Council of Chief State School Officers (CCSSO) approved a plan to conduct regular comparisons of the educational performance of the states rather than permit the federal government to preempt interstate performance comparisons. While initially opposed strongly to such techniques, the CCSSO is now determined to influence the sorts of performance measures used, including a deemphasis on SAT comparisons.

The initial statements of Secretary Bennett signaled the administration's continued emphasis on the bully pulpit. Upon his appointment, Bennett cited ten major issues he would address.[75] Later that month, President Reagan enumerated five broader, more easily digestible themes he and the new education secretary had agreed upon for the education agenda: choice, teachers, curriculum, setting, and parents.[76] One month after his appointment, Secretary Bennett delivered a more refined, yet still more memorable set of themes, his "three Cs": content, character, and choice.[77] This evolution indicates a growing sensitivity to the strategy of carefully articulating one's message in a format that can more easily be conveyed to the public. Each message contained similar content; Bennett's ten issues were subsumed within the elaborations of the president's five concerns and the three Cs.

Assessing the Impact of the Bully Pulpit

Although the administration's use of the bully pulpit has been its centerpiece of education policy, almost no research was found on the topic. An ERIC search revealed one piece that focused on the impact of task forces during previous administrations.[78] Weiss demonstrates that a bully pulpit strategy can have substantial impact on changing policymakers' assumptions or viewpoint about policy priorities.[79] She contends that such activities are effective in agenda setting and percolate indirectly into the policy process.

The Department of Education's assessment of the bully pulpit's impact has been handled more in a public relations vein than a scholarly one. The department published *The Nation Responds,* but its primary purpose was to reinforce the administration's message of optimism and to encourage continued state and local effort. The following quotation is indicative of the report's tone: "deep public concern about the Nation's future created a tidal wave of school reform which promises to renew American education."[80] Research on the impact of symbolism like "excellence" for guiding the policy agenda suggests the bully pulpit could be quite effective.[81]

Not only does the bully pulpit strategy seem to have impact upon the early stages of policymaking, but also it has an impact upon education research priorities and trends through indirect means.[82] More federally funded research has been directed at curricular content, academic standards, parent choice, and the excellence agenda as exemplified by the federal regulations on the NIE Center competition.

Another unresearched question concerns the origins of the themes for the bully pulpit. Certainly, the underlying message of returning influence to the state and local levels derives from the administration's New Federalism stance.[83] More directly, however, researchers and analysts from the conservative think tanks have played a very influential role as members and leaders of task forces. The Heritage Foundation, the Hoover Institution at Stanford, and American Enterprise Institute are three primary providers of the ideology, data, and strategies that form the administration's bully pulpit content.[84]

Also largely unnoticed is the administration's extensive use of political appointments within the Department of Education to disseminate its bully pulpit themes. For the first time, political appointees head the department's ten regional offices. Many education specialists have been replaced by "public information" specialists. According to Hanrahan and Kosterlitz, many research review panels have been completely released and former panelists replaced with "individuals less notable for their expertise in education than for their conservative views."[85] More effort should be expended to address these and related questions. The apparent success of bully pulpit strategies under this administration ensures their continued viability in the future.

RECENT NORMATIVE COMMENTARIES ON THE FEDERAL ROLE

The election of President Reagan caused a considerable increase in perspective pieces on the proper and probable federal role. Many of these federal role publications were normative arguments or attempts to extrapolate the future from the past. Ironically, none of the commentary prior to the National Commission on Excellence in Education report predicted the huge impact the "excellence" movement would have on the reallocation of federal versus state roles as developed in the previous discussion of the bully pulpit.

Several analysts have speculated on the direction and determinants of the future of the federal role in education.[86] Thomas posits five major determinants: the president; national political and economic conditions; the key issues of race relations, religion, and federal control; the Washington policy process; and administrative structure.[87] Thomas, Clark and Amiot, and Doyle all stress the crucial importance of President Reagan's leadership and ideological convictions.[88] Thomas observes that there is a shift in elite thinking to a view that too much reliance had been placed during 1965-1980 on federal education initiatives to improve national and economic problems.

Several of the writers, particularly Peterson and Rabe, stress that the education interest groups can play only a minor and marginal role in deflecting major determinants. Peterson and Rabe summarize the general consensus of the literature this way:

> While interest groups help sustain programs once they are enacted, and many help shape ways in which the legislation is formulated, the overall direction of education policy is surprisingly divorced from the play of group politics.[89]

Interest groups are viewed as a conservative force trying to preserve their programs in a largely fragmented and specialized way. Major education interest groups have reacted to the Reagan education ideology without being able to lead. Another force sparking interest group reaction is the Supreme Court decision in *Aguilar v. Felton,* banning the provision of federally funded remedial services in religiously affiliated schools. This decision could potentially upset the fragile coalition of public and private school organizations supporting existing delivery systems of federal categorical programs.

Given the Reagan administration's shift in policy, several researchers have explored the desirability and impact of a revamped federal role. Clark and Amiot, and Clark, Astuto, and Rooney summarized the Reagan approach as diminution, deregulation, decentralization, disestablishment of bureaucratic structure, and deemphasis.[90] They contended that the Reagan administration's impact will be fairly drastic. Prior to joining the U.S. Department of Education, Finn took the opposite view about probable impact because:

> a sorry blend of lackluster individuals, internal rivalries, failure of imagination, political timidity, blind spots, and yieldings to various federal pressures has prevented any coherent vision of a new federal role from forming. Far from resulting in the purposeful disassembly of the old role that Clark and Amiot think they see, these failings have led mostly to a kind of dull, depressing decrementalism.[91]

The kind of rhetoric employed in this debate is not buttressed by large-scale empirical surveys. The discussion thus far has pointed out that changes in Chapter 1 and 2 of ECIA are significant, but congressional momentum has shifted away from Reagan's federal education priorities ever since 1981.

No issue has been more symbolic of a new federal role than Reagan's repeated legislative requests for tuition tax credits to private school parents. James and Levin provided a rather complete overview of the numerous ramifications of this proposal, including legal, federal costs, potential beneficiaries, and the arguments in favor and against.[92] Tuition tax credits were defeated in the Senate and appear dead given Reagan's overall tax reform proposal of 1985. But it is the provision in this tax reform bill to end the deductibility of state and local taxes from federal income taxes that could have the biggest Reagan education impact. Ending state/local tax deductibility raises the price of increased state/local taxes to support education, and could dampen public willingness to support future tax increases.

Alternatives to the Reagan administration's conceptualization of the federal role have been proposed. For example, the Twentieth Century Fund advocated major federal initiatives to improve the attraction and retention of high quality teachers. The federal role in this area was quite strong from 1964 to 1972, but ended with the demise of the Education Professions Development Act. The only major federal initiative for teachers shifted to the National Science Foundation (NSF) after a 1983 statute. The involvement of NSF highlights a generic problem with all these federal role pieces—inattention to the numerous federal agencies involved in education. There are dozens of federal education and training programs, but the Department of Education administers only a handful of them. No one is analyzing the holistic impact or desirability of this fragmented nonsystem for delivering federal programs.

It is noteworthy that the highly visible school prayer issue has not been analyzed by academics who specialize in the federal education role. Pierard and Clouse provide some descriptions of the "New Right," but their main objective is to warn against the dangers of these groups.[93] Moreover, such major congressional issues as asbestos removal and cuts in federal child nutrition are not treated in any depth beyond normative argumentation. The research remains concentrated on the major federal grant programs that were once a part of ESEA.

Overall, the 1980 Reagan election has not been the critical turning point that Iannaccone or Clark and Amiot[94] foresaw if one looks only at federal education program structures and expenditures. But if one looks more closely at the federal bully pulpit and the high level of state initiatives for excellence, many of the Reagan goals have been accomplished. The federal level is no longer viewed as the prime engine of educational innovation.

SUMMARY AND IMPLICATIONS

The federal role in education has always been uncertain and subject to political controversy as well as the influence of broader social movements. At the very time the approaches to implementing the elementary/secondary education programs emanating from the Great Society initiatives seemed to realize a growing national consensus, the federal government, under the leadership of a conservative political coalition, attempted to turn federal policy in a new direction, using a set of bully pulpit strategies instead of regulations to achieve its objectives. This examination has reviewed some of the analytic tools available for researching the federal role in elementary and secondary education. It has also assessed a disparate, and often fugitive, literature on this federal role since the most recent research anthologies were published in the early 1980s.

This review of previously uncharted literature highlights several important developments. First, state and local implementation of the more mature federally sponsored categorical programs had by the early 1980s in many instances moved beyond the mutual adaptation stage generally portrayed in the research anthologies. The most recent national studies of these longer-standing programs portray reduced or more circumscribed intergovernmental conflicts compared to earlier assessments, accustomed rather than new or adjusting relationships, more emphasis on program improvement rather than on a strict compliance orientation, and highly tailored programs customized to fit the contours of local circumstances and capacities.

Second, it is still too early to assess fully state and local impacts of the streamlining of compensatory education requirements, the effects of the block grant, and the consequences of the easing of federal oversight across programmatic and regulatory strategies. The first wave of investigations were often undertaken by constituency groups and typically used exploratory case studies to examine the major programmatic reforms in ECIA. This initial surge of evaluations is soon to be followed by a wave of large-scale national assessments on state and local responses to the new or revised federal programmatic strategies.

Third, the Reagan administration's qualitatively different use of the bully pulpit as a major, independent policy strategy has been inadequately examined. There is broad recognition of the widespread public and professional reactions to the publication of *A Nation at Risk,* the issuance of the Wall Chart comparing state resources and college entrance scores, and other moral suasion devises. Nonetheless, to date, most of the commentary on these bully pulpit strategies has little if any empirical base and has been more public relations hype than systematic assessment.

Overall, subsequent research of the federal role in the 1980s can benefit a growing body of theoretical literature on differential federal strategies. Program evaluations will have to be designed to assess broad ranges of state and local responses to the New Federalism reforms. These evaluations will also have to be designed to examine programs that in many instances have become part of the fabric of state and local contexts and that, therefore, are likely to require careful specification of the conditions and contexts that affect state and local implementation.

Probably the greatest challenge for researchers of the federal role in elementary and secondary education will be to design and conduct systematic assessments of the origins and impacts of the modern use of the bully pulpit strategy. Only through such scholarship, and with the benefit of time's perspective, will the impacts of the Reagan administration's education policy be fully understood.

NOTES

1. The authors wish to thank Mary Moore and Paul Peterson for their valuable comments on earlier drafts of this article. The views and conclusions expressed here, however, are those of the authors. No official support or endorsement of the U.S. Department of Education is intended or should be inferred.

2. U.S. Department of Education, *The Fiscal Year 1986 Budget* (Washington, DC: Author, February 1985).

3. S. J. Peters, compiler. *Directory of Researchers in Educational Finance and Governance* (Stanford, CA: Institute for Research on Educational Finance and Governance, May 1984); C. Upshaw, compiler. *Directory of Researchers in Educational Finance and Governance* (Stanford, CA: Institute of Research on Educational Finance and Governance, August 1982).

4. The most recently published issue in U.S. Department of Education/Office of Planning, Budget and Evaluation, *Annual Evaluation Report Fiscal Year 1984* (Washington, DC: Author, 1985).

5. M. D. Tashjian and J. W. Keesling, *Data Bases Related to Federal Elementary and Secondary Education Programs* (Reston, VA: Advanced Technology, 1984).

6. Advisory Commission on Intergovernmental Relations, "Intergovernmentalizing the Classroom: Federal Involvement in Elementary and Secondary Education," in the series, *The Federal Role in the Federal System: The Dynamics of Growth* (Washington, DC: Author, March 1981); B. F. Birman and A. L. Ginsburg, "The Federal Role in Elementary and Secondary Education: New Directions and Continuing Concerns," *The Urban Lawyer* 14, 3 (1982): 471-500; C. F. Kaestle and M. S. Smith, "The Federal Role in Elementary and Secondary Education, 1940-1980" *Harvard Educational Review* 52, 4 (1982): 384-408; P. E. Peterson, "Background Paper" in *Making the Grade*, Report of the Twentieth Century Fund Task Force on Federal Elementary and Secondary Education Policy (New York: Twentieth Century Fund, 1983).

7. M. Kirst, "Teaching Policy and Federal Categorical Programs" (Stanford, CA: Institute for Research on Educational Finance and Governance, 1982). For other analyses of federal policy strategies, see A. H. Hastings, *The Strategies of Government Intervention: An Analysis of Federal Education and Health Care Policy* (Unpublished doctoral dissertation, University of Virginia, Charlottsville, 1982); H. M. Levin, "A Challenge for Action: National Leadership and Involvement in Educa-

tion," *IFG Policy Perspective* (Fall, 1983): 1-4; E. C. Mosher, "The Changing Responsibilities and Tactics of the Federal Government," *Public Administration Review* 40 (1980): 141-155; L. M. Salamon, "Rethinking Public Management: Third Party Government and the Changing Forms of Government Action," *Public Policy* 29 (1981): 255-275.

8. P. E. Peterson and K. K. Wong, "Toward a Differentiated Theory of Federalism: Education and Housing Policy in the 1980s," *Research in Urban Policy* 1 (1985): 301-324.

9. M. Grodzin, *The American System: A New View of Government in the United States* (Chicago: Rand McNalley, 1966); D. J. Elazar et al., *Cooperation and Conflict: Readings in American Federalism* (Itasca, IL: F. E. Peacock, 1969).

10. Peterson and Wong, "Toward a Differentiated Theory."

11. M. Derthick, *New Towns In-Town: Why a Federal Program Failed* (Washington, DC: Urban Institute, 1972); J. L. Pressman and A. Wildavsky, *Implementation* (Berkeley: University of California Press, 1973).

12. Peterson and Wong, "Toward a Differentiated Theory," p. 303.

13. J. E. Chubb, "Excessive Regulation: The Case of Federal Aid to Education," *Political Science Quarterly* 100, 2 (1985): 287-311.

14. M. E. Orland and R. J. Goettel, "States and the Implementation of Federal Categorical Programs in Education: A Heuristic Framework," *Educational Evaluation and Policy Analysis* 4, 2 (1982): 141-154.

15. Peterson and Wong argue that the one can determine the extent to which a policy is redistributive by estimating the degree to which those receiving the service are those paying for the service. If the two are completely different, the policy is an instance of pure redistribution. "Toward a Differentiated Theory," p. 306.

16. See, for example, T. W. Hartle and R. P. Holland, "The Changing Context of Federal Education Aid," *Education and Urban Society* 15, 4 (1983):408-431.

17. Kaestle and Smith, "The Federal Role," p. 390.

18. Peterson, "Background Paper," p. 149.

19. ACIR, "Intergovernmentalizing the Classroom," p. 11.

20. Birman and Ginsburg, "The Federal Role," pp. 484-485.

21. See also D. L. Kirp and H. R. Winslow, Jr., *Patchwork Quilt: The Diverse Educational Entitlements of Children* (Menlo Park, CA: SRI International, 1976); J. W. Meyer, "The Impact of the Centralization of Educational Funding and Control on State and Local Organizational Governance" (Stanford, CA: Institute for Research on Educational and Finance and Governance, August 1979).

22. ACIR, "Intergovernmentalizing the Classroom," p. 75.

23. Birman and Ginsburg, "The Federal Role," pp. 473, 484.

24. Kaestle and Smith, "The Federal Role," p. 405.

25. Peterson, "Background Paper," pp. 104-105.

26. *Ibid.*, pp. 145-146.

27. Kaestle and Smith, "The Federal Role," p. 405.

28. See also, Peterson and Wong, "Toward a Differentiated Theory."

29. See, for example, P. Berman and M. W. McLaughlin, *Federal Programs Supporting Educational Change, Vol. VIII: Implementing and Sustaining Innovations* (Santa Monica, CA: Rand Corporation, 1978); M. W. McLaughlin, "Implementation as Mutual Adaptation," in *Social Program Implementation*, W. Williams and R. F. Elmore, eds. (New York: Academic Press, 1976); M. W. McLaughlin and

P. Berman, "Macro and Micro Implementation" (Paper prepared for IMTEC Training Course, Federal Republic of Germany, June 1975).

30. *Ibid.*, p. 5.

31. Berman and McLaughlin, *Federal Programs Supporting Education,* p. 16.

32. H. M. Levin, "A Challenge for Action: National Leadership and Involvement in Education," *IFG Policy Perspectives* (Fall 1983): 1-4; Kirst, "Teaching Policy."

33. See, for example, H. M. Levin, "Federal Grants and Educational Equity," *Harvard Educational Review* 52, 4 (1982): 444-459.

34. H. J. Walberg, "Federal (Chapter 1) Education Spending and Effects on Poor Children" (Washington, DC: Learn, Inc., October 1984).

35. M. T. Moore et al., *The Interaction of Federal and Related State Education Programs,* Executive Summary (Washington, DC: Education Policy Research Institute, February 1983). The federal programs and civil rights provisions examined included: Titles I, IV, V and VII of ESEA; the Education for All Handicapped Children Act (P.L. 94-142); the Vocational Education Act; Title VI of the Civil Rights Act of 1964; Title IX of the Education Amendments of 1972; and Section 504 of the Rehabilitation Act of 1973. The state programs studied were analogous to federal programs, but funded at the state level. The eight states visited were: California, Louisiana, Massachusetts, Missouri, New Mexico, New York, Virginia, and Wyoming.

36. Moore et al., *The Interaction of Federal and Related State Education Programs,* p. 10.

37. *Ibid,* p. 12.

38. M. S. Knapp et al., *Cumulative Effects of Federal Education Policies on Schools and Districts* (Menlo Park, CA: SRI International, January 1983). The federal programs and civil rights provisions examined included Titles I and VII, ESEA; the Education for All Handicapped Children Act (P.L. 94-142); the Vocational Education Act; Title VI of the Civil Rights Act of 1964; Title IX of the Education Amendments of 1972; and Section 504 of the Rehabilitation Act of 1973. Where they existed, the study also documented local operation of the IndoChina Refugee Children Assistance Act, the Indian Education Act, and the Emergency School Aid Assistance Act. Also included in the study's scope were parallel state programs or requirements.

39. D. P. Crandall and S. F. Loucks, *A Roadmap for School Improvement, Vol. X: Executive Summary of the Study of Dissemination Efforts Supporting School Improvement* (Andover, MA: The Network, Inc., 1983). Among the federal programs examined in this study were the National Diffusion Network, Title IV-C Adoption Grants, and ESEA Title III.

40. D. P. Crandall, "Internal and External Improvement Approaches: Looking for the Right Blend" (Paper presented at the NIE-sponsored workshop. Strengthening the Connection of Dissemination and Improvement in Education, Washington, DC, June 25, 1984), p. 11.

41. B. L. Bessey et al., *A Study of State Management Practices: Looking Back at Title I and Toward Chapter 1,* Final Report (Palo Alto, CA: American Institutes for Research, August 1982), p. xvii.

42. *Ibid.,* p. xix.

43. Advanced Technology, *Local Operation of Title I, ESEA 1976-1982: A Resource Book* (McLean, VA: Author, June 1983). This study combined three meth-

odologies to report on local operation of the Title I program during the 1981-1982 school year and to compare this to earlier operation of the program: a mail questionnaire sent to approximately 2000 randomly selected school districts, structured interviews and document reviews in 100 nationally representative Title I districts, and case studies in 40 purposely selected Title I districts.

44. M. J. Gaffney and D. M. Schember, *Current Title I School and Student Selection Procedures and Implications for Implementing Chapter 1, ECIA* (McLean, VA: Advanced Technology, September 1982), p. 21.

45. See for example, Kaestle and Smith, "The Federal Role"; S. P. Mullin and A. A. Summers, "Is More Better? The Effectiveness of Spending on Compensatory Education," *Phi Delta Kappan* 64 (1983): 339-347.

46. V. Rezmovic and J. W. Keesling, *Paperwork and Administrative Burden for School Districts Under Title I* (McLean, VA: Advanced Technology, September 1983), p. 11.

47. U.S. Department of Education, *The Fiscal Year 1986 Budget,* pp. 52-53.

48. See, for example, Advanced Technology, *Local Operation of Title I, ESEA 1976-1982;* Bessie et al., *A Study of State Management Practices;* L. Darling-Hammond and E. L. Marks, *The New Federalism in Education: State Responses to the 1981 Education Consolidation and Improvement Act* (Santa Monica, CA: Rand Corporation, February 1983).

49. See, for example, M. Kirst and R. Jung, "The Utility of a Longitudinal Approach in Assessing Implementation: A Thirteen-Year View of Title I, ESEA," in *Studying Implementation: Methodological and Administrative Issues* (Chatham, NM: Chatham House, 1982), pp. 119-148; J. D. Sherman and M. A. Kutner, "Editors' Introduction," *Education and Urban Society* 16, 1 (1983): 3-5.

50. See, for example, P. J. Grey et al., *A Study of Contrasts: Effects of Education Consolidation and Improvement Act of 1981 on SEA and LEA Evaluation* (Portland, OR: Northwest Regional Educational Laboratory, 1982); J. W. Keesling, ed., *A Study of Intergovernmental Relations in Compensatory Education* (Reston, VA: Advanced Technology, 1985).

51. Children's Defense Fund, *An Interim Report on the Implementation of Chapter 1* (Washington, DC: Author, November 1984); J. C. Dougherty, *A Matter of Interpretation: Changes Under Chapter 1 of the Education Consolidation and Improvement Act* (Report prepared for the Subcommittee on Elementary, Secondary, and Vocational Education, Washington, DC: U.S. Congress, 1985); Lawyers' Committee for Civil Rights Under Law, *The First Year of Chapter 1* (Washington, DC: Author, 1984).

52. M. W. McLaughlin, P. M. Shields, and D. J. Rezabek, "State and Local Response to Chapter 1 of the Education Consolidation and Improvement Act, 1981" (Stanford, CA: Institute for Research on Educational Finance and Governance, April 1985).

53. National Institute of Education, "A Plan for a National Assessment of the ECIA Chapter 1 Program" (Washington, DC: Author, November 1984).

54. Summarized by M. Knapp and R. A. Cooperstein, "Charting a Course for Future Investigation of Educational Block Grants: A Reader's Guide to Current and Ongoing Research on Chapter 2" (Unpublished, Menlo Park, CA: SRI International, April 1984).

55. American Association of School Administrators, *The Impacts of Chapter 2 of the Education Consolidation and Improvement Act on Local Education Agencies* (Arlington, VA: Author, 1983); R. M. J. Kyle, *Kaleidoscopes: Emerging Patterns of Responses and Action in ECIA Case Studies of Chapter 2 in Selected States* (Washington, DC: E. H. White, July 1983).

56. M. Knapp, "Interim Report on the National Study of the Local Operations Under Chapter 2" (Paper presented at the annual meeting of the American Educational Research Association, Chicago, 1985).

57. A. H. Hastings, "Snipping the Strings: Local and State Administrators Discuss Chapter 2," *Phi Delta Kappan* 65, 3 (1983): 194-198; Kyle, *Kaleidoscopes.*

58. *Ibid.,* p. 183.

59. Knapp and Cooperstein, "Charting a Course."

60. R. K. Jung and R. M. Stonehill, "Big Districts and the Block Grant: A Cross-Time Assessment of the Fiscal Impacts," *Journal of Education Finance* 10, 3 (1985): 308-326.

61. Council of Great City Schools, *Trends in Federal Funding to Urban Schools: A Progress Report on the Reagan Years* (Washington, DC: Author, February 1983); American Association of School Administrators, *Private School Participation in Chapter 2 of the Education Consolidation and Improvement Act* (Arlington, VA: Author, April 1984).

62. For a fuller treatment of these early Chapter 2 studies and an explanation of the ongoing SRI national study, the reader is referred to Knapp and Cooperstein, "Charting a Course for Future Investigation"; and Southeastern Regional Council for Educational Improvement, *National Research and Evaluation Agenda: Chapter 2 Education Consolidation and Improvement Act* (Research Triangle Park, NC: Author, October 1984).

63. T. H. Bell, "Goals and Performance Priorities of the U.S. Department of Education for Fiscal Year 1984" (Washington, DC, 1983); J. A. Basile, "The Reagan FY 1985 Budget and Education" (Washington, DC: Federal Budget Report Inc., 1984).

64. R. Reagan, "Overview of Education Reform Issues," in *A Blueprint for Education Reform,* C. Marshner, ed. (Washington, DC: Free Congress Research and Education Foundation, 1984), p. 2

65. W. Greider, "The Education of David Stockman," in *Ladies and Gentlemen: The Presidents of the United States* (Boston: The Atlantic Monthly Company, 1984), pp. 105-128.

66. R. F. Elmore, "Education and Federalism: Doctrinal, Functional, and Strategic Views" (Stanford, CA: Institute for Research on Educational Finance and Governance, 1983).

67. T. H. Bell, "T. H. Bell (Interview)" *Education Board* 62, 3 (1981): 5-7.

68. H. Howe, "Two Views of the New Department of Education and Its First Secretary: View I," *Phi Delta Kappan* 61, 7 (1980): 446-447.

69. U.S. Department of Education, "Fact Sheet for *The Nation Responds: Recent Efforts to Improve Education*" (Press Release, May 11, 1984).

70. Basile, "The Reagan FY 1985 Budget and Education."

71. U.S. Department of Education, *The Nation Responds: Recent Efforts to Improve Education* (Washington, DC: Government Printing Office, May 1984), p. 11.

72. See, for example, R. Reagan, "Excellence and Opportunity: A Program of Support for American Education," *Phi Delta Kappan* (September 1984): 13-15; Bell, "Goals and Performance Priorities"; Basile, "The Reagan FY 1984 Budget and Education."

73. W. J. Bennett, "Address to the National Press Club" (Washington, DC: U.S. Department of Education, March 27, 1985).

74. T. Toch, "School Chiefs Endorse State-by-State Comparisons," *Education Week* 9, 12 (1984): 1, 16.

75. W. J. Bennett, "Statement by Secretary of Education William J. Bennett" (Press Statement, delivered February 11, 1985).

76. R. Reagan, "Remarks at the National Association of Independent Schools Annual Meeting. February 28, 1985," *Weekly Compilation of Presidential Documents* 21, 9 (Washington, DC: Government Printing Office, March 4, 1985): 232-237.

77. Bennett, "Address to the National Press Club."

78. T. E. Cronin and S. D. Greenberg, *The Presidential Advisory System,* Parts I-III (New York: Harper & Row, 1969).

79. C. H. Weiss, "The Many Meanings of Research Utilization," *Public Administration Review* 30, 5 (1979): 426-431.

80. U.S. Department of Education, *The Nation Responds,* p. 11.

81. M. Edelman, *The Symbolic Uses of Politics* (Urbana: University of Illinois Press, 1964).

82. Weiss, "The Many Meanings of Research Utilization."

83. M. Reagan, *The New Federalism* (New York: Oxford University Press, 1972).

84. E. M. Gardner, "The Education Crisis: Washington Shares the Blame," *Backgrounder* (Washington: The Heritage Foundation, May 11, 1984).

85. J. Hanrahan and J. Kosterlitz, "How the New Right Affects the U.S. Department of Education," *The Education Digest* 49, 7 (1984): 25-29.

86. See, for example, P. K. Piele, "Public Support for Public Schools: The Past, The Future, and The Federal Role," *Teachers College Record* 84 (1983): 690-707; F. M. Wirt, "Historical Givens, Alternative Futures, and Federal School Policy," *Teachers College Report* 84 (1983): 730-752; J. W. Guthrie, "The Future of Federal Education Policy," *Education and Urban Society* 14 (1982): 511-530.

87 N. C. Thomas, "The Development of Federal Activism in Education: A Contemporary Perspective," *Education and Urban Society* 15, 3 (1983): 271-290, p. 280.

88. W. C. Thomas, "The Development of Federal Activism"; Clark and Amiot, "The Disassembly of the Federal Role in Education"; D. P. Doyle, "Deregulation, the New Federalism, and Scarcity: The End of Additive Reform," *Phi Delta Kappan* (September 1982): 54-56.

89. P. E. Peterson and B. G. Rabe, "The Role of Interest Groups in the Formation of Educational Policy: Past Practices and Future Trends," *Teachers College Record* 84 (Spring 1983): 708-729, p. 724.

90. D. L. Clark and M. A. Amiot, "The Disassembly of the Federal Educational Role," *Education and Urban Society* 15, 3 (1983): 367-387; D. L. Clark, T. A. Astuto, and P. M. Rooney, "The Changing Structure of Federal Education Policy in the 1980s," *Phi Delta Kappan* 65, 3 (1983): 188-193.

91. C. E. Finn, Jr., "Reflections on the 'Disassembly of the Federal Educational Role,'" *Education and Urban Society* 15, 3 (1983): 389-396.

92. T. James and H. Levin, *Public Dollars for Private Schools* (Philadelphia: Temple University Press, 1983).

93. R. V. Pierard and Robert G. Clouse, "What's New About the New Right," *Contemporary Education* 54, 3 (1983): 194-200.

94. L. Iannaccone, "The Reagan Presidency," *Journal of Learning Disabilities* 14, 2 (1981): 55-59; D. L. Clark and M. A. Amiot, "End Note," *Education and Urban Society* 15, 3 (1983): 397-398.

CHAPTER FIVE

Educational Fiscal Policy and Judicial Deference

KERN ALEXANDER

By virtue of their offices, educational administrators, more often than not, find themselves on the side of the defendant state or local education agencies in school litigation. Most administrators regard much of the educational litigation as judicial encroachment on their prerogatives. Ironically, over the long run, such litigation has served to expand educational opportunities and to provide rationale for increased financing of the public schools. This review takes the position that current political trends toward a more conservative judiciary are harmful to expansion of educational opportunity and that judicial deference to administrative authority tends to be educationally counterproductive.

The nation has apparently developed a consensus that government has overinvested in educational and social programs and that the courts have generally exceeded their prerogatives by overextending the scope of civil rights protections. Sharp budgetary shifts and restraint at the federal executive and legislative levels enunciate a belief that the national purpose can best be served by budgetary reserve in educational and social programs. Concomitantly, there appears to be a generally accepted thrust toward a more conservative judiciary. Tax revolts in the various states resulting in reduction of taxing prerogative, such as in Massachusetts with Proposition 2½, evidence the pervasiveness of the strong sentiment to reduce government growth and spending. Certainly this cannot be all bad. Yet, from an educational administration point of view, the detriments may far outweigh the benefits, particularly when one realizes that growth of government and the alleged excess of governmental spending cannot be attributed to education.

In fact, the nation's commitment to education has been waning for several years as indicated by the reduced share of the Gross National Product which is now provided for education. During the last decade, total expenditures for K-12 education as a percentage of GNP declined from 4.2 to 3.7.[1] Although some of this decline is attributable to a leveling off

SOURCE: Kern Alexander, "Educational Fiscal Policy and Judicial Deference," *Educational Administration Quarterly*, Vol. 18, No. 3, pp. 131-149. Copyright © by The University Council for Educational Administration. Reprinted with permission.

of student population, other data suggest a general decline in public commitment. For example, instructional staff salaries in public schools, measured in constant 1979-80 dollars, have declined from $18,149 in 1969-70 to $16,813 in 1979-80. Total revenue receipts for elementary and secondary schools, when measured in constant dollars, have fallen about $5 billion during the last five years. During this same five-year period, revenue receipts per pupil in average daily attendance have risen only about one percent per year. In the last decade of financial contraction in education, both parents and educators have tended to look increasingly to the judiciary for relief for educational problems.

In the light of these observations, this review examines the inter-relationship between the judiciary and the economic welfare of the public education system. Further, the reviewer questions the prevailing political philosophy, which portends increased deference by the judiciary in educational affairs, that may reduce the financial commitment to education.

During 1981-82, two dozen bills have been introduced in Congress to limit the authority of the federal courts. Congressional attempts to place restrictions on the judiciary have come about as various members of Congress have viewed with increasing disfavor those rulings bearing on important social and economic issues, many of which touch education. Most notable among the attempts to limit judicial action was the antibus-ing rider attached to a bill which authorized funds for the U.S. Department of Justice. The attempt, of course, was to squeeze the department's budget so that the Justices would be unable to enforce civil rights claims.

In the face of this attitude toward the judiciary, the federal courts have, in recent years, tended to withdraw into a less assertive role. Harry T. Edwards commented in 1980 that, "the Federal courts continue to eschew an activist role, especially in the enforcement of individual rights."[2] As the role of judge-made law has diminished, there has been a concomitant burgeoning of regulations to restrict individual choice and local educational prerogative. Since the mid-60s, few major legislative advancements have been made that were not prefaced by positive judicial action establishing the philosophical rationale for the change. During this time, judicial initiative in educational matters provided educational relief for those denied their civil rights regardless of the fiscal consequences. Thus, it can be concluded that the call today to reduce the role of the judiciary can only have adverse effects on educational opportunity.

ECONOMIC CONSEQUENCES

In our society, many decisions of great relevance tend to acquire their importance from the economic balance sheet. One does not need to adhere entirely to the theory of economic determinism[3] to recognize that most significant educational changes in public schools transpire as a result of fiscal policy decisions or are made in an overall milieu of the prevailing economic condition. Indeed, the historical context in which the public schools were first founded held significant economic overtones. Cubberley described the creation of state schools as largely a battle for tax support to eliminate the pauper-school idea and to make schools entirely free.[4] The public school concept was premised on the notion that enough revenues would be collected through general taxation to operate schools, free of tuition and fees, where rich and poor alike could be educated in common.

Most significant court decisions in education have fiscal consequences which may alternatively please or distress various groups in our society. A decision by the courts, for example, to fiscally equalize funds among school districts may well help children in poorer school districts but yet correspondingly draw criticism from taxpayers in more wealthy areas of a state.

When major legislative policy decisions are made for education, there is an assumption of the accompanying public willingness to support the will of the majority. The politician's ability to set new directions for education is ultimately dependent on the public's desire to go along; the accountability of the legislator is much more direct and certain than that of the courts. On the other hand, in judicial theory, judge-made law may evolve from custom and societal preference. With court law, the proximate relationship to the people is more remote than with legislation. The result is that the courts may render decisions, to protect individual rights and freedoms, which if taken to public referendum would have failed because of economic or other consequences. Courts may well, though, give relief to a minority which could never win legislative approval. However, when this is done, judicial decisions may have substantial financial impact on the public treasury that may not have transpired through legislative channels.

In rendering decisions that have important financial implications, the courts have generally improved the quality of public education. A familiar early example was the decision in the 1874 Kalamazoo case where the Supreme Court of Michigan, without explicit statutory basis, held that school taxes could be assessed to establish a high school program.[5] The decision influenced the expansion of the public school upward to include preparation to enter college, a new role for public education. Although it was judicially innovative for its day, the Kalamazoo-type case today would hardly raise an eyebrow.

Assertiveness by the courts in matters of individual rights and freedoms has obviously had a profound impact on all governmental agencies and especially on education. Court decisions have resulted in greatly expanded educational opportunity and, in most instances, the economic consequences have been substantial.

Court decisions bearing on education may result in different economic consequences, including an increase or decrease in individual and/or public costs. Compulsory education[6] and child labor law cases resulted in an increased cost to individual children and their families because they were required to attend school during the working day, thus forgoing wages. Yet, economic advantage was also gained as the children utilized their education to acquire increased work skills and employment options resulting in augmented lifetime earnings. Correspondingly, public or social costs were increased because many children were compelled to attend public schools which were paid for with tax dollars. These costs were, however, offset by the taxes the state received back from the increased earning power of the former students as they contributed to the earning power of the work force. Educational cost consequences of various court decisions are apparent in many cases dealing with areas of education such as bilingual programs and special offerings for the handicapped. There are as well even more pervasive cost/benefit consequences such as those of racial segregation in the schools.

One can see, then, how court decisions expanding educational opportunity may produce economic cost benefits to both the individual and the state. Horace Mann recognized this and made the benefit argument one of his primary bases for advancing the cause of public education. It is worth noting that in 1848, long before economic science made the same discovery, he maintained that the primary ingredient in the development of the wealth of nations was the intellectual development of the human being. Mann warned that:

> . . . political economy, therefore, which busies interest about capital and labor, supply and demand, interest and rents, favorable and unfavorable balances of trade; but leaves out of account the element of wide-spread mental development, is nought but stupendous folly.[7]

In recent years, economists have been able to measure within a certain degree of acceptable tolerance the economic benefits derived from expansion of educational opportunity. The most widely used method is the rate of return approach that produces a percentage return to both the individual and state after costs and benefits are taken into account. Although it is difficult to show that any particular court decision has a definitive effect on rates of return to education, estimates of overall educational impact can be made as courts expand educational opportunity.[8] Thus, one may speak rather confidently that those court decisions that have substantially expanded opportunity have produced important economic benefits which will in the future yield returns many times greater than the original investment.[9]

One can think of a myriad of court decisions in education which have had significant financial overtones. A few, though, are particularly noteworthy and most useful for illustration purposes. Among these are cases involving racial segregation, bilingual education, special education for the handicapped, state school finance, and church-state issues.

RACIAL SEGREGATION IN SCHOOLS

The most manifestly justifiable of all judicial action touching on education is found in the long struggle to desegregate the public schools. Space here obviously will not allow even a surface explication of all the judicial, social, and economic ramifications of school desegregation. Suffice it to say, the economic overtones of this great human equality phenomenon have dominated social intercourse in this country for many years. Some mention of desegregation is, though, vastly important to this discussion since racial inequality in education still remains in some southern school districts and in a great many northern school districts as well. As Becker has noted, the economics of inequality is not only important to the individual, but also to the state and society.[10]

In one sense, whites have always placed a relatively high economic value on segregation. Before the Brown decision in 1954, southern whites were willing to expend funds to maintain separate and dual school facilities, a system more costly than a single system even though the black schools were markedly inferior to white schools. After Sweatt vs. Painter in 1950, when the Supreme Court held that blacks attending inferior state law school facilities must be admitted to the white state university, the cost of segregation became even greater. In this case, the Supreme Court was cognizant of not only the costs but also the benefits of equal educational opportunity when it observed that students at black, inferior, segregated law schools would have little opportunity to develop professionally and, in the future, to hold important legal positions in bench and bar. The Court, in requiring equal facilities for higher education programs, forced southern states to establish, at great cost, better black schools at all levels—elementary school, secondary school, and higher education. Deference by the courts resulted in little change; active intervention resulted in much improvement.

Prior to Sweatt, judicial deference to state legislative and local school board prerogatives resulted in a very low expenditure for black schools. Possibly the most glaring example of untoward judicial deference at the highest level having important financial overtones in denying equal educational opportunity was in Cumming vs. Richmond County Board of Education (1889).[11] In this infamous case, the school board claimed it did not have the tax resources to provide facilities for a black high school. Black high school students were advised by the board to attend private church affiliated schools. In an unfortunate decision, the U.S. Supreme Court refused to require that the local board maintain high school facilities for the black students, reasoning that the matter of education and taxation to support it was solely a state concern. The school district was allowed to close the black high school. Obviously, the Court's deference to state and local authority resulted in a blatant denial of educational opportunity and reduced the value of the human capital who were prevented from attending secondary school.

From 1954 to today, however, courts have not been disposed to allow short-range financial burdens or immediate public costs to excuse racial discrimination.[12] In each case where the Supreme Court has refused to defer to state legislative and administrative prerogative, the direct public costs for education were increased. But it can be seen that these costs were more than offset by the long-range benefits accruing to black students, individually, and to society.[13]

Before the 1954 Brown decision, white schools had much higher expenditure per pupil per year than black schools. Black teachers received lower salaries, the school year was generally shorter, and facilities were inferior. In Florida, for example, the expenditure per pupil for black students was only 39 percent of that for white students in 1940. Of course, this had changed significantly by 1950 when it had increased to 74 percent, but wide expenditure variations still existed between schools and school districts. By integrating the schools and equalizing the expenditure per pupil between black and white pupils, the U.S. Supreme Court extended not only the educational and social advantages of association with white children, but also significantly altered the economic condition of the South.[14] Today, the disparity in educational opportunity exists to a great extent in the North where hundreds of small school districts are segregated on both racial and economic bases.

Since the Brown decision in 1954, there has been a change in the benefits and costs of educational services for blacks. In addition, the actual earning differentials between black and white males have declined in the marketplace. Brown, it should be noted, had an impact throughout society and affected equal opportunity for blacks beyond the boundaries of education. Statistics may also be garnered to show that this increase in earning and consuming power of blacks has provided, in the two and a half decades since Brown, a stimulus to the American economy. For example, in 1955 the annual income of black males was 54 percent that of white males, and in 1978 the percentage had risen to 74 percent.[15] The effect being, as Horace Mann said, "to change a consumer into a producer" and, thus, to make the black American a better and more responsible consumer.

Some may reasonably argue that federal civil rights legislation has had a greater impact on the racial integration of the schools than has judicial action. Certainly, the Civil Rights Act of 1964 was a major instrument that was used by the U.S. Office of Education and the courts in bringing about desegregation. Yet, it was the judiciary with its initial interpretations of equal protection that provided the impetus and the sustenance for the movement toward racial equality in the public schools. Where the Supreme Court has moved boldly as in Swann vs. Charlotte-Mecklenburg,[16] integration has moved forward; where the Court has been reluctant as in Milliken vs. Bradley,[17] integration has been retarded.

One finds in Brown and its progeny an important change in the economic condition of the public school and of society generally. Had judicial deference been exercised in 1954 and in later decisions, not only would social justice have been delayed, but substantial economic loss to both the individual and society also would have resulted.

EDUCATING THE HANDICAPPED

A court decision that has greatly affected educational financing and school policy is Mills vs. Board of Education of District of Columbia.[18] Although generally viewed as a procedural due process case, Mills had important economic consequences for both the school district and the handicapped child.[19] Another landmark case, Pennsylvania Association of Retarded Children vs. Commonwealth of Pennsylvania[20] (the PARC case) in concert with Mills, helped add form and strength to the arguments of advocates for handicapped education. After the implementation of the PARC court decree, the state of Pennsylvania witnessed a significant increase in the number of programs available to retarded children.[21]

Before Mills was rendered in 1972, the federal government had made very little effort to education handicapped children. States had been more aggressive, several having had elements in their foundation programs or special categorical grants which provided for special education.

Nevertheless, educational opportunity for the handicapped was limited as schools systematically turned away children with handicaps because school districts claimed they did not have the resources to provide for such high-cost programs. Under general state statues which provide for creation and maintenance of public schools, the courts had typically ruled that the role of the school was purely educational and to provide services which mingled treatment with education was beyond the scope of the school prerogative. Further, it was a widely held belief that the inclusion of certain types of handicapped children in the classroom was disruptive and that their presence was detrimental to the education of others. In Mills, though, money was the root of the problem. Because of costs, from an estimated total of 22,000 retarded, emotionally disturbed, blind, deaf, and speech and learning disabled, only 4,000 were receiving special education services. In the face of this denial, the Federal District Court in the District of Columbia held that the Due Process Clause of the Fifth Amendment was elastic enough to provide equal protection, as envisioned under the Fourteenth Amendment, to handicapped children denied educational rights. The court in quoting an earlier Washington, D.C. decision stated:

> From these considerations the court draws the conclusion that the doctrine of equal educational opportunity—the equal protection clause in its application to public school education—is in its full sweep a component of due process binding on the District under the due process clause of the Fifth Amendment.[22]

The defendant school board maintained that the financial resources of the system were not adequate to sustain the burden of providing educational programs to meet the needs of all the handicapped children. The court took a dim view of this position and responded thusly:

> ... the District of Columbia's interest in educating the excluded children clearly must outweigh its interest in preserving its financial resources. If sufficient funds are not available to finance all of the services and programs that are needed and desirable in the system then the available funds must be expended equitably in such a manner that no child is entirely excluded from a publicly supported education consistent with his needs and ability to benefit therefrom.[23]

The lack of available funds could not be used as an excuse for nonperformance. The spectre of Cumming,[24] which denied equal opportunity to black children, would not be allowed to arise to similarly deprive the handicapped. The Mills[25] decision had a profound effect on the education of the handicapped in the United States, being the precursor of action by state legislatures across the country. Mills, too, provided the rationale for Congressional enactment of the pervasive PL. 94-142, the Education of All Handicapped Children Act.

Today, the precedents of Mills and PARC have set a pattern for judicial action in special education in many other jurisdictions. In New York, for example, Rebell reports that when Jose P vs. Ambach[26] was first initiated in 1979 that approximately 50,000 students were enrolled in special education programs in the City of New York, but by January 1, 1980, the number had risen to 60,000 and by September 1, 1980, to a total of 75,000 students. Additionally, as Rebell observed, hundreds of additional staff had been hired to accommodate the evaluation and educational needs of these children.[27]

Had the court in Mills deferred to the District of Columbia Board of Education or the PARC court have failed to act because of perceived financial exigency, the educational needs of the handicapped would have been long delayed or possibly never completely fulfilled.

THE LAU REMEDY

The bilingual education movement probably would not have amounted to much without the impetus provided by the 1974 U.S. Supreme Court decision, Lau vs. Nichols.[28] Certainly the Bilingual Education Act of 1968 was an indication of a degree of governmental interest in bilingual education, but it amounted to little monetarily, initially providing for only $7.5 million for demonstration projects. The program coasted along for six years with little increase in funding until the Lau decision, which caused a dramatic shift in government policy. *Fortune* magazine in September 1980 noted that it was the "Supreme Court that turned bilingual education from an experimental program into a permanent legal fixture. . . ."[29] The economic results of the Court's decision enunciated judicial philosophy that had dramatic effects on educational policy.

In Lau, the U.S. Supreme Court reversed the Ninth Circuit Court of Appeals and embraced the opinion of a dissenting judge by the name of Shirley Hufstedler who had maintained that "access to education offered by public schools is completely foreclosed to those children who cannot comprehend any of it."[30] Later as Secretary of Education, Hufstedler updated, formalized, and administered the so-called Lau remedies.

In the Lau decision, the Supreme Court used §601 of the Civil Rights Act of 1964 to require bilingual education in the San Francisco public schools, banning discrimination based "on the ground of race, color, or national origin" in "any program or activity receiving Federal financial assistance." According to the Court, §601 was violated when non-English speaking Chinese children were prevented from effectively participating in the educational program solely because of the language barrier. The decision, it should be emphasized, was based on the Civil Rights Act and not the equal protection clause of the Fourteenth Amendment. The San Francisco school district had a contractual obligation to abide by the requirements of the Civil Rights Act in order to receive federal funds. The district acquiesced to the rules in order to receive financial benefits, and the Court's legal foundation was found in statute. Judicial intervention was necessary to discover the intent of the Civil Rights Act with regard to bilingual education. This decision had important economic consequences for the public schools. As state and local authorities sought to comply with Lau, Congress increased appropriations for bilingual education. The total per year from all levels exceeded $450 million by 1981. Thus, the decision of the U.S. Supreme Court in overriding the judicial timidity of a lower court expended the nation's financial commitment to equal educational opportunity.

If the Supreme Court had deferred to the local education agency, not only Chinese children but also thousands of other children in need of bilingual instruction would have been denied educational benefits. Although many have criticized with some validity the subsequent federal regulations which accompanied the Congressional response to Lau, the fault does not lie with the rationale of the decision itself. Overzealous advocacy by bilingual proponents who wanted subjects taught in foreign languages for reasons ranging from nationalistic pride to cultural self-determinism produced some administrative growing pains that should not be placed at the feet of the Supreme Court. The Court's rationale, though, did greatly expand the educational opportunity for non-English speaking children. Judicial deference would have denied many children the education provided by the increase of federal, state, and local funds. Simple justice required the financial commitment.

STATE SCHOOL FINANCE

The impact of the judiciary on educational policy is nowhere more evident than in the "school finance" cases. Before the late 1960s, legislation regarding the distribution of school funds had been given a wide berth by the courts at both the state and federal levels. Where challenges to state school finance programs had been launched, the courts had maintained that the allocation of state revenues was a legislative prerogative that would not be invaded by the courts. The position of the courts was basically the same as the U.S. Supreme Court when it first refused to enter the "political thicket" of reapportionment.[31]

Likewise, the courts were generally hesitant to enter the arena of public school finance, clinging to the well-enunciated principle that legislative authority could not be superseded by the courts unless there were "clear and hostile discriminations against particular persons and classes."[32] Classification for purposes of taxation could not be arbitrary; errors of judgment resulting in underevaluation or overevaluation that were not intentional or systematic were not constitutionally offensive.[33]

Judicial hesitancy to invalidate legislative acts dealing with taxation emanated at least partly from an uncertainty as to what the needs of state government actually were. The U.S. Court of Appeals for the Ninth Circuit spoke of judicial deference in taxation as a matter of fitting the system of taxation to local conditions.

> Traditionally classification has been a device for fitting tax programs to local needs and usages in order to achieve an equitable distribution of the tax burden. It has, because of this, been pointed out that in taxation, even more than in other fields, legislatures possess the greatest freedom of classification. Since the members of a legislature necessarily enjoy a familiarity with local conditions which this court cannot have, the presumption of constitutionality can be overcome only by the most explicit demonstration that a classification is a hostile and oppressive discrimination against particular persons and classes.[34]

It was, therefore, possible to have intentional discrimination in taxation of great magnitude, but the courts refused to extend constitutional protection to include the distribution of public funds. Nonintervention of the judiciary with regard to the allocation of state school funds was virtually complete. It existed to the extent that few complaints were ever rendered contesting school finance formulas. Where plaintiffs persevered the familiar response of the courts was:

> It is generally held that the constitutional provisions requiring equality and uniformity relate to the levy of taxes and not to the distribution or application of the revenue derived therefrom; and hence statues relative to the distribution or application of such money cannot be held invalid on this ground.[35]

In the arena of state school finance, the doctrine of judicial deference is probably best summed by *Corpus Juris Secundum* which states:

> In the absence of constitutional regulation the method of apportioning and distributing a school fund, accruing from taxes or other revenue, rests in the wise discretion of the state legislature, which method, in the absence of abuse of discretion or violation of some constitutional provision, cannot be interfered with by the courts ... the fact that the fund is distributed unequally among different districts or political subdivisions does not render it invalid.[36]

This general attitude of the courts was drawn into question in 1968 in cases in Virginia[37] and Illinois[38] wherein plaintiffs complained that the "wise discretion" of the legislature had left great gaps in uniformity and equality of educational opportunity among school districts. Later, the more renowned Serrano case[39] was filed in California. The potential for educational, economic, and fiscal policy reform was profound as several states began to scramble to defend their systems of school financing. If plaintiffs in these cases prevailed, it meant not only a substantial redistribution of present state funds but also sizable increases in state revenues.

Federal courts in both Virginia and Illinois rejected plaintiffs' complaint, with the McInnis court in particular most clearly stating the deference rule, ". . . the courts have neither the knowledge, nor the means, nor the power to tailor the public moneys to fit the varying needs of these students throughout the state."[40]

In California, that state's supreme court responded quite differently by rejecting the deference doctrine and wading assertatively into the waters of state school fiscal policy. Judicial abstention to legislative control of state school fiscal policy would never be the same. As all know, the California court held in that historic case that a child's education could not be dependent on local taxpaying ability.

As a result of Serrano, positive educational benefit carried forward throughout the last decade as state legislatures examined and reexamined their school finance policies and court decisions were rendered in many states which continue to force legislative reassessment. This has transpired even in the face of the Rodriguez[41] decision in which the U.S. Supreme Court removed the equal protection clause as a viable ground on which to base complaints. In the Rodriguez case, the U.S. Supreme Court refused to grant plaintiffs relief under the equal protection clause of the Fourteenth Amendment. The issues were the fundamentality of education and the application of equal protection principles, but the sovereignty of the state's fiscal powers weighed heavily on the Supreme Court. Intervention in state legislative affairs involving taxation was a matter of separation of powers, and the Court was unwilling to go that far. The Court stated:

> We are asked to condemn the State's judgment in conferring on political subdivisions the power to tax local property to supply revenues for local interests. In so doing, appellees would have the Court intrude in an area in which it has traditionally deferred to state legislatures. This Court has often admonished against such interferences with the State's fiscal policies.[42]

Although the Court's abstention may have appeared justifiable on grounds of state legislative sovereignty over fiscal affairs, the cost to educational opportunity was probably very high. This decision virtually foreclosed all future school finance litigation under the equal protection clause, casting the issues of fiscal and educational need equalization back to the state constitutional level.

Most recently, state courts in Georgia[43] and Maryland[44] found that the current schemes of financing in those states violated the state constitutional provision. In other states, decisions have been rendered almost annually asserting judicial control over legislative prerogative. In 1977, Horton[45] in Connecticut; in 1978, Levittown School District[46] in New York; in 1981, Pauley[47] in West Virginia; and in 1980, Washakie County School District[48] in Wyoming, courts held that the respective state systems of school financing violated the state's own constitution. In each of these cases, plaintiffs alleged that the school distribution formula was constitutionally deficient, violating one or more state constitutional provisions. For example, in Connecticut, Wyoming, and New York, the finance formulae were found to fall short of requirements of the equal protection clauses of their respective constitutions. In West Virginia, the court held that the state's "thorough and efficient" clause made education a fundamental right. Thus, a discriminatory classification created by the school finance formula violated the equal protection clause of the West Virginia Constitution.

In a highly publicized decision, Robinson vs. Cahill,[49] rendered shortly after the U.S. Supreme Court's rejection of the plaintiff's claims in Rodriguez, the state Supreme Court of New Jersey demonstrated the full scope of judicial power. Here the court not only refused to defer to the legislature on school finance and educational policy matters, but also it boldly forced the legislature to levy a new income tax to support the increased costs of reform. The timing of this case was extremely important to school finance litigation because it opened new avenues of state constitutional relief after the federal constitutional remedies had been foreclosed by Rodriguez. The court in the Robinson case observed that the equal protection clause of a state's constitution can be more demanding than the equal protection clause of the United States Constitution, yet did not find it necessary to invoke this provision in requiring revision of New Jersey's school finance law. The case finally rested on the court's interpretation of the expansiveness of the "thorough and efficient" provision of the New Jersey constitution.

The significance of this type of State case is noted by Justice William J. Brennan, Associate Justice of the U.S. Supreme Court, in a law review article in 1977 where he observed that as the Supreme Court has withdrawn from expansion to equal protection guarantees, state courts have stepped in to fill the void by expanding state equal protection clauses to guarantee exercise of fundamental rights.[50] Brennan said that this is an "important and highly significant development for our constitutional jurisprudence."[51] Therefore, judicial deference by the U.S. Supreme Court has not necessarily been imitated at the state level. Decisions such as Robinson and the school finance cases which followed have led to a reassertion of the state judicial role in assuring constitutional rights under state constitutions.[52]

Such revitalization of the judicial role in states would be pointless and potentially harmful to our governmental system if it did not produce benefits to society through better educational programs. At the state level, changes in the structure of the finance program can produce dramatic local effects on both taxpayers and school children. In the instance of New Jersey, for example, the benefits to the judicial intervention far outweigh any perceived detriments. Lehne has reported that Robinson was responsible for producing a new public school law in 1974 which became the guiding statute for education in New Jersey and established requirements and procedures for adherence to the constitutional standards of "thorough and efficient."[53] Although Lehne ultimately concluded that Robinson probably did not result in an overall increase in expenditures for the public schools, several benefits were obviously attributable to the case. As a spinoff of the litigation, local school districts were required to define specific educational goals, shape programs to meet the goals, evaluate their progress, and institute corrective action where necessary. The Robinson decision (or decisions—Robinson ended up encompassing six state court decisions and five federal court opinions) affected education in several other ways as well: (1) it raised an awareness of educational problems and mobilized forces for improvements; (2) it required the state department of education to define educational standards for student performance; (3) it created a legislative process for the ongoing study of the financing, administration, and operation of the public schools; (4) it reformed the role of education in the total system of politics, elevating it to a higher level of importance; (5) it resulted in a new and improved equalization method for distributing state school monies; and (6) it produced additional fiscal effort by the state to support the public schools. Had the New Jersey Supreme Court refused to tread in the "bramble bush" of educational finance reform, it is doubtful that these achievements would have been realized.

Perhaps the most important benefit of such cases is that judicial intervention produces significant fiscal advantage for education—not directly, but as a result of the dramatization of the issues that the judiciary illuminates. In most states where school finance has been litigated, benefits have accrued to education simply because of the increased publicity and public visibility that accompanies such controversies.

CHURCH AND STATE

The harm of judicial deference visited on the public schools can be nowhere better demonstrated than in the matters involving the separation of church and state. Where courts have abstained from invoking constitutional guarantees under the "establishment clause" of the First Amendment, both taxpayers and public schools have tended to suffer. One need not be reminded of the great church and state controversies throughout history to recognize their impact on economic conditions. Much of the history of the Western World is merely the documentation of political and economic contests between religion and the sovereign. Every era, from the Constitutions of Clarendon of the twelfth century to the dissolution of monasteries of the sixteenth century and to Walz vs. Tax Commission[54] in the twentieth century, has had cases that involved taxation and the struggle for control of property between religion and state. The importance of the ecclesiastical connection with education and economics did not go unnoticed by the father of economics. Adam Smith, who, in his *Wealth of Nations*, devoted an entire chapter to the economic aspects of religious instruction.[55] Significantly, he observed that the state has only finite resources that the church seeks to acquire, and when it does, it diminishes the resources available for state purposes:

> The revenue of every established church, . . . , is a branch, . . of the general revenue of the state, which is thus diverted to a purpose very different from the defence of the state. . . .
>
> The more of this fund that is given to the church, the less, it is evident, can be spared to the state. It may be laid down as a certain maxim, that, all other things being supposed equal, the richer the church, the poorer must necessarily be, either the sovereign on the one hand, or the people on the other. . . .[56]

Such division of state resources applies to education in the United States as readily as to historical states of Adam Smith's experience. Originally, clergymen opposed the creation of public schools for fear of erosion of support for private schools, and the clergy generally felt that public schools contributed to an increase in "drunkedness, crime, juvenile depravity" and were generally "Godless."[57] As common schools became stronger, the church schools shifted their emphasis to division of the public treasury in order to increase the revenues for church-related schools.

Such proposals were advanced in many states, an example of which is documented in the state superintendent of Michigan's annual report in 1853. In this *Petition for a Division of the School Fund,* Catholic clergy devised a voucher plan in which the parent be left free to choose the teacher to whom he will entrust the education of his child, as he is left to choose his physician, his lawyer, etc.; that each person teaching any public school in the State should be entitled to draw from the public school fund, such sums as the law might provide for every child so taught. . . .[58]

Opposition protested that such a plan would place "the school fund of the state in the hands of religious bodies or sects. . . "[59] This particular forerunner of today's voucher bore no fruit for the church.

In more recent years, the church-related schools have launched vigorous campaigns to capture portions of state and federal funds. In several instances, the courts have acted affirmatively in stemming the diversion of public tax funds, but in several cases the courts have allowed enabling legislation to stand. Thus, judicial deference to legislative prerogative has resulted in the outflow of billions of dollars to parochial schools, funds which diminish public school resources and enhance the strength of religious organizations.

Such deferential treatment was given by the U.S. Supreme Court in Cochran vs. Louisiana State Board,[60] Everson vs. Board of Education,[61] and Board of Education vs. Allen.[62] In each instance, the court allowed legislation to stand that provided state aid to parochial schools. The rationale of the Court was particularly significant in Allen because it cast open the public treasury to parochial school use so long as the school could show that it provided secular as well as sectarian educational services.

In Allen and its precursors,[63] the Court adopted the doctrine of "child benefit" which is premised on the idea that the state, in providing public tax funds for parochial schools, actually benefits the child rather than the church. In accepting this defense, the Court allowed the state statutes in question to stand and, by its deference, established a precedent for other states to follow in aiding parochial schools. Shortly after Everson in 1947, over 20 states enacted statutes which allowed the use of public funds for transportation of parochial school students.

Similarly, over 20 years later after the Allen decision, proponents of aid to parochial schools launched a vigorous campaign in virtually all state legislatures to expand public funding of secular activities in religious schools. The Supreme Court in deferring to state action had refused to invoke the Establishment Clause of the First Amendment, paving the way for many state legislatures not only to provide books and transportation for parochial schools, but also to encourage categorical aid devices that directly aided parochial school operations.

As history has shown time and again, departure from strict adherence to the principle of separation results in overzealous pursuit of the public tax dollar by church interests, and this case was no exception. New state plans to aid parochial schools represented a range of approaches, including salary supplements for teachers of secular services, contracts for purchase of parochial school services, maintenance and repair grants, and tuition reimbursement. This deluge of statutes dividing the public treasury between public and parochial school interests was finally stemmed by several Supreme Court decisions that held such services constituted either enhancement of religion or excessive entanglement between church and state.[64]

More recently, the Supreme Court has held that auxiliary services and direct loans for instructional materials and equipment for parochial schools are unconstitutional.[65] In Nyquist, the Court has held that the income tax deductions for parents of children attending parochial schools violate the Establishment Clause.[66] Many believe this latter decision is the critical precedent in predicting how the Supreme Court will rule if the Congress enacts a law to provide tuition tax credits, provided that new Supreme Court appointments do not alter the Court's balance.

Should tuition tax credits be enacted and should the Supreme Court defer to Congressional action, then the basic structure of education in this country could be permanently altered. The economic effects of such judicial deference could possibly result in private and parochial schools acquiring a major share of federal funds for elementary and secondary education. Estimates range as high as seven billion dollars by 1986. Recently, in hearings before the House Education and Labor Committee, John E. Chapoton, Assistant Treasury Secretary, suggested that the money lost to the Treasury from such credits could possibly be taken from existing federal school aid programs in order to combat further federal budgetary deficits. Additionally, if such tax measures for parochial schools were allowed to stand at the federal level, there is little doubt that several state legislatures would shortly follow suit, further dividing the public treasury.

With this issue, the U.S. Supreme Court may truly be the court of last resort for public education. If the time comes when the Supreme Court is called to rule on the issue, a reversion to judicial deference with respect to Congressional prerogative would do untold damage to the public schools. Instead, the Court's active enforcement of the precedent it laid down in Nyquist, to wit:

> Special tax benefits, however, cannot be squared with the principle of neutrality established by the decisions of this Court. To the contrary, insofar as such benefits render assistance to parents who send their children to sectarian schools, their purpose and inevitable effect are to aid and advance those religious institutions. . . ,

would undoubtedly prevent division of public resources and political divisiveness.[67]

CONCLUSION

The extent to which judges can go in shaping society has long been debated. Some had maintained that judges must merely interpret the law as it is found, but not create it. At the base of all law, though, are broad general principles such as equity and social justice which may not be written into statute but are, nevertheless, the final standards of good or bad law. Cardozo once asserted that, "The final cause of law is the welfare of society."[58] Certainly where education is concerned, this goal is most obvious.

Failure of the courts to assert boldly their prerogatives generally results in harm to public education. Nonassertion may result in denial of educational opportunity to an individual child and concomittantly lend itself to a diminution of fiscal resources for education. Where the courts have refused to defer, educational opportunity has been expanded as in the desegregation cases. Similarly, decisions expanding the educational horizons for handicapped, bilingual, and economically deprived children have sparked public financial commitments for many children who would never have received educational services without such intervention. Further, drastic modifications in the structure of the free public schools could come about if courts stand aside and allow religious interests to divide and partition public revenues for their respective sectarian purposes. There is currently no evidence to indicate that the contest is not a zero sum game. In fact, judicial deference may well lead to political divisiveness that would be harmful not only to individual liberties, but also to the overall supply of financial resources for public education.

NOTES

1. R. L. Johns, E. L. Morphet, and K. Alexander, *Economics and Financing of Education* (Englewood Cliffs, N.J.: Prentice-Hall, 1982).

2. H. T. Edwards, *Higher Education and the Unholy Crusade Against Governmental Regulation* (Cambridge, MA: Institute for Educational Management, Harvard University, 1980), pp. 1-2.

3. D. Greenwald, *The McGraw-Hill Dictionary of Modern Economics,* 2nd ed. (New York: McGraw-Hill, 1973), p. 189.

4. E. P. Cubberley, *The History of Education* (Boston: Houghton Mifflin, 1920), pp. 676-677.

5. Stuart vs. School Dist. No. 1 of the Village of Kalamazoo, 39 Mich. 69 (1874).

6. Commonwealth vs. Bey, 166 Pa.Super. 136, 70 A.2d 693 (1950).

7. H. Mann, *The Capacities of Our Present School System to Improve the Pecuniary Condition and to Elevate the Intellectual and Moral Character of the Commonwealth,* from the 12th Report, Massachusetts (1848).

8. T. W. Schultz, ed., *Investment in Education* (Chicago: University of Chicago Press, 1972).

9. *Ibid.*

10. G. S. Becker, *The Economics of Discrimination,* 2nd ed. (Chicago: University of Chicago Press, 1971).

11. Cumming vs. Richmond County Board of Education, 175 U.S. 528, 20 S.Ct. 197 (1899).

12. Green vs. County School Board of New Kent County, 391 U.S. 430, 88 S.Ct. 1689 (1968); Alexander vs. Holmes, 396 U.S. 19, 90 S.Ct. 29 (1969); and Swann vs. Charlotte-Mecklenburg Board of Education, 402 U.S. 1. 91 S.Ct. 1267 (1971).

13. See Becker, *Economics of Discrimination.*

14. See R. A. Posner, *Economic Analysis of Law* (Boston: Little, Brown, 1977), pp. 529-530.

15. *Money Income of Families and Persons in the United States: 1978* (Current Population Reports, Bureau of Census, Series P-60, No. 123, G.P.O., June 1980), p. 279.

16. Swann vs. Charlotte-Mecklenburg Board of Education.

17. Milliken vs. Bradley, 418 U.S. 717, 94 S.Ct. 3112 (1974).

18. Mills vs. Board of Education of District of Columbia, 348 F. Supp. 866 (1972).

19. See K. Alexander, "Educating the Handicapped: Fiscal and Human Resources," in *Financing Special Education in the United States,* Vol. 4, Leadership Series in Special Education, A. M. Rehman and T. F. Riggin, eds. (St. Paul: University of Minnesota, 1976).

20. Pennsylvania Association of Retarded Children vs. Commonwealth of Pennsylvania, 334 F. Supp. 1257 (E.D.Pa. 1971), modified, 343 F. Supp. 279 (E.D.Pa. 1972).

21. M. A. Rebell, "Implementation of Court Mandates Concerning Special Education: The Problems and the Potential," *Journal of Law and Education* 10, 3 (July 1981): 340-343.

22. Bolling vs. Sharp, 344 U.S. 873, 73 S.Ct. 173 (1952).

23. Mills vs. Board of Education of District of Columbia.

24. Cumming vs. Richmond County Board of Education.

25. Mills vs. Board of Education of District of Columbia.

26. Rebell, "Implementation of Court Mandates"; and Jose P vs. Ambach, 279 C. 270, 3 EHLR 551:245 (E.D. N.Y. 1979).

27. Rebell, "Implementation of Court Mandates," pp. 352-353.

28. Lau vs. Nichols, 414 U.S. 563, 94 S.Ct. 786 (1974).

29. *Fortune* (September 22, 1980), p. 84.

30. *Ibid.*

31. Colegrove vs. Green, 328 U.S. 549 (1946).

32. Bell's Gap Railroad Co. vs. Pennsylvania, 134 U.S. 232 (1890).

33. Coutler vs. Louisville & Nashville Railroad Co., 196 U.S. 599 (1905).

34. Hess vs. Mullaney, 15 Alaska 40, 213 F.2d 635 (U.S.C.A. 9th Cir. 1954) *cert. denied,* 348 U.S. 836 (1954).

35. Dean vs. Coddington, 81 S.D. 140, 131 N.W.2d 700 (1964).

36. 79 C.J.S. §411.

37. Burruss vs. Wilkerson, 310 F. Supp. 572 (1969), *affirmed mem.* 397 U.S. 44, 90 S.Ct. 812 (1970).

38. McInnis vs. Shapiro, 393 F. Supp. 327 (1968); *affirmed mem.* 89 S.Ct. 1197 (1969).

39. Serrano vs. Priest, 6 Cal.3d 584, 487 P.2d 1241 (1971).

40. McInnis vs. Shapiro.

41. San Antonio Independent School District vs. Rodriguez, 411 U.S. 1, 93 S.Ct. 1278 *ret. denied,* 411 U.S. 959, 93 S.Ct. 1919 (1973).

42. *Ibid.*

43. Thomas vs. Stewart, Polk County Supreme Court, 1981; since reversed, Daniel vs. Thomas 285 S.E.2d 156 (1981).

44. Somerset County Board of Education vs. Hornbeck, trial court, 1981.

45. Horton vs. Meskill, 172 Conn. 615, 276 A.2d 359 (1977).

46. Board of Education, Levittown Union Free School District vs. Nyquist, 443 N.Y. S.2d 843 (1981).

47. Pauley vs. Kelly, 255 S.E.2d 859 (W.Va. 1979).

48. Washakie Co. Sch. District No. One vs. Herschler, 606 P.2d 310 (Wyo. 1980).

49. Robinson vs. Cahill, 62 N.J. 473, 303 A.2d 372, 287 (1973).

50. W. J. Brennan, Jr., "State Constitutions and the Protection of Individual Rights," *Harvard Law Review* 90 (January 1977): 489-504.

51. *Ibid.*

52. A. E. D. Howard, "State Courts and Constitutional Rights in the Day of the Burger Court," *Virginia Law Review* 62 (June 1976): 873-944.

53. R. Lehne, *The Quest for Justice, The Politics of School Finance Reform* (New York: Longman, 1978).

54. Walz vs. Tax Commission of the City of New York, 90 S.Ct. 1409 (1970).

55. A. Smith, *The Wealth of Nations, 1776* (New York: The Modern Library edition), pp. 740-768.

56. *Ibid.,* pp. 764-765.

57. Reverend M. H. Smith, "The Ark of God on a New Cart," in *Public Education in the United States: Readings,* Ellwood P. Cubberley, ed. (Boston: Houghton Mifflin Company, 1934), pp. 134-135.

58. *Report of the Superintendent of Public Instruction for Michigan,* 1853, pp. 190-191.

59. *Ibid.,* p. 205.

60. Cochran vs. Louisiana State Board, 281 U.S. 370, 50 S.Ct. 335 (1930).

61. Everson vs. Board of Education, 330 U.S. 1, 67 S.Ct. 504 (1947).

62. Board of Education vs. Allen, 392 U.S. 236, 88 S.Ct. 1923 (1968).

63. See: Cochran vs. Louisiana State Board of Education, and Everson vs. Board of Education.

64. Lemon vs. Kurtzman, 403 U.S. 602, 91 S.Ct. 2105 (1971); Committee for Public Education and Religious Liberty vs. Nyquist, 413 U.S. 756, 93 S.Ct. 2955 (1973); and Sloan vs. Lemon, 413 U.S. 825, 93 S.Ct. 2982 (1973).

65. Meek vs. Pittenger, 421 U.S. 350, 95 S.Ct. 1753 (1975).

66. Committee for Public Education and Religious Liberty vs. Nyquist.

67. Lemon vs. Kurtzman.

68. B. N. Cardozo, *The Nature of the Judicial Process* (New Haven, CT: Yale University Press, 921), p. 66.

PART TWO

Educational Organizations in Which Leaders Lead

As the schools moved into complex organization patterns—from one or two rooms to many, from one building to several—the organizational structures for education changed dramatically.

The existing organizational patterns that were known and understandable were industrial and military. These models called for very specific outcomes. Raw materials were to be converted into products. Raw recruits were to be taught how to become part of a fighting team. Likewise the schools had a comparable mission: to convert children (the raw materials) into citizens able to work, to use rudimentary life knowledge and skills, and to be good citizens. The schools were production lines and training camps. The final products were to be good Americans, who knew how to work, to use English, to practice the same values, and to pass on the nation secure and prosperous.

Each education practitioner had a place in the classical organization. A person's place in the hierarchy was very clear. From top to bottom everyone had a place: on top was the board, next was the superintendent, next (or lower on the charts) was the teacher (not a union), and finally was the student. A series of boxes connected with a solid line represented *authority*. The classical theory of power was next: no circles, no dotted lines, and no vague positions. There was a stable organization for stable times, values, expectations, and outcomes.

A static organization for dynamic, changing times was obsolete and is dysfunctional. Organizational experts began to study the nature of organizations as they existed to determine the ways in which they were functional and dysfunctional. The experts studied the military and industry. They studied various academic disciplines. A specialized field of education researchers developed to create an education administration speciality. The following annotations reflect some of the best thinking about the nature of education administration.

CHAPTER SIX

Toward an Integrative Theory of Power and Educational Organizations

RODNEY MUTH

On the assumption that power is central to social life, a power model is proposed and tested. The model is designed to address the problem of conceptual clarity in power studies and to provide an integrative mechanism for explaining divergent outcomes of power acts. Three studies that support the efficacy of the model suggest that the model has considerable heuristic and empirical potential.

The usefulness of the concept of power for the study of social life is indisputable[1]—it is ubiquitous in social relations of all kinds, a central element in organizations, and fundamental to schooling[2]—even though what power *is* and what power *includes* are the subjects of considerable debate.[3] The position taken here is that power is a basic, if not the most basic, element in human relations and that it is possible to construct parsimonious models of power that can account for divergent outcomes of power acts, regardless of the motives or perceptions involved, and which permit integration of competing power theories.[4]

The impetus for this article began years ago when the author noted, as had others,[5] that structural-functionalist and conflict views, two orientations that still dominate social theorizing and command ardent followings, relied quite heavily on the same variable—power—to explain opposing social outcomes—consensus versus conflict. Although not the only theories of power and its effects, the structural-functionalist and conflict theories convey opposing perspectives that have gained considerable support among both theoreticians and researchers. Each view is a normative perspective on social inequality and is concerned about the justice or injustice of these inequalities.[6] On the one hand, the structural-functionalist or consensus theorists, such as Durkheim, Weber, and Parsons, see social inequalities as functional to social order. In their view differentially distributed rewards secure social survival by ensuring that the best qualified fill the most instrumental positions in society and are

SOURCE: Rodney Muth, "Toward an Integrative Theory of Power and Educational Organizations," *Educational Administration Quarterly*, Vol. 20, No. 2, pp. 25-42. Copyright © by The University Council for Educational Administration. Reprinted with permission.

rewarded commensurately, a process to which most members of society readily assent. On the other hand, the conflict theorists, such as Marx, Mills, and Dahrendorf, raise the needs of individuals (or nonelite groups) above those of the system (which is designed and controlled by elites), emphasizing the conflicts created by the unequal distribution of valued goods, services, and status.

Integral to each perspective is the concept of power. For consensus theorists, power beneficially establishes order and regulates allocative processes and ultimately is enforced by Hobbes's omnipotent state. For the conflict theorists, power is used to deprive some of access to the "fruits of their labors" and precipitates a struggle (conflict) between the existing power structure and the powerless. The conflict theorists believe that powerful elites use their control of institutions and organizations to keep nonelites out of value-allocating processes, whereas consensus theorists believe that such structures keep society together, preventing the "war of each against all."

At least two problems arise in trying to integrate these divergent views. First, one element central to both theories is the concept of power, but the concept itself is quite ambiguous. Second, these theories are normative and at the very least require integration into a broader scheme or empirical model that usefully applies to schools and other organizations and that can help explain the divergent outcomes cited by both viewpoints.

ON POWER

Among social analysts, probably the first to examine the heuristic value of the concept of power was Max Weber who defined power as "the probability that one actor within a social relationship will be in a position to carry out his will despite resistance, regardless of the basis on which this probability rests."[7] Explicit in this view are several assumptions: power is relational, latent, and asymmetric, and according to Weber, it relies on the use of some form of force to transact a power interaction.

The first two assumptions are obvious. Without more than one actor, no relationship and no interaction exist. Weber also explicitly labeled power as a potential or probabilistic condition—one can have power and not use it, and just having power may alone be enough to affect another's behavior.[8] The second two assumptions, however, are problematic. Even though Weber defined power as based in force (one can "carry out his will despite resistance"), an actor's power relative to another varies with the circumstances and with the resources and needs of each actor as well as the actors' perceptions of the consequences of the interaction.[9] If, however, a coercive element remains essential to a definition of power, then arguments about situational asymmetry are moot. Yet, if power is an aspect of most social relations, as Weber rightly suggested, then to project such relations as ultimately supported by or dependent upon the threat or probable use of physical or mental violence is incompatible both with a variety of analyses and common sense.[10]

Clearly, then, definitions of types of power are closely related to the bases of power—the variety of resources that enable an actor to transact a power interaction successfully and thereby establish control. These resources necessarily go beyond Weber's imputation of force, punishment, or even subtle duress and may include rewards, the fulfillment of needs, and general symbol manipulation as in propaganda, or sophisticated advertising.[11] Critical is the point that Actor, the "power holder," must have a transactional medium sufficient to control Other, thereby signifying Actor's power relative to Other. What Actor's resources are, how they are used, and how their existence or expression is perceived[12] all determine the nature of the relationship[13] and move it from a state of power as potential to one of control.

Redefining Power and Control

Because power theorists have relied primarily on Weber's definition or slight paraphrases of it, many behaviors have been essentially excluded since such definitions ultimately rely on the use of coercion. In order to broaden the concept of power and thus (1) incorporate common usage, (2) permit definition of behavioral relations which may or may not be symmetrical, and (3) include coercive as well as noncoercive acts, power can be defined simply as the ability of an actor to affect the behavior of another actor.[14] Given this definition, power is relational, potential, and probably asymmetrical; *Ability* indicates the resource capacity necessary to exercise power; *actor* signifies any singular or plural body, human or otherwise; and *affect* includes maintenance of prior conditions or changes in them in intended directions. Power may remain latent, yet a power holder can still be described in terms of the ability to be powerful. Most importantly, this concept encompasses but does not rely upon coercion as a mode of effecting control.

If power is potential, then the behaviors produced by power acts must also be defined. The term *control* is parsimonious and incorporates the common understanding of a completed act of power. For instance, monopolies control markets, political machines control patronage, elections grant control to political parties, and disciplinary procedures control student behaviors. Control, then, designates the result of an act of power—it is the manifest acquiescence of one actor to the power of another. Power, however, can be present but remain latent. As a result, its latent and manifest aspects must, therefore, be differentiated. In this regard, see the power control matrix depicted in Figure 6.1. Thus, on the one hand, power indicates an ability to do something, like an individual's capacity to solve complex problems or play tennis. On the other hand, control demarcates performance—the degree to which an ability has been applied in the solution of a problem or the winning of a tennis match.

Subtypes of Power

To capture a full range of power-types, power can be depicted as a continuum (see Figure 6.2) extending from interactions that depend on the use of force to those that do not. At the coercive end of the continuum, Actor (A) has sufficient resources to compel Other (O) to behave as Actor wants. The Other so compelled may also have power, but it is insufficient to counteract Actor's. At the opposite end of the continuum, Actor still holds the preponderance of resources yet is unable or unwilling to force Other to submit. Other, however, derives power from the ability to accept or reject Actor's power attempt. At the middle of the continuum is authority that, depending on the predominating nature of the relationship, can assume characteristics of either pole. Although coercion and influence occupy the poles, with authority in the middle, none of these power-types exists in isolation. Indeed, all three may be present to some degree in any setting, and movement in any direction along the continuum will increase one type of power while decreasing the effects (although not necessarily the quantity) of the other types.

Coercion. As a subtype of power, coercion closely approximates Weber's conception of power and is defined as the ability of an actor to affect another's behavior, regardless of the other's wishes. In this case, Actor gains control of Other's behavior by using force, ultimately physical or mental violence, to translate power into control. Other's resistance to Actor's demands ceases and Actor's control of Other is manifest when Other capitulates to Actor's coercion. This relationship is clearly asymmetric; Actor has superior resources and can enforce demands. As a result, Actor's ability to affect Other's behavior is all but indisputable by Other. In a prison, for example, even though Other may choose to escape or die rather than acquiesce, until these presumably unintended consequences occur, Actor has power and control in relation to Other.[15] Aside from choosing or being able to escape or die, Other's only alternative is to capitulate. In this situation, it can be inferred that Actor holds most of the relevant resources while Other has none or relatively few. Actor simply tells Other what to do, and Other, having minimal realistic

	Other Responds As Actor Intends	Other Does Not Respond As Actor Intends
Actor Acts	*Control Observed:* Actor's power-type inferred from Actor's and Other's behaviors	*No Control Observed:* Actor's and Other's behaviors suggest that Actor is not sufficiently powerful relative to Other in this instance
Actor Does Not Act	*Control Inferred:* Both Actor's power and and control relative to Other inferred from Other's behavior	*No Control Observed or Inferred:* No inferences about Actor's power relative to Other possible

Figure 6.1: A Power-Control Matrix

options, does as directed. It is at this end of the continuum that conflict theorists concentrate their analyses.[16]

Authority. According to Weber, authority is legitimate power, a distinction accepted here. Authority is not, however, the legitimation or willing acceptance of acts of power which ultimately rely on force. Instead, authority is defined as the legitimation of an actor's ability to affect another's behavior. In other words, Other voluntarily, willingly allows Actor to command and then follows such commands or directives. Although Other yields some will to Actor, Other can withdraw from the relationship if Actor oversteps Other's area of voluntary acceptance.[17] If the relationship is to remain authoritative, then Actor cannot force Other to maintain it unless Other has few alternatives and is more dependent on the relationship with Actor than is Actor. If that is so, the relationship may become more coercive.

Typical authority relations are those between employers and employees. Teachers and administrators, for example, receive wages for performing activities authorized by boards of education. In so doing, each party gives up some freedom and discretion; however, should the board invoke other, nonlegitimated forms of power to try to control its employees' behaviors, or more of them, they may file grievances, strike, or seek alternative employment. Occupying the middle of the power con-

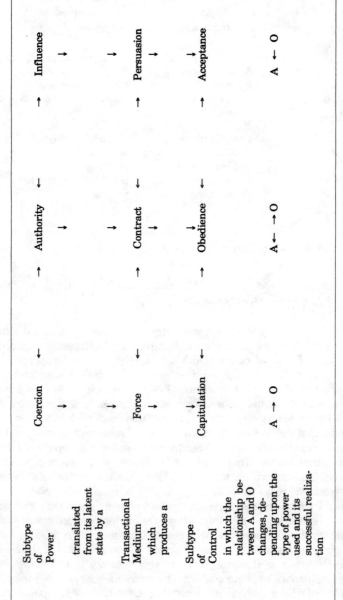

Figure 6.2: Power-Control Continuum

tinuum, the authority-obedience relationship is one in which Actor's and Other's power, in terms of their agreements on mutually acceptable behaviors, is more symmetric than asymmetric (see Figure 6.2). Authoritative relationships, as defined here, usually depend on normative expectations and similar forms of behavioral regulation.[18]

Influence. The last subtype of power defined here is influence—the ability of an actor, without recourse to force or legitimation, to affect another's behavior. Persuasive acts—including transactional media like referent modeling, expert knowledge,[19] public relations, and propaganda—convince Other that behaving as Actor desires is beneficial. Thus, when Other accepts Actor's power attempt, Actor achieves control, that is, the consonance of Other's behavior with Actor's wishes.

Unlike coercion or authority, influence depends on what Other wants. A principal, for instance, may want a teacher who is quite knowledgeable about contractual provisions to do something more than is normally expected. Having neither the authority to direct the teacher to behave as wished, nor the desire to force the teacher to do so, the principal seeks to persuade the teacher to do what is preferred, perhaps by accommodating on another point of some importance to the teacher. In this type of power relationship, persuasion and incentives are the means of transacting the relationship, simultaneously changing its symmetry and establishing Actor's dependence upon Other's ability or desire to accept or reject Actor's power.

SOME EMPIRICAL APPLICATIONS

At the outset of this article, it was suggested that an empirical model is needed to test the assumption that conflict and consensus theories can be integrated with power as the central element. Thus, in order to complete the empirical model (see Figure 6.3), conflict is defined as disagreement about the outcome of behaviors in a relationship, and consensus is defined as agreement about the outcome of behaviors in a relationship. Of course, conflict and consensus occupy the two poles of this second continuum. When the power and conflict-consensus continua are joined, several hypotheses can be derived: coercion and influence are inversely related, coercion and conflict are positively related, and influence and consensus are positively related. Further, given the nature of authority and its place on the power continuum as discussed, authority relates positively both to coercion and influence, relates positively to conflict to the degree that it is viewed as coercive, and relates positively to consensus to the degree that it is seen as influential.

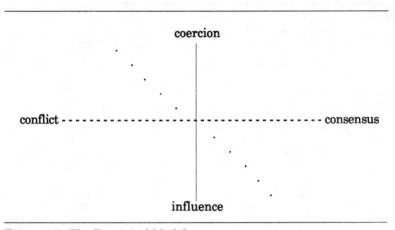

Figure 6.3: The Empirical Model

SOURCE: R. Muth, "Teacher Perceptions of Power, Conflict and Concensus," *Administrator's Notebook* 21, 4 (1973): 1.

NOTE: Each of the intersect points above represents a theoretically possible instance of a power behavior which results in a degree of either conflict or consensus.

STUDIES OF POWER, CONFLICT AND CONSENSUS

As was first reported in 1973, the model displayed in Figure 6.3 was used to relate power behaviors of the principals in 35 high schools in the Midwest to the degree of conflict or consensus perceived by teachers (N = 366) in those schools.[20] The rows in Table 6.1 labeled 1971 show that the more coercive principals tended to be, the greater the conflict teachers perceived relative to the two conflict-consensus factors: policy (matters vital to the functioning of the school) conflict ($r = .542$, $p < .005$) and routine (various structural restrictions) conflict ($r = .423$, $p < .005$). The more influential principals tended to be, the less conflict (greater consensus)[21] their teachers reported ($r = -.550$ and $-.454$, respectively, $p < .005$). Because authority was assumed to be part of the normal, shared expectations in school organizations, its impact on conflict and consensus was expected to be small as the correlations between authority and conflict over policies or routine indicated ($r = -.078$ and $-.059$, respectively, $p > .05$). Further, the hypothesized power continuum (see Figure 6.2) was verified: coercion and influence were negatively related ($r = -.529$, $p < .005$); coercion and authority were positively related ($r = .121$, $p < .005$); and authority and influence were positively related ($r = .413$, $p < .005$).

TABLE 6.1
Correlations: Power and Outcome Variables[a]

Variables		Influence	Authority	Coercion	Policy Conflict	Routine Conflict	Evaluation Conflict	Involvement	Effectiveness
Influence		1.000							
Authority	1971	.413	1.000						
	1977	.568							
Coercion	1971	-.529	.121[c]	1.000					
	1977	-.377	.140						
	1979	-.41							
Policy conflict	1971	-.550	-.078[b]	.542	1.000				
	1977	-.552	-.208	.495					
Routine conflict	1971	-.454	-.059[b]	.423	.703	1.000			
	1977	-.456	-.239	.429	.727				
Evaluation conflict	1977	-.429	-.212	.388	.650	.521	1.000		
Involvement	1979	.34		-.05[b]				1.000	
Effectiveness	1979	.60		-.35				.42	1.000

a. The dates for the rows indicate the time at which the data were collected for each study. The 1971 study surveyed 366 teachers, and the 1977 surveyed 414 teachers. The 1979 study surveyed 372 college faculty members, although the correlations reported here are for 269 subjects who completed all aspects of the survey.

b. $p < .05$

c. $p < .05$

For all other coefficients, $p < .01$.

Moreover, among the many multivariate tests conducted, canonical analyses confirmed the expected relationships between the two continua. When combined, they accounted for 40% of the variance in the five variables (R = .636, χ^2 = 187.95, p < .005) and indicated that the removal of either influence (R = .570, χ^2 = .143.06, p < .005) or coercion (R = .582, χ^2 = .150.70, p < .005) caused the canonical weights for authority to increase in magnitude and assume the sign of the deleted variable relative to policy or routine conflict. All of the above relationships held, even when the primary variables were regressed on a variety of organizational variables and demographic characteristics.

A replication in 1977 repeated the prior study (1971) with 414 teachers from 37 high schools in the Midwest, and it was concluded on the basis of the 1977 study that the model had been validated (see Table 6.1, rows labeled 1977).[22] That is, each of the hypotheses was reconfirmed following numerous multivariate analyses, an example of which is displayed in Table 6.2. This study also added another conflict variable, evaluation conflict, based on the implications of the power model for principal-teacher interactions in this area and found the expected relationships. The new variable was related positively to coercion (r = .388, p < .001), and it related negatively to influence (r = −.429, p < .001) and authority (r = −.212, p < .001). Thus, teachers who felt that their evaluations were inappropriate also had principals who behaved more coercively and less influentially than was the case for teachers who felt that their evaluations were appropriate [from the original study, not tabled here: β = .312 (Coercion), β = .245 (Influence); R = .501, F = 45.8 p < .005].

Power, Involvement, and Organizational Effectiveness

A study completed in 1980 investigated the power model's ability to predict professional job involvement and organizational effectiveness in seven private colleges in Andhra Pradesh, India.[23] Using the responses of 372 faculty members, this study examined the power behaviors of college administrators, and it was found that coercion and influence were inversely related (r = −.41, p < .001; see Table 6.1, the row for 1979). Poor factor loadings, explainable in part by cultural orientations, eliminated the authority factor from the analyses: in any event, the range of the underlying continuum was again confirmed.

This study also hypothesized that coercion would relate negatively and influence positively to job involvement.[24] It was further hypothesized that coercion would be negatively related and influence positively related to organizational effectiveness. Originally, effectiveness and its scales were

TABLE 6.2
Regression of Policy Conflict/Routine Conflict
on Influence, Authority, and Coercion

Variable			Regression Coefficient	Beta	F	p
Influence/policy	1971		−.56	−.395	45.51	<.005
conflict	1977		−.60	−.408	53.02	<.005
Authority/policy	1971		.07	.046	.84	
conflict	1977		−.04	−.024	.22	
Coercion/policy	1971		.49	.328	37.19	<.005
conflict	1977		.58	.344	54.61	<.005
Constants	1971	15.55				
	1977	15.35				
Influence/routine	1971		−.49	−.327	25.94	<.005
conflict	1977		−.28	−.226	13.82	<.005
Authority/routine	1971		.06	.043	.61	<.01
conflict	1977		−.20	−.162	8.16	<.01
Coercion/routine	1971		.44	.275	21.82	<.005
conflict	1977		.52	.367	52.86	<.005
Constants	1971	14.69				
	1977	13.48				
Coefficient of determination (R^2)	1971		.392/.210		77.63/44.73	<.005
	1977		.401/.299		91.58/58.73	<.005

modeled on Parson's theory of organizational effectiveness: adaptation, goal attainment, pattern maintenance, and integration.[25]

As shown in Table 6.1, coercion and job involvement were inversely related, although not significantly ($r = -.05$, $p > .05$), and influence and involvement were positively correlated ($r = .34$, $p < .001$); coercion and influence correlated as expected with organizational effectiveness ($r = -.35$ and $.60$, respectively, $p < .001$); and involvement and effectiveness were positively related ($r = .42$, $p < .001$). As the analysis in Table 6.3 shows, when organizational effectiveness was regressed on coercion, influence, and involvement ($R = .653$, $p < .001$), the presence of influence contributed most to the predication of college effectiveness, and faculty involvement was the next most important determinant in this relationship. Coercion was the weakest of the predictors ($\beta = -.153$, $p < .01$). Thus, the more that administrators behaved influentially and the more that

TABLE 6.3
Regression of Effectiveness on Coercion, Influence, and Involement

Variable	Regression Coefficient	Standard Error	Beta	F
Coercion	−.414	.139	−.153	8.84*
Influence	1.428	.175	.446	66.66**
Involvement	.590	.114	.257	26.69**
Constant	61.098			
Coefficient of determination (R^2)			.427	
Standard error of estimate			11.880	
Overall equation				65.71**

*p <.01
**p <.001

professors felt involved in their work, the more the professors saw their colleges as operating effectively. Additionally, it was found through path analyses that involvement mediated influence somewhat, indicated that these two variables tend to reinforce one another. Conversely, coercion was not mediated by involvement, and it directly and adversely affected college effectiveness.

SOME THEORETICAL IMPLICATIONS

The three studies just discussed were designed to define, clarify, and test an empirical model of power. Following Lenski's notion that empirical studies can be used to integrate normative theories,[26] the three studies cited here began with the assumption that acts of power would produce either conflict or consensus depending on the nature of the power acts. Other connections between power and various outcome variables have suggested that power might alienate one from or heighten one's commitment to an organization. Finally, it was assumed that power would also affect organizational effectiveness positively or negatively, again depending upon the type of power used and how it was perceived. From these assumptions, hypotheses were developed and tested, the results of which suggest some general theoretical linkages. These are outlined below, along with some sample hypotheses:

Premises

A_1 Power produces *both* conflict and consensus.
A_2 Power produces *both* alienation and commitment.
A_3 Power produces *both* ineffectiveness and effectiveness.

Propositions and Hypotheses[27]

P_1 The greater the coercion, the greater the conflict.
    H_1 The more repressive the administration of a school (system), the greater the number of grievances filed.
P_2 The greater the influence, the greater the consensus.
    H_2 The greater the use of expert knowledge by a supervisor, the more readily a teacher will adopt an alternative program or activity.
P_3 The greater the coercion, the greater the alienation.
    H_3 The more repressive a school environment, the greater the number of teacher and student absences.
P_4 The greater the influence, the greater the commitment.
    H_4 The more that teachers help to determine program or activity changes, the more likely they will adopt and use such changes.
P_5 The greater the coercion, the less the effectiveness.
    H_5 The more repressive a school environment, the lower the student achievement.
P_6 The greater the influence, the greater the effectiveness.
    H_6 The more a community supports school activities, the greater the number of students who will participate in such activities.

Derivations and Hypotheses

D_1 The greater the conflict, the less the commitment.
    H_7 The greater the differences among teachers' expectations for student performance, the less teachers will engage in program improvement activities.
D_2 The greater the consensus, the greater the commitment.
    H_8 The greater the agreement on short-term goals for teaching improvement, the higher the participation of teachers in targeted staff development activities.
D_3 The greater the conflict, the less the effectiveness.
    H_9 The greater the dissension among bargaining unit members about negotiating priorities, the less likely the unit will effect desired changes in its existing contract.
D_4 The greater the consensus, the greater the effectiveness.

H_{10} The more a supervisor and teacher agree on the process of evaluation, the more likely recommendations from the evaluations will be followed.

D_5 The greater the alienation, the less the effectiveness.

H_{11} The more a teacher is disaffected in terms of role expectations, the less productive that teacher's role performance will be.

D_6 The greater the commitment, the greater the effectiveness.

H_{12} The more a school (system) demonstrates its support for innovation, the greater the frequency of innovative behaviors.

The above sample hypotheses only begin to illustrate the heuristic potential of the power model outlined here. Other hypotheses about the effects of the three subtypes of power, alone or in combination, as well as other subtypes of power, which might easily be added to the model, can be generated and tested.[28] More usefully, the model can be employed to integrate other approaches to the study of power and organizations. The greatest value of the power continuum lies in its capacity as a heuristic and empirical tool. The power model advanced here, and power, generally, has considerable explanatory and integrative power and can assist the movement toward needed conceptual clarity and theoretical synthesis.

NOTES

1. Even though J. March, "The Power of Power," in *Varieties of Political Theory*, D. Easton, ed. (Englewood Cliffs, NJ: Prentice-Hall, 1966), pp. 39-70, suggests that "power is a disappointing concept" (p. 70)—recanting his earlier position, according to J. Nagel, *The Descriptive Analysis of Power* (New Haven, CT: Yale University Press, 1975), p. 5—the weight of the continuing and recent attention to the concept of power underscores its utility for the analysis of social behaviors. In this tradition, see R. N. Adams, *Energy and Structure: A Theory of Social Power* (Austin: University of Texas Press, 1975); D. V. J. Bell, *Power, Influence, and Authority* (New York: Oxford University Press, 1975); D. Cartwright, ed., *Studies in Social Power* (Ann Arbor: University of Michigan, Institute for Social Research, 1959); A. H. Henderson, *Social Power* (New York: Praeger, 1981); S. Lukes, *Power: A Radical View* (London: Macmillan Ltd., 1974); J. Pfeffer, *Power in Organizations* (Marshfield, MA.: Pitman, 1981); P. G. Swingle, *The Management of Power* (Hillsdale, N.J.: Lawrence Erlbaum, 1976); and D. H. Wrong, *Power: Its Forms, Bases, and Uses* (Oxford: Basil Blackwell, 1979). As D. Nyberg, *Power Over Power* (Ithaca, NY: Cornell University Press, 1981), drawing on Bertrand Russell, has suggested, "power is *a* fundamental concept in social science, if not *the* fundamental concept" (p. 40).

2. A most persuasive case in regard to schooling and power has been made in a series of articles and papers written, either individually or jointly, by Mitchell and Spady, the essence of which can be found in D. E. Mitchell and W. G. Spady,

"Authority, Power, and the Legitimation of Social Control," *Educational Administration Quarterly* 19, 1 (Winter 1983): 5 -33. As N. J. Boyan, "A Constitutional Perspective on Authority" (Paper presented at the American Educational Research Association Annual Meeting, Los Angeles, California, April 1981), suggests in an analysis of some of their earlier writings, their arguments are complex. Yet, their position on power and authority is problematic: first, their scheme weighs heavy with terms—such as social power, coercive constraint, pure authority, authority-based control, force, persuasion, social control, and so on—the definitions of and the relations among which are not always clear; second, they claim that authority and power are different phenomena while implicitly and explicitly stating that both produce the same outcome—social control; third, they use etymology to support their perspective, apparently ignoring the mutability of language and the importance of contemporary meaning to contemporary action; and, finally, their model is basically normative—it expresses their preferences for how authority ought to work, especially in schools, but it does not suggest how authority does work.

3. One of the best recent treatments of the analytical history of power and its uses in various disciplines can be found in S. H. Ng, *The Social Psychology of Power* (London: Academic Press, 1980).

4. See, for example, G. Lenski, *Power and Privilege* (New York: McGraw-Hill, 1966), especially Ch. 1, in which he suggests the need for empirical models that can explain social phenomena as opposed to those that state preferences for particular social conditions, as normative theories do.

5. See S. Ossowski, *Class Structure in the Social Consciousness*, S. Patterson, trans. (New York: Free Press, 1963); and P. van den Berghe, "Dialectic and Functionalism: Toward a Theoretical Synthesis," *American Sociological Review* 28 (1963): 695-705.

6. Lenski, *Power and Privilege*, p. 17.

7. M. Weber, *The Theory of Social and Economic Organizations*, A. M. Henderson and T. Parsons, trans. (New York: Free Press, 1947), p. 152. For similar definitions by authors with differing perspectives, see A. Etzioni, *A Comparative Analysis of Complex Organizations* (New York: Free Press, 1961), pp. 4-5; H. Gerth and C. W. Mills, *Character and Social Structure* (New York: Harcourt, Brace & World, 1953), p. 195; R. A. Dahl, "The Concept of Power," *Behavioral Science* 2 (1957): 201-215; T. Parsons, *The Social System* (New York: Free Press, 1951), p. 121; C. W. Mills, *The Power Elite* (New York: Oxford University Press, 1959), p. 9; and J. Hage, *Theories of Organizations* (New York: John Wiley, 1980), p. 54.

8. As A. M. Rose, *The Power Structure* (New York: Oxford University Press, 1967), pp. 45-53, points out, behaviors may be motivated solely by perceptions rather than the use of power. Weber anticipated this in his definition: power itself can be one "basis" of power. See also D. Katz and R. L. Kahn, *The Social Psychology of Organizations* (New York: John Wiley, 1966), pp. 219-220; and F. E. Oppenheim, *Dimensions of Freedom* (New York: St. Martin's Press, 1961), p. 100, on the potential nature of the concept of power.

9. While some theorists posit that power is a zero-sum phenomenon, T. Parsons critiques this assumption in *Structure and Process in Modern Societies* (New York: Free Press, 1960), pp. 219-222. For more recent discussions, see Hage, *Theories of Organizations*, pp. 55-56; R. H. Hall, *Organizations: Structure and Process*, 2nd ed. (Englewood Cliffs, NJ: Prentice-Hall, 1977), pp. 199-200; and S. Bacharach and E.

J. Lawler, *Power and Politics in Organizations* (San Francisco: Jossey-Bass, 1980), pp. 105-108.

10. See, for example, P. M. Blau, *Exchange and Power in Social Life* (New York: John Wiley, 1964), in which he suggests that the multiple and complex power relations between spouses may contain elements of force but most often do not. Oppenheim, *Dimensions of Freedom*, pp. 91-92, cautions that power should describe those relations which involve influence and other types of power supported by prestige, authority, or charisma as well as those which involve submission to duress.

11. J. P. R. French and B. Raven, "The Bases of Social Power," in *Group Dynamics*, 3rd ed., D. Cartwright and A. Zander, eds. (New York: Harper & Row, 1968), pp. 259-269, advance five bases of power, the traditional "bases" discussed most often in the literature. See all F. E. Oppenheim, "'Power' Revisited," *The Journal of Politics* 40 (1978): 590, for a discussion of the use of rewards that cannot be refused. For additional considerations, see Pfeffer, *Power in Organizations,* and Bacharach and Lawler, *Power and Politics.*

12. R. L. Peabody, "Perceptions of Organizational Authority: A Comparative Analysis," *Administrative Science Quarterly* 6 (1962): 463-482. After all, to deny Other's view of the mode used would deny the relational nature of power and rule out various personality variables that may predispose Other to certain kinds of power acts.

13. See, for example, R. Presthus, *The Organizational Society* (New York: Random House, 1962), in which he discusses patterns of accommodation to the authoritarian character of organizations; Etzioni's *Complex Organizations* in which he outlines the nature of involvement in organizations induced by the type of power used to secure compliance; and Lukes, *Power: A Radical View,* in which he suggests that people's wants may be a product of the system, not their own "free" choice.

14. For similar definitions, see A. L. Stinchcombe, *Constructing Social Theories* (New York: Harcourt, Brace & World, 1968), p. 157; Dahl, "The Concept of Power," pp. 202-203; and F. E. Oppenheim, *Political Concepts: A Reconstruction* (Chicago: University of Chicago Press, 1981), pp. 10-11.

15. Oppenheim, *Dimensions of Freedom,* argues, however, that one must distinguish between physical and mental "unfreedom."

16. R. Dahrendorf, *Class and Class Conflict in Industrial Society* (Stanford: Stanford University Press, 1959), p. 158. Dahrendorf, among others, argues that wealth is a primary resource which can be used to force compliance.

17. This "area of voluntary acceptance" is similar to Barnard's "zone of indifference" in which he indicates that individuals accept orders without consciously questioning them: C. Barnard, *The Function of the Executive* (Cambridge, MA: Harvard University Press, 1938), p. 167. Yet, voluntary acceptance as used here is broader than Barnard's "zone" and includes all parts of the relationship between Other and Actor which are "legitimated."

18. See, for instance, J. Blake and K. Davis, "Norms, Values, and Sanctions," in *Handbook of Modern Sociology*, R. E. L. Faris, ed. (Chicago: Rand McNally, 1964), pp. 456-484.

19. Blau, *Exchange and Power,* suggests that even expert knowledge can be used coercively if Other builds up sufficient obligations in relation to Actor's expertise.

20. R. Muth, "Teacher Perception of Power, Conflict and Consensus," *Administrator's Notebook* 21, 4 (1973): 1-4. The scales used in this study and the next one

referred to can be found in E. F. DeRoche, *Evaluating School Programs and Personnel* (New York: Allyn & Bacon, 1979).

21. The conflict-consensus scales were scored on a "real" vs. "ideal" basis with the absolute difference used as a measure of conflict. Thus, the power variables were related only to the conflict variables.

22. C. G. Thom, "The Relationship Between Principals' Power Behaviors and Their Evaluations of Teacher Performance" (Unpublished doctoral dissertation, Marquette University, 1977).

23. M. Devadoss, "Power, Involvement, and Effectiveness in Seven Private Colleges, Andhra Pradesh, India" (Unpublished doctoral dissertation, Fordham University, 1980).

24. Etzioni, *Complex Organizations;* M. E. Brown, "Identification and Some Conditions of Organizational Involvement," *Administrative Science Quarterly* 14 (1969): 346-355; J. L. Franklin, "Power and Commitment: An Empirical Assessment," *Human Relations* 28 (1975): 737-753; and R. S. Schuler, "Determinants of Job Involvement, Individual vs. Organizational: An Extension of the Literature" (Paper presented at the Academy of Management, New Orleans, Louisiana, August 1975).

25. T. Parsons, "General Theory in Sociology," in *Sociology Today: Problems and Prospects,* R. K. Merton, L. Broom, and L. S. Cottrell, Jr., eds. (New York: Basic Books, 1959), pp. 3-38.

26. Lenski, *Power and Privilege.*

27. Due to space limitations and because the concept of authority is complex, propositions and hypotheses based on authority have been eliminated from consideration here. Also, while each of the propositions has its logical inverse, these remain unstated here for reasons of simplicity.

28. Recent discussion about "loosely coupled" organizations and "organized anarchies" provide fertile ground for analyses of power because, as M. Crozier, *The Bureaucratic Phenomenon* (Chicago: University of Chicago Press, 1964), points out, areas of uncertainty are ripe for the growth and display of power. See J. G. March and J. P. Olsen, *Ambiguity and Choice in Organizations* (Bergen, Norway: Universitetsforlaget, 1976); and K. Weick, "Educational Organizations as Loosely Coupled Systems," *Administrative Science Quarterly* 21 (1976): 1-19.

CHAPTER SEVEN

A Perspective on Organizational Cultures and Organizational Belief Structure

JAMES A. CONWAY

Currently school organizations are under pressure to achieve excellence. To accomplish this, organizational transformations must occur which require in-depth changes in the organizational culture of schools. This perspective addresses the study of organizational cultures and focuses on the ways that beliefs and value are structured in school organizations. An analogy between cognitive systems and organizational belief systems is constructed to conduct this analysis.

Over the past decade the schools in the United States have found themselves immersed in a sea of troubles. Some 39 commissions, committees, and self-appointed critics have identified our educational system as one beset with critical problems. Concurrently, the effective school/effective principal movement has identified a number of tasks that schools need address as they make an effort to increase their effectiveness as educating institutions.

Also occurring at this time has been a parallel examination of American business and its productivity. This has resulted in a literature of comparisons with Japan[1] and a literature focused on characteristics of excellence.[2] Out of this America has rediscovered the concept of culture, and come to acknowledge that organizations possess a culture as do departments and other natural work units. This literature has made clear that the beliefs and values of companies or schools of excellence are fundamental to their productivity. Ouchi's studies of "Theory Z" organizations underscore the need for a company philosophy of commitment to quality values.[3] Pascale and Athos talk to superordinate goals which reflect a similar value orientation;[4] and Peters and Waterman emphasize the commitment to quality service, individual initiative, and risk taking as key company values.[5]

It is not surprising to find excellence where such company values and personnel characteristics exist. It is also likely that effective schools will

SOURCE: James A. Conway, "A Perspective on Organizational Cultures and Organizational Belief Structure," *Educational Administration Quarterly*, Vol. 21, No. 4, pp. 7-25. Copyright © by The University Council for Educational Administration. Reprinted with permission.

demonstrate a similar set of values. Therefore it is to be expected that emphasis will be given any organizational culture that manifests such value sets. And, indeed, that has been the methodology of this era of studies, i.e., to locate organizations of high productivity or excellence and compare the patterns of beliefs and values with those less productive; to observe the principals of effective schools in action and infer or generalize to the needed behaviors for all such organizations.

Nor is it surprising, then, to see the rediscovery of the culture concept when excellence tends to be defined in terms of *what* these organizations do and *how* they believe. This is consistent with the earliest days of anthropology when Tyler defined culture as "that complex whole which includes knowledge, belief, art, morals, law, custom, and any other capabilities and habits acquired by man as a member of society."[6] The essence of that definition is still found in the more recent applications of culture to organizations. For example, Stonich describes culture as:

> a pattern of beliefs and expectations shared by members of an organization. These beliefs and expectations produce rules for behavior—norms—that powerfully shape the behavior of individuals and groups in the organization.[7]

Pettigrew recognized the more diversified nature of the concept by adding to the *content* the *events* that make culture visible:

> While providing a general sense of orientation, culture treated as a unitary concept in this way lacks analytical bite. A potentially more fruitful approach is to regard culture as the source of a family of concepts. The offsprings of the concept of culture I have in mind are symbol, language, ideology, belief, ritual and myth.[8]

What has been typical in this literature has been a view of culture as the subjective or "man made" component of environment in contrast to the "natural" environment. Emphasis has been on the ideological content, i.e., the beliefs and values of the organization as these become manifest through examination of the tools, symbols, customs, rites, and language. In like manner, the organization's culture becomes more evident through the heroes of the organization who "personify the culture's value and as such provide tangible role models for employees to follow."[9] Finally, this ideological content is made visible in the company rituals that convey the organizational expectations to employees.[10]

At this point, it is necessary to interrupt the flow and return once more to the schools and organizations of this era. What the organizational culture studies tell us about these organizations is that *if* they have the appropriate ideology, *if* they possess the value and belief orientations of those organizations already identified as excellent, *then* these less productive organizations will also be able to join the ranks of the exceptional. In essence these studies are analogous to a study of "natural" athletes and finding that they have certain attitudes of self-adequacy and beliefs that they are capable of winning; therefore, if you want to be an exceptional athlete, all you have to do is transform yourself to be like these "naturals." And this is the crux of the problem, the flaw in the method—it may work if you are already a "natural," if you possess the physical prowess to back up the beliefs, but if you are not, how do you transform yourself? In addition, are these exceptional athletes in possession of the traits or characteristics necessary for further "self-transformation"?

We seem to be asking schools that are now considered mediocre or poor to become excellent by transforming themselves, by emulating the value orientations of schools of excellence. We are asking them to undergo culture change, which means a fundamental change in values and value orientation. If this is the case, we need to understand what it is about organizations that contributes to that type of transformation. We are asking schools to restructure themselves and their culture, to go through an organizational learning of the most difficult type.

ORGANIZATIONAL LEARNING

Various authors have looked at learning as an organizational variable and have identified at least two fundamental types. At the simpler level there is that learning in which the organization (or organism) recognizes a deviation from some expected set of outcomes and corrects the error by doing more of the same, but either doing it more efficiently or with greater effort. This was the fundamental approach to the "cult of efficiency" as associated with Frederick Taylor. A man could learn to carry *more* bricks for *longer* periods if he could find more energy-efficient ways to hoist and carry the load. In applying this to organizations, Argyis and Schon define this as single-loop learning wherein

> members of the organization carry out a collaborative inquiry through which they discover sources of error, invent new strategies designed to correct error, produce these strategies, and evaluate and generalize the results.[11]

It is likely that the response of a school to a problem of below-average mathematics achievement would be an approach of single-loop learning. The analysis of the problem is that the youngsters are not receiving sufficient instruction; the inquiry might find teachers being interrupted by announcements, students being taken from classes for special subjects, heightened incidences of absence and tardiness so that the conclusion is to control time for instruction (time on task). To correct, the school tries to decrease the distractions and increase the length of the school day.

The other end of the spectrum is seen as double-loop learning by Argyis and Schon,[12] deutero-learning by Bateson,[13] and reconstructive learning by Friedlander.[14] This type of learning is an in-depth change in the organization:

> In reconstructive learning the organism questions its premises, purposes, values. For individuals these are represented in one's goals, principals, life-style, beliefs. For the organization they are represented by its goals, policies, and norms. . . . Reconstructive learning calls for in-depth confrontation of old patterns and the development of radically different ones. It suggests the construction of new goals, policies, norms, styles rather than simple modification of the old.[15]

It is this type of learning that is being asked of schools as they prepare themselves to meet the challenges of the criticisms. Culture change is reconstructive learning. Without an appropriate culture, the inventions will not take root. And if or when they finally do take root they promote still further change in the system. As Perrow has indicated: "When a long range view is taken, the cultural system seems determinate; when a medium range view is taken, the technological system is determinate; in the short run, the structure may appear to be the most important."[16] Perrow goes on to say that in organizations which are established to change people (as with hospitals or schools) the influence of cultural definitions is most apparent and basic. Changes in technology are embedded in a culture which requires consideration if the technological changes are to "take."[17]

The question now is how to better understand organizational cultures and culture change. As already stated, the culture in an organization is composed of patterns of beliefs and expectations. This ideological content is the social magnet that links individuals in committees and departments and also links the committees, departments, and people in the organization. While there are separate and distinct cultures for individual departments, there is also an overarching culture which is captured in the organization's philosophy and values. These various cultures and subcultures are made visible through the company goals, the organizational and unit policies, the rules, the conveyors of meanings such as rites and rituals, language, symbols, and heroes. But there is a third element which has not been given significant attention as it does not rise to a level of importance until the need for culture change occurs. The element is evident in Geertz's conception of culture as "a system of meanings embodied in symbols which are generally shared among the members of a social group, who use them to perform vital mental activities."[18] Geertz's definition incorporates the key word *system*. In this system refers to the *way* that the beliefs and values are ordered, arranged, and linked. System here is concerned with the interrelationships of the beliefs and values no matter how logical or illogical. If an organization is expected to *reconstruct* itself, it needs to be aware of its cultural *system*. The intent of this article is to address this imbalance in the study of organizational cultures and focus on the *way that beliefs and values are structured* in the organization or its parts.

In order to conduct this analysis, it appears useful to address the topic from the perspective of the way that *cognitive systems* function in individuals. In so doing, the intent is not to anthropomorphize the organization, but, rather, to use the analogy as a starting point for developing the conceptual argument. The use of analogy as a device for initiating creative thought[19] and for theory-building is well accepted.[20] This particular analogue seems especially appropriate as it deals with a system of beliefs in the organism and how those beliefs come to be recognized as a system that is either open or not open to change. The framework to be used is attributed to Milton Rokeach and his works on the structure of cognitive systems.[21] The basic Rokeachian framework shall first be described briefly, and then will be elaborated as the organizational analogy is constructed.

ROKEACH AND COGNITIVE SYSTEMS

It was in the 1950s that Rokeach published a series of works testing his conceptualization of individual cognitive system orientation. His early thinking about rigidity, ethnocentrism, and authoritarianism led him to conclude that those concepts were interrelated but insufficient to explain certain phenomena. For example, the California Studies of Adorno, Frenkel-Brunswik, Levinson, and Sanford culminated in the construction of the F-Scale, an instrument to measure an individual's propensity toward fascism. The California authors labeled the "high F" person as an "Authoritarian Personality."[22] Administrations of the F-Scale to English-speaking communists were conducted and the findings showed these persons as low in the authoritarian trait. This seemed contrary to knowledge of a communist cell and a cell mentality wherein strict adherence to an authority of the State or the cell leader was common. This led Rokeach to comment that the F-Scale appeared to measure only "rightist" authoritarianism. The scale was content related, that is, it measured a set of beliefs about fascism such that agreement with those beliefs could well predict an authoritarian outlook. But where the beliefs were contrary to the individual's, even though that person tended toward an authoritarian orientation in behavior, then predictability fell.[23] This led Rokeach to postulate that content was only one predictor for this type of personality; a more basic predictor was the interrelationship of the individual's beliefs *without regard to their content*. This facet of the cognitive system was explicated in his theoretical work on "dogmatism" as a fundamental hypothetical cognitive state.[24] He suggested that all cognitive systems could be conceived of as a set of beliefs organized on three basic dimensions that describe the organization of the structurally arranged parts. The basic structure of the beliefs may be considered as a continuum that ranges from "open" at one end to "closed" at the other with the closed end constituting high dogmatism. Each of the three dimensions describes an aspect of the closedness of the belief system structure.[25] These are defined briefly in Table 7.1.

Since it is possible to consider an organization as a system with a cognate analog of organizational learning, then it may be appropriate to apply Rokeach's perspective on the structure of cognitive systems to the organization. It is through the application and development of this analogy that the imbalance in organizational culture shall be clarified. In the sections that follow, the three dimensions (from Table 7.1) shall be clarified as they are applied to the organization.

BELIEF STRUCTURE IN ORGANIZATIONS

The Belief-Disbelief Dimension

It is suggested that in organizations, as in individuals or living organisms, there are two systems operating, one of beliefs and another of disbeliefs. These systems are parallel but not symmetrical. For every belief held in an organization, as in the wisdom of consensus decision making, there are a *series* of beliefs about ways for arriving at decisions that are considered inappropriate or even false for that organization. Thus the disbelief subsystem on decision making might contain hundreds of entries for a single belief in the parallel belief system. Paraphrasing Rokeach[26] in the application of this concept to organizations, it is asserted that:

(a) *the belief system* represented all the beliefs, sets, expectancies, or hypotheses, stated or implicit, that a group or organization at a given time accepts as true of the environment in which it exists; and

(b) *the disbelief system* is composed of a series of subsystems rather than merely a single system, and contains all the disbeliefs, sets, expec-

TABLE 7.1
Simplified Definitions of Cognitive System Dimensions

A. Belief system:	all the beliefs, sets, expectancies, or hypotheses, conscious and unconscious, held as true at a given time.
B. Disbelief system:	a series of subsystems containing all the sets, expectancies, or hypotheses conscious and unconscious that are rejected as false at a given time.
C. Belief-Disbelief system:	an organization of parts that may or may not be logically interrelated but a potential for communication exists.
D. Dimension 1:	the organization along a belief-disbelief continuum.
E. Dimension 2:	the organization along a central-peripheral range of regions or layers. The three basic layers are:
a. Central region:	that layer containing the "primitive beliefs," i.e., those beliefs acquired about the nature of the physical world, self, and others.
b. Intermediate region:	beliefs about the nature of authority and how others line up with that authority.
c. Peripheral region:	beliefs derived from authority and the nature of authority.
F. Dimension 3:	the organization along a time-perspective. Beliefs about the relationships and interrelationships of past, present, and future.

NOTE: Definitions are abstracted from M. Rokeach, *The Open and Closed Mind* (New York: Basic Books, 1960), Chapter 2.

tancies, stated or implied, that, to one degree or another, a group or subgroup at a given time rejects as false.

The combined systems of beliefs and disbeliefs as these occur in the organization shall be referred to as the "organizational belief structure." Besides its parallel and asymmetrical arrangement, each dimension also has several additional properties that contribute to an understanding of the structural aspect of the organization's culture.

1. Isolation. As an outsider views an organization it may be possible to ascertain beliefs that are mutually held but unknown to subunits adhering to these beliefs. It might likewise be possible to identify where logically contradictory beliefs co-exist in the same system, again either unknown to the parts or, if known, perhaps perceived as irrelevant or even simply denied. Goldner identified both of these positions in his comparative study of belief systems in the Catholic Church and industry.[27] These examples point to the existence of isolation of beliefs or disbeliefs among adherents in the organization.

When a system chooses to accentuate differences within the system rather than similarities, then isolation will be more likely to occur. It may well be that highly departmentalized universities or high schools, as well as elementary schools employing the "self-contained classroom" as an organizing concept, make themselves particularly susceptible to organizational isolation.[28] This structural isolation of the parts is a cultural counterpart to a loosely coupled system of bureaucratic linkages.[29] If so, it fosters an apparent contradiction. Loosely coupled systems are considered "better able to adapt to the organizational contingencies described by contingency theory than can more structured, more tightly coupled organizations."[30] But by the cultural system perspective it would seem more logical to expect an isolation of parts within and between the belief and disbelief systems *to resist* change, since *isolation* is a basic property of closedness in a system. *Closedness* in an organizational belief structure means the *system is resistant to change;* it will tend to promote or sustain internal isolation in order to protect and maintain intact its organizational belief structure.

How can this paradox be rationalized? Loosely coupled systems apparently adapt *because there is isolation,* not despite the isolation. The change is a change in parts, in the units or subunits and not in the total system.[31] As long as departments or teachers need not share their beliefs they are free to adapt and modify practices or not, as they may wish. It is not unusual to run through a description of teachers in a single school, even at a single grade level, and find one described as traditional, the next as innovative, and a third as working from the "dark ages." The system not only tolerates isolated teaching philosophies but may even encourage such variation. *Total system change* is a different issue. A coordinated movement for change is almost impossible for a loosely coupled organization.[32] If it does occur it is probably accomplished through a relatively authoritarian process that Rokeach labels "party-line" change.

2. *Differentiation.* Belief-disbelief systems vary in terms of the degree of richness of knowledge and in the detail of the beliefs and disbeliefs. It is reasonable to expect that systems will vary in their support and encouragement of differentiated beliefs. In systems theory this is an aspect of requisite variety or the extent to which there is belief-readiness in the system. As a school moves to a single learning style or belief it decreases the opportunity for its clients to find a match for the individual styles among the client group. During the early days of "open education" it was not surprising to find youngsters working at study carrels in the halls of the school. These youngsters had difficulty in adapting to the noise and

commotion of the open-spaced areas, for the school had not anticipated this press for variant beliefs and thus had not built opportunities for other styles into the basic design.

3. Narrowness. A restricted range of disbeliefs is the extension of low differentiation of beliefs. Some schools will categorize all programs that deal with human values as undesirable. They can see no differences between teaching *for* values and teaching *about* values. Social studies is as evil as is socialism as long as the word *social* is present. Some schools will tolerate no mention of human relations nor anything that faintly resembles such. A suggestion for an alternative faculty structure is sometimes labeled reorganization and reorganization somehow means retrenchment so that the members shun any examination of benefits or costs of a matrix versus divisional arrangement. In many cases the products, programs, or positions involved with a reorganization will not be examined at all, but simply denounced or dismissed at first mention. This tendency to lump or cluster disbeliefs is another indication of closedness, of resistance to considering different possible beliefs for system integration and growth. Closed organizational belief structures tend to view their organizational world in dichotomies of "we" versus "they." The "they" are the enemies to be resisted or the outsiders to be avoided. It might be hypothesized that the frequency of 'we-they" talk and its diffusion through the system is indicative of the relative closedness of the organization and its resistance to externally influenced change.

The Central-Peripheral Dimension

A second dimension that Rokeach considers as organizing the belief-disbelief structure is the central-peripheral range. As applied to an organization this is a hierarchy of examined beliefs and disbeliefs that constitute the world map of the organization.

1. The central region. This core level is the most hidden yet also the most significant sector of beliefs. In an organization this region would include the "primitive" beliefs that the sub-groups have about the nature of organization. This is the level of "social paradigm" for Litterer and Young[34] and for Schein the "culture paradigm" of the organization.[35] It is the set of basic assumptions that the group or organization has evolved and *unconsciously* adheres to. Schein argues that the core assumptions around which cultural paradigms form are those beliefs about:

(1) the organization's relationship to its environment: Do members view the relationship as dominance/submission? as harmonizing? as controllable?

(2) the nature of reality and truth: Is truth revealed or discovered? How is time perceived? Space?

(3) the nature of human nature: Are people good, bad, or mixed? What are key "human" attributes?

(4) the nature of human activity: Why do people work? What is "right" or "wrong" in the organization?

(5) the nature of human relationships: Is life cooperative or competitive? Which is primary, the group or the individual?[36]

It is not often that systems spend time examining their commonly held "primitive" beliefs. This region is least examined yet most basic to the system, but is also least susceptible to change.[37]

2. *The intermediate region.* Rokeach describes this region as containing the sets of beliefs derived from the primitive beliefs about the nature of authority and the uses of authority.[38] All individuals and collectivities rely upon authority in one way or another. Authority is a source for information. In the organization it may be significant to view who or what the organization has selected for its authorities. Are the authorities for the organization past members? Are previous teachers or administrators considered as organizational heroes? Is research as a process and the findings of research considered part of authority?

This region not only contains beliefs about its "heroes," but it also contains a set of "antiheros." These are the figures that carry negative authority for the group. The negative authorities may help a group decide what is false; that is, convince them to reject a proposition or a proposal. For some schools that may be Skinnerian psychology, or the previous superintendent, or that "ivory-towered institution" on the hill, or the State.

3. *The peripheral region.* This region contains all the beliefs and disbeliefs derived from authority and the nature of authority. This is where the social map finds closure. For Litterer and Young this region would show the "management paradigm," which they say in business are of three types: the entrepreneurial, the scientific, and the humanistic.[39] From another perspective the contents of this region make up what is referred to as a company's ideology.[40]

The content and arrangements of this hierarchy of regions is only half of the picture. The missing segment is the "structural interconnections" within the peripheral region and between regions.[41] The question is whether or not new information can enter the regions to effect (1) a reorganization of beliefs, (2) a revision of ideology, and (3) a repatterning of paradigms. The extent to which an organization filters information to protect and maintain intact the primitive beliefs of the central region is predictive of the closedness of the system. Mechanisms for protection are generally related to isolation (loose coupling) in the system. For example, specialization is a mechanism that decreases the likelihood that units will have high awareness of one another and which, relatedly, fosters low differentiation in the disbelief system. In the organization this decreases the likelihood that information received by one unit will be passed on to other appropriate units. Some units have misused "executive sessions" and thus unconsciously isolate themselves from those above or from their constituencies. University students may lose confidence in their professors when they find themselves excluded from departmental deliberations. Disgruntled taxpayers may misinterpret board actions when the board excludes their representatives from discussions.

Another form of isolation is seen in a case described in Argyis and Schon[42] in which a game of "distancing" effectively walled off the Dean of a faculty and prevented an impending change in the structure of that organization. Messages from dissatisfied students were not being "heard" by an apparently fractionated faculty. A new dean was brought in but he was soon rendered ineffective by faculty.

> The stance of most of the senior faculty when the dean first arrived was to distance themselves from any responsibility about the issues of planning and redesign. When the dean asked for help and cooperation, the most frequent response he received was, "The task of redesigning the school is a deanly decision." The dean struggled several times to make such decisions at least a function of the senior faculty, but when he called meetings for that purpose the senior faculty operated beautifully to cancel each other out. They used such devices as polarizing issues, making assertions in ways that make the issues untestable, one-upping each other . . . and so on.[43]

Isolation of executives may also occur as a function of the organizational pyramidal or bureaucratic structure. This is quite different from the group norm to isolate as in the dean's case. While different, it still promotes an effective closedness in the system for maintaining the status quo. The physical and psychological distance that is bureaucratically induced "takes a toll on communication and criticism upward because the absences of contact guarantees the absence of communication, especially of insensitive information."[44]

The Time-Perspective Dimension

Citing Frank[45] and Lewin,[46] Rokeach proposes a third dimension of the belief-disbelief system: a time perspective.[47] Rokeach's position is that the organism's tendency to fixate on either the past *or* present *or* future without concern for the connections across time is indicative of a narrow time perspective. On the other side is the broad perspective, characteristic of openness, wherein the balance of time is understood and beliefs can be placed in the time orientation from past to future. The organization that chooses to denigrate its traditions and avoid its prehistory demonstrates narrowing.[48] The dissolution or denigration of planning functions may also signal a decreasing breadth in the time perspective dimension. A third example of such narrowing is characterized by a society and its organizations that adopt the "now generation attitude" as a predominant force. As personnel concern themselves with issues of immediate benefit with little or no regard for long range implications, they demonstrate that these future time periods have been isolated in a disbelief region; additional narrowing occurs when this same group refuses to look at past behaviors that were similar with the negative effects they had on personnel and organization.

RECAPITULATION AND MODEL CLARIFICATION

To date it seems that organizational culture has generally been relegated to inquiries focusing on the content of the ideology of the system.[49] While knowing the dominant metaphor of an organization or knowing its primary philosophical direction could be important, the use of organization belief structure as a culture dimension for understanding an organization's receptivity to change is at least equally critical. By looking at organizational belief structures as ranging from open to closed it may be possible to discern opportunities for increasing the likelihood of the organization receiving and acting on new technologies as well as needed conservation of resources through reorganizations.

Using Rokeach's conceptualization for individual cognitive systems as a model, it has been argued that organizations also possess a collective belief-disbelief system designated as the organizational belief structure. This structure varies across three interrelated dimensions.

The first dimension entails the internal differentiation, isolation, and breadth of distribution of beliefs and disbeliefs. The second dimension is an ordering of the system belief-disbelief orientation from a central core of unexamined primitive beliefs to the more transient peripheral region encompassing the management paradigm and related beliefs. The third dimension is the time perspective which can range from narrow to broad. Each of the dimensions contribute to the extent to which the belief structure is *open* or *closed*.

Indicators of Structural Open-Closedness

The relative openness of the organizational belief structure is related to certain indicators for the system and the dimensions. First, again paraphrasing Rokeach, the openness or closedness of the belief structure may be viewed in terms of the permeability of the structure to information.

> A basic characteristic that defines the extent to which an organization's system is open or closed is the extent to which the organization can receive, evaluate, and act on relevant information received from the outside on its own intrinsic merits, unencumbered by irrelevant factors in the situation arising from within the system or from the outside.[50]

An interesting view of closedness on this characteristic is seen in the concept of organizational "knowledge disavowal." Saltman relates the example of a firm committing itself to a new product. When the market research indicated results *better than anticipated,* the firm rejected (disavowed) the studies as too optimistic, perhaps because it had not anticipated and could not alter its production to meet the more salubrious predictions.[51]

Another form of knowledge disavowal was evident in an experimental study by Conway[52] in which groups were formed with all members being predominantly closed in beliefs, or all open in beliefs, or half the members open and half closed. When confronted with a problem the predominantly closed groups used silence as a way of avoiding coming to grips with a potentially threatening problem. These groups unconsciously adopted a closedlike structure that found belief-avoidance (silence) as an operating mechanism. While organizations are not likely to be composed entirely of "closed-minded" persons, organizational members may nevertheless employ selective information avoidance across departments or across levels of the organization as a way of maintaining intact the structure of that organization. Janis analyzed the behaviors of the Kennedy Cabinet at the time of the decision to invade the Bay of Pigs. He found that group used silence to avoid critical discussions that might upset the ultra-cohesiveness of that cabinet. This phenomenon of "groupthink" is another form of closed behavior at the group level.[53]

Most organizations will be composed of a variety of personalities some closed, others open, and the great majority somewhere in-between. In

Conway's mixed groups a different type of behavior proved as effective as silence in warding off a problem solution that was potentially threatening to the central beliefs of the members. The mixed groups used excessive *noise* to effect the same ends a silence.[54] Despite the fact that the correct solution to the problem being worked on by the experimental "mixed" group was voiced more than once during the problem-solving period, this type of group tended not to "hear" the solution. The group members did not attend to it and continued to talk with one another, raising multiple irrelevancies in the process, and sustained that excessive conversation to the conclusion of the period without solution success.[55]

Meetings are critical nodes for organizational coordination, decision making, problem solving, and change. If meeting behavior shows an isolation of beliefs and disbeliefs, whether through extreme silence or excessive talk, then the culture structure may be signaling a tendency toward closedness.

One final indicator of organizational belief structure openness or closedness is the breadth of the system's time perspective. When an organization is willing and able to set new beliefs into the perspective of its founding traditions, then there is indication of a reasonably broad *time perspective* and system openness. The organization that acts to cut off or deny the past, or the future, has narrowed its time dimension and decreased the likelihood of internal examination of beliefs. A system with high turnover, or one that encourages the early retirement of workers, is in danger of decreasing its organizational memory and, with it narrowing its organizational time perspective. So, too, with a rejection of long-range planning which articulates present behaviors and choices with predictions about probable futures.

During the conflict-ridden 1960s the extremes in student behaviors forced schools to examine disbeliefs and adopt a more future-oriented time perspective than had heretofore been the case. The culture belief structures of the schools and universities were *forced* to change—and changes did occur. Now we are in a period of rationality and debate. Schools are being *asked* to change; studies of schooling show need and the effective schools research shows direction. But a question still begs to be answered: The studies have identified schools with a set of beliefs that happen to coincide with high achievement—do these schools also possess the characteristics for transforming themselves should new directions be identified? Are we setting out the appropriate models of organizational cultures?

Geertz contends that cultures are created and sustained, transmitted and changed, through social interaction, through message exchanges, through communication.[56] Where a set of beliefs are already in place, and where those beliefs are currently consistent with the culture content identified as supporting "effective schooling," then that organization will find its place among the identifiably excellent. But should that organization act to inhibit exchange and examination of beliefs or disbeliefs, either consciously or unconsciously, then that organization is unlikely to sustain itself in a society that is under constant change. Furthermore, should research findings show new formats for effectiveness that demand fundamental shifts in the organizational culture, then these so-called effective schools may show themselves as closed to the new data and unable to reshape the organization for meeting the new demands. These model schools need to be reanalyzed or historically studied to determine to what extent their organizational belief structures are open to sustaining the excellence that is presently there.

NOTES

1. While a plethora of works exist, the most prominent have been W. Ouchi, *Theory Z* (Reading, MA: Addison-Wesley, 1981) and R. Pascale, and A. Athos, *The Art of Japanese Management* (New York: Simon and Schuster, 1981).

2. T. J. Peters and R. H. Waterman, Jr., *In Search of Excellence: Lessons from America's Best Run Companies* (New York: Harper & Row, 1982) and T. E. Deal and A. Kennedy, *Corporate Cultures: The Rites and Rituals of Corporate Life* (Reading, MA: Addison-Wesley, 1982).

3. Ouchi, *Theory Z.*

4. Pascale and Athos. *The Art of Japanese Management.*

5. Peters and Waterman, *In Search of Excellence.*

6. Quoted in D. J. Boorstein, *The Discoverers* (New York: Random House, 1983), p. 647.

7. P. J. Stonich, ed., *Implementing Strategy: Making Strategy Happen* (Cambridge, MA: Ballinger, 1982), p. 35.

8. A. M. Pettigrew, "On Studying Organization Cultures," *Administrative Science Quarterly*, 24 (1979): 574.

9. Deal and Kennedy, *Corporate Cultures*, p. 14.

10. H. N. Trice and J. M. Beyers, "Studying Organization Cultures Through Rites and Ceremonials," *Academy of Management Review* (forthcoming).

11. C. Argyis and D. A. Schon, *Organizational Learning* (Reading, MA: Addison-Wesley, 1978).

12. *Ibid.*

13. G. Bateson, *Steps to an Ecology of Mind* (New York: Ballentine, 1972).

14. F. Friedlander, "Patterns of Individual and Organizational Learning," S. Srivasta and Associates, eds., *The Executive Mind* (San Francisco: Jossey-Bass, 1983).

15. *Ibid.*, p. 193.

16. C. Perrow, "Hospitals: Technology, Structure and Goals," in J. G. March, ed., *Handbook of Organizations* (Chicago: Rand McNally, 1965).

17. *Ibid.*

18. C. Geertz, *The Interpretation of Cultures: Selected Essays* (New York: Basic Books, 1973).

19. E. deBono, *Lateral Thinking for Management* (London: American Management Society, 1971).

20. H. Simon and A. Newell, "The Uses and Limitations of Models," in M. Marx, ed., *Theories in Contemporary Psychology* (New York: Macmillan, 1963).

21. M. Rokeach, *The Open and Closed Mind* (New York: Basic Books, 1960) also Idem, "The Nature and Meaning of Dogmatism," *Psychological Review* 61, 3 (1954): 194-204.

22. T. W. Adorno, E. Frenkel-Brunswick, D. J. Levinson, and R. N. Sanford, *The Authorization Personality* (New York: Harper, 1950).

23. Rokeach, *The Open and Closed Mind*.

24. *Ibid.*

25. *Ibid.*

26. *Ibid.*

27. F. H. Goldner, "Internal Belief Systems and Ideologies About the Organizational Structure of Church and Industry," in C. J. Lammers and D. J. Hickson, eds. *Organizations Alike and Unlike* (London: Routledge & Kegan Paul, 1979), pp. 124-136.

28. J. I. Goodlad, *A Place Called School* (New York: McGraw-Hill, 1984).

29. K. E. Weick, "Educational Organizations as Loosely Coupled Systems," *Administrative Science Quarterly* 21 (1976): 1-19.

30. F. W. Lutz, "Tightening Up Loose Coupling in Organizations of Higher Education," *Administrative Science Quarterly* 27 (1982): 653. Also see W. A. Firestone, and R. E. Herriott, "Two Images of Schools Organization: An Explication and Illustrative Empirical Test," *Educational Administration Quarterly* 18, 2 (1982): 39-59.

31. J. M. Beyer and H. M. Trice, "The Utilization Process: A Conceptual Framework and Synthesis of Empirical Findings," *Administrative Science Quarterly* 27 (1982): 591-622.

32. In an article by A. D. Meyer, "Adaptive to Environmental Jolts," *Administrative Science Quarterly,* 27 (1982): 515-537, comparing hospital responses to the environmental jolt of a doctors' strike, a hospital (Community Hospital) was depicted as perceiving itself as an entrepreneurial mob, as an organized anarchy, as loosely coupled in structure. This same hospital was found to be highly anticipatory of environmental jolts and high in total system learning. This is apparently contradictory to the argument above of non-total system change in loosely coupled organizations. However, the organization was also described as "a richly connected network of informal power" where work was coordinated and resources reallocated by "means of impromptu agreements that were negotiated informally",(p. 526). In other words, this apparently loosely structured organization was actually well connected through its informal systems.

33. Rokeach, *The Open and Closed Mind*.

34. J. Litterer and S. Young, "The Development of Managerial Reflective Skills" (Amherst: University of Massachusetts, 1980), mimeo.

35. E. Schein, "Coming to a New Awareness of Organizational Culture," *Sloan Management Review* (Winter 1984): 3-16.

36. *Ibid.*

37. J. M. Bartunek, "Changing Interpretive Schemes and Organizational Restructuring: The Example of a Religious Order," *Administrative Science Quarterly* 29 (1984): 355-372.

38. Rokeach, *The Open and Closed Mind.*

39. Litterer and Young, "The Development of Managerial Reflective Skills."

40. J. M. Beyer, "Ideologies, Values and Decision-Making in Organizations," in P. C. Nystrom and W. H. Starbuck, eds., *Handbook of Organizational Design,* 2 (Oxford: Oxford University Press, 1981), pp. 166-202.

41. Rokeach, *The Open and Closed Mind.*

42. Argyis and Schon, *Organizational Learning.*

43. *Ibid.,* p. 148.

44. R. E. Kaplan, W. H. Drath; and J. R. Kofodimos, "Power and Getting Criticism," *Issues and Observations, Center for Creative Leadership,* 4, 3 (August 1984): 3.

45. L. K. Frank, "Time Perspectives," *Journal of Social Philosophy* 4 (1939): 293-312.

46. K. Lewin, "Time Perspectives and Morale," in *Civilian Morale,* G. B. Watson, ed. (Boston: Houghton-Mifflin, 1942).

47. Rokeach, *The Open and Closed Mind.*

48. Goldner, "Internal Belief System and Ideologies."

49. Beyer, "Ideologies, Values and Decision Making Organizations"; also see W. H. Starbuck, Guest Editor, Issue on "Organizational Ideology," *Journal of Management Studies* 18 (1982).

50. Rokeach, *The Open and Closed Mind,* A paraphrase from p. 57.

51. G. Zaltman, "Knowledge Disavowal," Paper presented at the Conference on Producing Useful Knowledge for Organizations, Pittsburgh, Pa. (Oct. 28-30, 1982).

52. J. A. Conway, "Problem Solving in Small Groups as a Function of 'Open' and 'Closed' Individual Belief Systems," *Organizational Behavior and Human Performance* 2, 4 (November, 1967): 394-405.

53. I. L. Janis, *Victims of Groupthink* (Boston: Houghton-Mifflin, 1972).

54. Conway, "Problem Solving in Small Groups."

55. *Ibid.*

56. Geertz, *Interpretation of Cultures.*

CHAPTER EIGHT

Effective Schools and School Improvement: A Comparative Analysis of Two Lines of Inquiry

DAVID L. CLARK, LINDA S. LOTTO, and TERRY A. ASTUTO

The authors studied the school improvement literature and the school effectiveness literature. Their review was of the history and the consensus of the two lines of inquiry. The underlying question is whether the findings and generalizations of the two sets of findings can be used side by side by researchers administrators to determine how schools can change to improve more effective instruction. Both kinds of research have had similar inputs and process variables. Examples include leadership, school climate, teachers, students, curriculum materials, finances, and school-community relations.

Distinct traditions of educational inquiry have evolved in the study of school effectiveness and school improvement. After years of equivocation about the role of schooling in student achievement, the school-effectiveness literature has recently taken on a prescriptive tone; not only is schooling argued to matter, but also specific characteristics are cited as associated with successful student outcomes. This perspective has emerged from the stimulus of inquirers who have searched for and documented the characteristics of what have been termed instructionally effective schools (IESs). The school improvement (SI) literature is not characterized by the litany of factors associated with IESs, but recent aggregations of the school improvement research indicate that the agreement on variables affecting educational change programs in schools and school systems is nearly as high as that in the school effectiveness literature. The history and the intra- and inter-literature consensus of these two lines of inquiry will be examined in this review. The purpose is to determine whether the findings and generalizations of these bodies of

SOURCE: David L. Clark, Linda S. Lotto, and Terry A. Astuto, "Effective Schools and School Improvement: A Comparative Analysis of Two Lines of Inquiry," *Educational Administration Quarterly*, Vol. 20, No. 3, pp. 41-68. Copyright © by The University Council for Educational Administration. Reprinted with permission.

research can be used conjointly in order to understand how schools strive to change to attain more effective instructional outcomes.

A reasonable initial question for the reader is, "Why should these literatures conjoin?" The outcome variable of central interest to the school effectiveness researcher has been a measure of student achievement; for the school improvement researcher, it has been a measure of level of adoption of an innovation by a school or school system. The inquirers are, in fact, in pursuit of different questions. In the former case, the question is whether altering resources, processes, and organizational arrangements will affect student outcomes. In the latter case, the issue is whether schools can change and, if they can, how they do it.

However, although investigating distinguishable questions using disparate outcome variables, these traditions of educational research have shared input and process variables. They have examined leadership, school climate, teachers, students, curricular materials, patterns of curricular organization, instructional tactics and strategies, financial resources, facilities and equipment, and parental and school-community involvement in education. Concern with leadership, for example, directed the school effectiveness inquirers to the issue of whether the behaviors or expectations of the principal were distinguishable in effective and less effective schools. The school improvement researchers examined the impact of the school leader on the ability of the unit to invent, adopt, or adapt practices that would make the school more responsive to contemporary knowledge in education—including, of course, the recently popularized version of an instructionally effective school. The contention here is that this degree of overlap in input and process variables justifies a comparative analysis of these bodies of literature. Thus, it is the intent to:

(1) Examine the two traditions of research singly for findings and generalizations;

(2) Review the conceptual and technical adequacy of the research; and

(3) Assert the generalizations that policy makers and practitioners might reasonably infer about what affects school success and how schools change.

EFFECTIVE SCHOOLS RESEARCH

During the school year 1970-71, George Weber, the associate director of the Council for Basic Education, undertook a modest study to resolve an enigma that had troubled him for some time. He knew, on the one hand, that reading achievement in inner-city schools was low, "both relatively and absolutely," i.e., "relative to other schools in other areas" and "in terms of the requirements of other grades."[1] These "facts" about low achievement were accepted so generally and consistently that most lay persons and even school people had come to believe that such achievement was all that could be expected. But, on the other hand, Weber thought that was not so: "I had seen for myself one inner-city school and had heard reports of several others in which reading achievement was *not* relatively low, in which it was, indeed, about the national average or better."[2]

Weber set out to find some successful inner-city schools. He identified two schools in New York City, one in Kansas City, and one in Los Angeles that met his definition of a successful inner-city school: i.e., first, that the "school was a nonselective public school in the central part of a large city that is attended by very poor children," and, second, that "the school [had] to achieve a national grade norm score as a median" and have a low percentage of gross failures.[3]

After visiting and studying the four schools, Weber concluded that there were eight factors in these schools that were not usually present in unsuccessful urban schools:

(1) strong administration leadership—in three cases it was the building principal and in one an area superintendent;

(2) high expectations for student achievement;

(3) positive school atmosphere—a sense of order, purpose, and a pleasure in learning;

(4) a strong emphasis on reading;

(5) additional reading personnel;

(6) use of phonetics;

(7) individualization of instruction;

(8) regular evaluation of pupil progress.[4]

Why pay so much attention to a study conducted a dozen years ago that has been followed, if not superseded, by so many other empirical investigations of effective schools? Because Weber was there first. His study was a demarcation between the quantitatively oriented school effectiveness studies of the 1960s that relied chiefly on large sample, correlational analyses of school factors and outcomes and the search for successful schools studies of the 1970s that used observational, case study methodology. His findings will be used as a benchmark against which to discuss the research that preceded and followed his inquiry.

The Quantitative Studies of the Determinants
of Educational Effectiveness

Pre-1970. As George Weber was in the midst of his field studies, the President's Commission on School Finance funded The Rand Corporation to conduct an interdisciplinary study by that Corporation. The Commission sought answers to a policy question: What resources, processes, and organizational arrangements affect student outcomes in school? The Rand team in its final report attempted to meet an even broader goal, that was to assess "what is known at present about the determinants of educational effectiveness."[5] This comprehensive review included: (1) input-output studies—as, for example, the Coleman Report; (2) process studies of how resources were applied to students; (3) organizational studies—primarily case studies of school systems and schools; (4) evaluation studies—most often evaluations of federal interventions; and (5) experiential studies that the authors defined as "reform" literature describing "how the school system works and what it does to those on the inside, particularly students."[6] They did not describe their study as such in 1972, but in 1984 parlance, they conducted a meta-analysis of the determinants of educational effectiveness.

The findings of the Rand study held out little hope for the school reformers. The key proposition of the study was that, "Research has not identified a variant of the existing system that is consistently related to students' educational outcomes."[7] By a variant in the system, the researchers included school resources, processes, organization, and aggregate levels of funding. In their own words, Averch et al. stated:

> We must emphasize that we are not suggesting that nothing makes a difference, or that nothing "works." Rather we are saying that research has found nothing that consistently and unambiguously makes a difference in student outcomes.[8]

Confronted with these data, they commended for the consideration of the President's Commission two policy implications:

> Increasing expenditures on traditional educational practices is not likely to improve educational outcomes substantially.

> There seem to be opportunities for significant redirections and in some cases reductions in educational expenditures without deterioration in educational outcomes.[9]

The conclusions of the Averch team were considerably more pessimistic than those of the Coleman report, although the latter is often portrayed as the landmark empirical study that demonstrated that schools make little difference in pupil achievement. As Coleman has pointed out frequently, that was not what his study demonstrated. The Coleman report noted that, "differences between schools account for only a small fraction of differences in pupil achievement."[10] But it did go on to conclude that:

> The schools do differ, however, in their relation to the various racial and ethnic groups. . . . The achievement of minority pupils depends more on the schools they attend than does the achievement of majority pupils. This indicates that it is for the most disadvantaged children that improvements in school quality will make the most difference in achievement.[11]

Coleman noted further that differences in pupil achievement were related to teacher quality (score on verbal skills tests and educational background), the educational background and aspirations of other students in the school, and, at least in the case of minority students, to some instructional facilities such as science laboratories. Averch et al. dismissed these relationships citing the subsequent critiques of Coleman's work and contradictory findings in other school effectiveness studies.

Post-1970. Richard Murnane updated the review of the quantitative studies of school effectiveness through the 1970s.[12] He argued that the more recent studies incorporated methlological improvements that allowed them to be more sensitive to the relationship between school resources and the quality of education. Specifically, these later studies used the individual child as the unit of observation, progress instead of achievement level as the measure of effectiveness, and a broader and more sophisticated definition of school resources and their delivery to each child. His conclusion based on this research differed from that of the Averch et al. study:

> It provides clear support for the belief of most Americans—that schools matter. . . . There is no unequivocal consensus regarding the role of any school resource in contributing to school achievement. However, a judicious interpretation of the evidence (including the research methodology as well as the pattern of coefficient estimates) does suggest some tentative conclusions.[13]

The tentative conclusions of the Murnane review strike a familiar chord with the Coleman study, to wit:

Quantitative research on school effectiveness began with a broadly specified input-output model that was agnostic on the role played by particular school resources. In the model, a large number of resources were created in a parallel fashion. A critical survey of this research indicates that the primary resources are teachers and students. . . . Physical facilities, class size, curricular and instructional strategies can be seen as secondary resources that affect learning through their influence on the behavior of teachers and students.[14]

Attributes of teachers noted as being related to student achievement included: (1) intellectual skills as measured by a verbal ability test, (2) quality of college attended, (3) teaching experience, (4) high expectations held by the teacher for students, and (5) voluntary participation in postgraduate education. Murnane argued that research on peer groups, predominantly at the elementary school level, indicated that: (1) elementary school children with low skill levels were benefited by attending schools in which the average achievement level was relatively high, (2) elementary school children from low socioeconomic status families made more progress if they attended schools with relatively high SES student bodies, and (3) the disadvantage that accrued to either high achieving or high SES students was small in schools in which low achieving or low SES children were added.

Summary. The yield of school effects correlated with school outcomes from the traditional school effectiveness studies has been modest. Looking across this body of research for the past quarter century, the most significant finding probably is, as Murnane noted, a reaffirmation of the long-held belief that "schools matter." The things of schools that matter are people. Teachers make a difference. The difference is sufficiently powerful that even the crude measures of teacher characteristics that have been employed reflect the difference. Fellow students also make a difference. The school effects that can be documented impact most powerfully on the most disadvantaged children.

Search for Instructionally Effective Schools

As was noted earlier, the focus of research activity on effective schools changed in the 1970s from large sample, correlational studies of schools to descriptive case studies of individual schools that had exhibited success in student achievement beyond what would have been predicted by the socioeconomic status of their student populations. The Weber case studies foreshadowed the approach that produced the findings that dominated this period of inquiry.

The spokesperson for the instructionally effective schools (IES) research of the past decade was Ronald Edmonds. He redefined the target of study and concern about effective schools employing a definition not dissimilar from that used by Weber. Edmonds defined an instructionally effective school as one that "brings the children of the poor to those minimal masteries of basic school skills that now describe minimally successful pupil performance for the children of the middle class."[15] This definition refocused the policy issue of effective schools on what Edmonds and many of his colleagues regarded as the central issue confronting American education—schools that are effective for children from socio-economically disadvantaged homes. Obviously it narrowed the target schools, the target population of students within these schools, and the measure of achievement applied to the schools. The context of the IES studies and the reform movement attached to them was specified by Edmonds thusly:

> I measure our progress as a social order by our willingness to advance the equity interests of the least among us. . . . Inequity in American education derives . . . from our failure to educate the children of the poor. *Education* in this context refers to early acquisition of those basic school skills that assure pupils successful access to the next level of schooling. If that seems too modest a standard, note that as of now the schools that teach the children of the poor are dismal failures even by such a modest standard. Thus, to raise a generation of children whose schools meet such a standard would be an advance in equity of the first order. I offer this standard . . . to note that its attainment is far more a matter of politics than of social science.[16]

Edmonds, as Weber before him, believed that effective schools existed—he and his colleagues had viewed them and documented their attainments in his early study of the Detroit Model Cities program and the reanalysis of the Equal Educational Opportunity Survey data in the Northeastern quadrant of the United States. His political argument with those who quibbled about the identification of IESs was unyielding:

> How many effective schools would you have to see to be persuaded of the educability of poor children? If your answer is more than one, then I submit that you have reasons of your own for preferring to believe that basic pupil performance derives from family background instead of school response to family background.[17]

The "search for instructionally effective schools" studies generated a consensus about a cluster of factors noted as characteristic of such schools:

(1) strong administrative leadership;

(2) a climate of expectation for satisfactory student achievement;

(3) an orderly but not oppressive school climate;

(4) a focus on pupil acquisition of basic school skills;

(5) a system for continuous monitoring of pupil progress; and

(6) resources that can be focused on the fundamental learning objectives of the school.

A second strand of educational research activity in the 1970s complemented and extended the case study literature on effective schools by documenting and publicizing verifiable findings in the category labeled as "process studies" by Averch et al. The Rand report had argued that research on how resources are applied to students (e.g., studies of the teaching process) might, although it had not, contribute to an understanding of the determinants of school effectiveness. Now it had. The disappointing trail of conflicting findings and ambiguous conclusions reported by Averch et al. was replaced by a consensus about the impact of the use of particular resources on school effectiveness, e.g., engaged learning time and structured classroom activities.

Donald MacKenzie contended that the 1970s, in contrast with the preceding decade of research, saw a confluence of findings from the case study or IES approach, the process studies, and the evaluation of federal programs.[18] Add this to the Murnane argument that the quantitative studies of the 1970s supported relationships between people variables and school outcomes, and the conclusion seems to be that what was known about effective schools was considerably more interesting in 1983 than it was in 1970. MacKenzie's summary of the dimensions of effective schooling growing out of the case study, process, and evaluation literatures is presented in Table 8.1.[19] The distinction he has drawn between the "core" and "facilitating" elements reflects simply the frequency with which each element was reported in the school effectiveness literature.

What Do We Know About School Effectiveness?

MacKenzie, in his thoughtful review of the school effectiveness literature, wished to avoid a new litany of factors. He cited Purkey and Smith's admonition that effective schools were vital, changing, interacting groups of people not to be represented by checklists of ingredients but, rather, by a "syndrome" or "culture" of mutually reinforcing expectations and activities.[20] The problem is that, when one finally comes to a summary section, expectations are held out for authors. However, no matter how the a priori demurs are phrased, the anticipated synthesis of research findings loses the feel of a syndrome or culture. Following is a best guess about what is "known" from the school effectiveness literature. These

TABLE 8.1
Dimensions of Effective Schools and Schooling

Core Elements	*Facilitating Elements*

Leadership

- Positive climate and overall atmosphere
- Goal-focused activities toward clear, attainable and relevant objectives
- Teacher-directed classroom management and decision-making
- In-service staff training for effective teaching

- Shared consensus on values and goals
- Long-range planning and coordination
- Stability and continuity of key staff
- District-level support for school improvement

Efficacy

- High and positive achievement expectations with a constant press for excellence
- Visible rewards for academic excellence and growth
- Cooperative activity and group interaction in the classroom
- Total staff involvement with school improvement
- Autonomy and flexibility to implement adaptive practices
- Appropriate levels of difficulty for learning tasks
- Teacher empathy, rapport, and personal interaction with students

- Emphasis on homework and study
- Positive accountability; acceptance of responsibility for learning outcomes
- Strategies to avoid nonpromotion of students
- Deemphasis of strict ability grouping; interaction with more accomplished peers

Efficiency

- Effective use of instructional time; amount and intensity of engagement in school learning
- Orderly and disciplined school and classroom environments
- Continuous diagnosis, evaluation, and feedback
- Well-structured classroom activities

- Opportunities for individualized work
- Number and variety of opportunities to learn

Efficiency

- Instruction guided by content coverage
- Schoolwide emphasis on basic and higher order skills

SOURCE: Adapted from MacKenzie, D., "Research for School Improvement: An Appraisal of Some Recent Trends." *Educational Researcher* 12, 4 (1983): 8.

have been labeled propositions in the sense of that term implying, stated for the purpose of discussion.

Proposition 1. Schools differ in effectiveness: consequently, they matter. They matter to all children. They matter especially to children who have fewer learning opportunities outside school.

Proposition 2. People matter most in schools:

(a) Teachers affect student learning by the expectations they hold for student performance and for their own teaching performance;

(b) Students affect one another by their level of achievement, behavioral standards, and expectations;

(c) Building level administrators make a difference in setting a climate within the building and supporting the work of teachers; and

(d) System level administrators affect building level leadership by offering psychological and material support. They develop consensus around a raison d'être for the school district.

Proposition 3. Schools that matter can be characterized as (1) focusing on academic achievement of students, (2) maintaining high expectations for student achievement, (3) allocating and utilizing academic learning time efficiently and effectively, (4) maintaining an orderly and supportive school climate, (5) providing learning opportunities for teachers as well as students, and (6) using regular programs of evaluation and feedback to students.

Proposition 4. Why effective schools exist, are sustained, fail to emerge, or fail over time is unclear. Exogenous shocks to, and support mechanisms for, schools and systems undoubtedly assist in the creation of more effective schools. The key, however, lies in the people who populate particular schools at particular times and their interaction within these organizations. The search for excellence in schools is the search for excellence in people.

SCHOOL IMPROVEMENT RESEARCH

The basic message to be derived from the research on school improvement is as unambiguous and optimistic as that of the school effectiveness research:

(1) Public schools and school systems can and do improve;

(2) School improvement programs (federal, state, and local) work; and
(3) Professional educationists are capable of effecting positive educational changes.

This message emerges from a tradition of school improvement literature that has spanned more than 50 years beginning with Paul Mort's studies of educational change in Pennsylvania schools in the 1930s.[21] The cumulative result of this research has been the clarification and specification of factors related to effective school improvement practices. In the most recent major study in the field, "A Study of Dissemination Efforts Supporting School Improvement" (DESSI) by The Network, Inc., Huberman and Crandall observed, "the main ingredients of successful local innovation are coming clearer as each successive study replicates and refines them."[22] The "main ingredients" were found in the variable clusters typically employed in the school improvement literature, i.e., processes, people, innovations, and resources. In this section, these clusters will be employed to search for supportable responses to the following questions:

(1) What processes and procedures facilitate effective school improvement programs?
(2 How do people affect the school improvement process?
(3) What characteristics of an innovation influence successful dissemination, utilization, and institutionalization?
(4) What resources are required to support a school improvement program?

Processes and Procedures

"Change is a process, not an event."[23] The interactive phases of the process are described typically as adoption, implementation, and continuation or institutionalization. Each phase is affected by organizational choices about who will participate and how they will participate in choosing, planning about, carrying out, and evaluating any school improvement product, practice, or program.

Earlier research on adoption emphasized "grass roots" involvement in the early phase of the change process. In fact, the belief evolved that teachers not only had to be involved in the adoption decision, but they also had to be involved in the creation and/or adaptation of the innovation itself.[24] More recent studies have focused on the pivotal role of the administrator, especially the chief school administrator, in the decision to adopt, and they have emphasized teachers' involvement in implementation and institutionalization. Teachers want and need to participate in planning for and decision making about implementation, not adoption.

Teachers' concerns focus at the point of effective action—the classroom. Required changes in teaching behavior, the effectiveness of the innovation in attaining positive student outcomes, and personal and professional incentives for change capture the attention of teachers during the implementation stage. This is the point in the process when active teacher participation in planning and decision making is always useful and often imperative.[25]

One of the reasons cited in the earlier literature for involving teachers in the decision to adopt was to build commitment for the innovation on the part of the user. The commitment of teachers to a new practice or product continues to be identified as an important factor. However, commitment and a sense of ownership are developed through use of the new practice accompanied by continuous assistance and support. Even if commitment is evident prior to initial efforts to implement, practice time to increase mastery and continuous support and assistance are required for effective implementation. And successful implementation is requisite to continued commitment. In discussing the agenda of teachers, Huberman, Miles, et al. have noted:

> What matters to [teachers] are the demands made by the innovation on their present skills and on the way they run their classrooms, the initial and ongoing assistance they have available, the degree they feel committed to the practice as they get on top of it, the possibility of settling down into a phase of masterful, impact-producing use, and the likelihood of deriving some skills and materials that are transferable to other parts of their yearly repertoire.[26]

The commitment of teachers is not a prerequisite to implementation; commitment can be formed through the process of implementation. This recent finding suggests that the decision to adopt lies chiefly in the hands of administrators, and, consequently, early commitment to the innovation is more important for administrators than teachers.

Recent change studies have placed increased emphasis on the importance of the implementation stage. If planning for implementation is minimized, logistical shortcomings are likely to defeat the users. If the process is hyperrational, the prescriptive plan of action often becomes the focus of attention for central administrators, and users' needs are lost in the process. Implementation is a fragile phase of the road to institutionalization because, as Fullan has noted, "educational change is a process of coming to grips with the *multiple* realities of the people who are the main participants in implementing change."[27] Unfortunately for those who would attempt to facilitate the change process, the multiple realities are often conflictual. Each participant in the process from the inventor to the implementer can find a myriad of perfectly good reasons for denying the ability, good will, and commitment of the other. The incentives for administrators are often perceived as neutral reinforcers or disincentives by teachers, and the same is true in reverse. Effective planning provides for people time. It provides time for users to behave like disbelievers, to test and fail and test again. The focus of the planning for implementation must be on the users and their need to work with the innovation.

People

District level administrators. Fullan summarized the role of the district administrators in the change process thusly: "The district administrator [by which he means the chief executive officer and his immediate subordinates] is the single most important individual for setting the expectations and tone of the pattern of change within the local district."[28] Loucks et al.[29] noted that a key element in successful implementation was the commitment, involvement, and active support of the superintendent. Huberman and Crandall reported that central office staff other than the superintendent were often key actors in successful school improvement initiatives:

> Field study data suggested that in successful projects involving major practice change, principals were often accelerators in cars being driven by central office administrators who provided most of the thrust, resources, and pressure, resulting in significant and durable outcomes. The pivotal role of *central office personnel* thereby emerges.[30]

Effective district level administrative involvement seems to include strong initial commitment to the change in the adoption stage, continued general support and assistance in the implementation stage, and specific support and assistance in implementation by personnel described by Loucks et al. as "local facilitators":

> The local facilitator, a role which previous research has all but ignored, emerged as an important player in nearly half of the sites. This person, usually a project director, curriculum coordinator, or federal program coordinator, was often the direct link between the practice and the teachers, arranging training, providing resources, and spending time in the classrooms.[31]

The active involvement of the district level administrator provides a signal to teachers. Evidence of the district administrator's interest in the practice can convince teachers that the effort should be taken seriously.

However, active involvement means just that. General support or verbal support alone is insufficient. Specific support throughout the implementation process is what is necessary. Change at the districtwide level is not possible without the support, encouragement, and involvement of the district administrator, and this support includes the provision of resources and training opportunities as well as communicating the expectation that the schools will be successful in implementing the new practice or program.

Building administrators. Congruent with the school effectiveness research, the school improvement literature has emphasized the importance of leadership on the part of the building principal. Berman and McLaughlin[32] reported a positive relationship between active support by the principal and successful program implementation. The Research and Development Utilization (RDU) Program evaluation failed to confirm this relationship.[33] The RDU researchers did equivocate, however, by noting that facilitating actions on the part of the principals were associated with success in implementation processes. The RDU data seem to suggest that the principal need not be a direct instructional leader but should at least be generally supportive of the school improvement effort. Nevertheless, the DESSI study researchers noted that:

> Principals played major communication roles, both with and among school staff, and with others in the district and in the community. They also coordinated use of the practices at the building level, organized resources, rearranged schedules, and engaged and managed personnel.[34]

School improvement research has documented the ability of the principal to influence change. This influence is often communicated through suasion and the assertion of high expectations. Principals who become involved in change are more likely to function in a facilitative, coordinative role rather than in a directive role. The actions taken by effective principals include: (1) communicating the importance and the likelihood of successful implementation, (2) providing or arranging for the training and materials necessary for successful implementation, and (3) scheduling time for teachers to work with and on the new program or practice.

Teachers. Successful implementation has also been associated with school improvement programs that enhance the quality of the work life of teachers. Unsurprisingly, though often neglected, the innovation has to work for teachers as well as students. The teachers' involvement in school improvement activities has to "fit" as a regular part of their daily work. The school improvement effort works best in a school climate that provides teacher-to-teacher and teacher-to-external assister contacts focused on the innovation.

Studies of the relationship between teacher characteristics (e.g., experience and education) and effective change have produced inconsistent findings with one exception, that is, the teachers' sense of efficacy. The belief by teachers that they can be effective in teaching students and improving practice facilitates implementation of school improvement programs.[35]

Teachers are willing to and do implement school improvement programs when they are provided on-going training, assistance, and the time for mastery of a new practice. Teachers are also willing to and do use new materials that pass a practicality ethic,[36] i.e., are judged to be of high quality, possible to implement, significantly different from current practice, and balanced in terms of personal and professional benefits and costs. To continue the use of a new practice, teachers must perceive direct and concrete benefits—both to students and to themselves.

External assisters. Fifteen years ago, Havelock argued the importance of a link between the resource (R & D) and user systems in order for change to occur.[37] Despite conflicting evidence from some studies, the value of external assisters in the school improvement process has remained basically unchallenged. The activities of external assisters that are effective in supporting school improvement programs have been specified through subsequent research. Because of the resocialization needs of the change process, external assisters must have continuous contact with the school-level implementers. To be effective at the school level, the assistance offered must be personal and practical. In addition to technical expertise, external facilitators must be knowledgeable of the change process and be sensitive to the critical role played by building and district level administrators.

In the DESSI study, it was noted that external assisters were most effective at the school level, for example, "their major contribution to school improvement appears to be preparing a congenial environment for the new practice (ensuring that resources, facilities, and so forth are in place), rather than assisting with the content of the new practice."[38] Huberman and Crandall also observed that the skills and characteristics of individual external assisters may match more closely with different organizational levels and/or different task requirements during the adoption, implementation, and institutionalization stages. Some assisters may be more effective with individual teachers working on technical mastery while others may be more effective with district superintendents in securing external funding.[39]

School board and community. As comforting as it is to picture the school board, parents, and community involved as vital links in school change efforts, the research on school improvement has suggested otherwise:

> by far the most prevalent case is that school boards and communities do not initiate or have any major role in deciding about innovative programs.[40]

Fullan hastened to add that: (1) communities can become powerful in the smaller number of cases when they become aroused; (2) if ignored, communities may subsequently reject innovations about which they were uninformed; and (3) communities have been documented as rejecters of ill-conceived innovations when the results of such efforts became obvious to them. In sum, most communities most of the time do not participate actively in the adoption and implementation processes of educational change. Communities and parents appear to be more effective at preventing change than promoting it.

Final note. Before moving from people to the innovation itself, it might be useful to be reminded that school improvement is a complicated process, precisely because it revolves around people and people resist cubby holes and generalizations. Loucks et al. have noted:

> We originally looked for contributors that were unique to each of the role groups: teachers, administrators, local and external facilitators. What we found instead was a set of assistance functions that needed to be assumed by someone in order for implementation to occur . . . What we found was a *constellation of actors* taking on various functions to result in a fully supportive effort. Some combinations appeared to work better than others . . . There are some functions that a particular role group plays out best . . . But our findings indicate that the *configurations of assistance* are endless, and for each situation a unique combination of players can be called upon to supply all the necessary functions.[41]

Characteristics of the Innovation

Simple changes are the ones school systems are least likely to adopt and implement successfully. That finding runs counter to earlier results. Paul observed that the relative advantage, complexity, and compatibility of an innovation did influence implementation, and he offered three propositions in this regard:

(1) The greater the relative advantage of the innovation, then the greater the likelihood of implementation;

(2) The greater the complexity of an innovation, then the less likely it will be implemented and the less likely it is trivial; and

(3) The greater the compatibility of an innovation, then the greater the likelihood of implementation and the greater the likelihood that it is trivial.[42]

However, Berman and McLaughlin[43] found that the larger the scope of the project, the greater the chance for success. In addition, the study of the RDU program identified product quality, complexity, and difficulty of implementation as positive factors in adoption.[44] The consensus of current research in the field is that an innovation is more likely to be *adopted* if it is perceived as having (1) relative advantage (it is better than current practice and worth the effort), (2) compatibility (it is consistent with beliefs and past experience with change efforts), (3) simplicity (it is easy to understand and use), and (4) legitimacy (it is sponsored by a believable colleague). An innovation is more likely to be *implemented* if it (1) addresses a specific need, (2) exhibits clarity in purpose and technique, (3) is complex (it is perceived as ambitious), and (4) is characterized by quality and practicality. The point that was clarified in the later research is that the perceived relative advantage of complex change outweighs the obvious advantage of simplicity. A change has to be worth the effort to attract the energy of adopters. Based on the current research, three different propositions can be offered:

(1) The greater the relative advantage of the innovation, then the greater the likelihood of implementation;

(2) The greater the complexity of the innovation, then the greater the relative advantage and the greater the likelihood of implementation, provided that personal and professional benefits and costs are balanced; and

(3) The greater the quality and practicality of the innovation, then the greater the likelihood of implementation.

Clearly the probability of an innovation having all of the optimal characteristics for implementation are low. As a result, trade-offs are involved. The important point is that knowledge about the key characteristics of innovations and their effect on implementation helps designers to invent and devise appropriate change strategies on the basis of predicted responses.

Resources

People and dollars affect the success of school improvement efforts. Implementation requires effective staff development that combines (1) task-specific training activities, (2) on-going continuous support for the implementers, and (3) opportunities for regular meetings and interaction among teachers, administrators, and external assisters.

Staff development, like change itself, can be described as a process, not as an event. It needs to begin at the preimplementation stage, be tooled to fit the innovation, and continue on through institutionalization. The focus of staff development must be not only on the development of new skills, but also on the development of new concepts and behaviors in a supportive organizational climate. Interactions among teachers, between teachers and administrators, and between teachers and external facilitators provide opportunities to derive the technical and psychological support that enhances effective implementation. Teachers report that they learn best from other teachers. Teacher-teacher interactions provide for technical and psychological support as well as personal reinforcement. Assistance from external facilitators is viewed as helpful by teachers when it is practical and concrete. Assistance from administrators emphasizes to teachers the importance of their efforts to the organization and is a source of personal reinforcement. Huberman and Crandall have observed that "innovations entailing significant practice change live and die by the amount of assistance they receive."[45]

The earliest studies of educational change naively correlated school district expenditures and successful change efforts. These so-called cost-quality studies ignored the effect of community characteristics on either educational processes or outcomes. More recent studies have found difficulty in establishing any relationship between dollars and effective change efforts. That seems an almost equally naive conclusion. The research is clear that external facilitators, internal facilitators, materials, time for teacher planning and interaction, and time for teachers to implement the innovation are all important components of a successful school improvement program. These conditions all require the expenditure of funds. Slack resources are vital to provide the required human and material resources to support change efforts, and resource support may be a significant motivator in signaling the importance of a new program or practice. Fullan, in his review of the school improvement literature, argued that there is little doubt that the availability of funds external to the district is a "powerful stimulant for adoption."[46] The relationship of additional resources to successful implementation is, however, more complex since innovations and districts vary widely in the need for additional assistance during the implementation phase. Some innovations, for example, require extensive staff development and others do not; some districts have ample staff development resources and others do not. Again, Fullan provides a common sense summary of the issue: "Additional resources for educational reform . . . provide the margin for implementation support in many school districts."[47]

What Do We Know About School Improvement?

Research on educational change has clarified and specified some of the ingredients necessary for school improvement. As with the effective school, effective school improvement programs are probably best represented as a "syndrome" or "culture" of mutually reinforcing expectations and activities. For the purpose of bringing together the research findings of the school improvement literature, a set of propositions—statements for discussion—are again offered:

Proposition 1. Public schools, individual classrooms, and school systems can and do improve, and the factors facilitating school improvement are neither so exotic, unusual, or expensive that they are beyond the grasp of extraordinary leaders in ordinary situations.

Proposition 2. People matter most in school improvement programs:

(a) Teachers can and will implement new practices and programs given active leadership from building and central office administrators, a chance for planning the implementation process, appropriate training, opportunities for interaction, breathing space to try and fail, and continuous assistance and support;

(b) Building level administrators make a difference in school improvement programs by establishing a climate of expectations that teachers will successfully improve practice and by providing on-site coordination, communication, assistance, and support;

(c) District level administrators affect school improvement programs by exhibiting active backing in the form of communicated expectations for success, psychological support, needed resources, and local facilitation assistance; and

(d) External assisters are most effective at the school level providing concrete and practical assistance on implementation issues, such as planning, scheduling, problem solving, and follow through.

Proposition 3. An innovation is more likely to be adopted and implemented if it is perceived as having relative advantage, compatibility, simplicity, and legitimacy. Implementation is more effectiveness when the innovation focuses on a specific need and demonstrates clarity in purpose and techniques.

Proposition 4. Specific resources are necessary to support effective school improvement programs:

(a) staff development programs that are task-specific and provide on-going, continuous assistance and support; and

(b) monetary resources that are adequate to provide the people, materials, and time needed in the program.

A CRITICAL ASSESSMENT OF THE KNOWLEDGE BASE

No inquiry is unassailable. The knowledge base that accumulates from any tradition of inquiry needs to be interpreted by users on the basis of the confidence they feel in the findings for the uses to which they will put the findings. The gravity of error in findings of questionable validity or reliability depends upon the nature of those uses.

As a knowledge base gains visibility, and practitioners and researchers assert its authoritativeness, it attracts criticism. The IES literature has suffered that fate recently; it is both highly visible and vulnerable in some obvious respects. The school improvement research is less visible and has a stronger, richer tradition of findings based upon a more representative contribution by the total educational research community—both methodologically and substantively. It is important to note and summarize the recent criticisms of these bodies of research literature and then discuss some model biases that may be affecting these fields of inquiry. This discussion is included not to discourage use of the findings from these fields but, rather, to assist the reader in interpreting the findings.

Classical Research Criticisms

In the past two years, there have been several reports addressing weaknesses of the IES and SI research bases.[48] The strongest cautionary notes struck by these commentators are noted briefly below:

(1) *Sample bias*—The IES literature concentrates almost exclusively on the urban schools serving students from low socioeconomic status homes. The SI research is concentrated in suburban schools. Since both literatures overrepresent federal projects, they tend to evaluate single programs and overlook interactions with other innovative programs in operation in the district or school. Neither can be argued to be representative of the broad population of schools and school programs to which the findings are often generalized.

(2) *Units and levels of analysis*—The IES research has been conducted almost solely at the school level and in elementary schools. The SI research has historically included school and district level analyses and,

more recently, in the RDU and DESSI studies, has used the teacher and the classroom as a unit of analysis.

(3) *Methodological narrowness*—Little longitudinal data have been gathered by either IES or SI researchers. In the former instance, Rutter[49] can be noted as an exception, and the DESSI and RDU case studies supplied limited longitudinal data on some SI programs. The difficulty in dealing with the lists of critical factors generated by these researchers as a syndrome or culture lies in the dearth of information about how effective schools and school improvement programs emerge, sustain themselves, and/or die over time. The lack of longitudinal data has left the IES findings defenseless against the charge that most such schools are transitory, even random or accidental abberations.

(4) *Outcome measures*—The SI studies have diffuse outcome measures ranging from adoption to implementation to impact on students. The IES studies have a narrow, almost singular, focus on basic skills achievement. This makes intra- and interliterature comparison of findings difficult. Ralph and Fennessey argued that the problems of IES researchers with outcome measures included actual fraud in test-giving as well as inadequate analytic techniques.[50]

(5) *Methodological carelessness*—The IES studies are at best described as case studies, and at worst referred to as anecdotal descriptions. Many of these reports are so lacking in rigor that what the researcher did and found cannot be assessed by the user. The school improvement studies have employed chiefly case study and evaluation designs that have maintained reasonable state-of-the-art standards of rigor.

(7) *Intervening variables and random errors*—Many of the IES studies can be criticized for paying too little attention to the control or assessment of nonschool variables and for failing to account for random error in comparing schools. In the former category, Ralph and Fennessey cited two major IES studies that failed to account adequately for the socioeconomic background of students in the so-called effective schools.[51] In the latter group, Ralph and Fennessey noted that a follow-up of the Weber study by the Massachusetts State Department of Education suggested that the Weber "schools were simply products of chance variation, i.e., false positives."[52] The SI research, with the exception of its early cost-quality studies has not been as vulnerable to such criticism.

What do these criticisms mean from a user's point of view? That clearly depends upon the user and the use. If one is contemplating an effective schools improvement effort at the high school level, the evidence from the IES studies on the role of the principal is highly suspect. The SI emphasis on external assisters may be an unnecessary overemphasis for a locally generated change project. The evidence on external assisters came from the evaluation of federal improvement programs that mandated their inclusion in projects. As a result, these evaluations may well have exaggerated the necessity of the external assister.

Having a feel for the research literature one is working with provides a tool to test the fittingness of findings. Having a feel for the local context for policy and decision making provides a test of the seriousness of the consequences of error inherent in using findings that are problematic. The current significance of the issue of use for policy formulation and decision making is higher in the instance of the IES literature since local and state-based school improvement efforts involving thousands of school districts are turning to these findings for policy guidance.

Model Bias in IES, SI Inquiry

The classical criticisms of a research literature tend to emphasize where the researcher looks (1 and 2 above), with which tools and techniques (s)he observes (3 and 4), and with what care or rigor the observation takes place (5 and 6). Equally pertinent are questions about what the researcher looks for and, at a more complicated level, what the researcher believes in enough to be able to see.

For example, most observers of IESs would probably not have discovered the "use of phonics" as one of eight critical variables distinguishing urban elementary schools that were successful in teaching reading.[53] As a reader explores the summary of the Weber report, (s)he may well have discounted that unusual variable or even attributed its appearance, as these authors did, to a program emphasis of the Council on Basic Education in 1971. This is neither an example of dishonest reporting by the observer nor of propagandizing, just an example of "believing is seeing."

These two literatures have shared common models of organizations and change, on the one hand, and causality, on the other, that have influenced what has been seen. Until quite recently, these research areas assumed:

(1) a rational bureaucratic view of organizations and organizing;

(2) a classical view of leadership, efficiency, and accountability;

(3) a goal-based view of intra- and inter-organizational planning for change and school improvement; and

(4) a relationship of linear causality between identifiable independent and dependent variables in effective schools and school improvement.

Has this made a difference in what has been seen and recorded? Yes. For example, earlier—and some current—SI studies discounted instances of implementation and institutionalization that had low fidelity to the original innovation. In contrast, Berman's introduction of the concept of adaptive implementation[54] as "ordinary" local behavior led SI researchers to begin looking for and seeing these adaptations as important and successful instances of implementation. The same broadening of perspective had occurred several years earlier in the evaluation community when Scriven introduced goal-free evaluation.[55] With the assumptions and tools of adaptive implementation and goal-free evaluation, the observer can see and record previously unnoticed instances of implementation as well as intricate and informative processes of adaptation and unanticipated outcomes that earlier models closed from view.

March,[56] Weick,[57] and Peters and Waterman[58] have argued that in effective organizations there is what they have termed a "bias for action." The peculiar characteristic of this bias is that it asserts that action in organizations frequently precedes intent. Organizations, these theorists contend, often discover preferences by acting. In contrast, the IES literature in particular has interpreted effective schools as well-ordered bureaucracies that work. Could they not just as reasonably be schools with active, committed people who try to discover techniques that work which they retrospectively weave into a more rational schema?

Do high expectations for student success "cause" high pupil achievement or does high achievement result in high expectations for student performance? One only has to deal with this issue if it is assumed that linear causality is found frequently in organizations. Many organizational theorists would subscribe to Weick's argument that:

> When any two events are related interdependently, designating one of those two cause and the other effect is an arbitrary designation. . . . In any causal loop no variable is any more or less important than any other variable. No variable in a loop controls other variables without itself being controlled by them.[59]

The syndrome that has eluded IES researchers may lie in the mutual causality that most people find in their daily lives in workplaces.

Again, the authors wish to simply suggest that, as they did with the classical research criticisms, readers and users should recognize where research is coming from. Early educational change studies employed views of organizational functioning appropriate to the time period in which they were conducted; they were hyperrational. More recent literature, such as DESSI, House,[60] and Fullan,[61] has provided more diverse perspectives. Nonetheless, the IES studies have continued, for the most part, to be dominated by conservative organizational perspectives. The guess is that they overemphasize the significance of bureaucratic characteristics in recording either their presence or absence.

Summary

Since the inferential limits of the IES and SI research are about to be stretched to their breaking point in the final section of this article, both the readers and authors are probably well-advised to recognize the metes and bounds of this knowledge base. Researchers and theorists who have worked in the IES and SI fields have at the very least provided what Ralph and Fennessey described as "a rhetoric of reform . . . a set of normative principles."[62] The authors would argue that the normative principles might be treated tentatively but that the total package of description and findings offers a practitioner's guide to action that exceeds substantially the accumulated experience of any individual. Limitations of theory and technique should lead anyone away from approaching this literature as a recipe for school success. But there is much to be learned and examined in these literatures that will illuminate options for effective practice.

LESSONS FROM AMERICA'S BEST-RUN SCHOOLS

Thomas Peters and Robert Waterman unleashed a blockbuster best seller in 1982 about America's best-run companies, *In Search of Excellence*.[63] The book is an articulate and relaxed summary of what the authors learned by visiting 35-40 successful companies, serving as consultants for many years to both successful and unsuccessful firms, and reviewing rather carefully contemporary theory and thought about organizations. They began their presentation by noting and commenting very briefly on attributes they asserted characterized excellent companies. It is the authors' desire to close by attempting the same brief summary for schools. The previous section of the article is commended to the reader for qualifications and reservations. Beyond this point, the reader is on his or her own.

(1) *Commitment.* Good schools project a raison d'être. The school's mission that is asserted by individual staff members may seem imprecise, but collectively the staff has arrived at an agreed upon set of behaviors and outcomes that are sufficiently specific to acculturate new organizational members and control the behavior of veteran members. They are organizations with a sense of themselves.

(2) *Expectations.* Good schools and school systems are populated by confident people who expect others to perform to their personal level of quality. The attitude of success crosses categories and feeds on itself. Teachers expect students to achieve. Students know they are expected to

achieve, and they expect, in turn, to have involved, competent teachers. Principals are surprised by teachers who fail. Teachers are surprised by administrators who ask little of themselves and others.

(3) *Action.* People in good schools do things. They have a bias for action, a proclivity for success, and a sense of opportunism. They plan for now, seize decision options when they arise, try new ideas, drop bad trials, and play within their strengths. Good school systems and schools have learned how to avoid talking new ideas to death. Critics of the IES movement pointed to its vague internal structure. Good schools invent a structure and improve their practice. The alternative public schools movement of the late 1970s flourished and succeeded because educators in those sites preferred to try new possibilities for success rather than live with old possibilities that had failed.

(4) *Leadership.* The IES literature hammered at the role of the principal as a key factor in school effectiveness. The SI research singled out the chief school administrator as the key to adoption and her or his staff as critical internal assisters. They are probably both right and incomplete. Peters and Waterman pressed the point that "innovative companies foster many leaders and many innovators throughout the organization."[64] People with high levels of efficacy and expectancy who are trying and experimenting cannot be restricted to designated leadership positions. Effective educational organizations spawn primary work groups and individual "champions" in unusual numbers. The designated leaders create an environment for trial and a tolerance for failure so that leaders can emerge and be sustained at all levels of the school system.

(5) *Focus.* Good schools pay attention to the task at hand. Student achievement in the classroom commands the attention of teachers and administrators. More classroom time is allotted to academic learning; more of the allotted time is engaged in academic learning time for students. Staff development programs concentrate on classroom-oriented skills and understandings. Good schools know what their core tasks are and focus on those jobs. Like successful companies, they "stick to the knitting."[65]

(6) *Climate.* At a minimum, good schools maintain an orderly and safe environment for students and teachers. But they are much more than orderly. Time after time observers report that the organizational climate in successful schools is obvious but hard to specify. Successful schools work for all people in the building. They are not schools for students; nor are they schools for teachers and administrators. They work for adults and children and adolescents. The SI literature emphasizes that successful innovations have to fit teacher need. That sounds selfish. One is inclined to say, Who cares about teachers if it works for students? The point is you cannot have one condition without the other. Good schools are good places to live and work, for everybody.

(7) *Slack.* Good schools have a reasonable level of human resources and slack time. In the IES literature, this shows up in a high ratio of adults to children in the building. In the SI literature, the importance of internal and external assisters is emphasized. Both literatures describe the necessity of time for teachers to participate in staff development activity and to incorporate new practices into their already crowded professional lives. Good practice is facilitated by a reasonable level of organizational redundancy and slack at the classroom level. Tolerance for failure, encouragement of experimentation, and the capacity to invent and adapt innovations are not achievable in organizational settings where effectiveness is regularly traded off for efficiency.

Do these attributes strike you as ordinary—even unsurprising? We hope so. Ordinary conditions would appear to be attainable. Most American schools are not excellent, just ordinary. Imagine that they could become ordinarily excellent.

NOTES

1. G. Weber, *Inner-City Children Can Be Taught to Read: Four Successful Schools,* Occasional Papers, Number Eighteen (Washington, DC: Council for Basic Education, 1971), p. 1.

2. *Ibid.,* p. 1.

3. *Ibid.,* p. 5.

4. *Ibid.,* pp. 25-28.

5. H. A. Averch, S. J. Carroll. T. S. Donaldson, H. J. Kiesling, and J. Pincus, *How Effective Is Schooling? A Critical Review and Synthesis of Research Findings* (Santa Monica, CA: Rand Corporation, 1972), p. iii.

6. *Ibid.,* p. vi.

7. *Ibid.,* p. x.

8. *Ibid.*

9. *Ibid.,* pp. xii, xiii.

10. J. S. Coleman, *Equality of Educational Opportunity* (Washington, DC: U.S. Government Printing Office, 1966), p. 22.

11. *Ibid.,* p. 22.

12. R. J. Murnane, "Interpreting the Evidence on School Effectiveness," *Teachers College Record* 83, 1 (Fall 1981).

13. *Ibid.,* pp. 20-21.

14. *Ibid.,* p. 27.

15. R. Edmonds, "Effective Schools for the Urban Poor," *Educational Leadership* 37, 1 (October 1979): 16.

16. *Ibid.,* p. 15.

17. *Ibid.,* pp. 22-23.

18. D. MacKenzie, "Research for School Improvement: An Appraisal of Some Recent Trends," *Educational Researcher* 12, 4 (April 1983).

19. *Ibid.*, p. 8.

20. *Ibid.*

21. P. R. Mort and F. G. Cornell, *American Schools in Transition* (New York: Bureau of Publications, Teachers College, Columbia University, 1941).

22. A. M. Huberman and D. P. Crandall, *People, Policies, and Practices: Examining the Chain of Social Improvement, Volume IX: Implications for Action* (Andover, MA: The Network, Inc., 1982), p. 80.

23. M. Fullan, *The Meaning of Educational Change* (New York: Teachers College Press, 1982), p. 41.

24. P. Berman and M. McLaughlin, *Federal Programs Supporting Educational Change, Volume IV: The Findings in Review* (Santa Monica, CA: Rand Corporation, 1975).

25. A. M. Huberman and M. B. Miles, *People, Policies, and Practices: Examining the Chain of School Improvement, Volume IV: Innovation Up Close: A Field Study in Twelve School Settings* (Andover, MA: The Network, Inc., 1982), p. 440; also see Chapters 7 and 8.

26. *Ibid.*, p. 440.

27. Fullan, *The Meaning of Educational Change*, p. 82.

28. *Ibid.*, p. 159.

29. S. F. Loucks, J. E. Bauchner, D. P. Crandall, W. H. Schmidt, and J. W. Eiseman, *People, Policies, and Practices: Examining the Chain of School Improvement, Volume I: Setting the Stage for a Study of School Improvement* (Andover, MA: The Network, Inc., 1982).

30. Huberman and Crandall, *Implications for Action*, p. 82.

31. Loucks et al., *Setting the Stage*, p. 42.

32. Berman and McLaughlin, *Federal Programs Supporting Educational Change, Volume VII: Factors Affecting Implementation and Continuation* (Santa Monica, CA: Rand Corporation, 1977), p. 124.

33. K. S. Louis and S. Rosenblum, *Linking R & D with Schools: A Program and Its Implications for Dissemination* (Washington, DC: National Institute of Education, 1981).

34. Loucks et al., *Setting the Stage*, p. 42.

35. Fullan, *The Meaning of Educational Change*, Chapter 7: Berman and McLaughlin, *Factors Affecting Implementation and Continuation*, p. 136.

36. Fullan, *The Meaning of Educational Change*, p. 136.

37. R. G. Havelock, *Planning for Innovation through Dissemination and Utilization of Knowledge* (Ann Arbor, MI: Center for Research on Utilization of Scientific Knowledge, 1969).

38. P. L. Cox, "Complementary Roles in Successful Change," *Educational Leadership* 41, 3 (November 1983): 12.

39. Huberman and Crandall, *Implications for Action*, pp. 55, 82-83.

40. Fullan, *The Meaning of Educational Change*, p. 194.

41. Loucks et al., *Setting the Stage*, p. 153.

42. D. A. Paul, "Change Processes at the Elementary, Secondary, and Post-Secondary Levels of Education," in *Linking Processes in Educational Improvement*, N. Nash and J. Culberton, eds. (Columbus, OH: University Council for Educational Administration, 1977), p. 52.

43. Berman and McLaughlin, *Factors Affecting Implementation and Continuation*, p. 88.

44. P. D. Hood, *The Role of Linking Agents in School Improvement: A Review, Analysis, and Synthesis of Recent Studies* (San Francisco: Far West Laboratory, December 1982), pp. 3.38, 3.43-3.45, 4.61.

45. Huberman and Crandall, *Implications for Action*, p. 76.

46. Fullan, *The Meaning of Educational Change*, p. 49.

47. *Ibid.*, p. 75.

48. P. Berman, "Educational Change: An Implementation Paradigm," in *Improving Schools: Using What We Know*, R. Lehming and M. Kane, eds. (Beverly Hills, CA: Sage, 1981); D. MacKenzie, "Research for School Improvement: An Appraisal of Some Recent Trends," *Educational Researcher* 12, 4 (April 1983); S. C. Purkey and M. S. Smith, *Effective Schools: A Review* (Madison: Wisconsin Center for Education Research, School of Education, University of Wisconsin, September 1982); J. H. Ralph and J. Fennessey, "Science or Reform: Some Questions About the Effective Schools Model," *Phi Delta Kappan* 64, 10 (June 1983): 689-694; B. Rowan, S. T. Bossert, and D. C. Dwyer, "Research on Effective Schools: A Cautionary Note," *Educational Researcher* 12, 4 (April 1983): 24-31.

49. M. Rutter, B. Maughham, P. Mortimer, J. Ouston, and A. Smith, *Fifteen Thousand Hours: Secondary Schools and Their Effects on Children* (Cambridge, MA: Harvard University Press, 1979).

50. Ralph and Fennessey, "Science or Reform," pp. 692-693.

51. *Ibid.*, p. 692.

52. *Ibid.*

53. Weber, *Inner City Children Can Be Taught To Read*.

54. P. Berman, *Thinking About Implementation Design: Matching Strategies to Situations* (Santa Monica, CA: Rand Corporation, 1978).

55. M. Scriven, "Prose and Cons About Goal-Free Evaluation," *Evaluation Comment* (December 1972).

56. J. G. March, "Model Bias in Social Action," *Review of Educational Research* 42, 4 (Fall 1972): 413-429.

57. K. E. Weick, *The Social Psychology of Organizing* (Reading, MA: Addison-Wesley, 1979), pp. 245-246.

58. T. Peters and R. Waterman, *In Search of Excellence: Lessons from America's Best-Run Companies* (New York: Harper and Row, 1982), pp. 119-155.

59. Weick, *The Social Psychology of Organizing*, p. 77.

60. E. R. House, "Three Perspectives on Innovation: Technological, Political, and Cultural," in *Improving Schools: Using What We Know*, R. Lehming and M. Kane, eds. (Beverly Hills, CA: Sage, 1981).

61. Fullan, *The Meaning of Educational Change*.

62. Ralph and Fennessey, "Science or Reform," p. 693.

63. Peters and Waterman, *In Search of Excellence*.

64. *Ibid.*, p. 14.

65. *Ibid.*, p. 15.

CHAPTER NINE

Multicultural Education and Urban Schools from a Sociohistorical Perspective: Internalizing Multiculturalism

H. PRENTICE BAPTISTE, Jr.

The article explains multicultural education in terms of a sociohistorical examination of American society. To explain the relationships between diverse social, racial, cultural, and ethnic groups, the author discusses Americanization, the melting pot, and cultural pluralism. He provides a typology of multiculturalism to guide the observation and analysis of education in various settings.

A definitive clarification of multicultural education lies in a sociohistorical look at our society. The national society of our country has been examined and analyzed from a sociological perspective on several occasions. Each of these analyses dealt with the various kinds of people, that is, the diversity of groups that constituted the population of this country. A few sociologists, such as Gunnar Myrdal of *American Dilemma*[1] and Talcott Parsons, presented explanations of the interactive relationship among the various cultural, racial, and ethnic groups.

The three sociological concepts that have primarily been utilized to explain the interactive relationship among the various social, racial, cultural, and ethnic groups are Americanization, melting pot, and cultural pluralism. These concepts are dissimilar in their intent for members of various social groups.

The Americanization Concept

The proponents of the Americanization process during the late 1800s and early 1900s were concerned about the influx of more than 20 million Eastern and Southern European immigrants to the United States. These immigrants were not only viewed as poor, but also of culturally and

SOURCE: H. Prentice Baptiste, Jr., "Multicultural Education and Urban Schools from a Sociohistorical Perspective: Internalizing Multiculturalism," *Journal of Educational Equity and Leadership*, Vol. 6, No. 4, pp. 295-312. Copyright © by The University Council for Educational Administration. Reprinted with permission.

racially inferior stock. Cubberly, a distinguished educational leader, in his book, *Changing Conceptions of Education,*[2] wrote that

> the southern and eastern Europeans are a very different type from the north Europeans, who preceded them. Illiterate, docile, lacking in self-reliance and initiative and possessing none of the Anglo-Teutonic conceptions of law, order and government, their coming has served to dilute tremendously our national stock, and corrupt our civic life. . . .
>
> Our task is to break up their groups or settlements, to assimilate and to amalgamate these people as part of our American race, and to implant in their children, so far as can be done, the Anglo-Saxon conceptions of righteousness, law and order and popular government, and to awaken in them reverence for our democratic institutions and for those things in our national life which we as people hold to be of abiding worth.

Cubberly's stature in the educational community led to an unquestionable acceptance of his ideas and beliefs. Educational systems operationalized his philosophy in an assimilation process of immigrants' children, which debased them of their cultural heritage as they were Americanized.

This process did not leave out their parents. Theodore Roosevelt[3] shared the xenophobic views of Cubberly and utilized his political influence to enhance the Americanization process. He denounced the idea of hyphenated Americans—Irish-Americans, Polish-Americans, and so on. This he considered to be disloyal to the country because he perceived it as holding allegiance both to America and to something else. His uncompromising position coerced many immigrants to forsake their heritage, their roots, for the new and "better" life. The Americanization phenomenon was an assimilation process of Anglo-Saxon cultural imperialism.

The Melting Pot

The melting pot theory was not synonymous with the Americanization process. The objectives of these two concepts were distinctly different. Promotion of Nordic Anglo-Saxon superiority in all aspects of life along with promotion of the inherent inferiority of non-Nordic origins of life was the essence of the Americanization process, whereas the melting pot theory proposed that a new "hybrid" group would emerge from the various distinct sociocultural groups. The sine qua non of this theory was that all groups would contribute on a parity basis to the production of a unique and superior American race. However, the mutual mixing of the diverse groups of this country was not allowed to occur and did not take place. Subsequently, we had the myth of the melting pot. As stated by Pratte[4]

> When a metaphor is no longer believed to be an "as if" vehicle for organizing our thinking and is taken to be a literal statement, a myth has been born.

It was in the early 1900s when this myth received its greatest impetus. The Broadway play entitled *The Melting Pot,* by Israel Zangwill, transformed the ideal to a myth by implying this amalgamation was a fact of American life, not an ideal by which we might judge our attempts to achieve a very difficult goal.

Cultural Pluralism

The concept of cultural pluralism is not new. However, of the three, it is possibly the least understood. One of its most able proponents—Horace Kallen[5]—met with fierce opposition when he presented his theory of cultural pluralism as an ideal sociological model for our society. He believed that the various cultural groups of our society could maintain their identity while coexisting in a mutually supportive system. He argued that cultural pluralism did not necessarily lead to disunity. Kallen's conception of cultural pluralism did not mean that our country would become a "mosaic of cultures." He stated in the early 1920s that there was a mainstream American culture that was historically not monolithic but pluralistic. Kallen believed that this pluralism had its roots in the founding of America, its basic political documents (the Declaration of Independence and the Constitution), the frontier tradition, the way in which the American people settled on this continent, and the values they developed. He believed cultural pluralism was intrinsic to what he called "the American idea."

In his book, *Cultural Pluralism and the American Idea,* Kallen[6] presented his idea of Americanization. Kallen wrote that Americanization means the acceptance by all Americans, native and foreign born, of "an over-arching culture based on the 'American idea.'" This overarching American culture is pluralistic because it reflects a pluralistic society. Pluralism is the essence of its strength and attraction. Kallen believed that cultures "live and grow in and through the individual, and their vitality is a function of individual diversities of interests and associations. Pluralism is the sine qua non of their persistence and prosperous growth."

A COMPARATIVE ANALYSIS

The previously discussed sociological concepts had their strong proponents and followers during the early part of the twentieth century. It is of interest that the real winner (Americanism) was never publicly attested to by the masses, that the alleged winner (melting pot) was a psychological myth, and that the loser (cultural pluralism) has since reemerged. Furthermore, each of the sociological concepts—Americanism, melting pot, cultural pluralism—promoted during the early twentieth century explicitly or implicitly supported racism. Each concept was politically motivated, and the public school system had a role in the operationalizing or nonoperationalizing of the concepts.

The hindsight of contemporary history allows us to realize that the Americanization process as proposed by Cubberly and others became the modus operandi for the socialization of inhabitants of the United States. Our institutions—public schools, government entities, and so on—exuded copiously the values and attitudes of Anglo-Americans to the detriment of any other group's values and attitudes. The Anglicization of non-Anglos' names, lifestyles, family practices, speech patterns, and so on surreptitiously became the order of the times. In spite of the ideal society as presented in Zangwill's play *The Melting Pot,* which found strong support in the masses of Americans, the real winner as to the accepted values, lifestyles, and social practices was Americanism.

It may come as a surprise to some that none of these sociological concepts was devoid of racism. Proponents of the melting pot theory did not intend for the amalgamation or melting process to include people of color or our visible ethnics. Actually, Afro-Americans, Asian Americans, Native Americans, and Mexican Americans, although very numerous in these United States during the turn of the century, were not included in the theories of Americanization, melting pot, and cultural pluralism. The focus of these conceptual theories were the immigrants from Southern and Eastern Europe. It was not the intent of these conceptual theories to provide any equitable relationship between people of color and White people. Therefore, each theory had a definite racist nature.

This is a political society. The basis of its operation is majority rule within a political democracy. Paramount to this political democracy is the inequitable distribution of goods, values, status, and power. Because politics is the management of conflict that results when different groups are in dispute over scarce resources, power, and status, an identification of the opposing groups must be made, and an interpretation of their stakes and stands must be give.[7] The Americanization idea explicitly stated its political position as Krug[8] describes Fairchild's argument in this way:

While the racial makeup of the American people would be hard to define, an American nationality did exist, based on Nordic or Anglo-Saxon cultural values and mores. The American nation, according to Fairchild, was formed principally by immigrants from England, Ireland, Germany, and the Scandinavian countries. But "beginning about 1882," he wrote, "the immigration problem in the United States has become increasingly a racial problem in two distinct ways. First by altering profoundly the Nordic predominance in the American population, and second by introducing various new elements which are so different from any of the old ingredients that even small quantities are deeply significant." These "new elements" consisted of Italians, Poles, and Jews, who were coming to the United States in large numbers. "The American People," Fairchild argued, "have since the revolution resisted any threat of dilution by a widely different race and must continue to do so in the case of large-scale immigration. If they fail to do so, the American nation would face the beginning of the process of mongrelization."

The "melting pot" idea, according to Fairchild, was "slowly, insidiously, irresistibly eating away the very heart of the United States. What was being melted in the great Melting Pot, losing all form and symmetry, all beauty and character, and nobility and usefulness, was the American nationality itself."

What the immigrants had to be told, with great kindness and full consideration, according to Fairchild, was that they were welcome to the United States under the condition that they would renounce their respective cultural values and embrace the dominant culture forged by the predominantly Nordic American people since its independence." The American public schools must be made the effective tools of achieving this objective, at least as far as the children of the immigrants were concerned, and this process must be accomplished as fast as possible.

Neither the melting pot nor the cultural pluralism theorists provided clear explanations for dealing with the political context of our society. Their single-minded focus on the "amalgamation" or "unity in diversity" of the various White cultural/ethnic groups blinded them to the reality of the political obstacles that stood in the way of such noble endeavors. As Pratte pointed out,

> the melting pot ideology made two assumptions: first, that immigrant groups in American society were unwilling to pay the price of Americanization and did not want to "make it" on WASP terms; second, that the American culture was accepting and tolerant enough of "foreign ways" to allow for the fusion and emergence of a "new American."[9]

Basically, each assumption was faulty. Kallen maintained that the majority culture would benefit from the coexistence and constant interaction with the various cultural/ethnic groups; whereas, the various cultural/

ethnic groups would accept and cherish the "common" elements of American cultural, political, and social mores as represented by the public schools. However, through their own efforts, they would support supplemental education for their children to preserve their ethnic cultural awareness and values. Kallen's theory failed to consider the intolerant attitude of the Americanists and the willingness of the immigrant groups to forsake their cultural and ethnic heritage. Kallen's theory of cultural pluralism ignored, to its detriment, the political nature of our society.

REDISCOVERY OF CULTURAL PLURALISM

Surely scholars writing in 2086 will have a clearer perspective as to what led to a broader acceptance of the ideal of cultural pluralism during the 1980s. Nevertheless, without the benefit of their time lag, I would like briefly to submit my reasons for the rediscovery of cultural pluralism. It has become obvious to many Americans that Americanization was a denigrating, ethnocentric process, which forced many individuals to scoff at or reject their heritage. Also, numerous publications had led to the renouncement of the melting-pot theory as a myth.[10] These observations paved the way for the acceptance of cultural pluralism via the demise of the Americanization process and the melting-pot theory. However, certain proactive actions such as (a) the emergence of self-determination by minority ethnic groups, (b) the *Brown vs. Topeka* Supreme Court decision of 1954, (c) civil rights legislation, (d) the emergence of ethnicity, (e) the impact of mass media, and (f) the sociopolitical climate of our country led to the rediscovery of the cultural pluralism ideal as a viable alternative philosophical goal governing the interrelationship of the various cultural/ethnic groups within our country.

In his publication, *The Rise of the Unmeltable Ethnics,* Novak[11] presents an eloquent case for White ethnic groups who failed to melt and who also rejected the Americanization process. These groups have maintained their ethnicity. They believed that being a hyphenated American is perfectly all right. Actually, they will argue that being an American is being the composite product of several cultures. The intense resurgence of ethnicity by numerous groups—Afro-Americans, Polish Americans, Italian Americans, and so-on—during the 1970s led several writers to refer to it as the decade of the ethnics.

The mass media, especially television, has been a significant catalyst in the resurgence of cultural pluralism. The consciousness of Americans was raised via the television exposure of Martin Luther King's marches for freedom, segregationists taunting Black students entering Little Rock High School, Jewish Americans being taunted in Cicero, and programs

such as *Roots,* and *Holocaust.* These and many other televised examples
of racism, ethnocentrism, discrimination, and other forms of dehuman-
ization served a significant function in the recognition and acceptance of
all groups. There is no question about the sociopolitical climate of our
society being more receptive of cultural pluralism during this time than
any other time in our history.

The concept of cultural pluralism that emerged in the 1960s was not
the same as the one espoused by Kallen in the early 1900s. Nor was the
impetus the same. Furthermore, the ambiguity of the 1960s concept has
been greater. The ambiguity of the concept has been extensively discussed
in the writings of Pratte (1979), Green (1966), and Pacheco (1977). Each
of these writers agreed that cultural pluralism refers to a theory of society;
however, the often-raised question is "should the theory be viewed as
descriptive or prescriptive?" My response is that it is both. It has also
been stated that there are different conceptual theories of cultural
pluralism. Several that have recently appeared in the literature are
democratic pluralism, insular pluralism, modified pluralism, and open
society.

Democratic pluralism is descriptive. It refers to a concept of cultural
pluralism in which there is a balance of power between competing and
overlapping religious, cultural, ethnic, economic, and geographical group-
ings. Pacheco[12] states that

> each group has some interests which it protects and fosters and each has
> some say in shaping social decisions which are all biding on all groups that
> make up the society. Common to all groups is a set of political values and
> beliefs which serve to maintain the entire social system through accommoda-
> tion and resolution to conflicts via appropriate channels.

This description has largely been accepted as the form of political organization that exists in our society.

Insular pluralism is descriptive of the relationships among various
social groups. The subgroups of the society as much as possible live in
isolation from one another. Each group places restrictions on the amount
and kind of associations its members may have with outsiders. As Green
(1966) and Pratte (1979) have pointed out in separate writings, the
various social groups will allow their members to develop primary and
secondary relationships within their respective groups, however, inter-
group associations and relationships may exist only at the level of polity.
Although this form of cultural pluralism professes a respect and recognition of cultural diversity within society, it is very restrictive of each
individual. The individual is confined to the social and cultural confines
of his or her cultural group regardless of the wishes of the individual.
Thus, insular pluralism allows each group to maintain its community

and culture while supporting the social value of freedom of association for groups but not for individuals.

The modified or halfway pluralism is not too different from insular pluralism; however, it encourages a high degree of functional contact between members of various cultural groups at the level of secondary associations. Pratte's criticism of this form of cultural pluralism is as follows:

> The fundamental difficulty inherent in the dynamics of the model of halfway pluralism is that the increased contact among groups on the secondary level of association may and often does promote cultural assimilation. (p. 129)

Pratte fails to acknowledge the possibility of acculturation. In cultural acculturation, the individuals retain and maintain their primary cultural heritage and experience while acquiring the skills and knowledge of another or other cultures. Thus, the individuals are able to function effectively in their primary culture and other cultures also. The faultiness of Pratte's reasoning lies in his belief that primary and secondary associations of members from various cultures can only culminate in an assimilation process. His writings implied that an individual can only function in one culture and that in order to function in another cultural setting, one will lose the ability to function in one's primary culture. Banks's[13] typology model on ethnicity addresses the hypothesis that an individual may function effectively in two or more cultures; however, more important, Banks's typology opens the door for the exploration of ways for facilitating the acculturation process. Some research utilizing Banks's model lends support to the acculturation process.[14]

The concept of cultural pluralism as an open society appears both descriptive and prescriptive. However, there is confusion because some observers believe our society is moving toward an open society and therefore, away from cultural pluralism. One such observer, Green[15] believes that an open society is one in which cultural groups and differences are irrelevant and eliminated. This has an apparent similarity to Talcott Parsons's prediction of the disappearance of ethnic groups from American society during the twentieth century. Green's assertion that we are moving toward an open society in the United States is highly questionable, when on examination one realizes his concept of an open society eliminates the significance of cultural groups, much less the reality of their present and future existence.

In the ASCD 1974 yearbook,[16] we are introduced to another definition of an open society. This definition includes the very essence of cultural pluralism because it is descriptive and prescriptive. It describes an open society in which a variety of cultures, value systems, and life styles not only coexist but are nurtured. . . . The major concern of the society at large, and of the schools in particular, would be for full participation of all human beings with rights which are not dependent on race, ethnicity, sex, or social class. Individual and group differences would be prized, not merely accepted or grudgingly tolerated, and every person would have equal access to what they want from and can give to the society.

ASCD's open society concept of cultural pluralism is relevant to the contemporary meaning and philosophical intent of cultural pluralism. This concept of cultural pluralism is both descriptive and prescriptive. It is descriptive in that it recognizes the real social structure of this society, that is, the existence of cultural diversity as evident by the various cultural ethnic groups, and their relationship to certain national institu- tions and value systems of this country.

It is prescriptive because it dares to say what ought to be. That is, cultural diversity should not only be recognized but also valued at both the group and personal levels; that not only is equitable treatment received by all, but equitable accessibility provided to all for societal rights and privileges.

MULTICULTURALISM

The concept of cultural pluralism led to the emergence of multicul- turalism. Multiculturalism refers to a process of education that affiliates itself not only with the descriptive nature but, more important, to the prescriptive nature of cultural pluralism. This prescriptive nature of cultural pluralism is manifested in numerous statements and definitions of multiculturalism (multicultural education) as illustrated in the follow- ing definition:

Multiculturalism should help students develop a better understanding of their own backgrounds and of other groups that compose our society. Through this process the program should help students to respect and appreciate cultural diversity, overcome ethnocentric and prejudicial attitudes and un- derstand the socio-historical, economic and psychological factors that have produced the contemporary conditions of ethnic polarization, inequality and alienation. It should also foster their ability to critically analyze and make intelligent decisions about real-life problems and issues through a process of democratic, diological inquiry. Finally, it should help them conceptualize and aspire toward a vision of a better society and acquire the necessary knowl- edge, understanding, and skills to enable them to move society toward greater equality and freedom, the eradication of degrading poverty and dehumanizing dependency, and the development of meaningful identity for all people.[17]

Common to definitions and statements of multiculturalism is what should or ought to be and the implicitness of their relationship to the development of an ideal society. Therefore, education that is truly reflective of cultural pluralism will be guided by the prescriptive statement of multiculturalism. Thus, the purpose of multiculturalism becomes that of ascertaining the ideal culturally pluralistic society. Unfortunately, that has not been the case. A brief exploration of the 1960s sociological direction will give ample evidence to support my calling them a "blaming the victim" position.

The Sociology of "Blaming the Victim"

In spite of the 1954 Supreme Court decision *(Brown vs. Topeka)*, the sociology of the 1950s-1960s did not support equity educational programs for all students. As a matter of fact, the sociology of this period presented a repertoire of studies to rationalize inequality.

The noted leaders of this racist and oppressive sociology were as follows:

James Coleman—*Equality of Educational Opportunity Study* (1966);
Daniel Patrick Moynihan—"Benign Neglect" (1965);
Arthur Jensen—*How Much Can We Boost IQ and Scholastic Achievement?* (1969); and
C. S. Jencks—*Inequality: A Reassessment of the Effect of Family and Schooling in America* (1972).

In the study of *Equality of Educational Opportunity,* Coleman[18] reported the following: Black students had access to educational resources that were very nearly equal to the resources that White students had, thus making our schools seem more equal than they were thought to be at that time. However, Black students scored substantially below Whites. He further reported that affluent students performed much better than poor students. The significance of Coleman's report is that it lets schools off the hook—that is, schools were blameless for the nonperformance of Black and poor children.

Moynihan[19] stated that benign neglect was the best our society could do. Moynihan argued that the poor are characterized by intrinsic disabilities that account for their low standing in our social order. He further argued that school reform is wasted on the poor since only massive intervention in the life of the poor would eliminate the intrinsic disabilities from which they suffer.

Jensen[20] and his followers (Shockley, Banzield, Hernstein), utilizing the pseudoscience of IQ with the trickery of statistical manipulations, raised the old nurture-nature debate of learning disability. Jensen argued that the failure of recent compensatory efforts to produce lasting effects on children's IQs and achievement suggest that the premises on which these efforts have been based should be reexamined. Jensen did not mean that the ethnocentric value system that gave rise to compensatory education should be examined. Nor did he mean that the racist process of forcing Black and poor children to fit the cultural mold of middle-class Anglo children should be examined. He was raising the age-old argument: Which contributed more to IQ development—genetics or environment?

Jensen buttressed his case for IQ development being heavily determined by genetics on Sir Burt's twin studies. Recently, Burt's twin studies have been severely questioned and possibly represent the most blatant scientific farce of the twentieth century.[21] It appears as if Sir Burt fabricated the studies and "cited collaborators" to further his own ideas of White supremacy. Thus, the cornerstone of Jensen's "genetic determination argument" has been unceremoniously removed.

Jencks's study, *Inequality,*[22] gave wide support to those sociological parameters of "blaming the victim" for their ills. He promoted the causal relationship between being poor, minority status, coming from broken homes, and seemingly low intelligence and low school achievement. A critical analysis of the works of Coleman (1966), Moynihan (1965), Jensen (1969), Jencks (1972), and others will lead one to the conclusion that all statistical weapons were being aimed at the victim.

A Sociology of Equity Education

It was not until the 1970s that other sociological premises, questions, and perspectives regarding the education of Black, poor, and urban youth began to be systematically investigated. This sociological inquiry has focused on the process of schooling. This new inquiry removes the burden of responsibility from the victim and places it where it rightfully belongs, on the educational system.

In the 1980s, however, we see federal institutions continuing their compensatory education programs even with budget cuts while Secretary of Education William Bennett "Getting Particular"[23] wishes to make our students "more American." The same paradox can be seen in other entities, specifically in teacher education programs. The remainder of this article will discuss levels of multiculturalism as they exist today.

TYPOLOGY OF MULTICULTURALISM[24]

Description

In this section, typology levels of multiculturalism that one may observe in a school, a teacher, a classroom, or some educational entity will be described. These conceptual levels are also reflective of the evolvement of multicultural education during the 1960s and 1970s.[25] However, the typology levels focus on the developmental sequence that an educational entity will undergo as it becomes ensconced in the philosophical orientation of multiculturalism. According to this typology, any educational equity involved in multiculturalism can be categorized into one of the ascribed conceptual levels of multiculturalism.

My hypothesis is that educational entities may exemplify three levels of multiculturalism. These levels are distinct with readily identifiable parameters or characteristics. Additionally, these conceptual levels differ qualitatively and quantitatively with respect to multiculturalism. There is a qualitative variation in the levels as to emphasis on product, process, or philosophy. The extent of this variation (quantity) as to the amount of product, process, and philosophy is also distinctive for each level.

Basically all educational components or entities can be observed to have the same kind of characteristic when at Level One. All educational components such as teacher educational programs, school districts or schools, service departments (counseling, library, and so on), academic departments (social studies, language arts, science, and so on), elementary or secondary classrooms, and educators (administrators, teachers, counselors, and so on) will display similar kinds of characteristics. For illustrative purposes as to how these characteristics may manifest themselves, I have chosen two educational components—teacher education programs and classroom instruction in a K-12 setting.

My direct involvement in teacher education programs at several universities and in two national research studies led to my first observations regarding the evolution of multiculturalism in a teacher education program. It became obvious that the extent of multiculturalism had a distinct qualitative dimension as well as a quantitative one. Quite obviously, teacher education programs would differ in the number of cultural/ethnic groups, number of workshops, courses, or programs devoted to multiculturalism, ethnic/cultural makeup of faculty and students, amount of funds budgeted for multiculturalism, and so forth. This is the quantitative dimension. However, a more salient feature appeared missing in most teacher education programs. This feature is the qualitative dimension. Further exploration of the educational arena reveals the omission or paucity of the qualitative dimension in other educational entities or components. The qualitative dimension of multiculturalism may be divided into three conceptual levels. Thus, the typology model, which is presented later in this article, is primarily based on this dimension, although not without the quantitative dimension. Also, it is along the qualitative dimension that internalization of multiculturalism must occur if educational equity and the prescriptive aspects of multiculturalism are going to be achieved.

The purpose of the typology is to help facilitate research in multiculturalism and also to aid in the intrinsic operatization (internalization) of multiculturalism in educational entities or components. It is my hypothesis that the internalization of multiculturalism in an educational entity can occur on at least three conceptual levels. Each level has a distinct set of characteristics that may be utilized to identify which conceptual level of the qualitative dimension of multiculturalism the educational entity has reached.

Level One is characterized by a single cultural or ethnic emphasis such as ethnic- or cultural-specific courses, celebration of cultural or ethnic holidays, and fragmented and unrelated topics on various cultural groups in the curriculum. Furthermore, Level One is characterized by such tangibles as workshops, seminars, or courses on specific minority or ethnic groups coupled with a lack of clear-cut programmatic goals or objectives. The additive notion is usually in vogue. During this period, the dominating feature for incorporating multiculturalism is the addition of courses (usually on one of the visible minority ethnic groups), conferences, or workshops. These tangibles are obviously paraded to suggest something more than the real intent of the program. Often these cultural/ethnic emphases are for specific populations and are geographically limited. Perhaps the most salient characteristics of Level One are its reaction posture and lack of institutionalization. These tangible cultural/ethnic displays are the result of external pressures brought about, for example, by interest groups, social pressures, or community groups.

Level Two is characterized by a confluent relationship between product and process. The seminal qualitative difference between Levels One and Two is that the tangible products are embedded in a matrix of process. In this period, there is a theoretical referent link with practice. Multiculturalism takes on a broader base in its incorporation into the educational entity. Generic components of multicultural education are identified along with strategies for incorporating them into the entire educational entity or program. In addition, steps are taken to institutionalize various facets of multiculturalism. Specific courses and related experiences become a formalized part of the educational program. This level forms a broad conceptual framework that guides the amalgamation of the elements and principles of multiculturalism with the core components of the educational program.

Attainment of Level Three represents a highly sophisticated internalization of the process of multiculturalism combined with a philosophical orientation that permeates all components of the educational entity. This pervasive quality will cause all facets of the educational entity to be governed by the accepted concepts, principles, and goals of multiculturalism. The attainment of Level Three by an educational entity surmises that it has emerged from Level One (product) and Level Two (product/processes) to a sophisticated and regenerative conceptual knowledge base for multiculturalism.

These levels are sequential, however; Levels Two and Three must be viewed as eclectic mixtures of those elements from the previous level (see Figure 9.1).

Research

Presently, I am conducting several studies on the internalization of multiculturalism. Utilizing my typology of multiculturalism as a guide, several appropriate instruments have been developed to aid in determining the extent to which the internalizing of multiculturalism has occurred in two selected educational entities. At this time, I will present preliminary data and results from my research into the internalization of multiculturalism by teacher education programs and public school teachers.

The teacher education program entity was selected as a starting point for my research because of its significant role in the training of our teachers for the public schools. Furthermore, the American Association of Colleges for Teacher Education (AACTE), along with numerous other teacher associations and state departments of education, have stressed, through position papers, certification requirements, legislative mandates, and accreditation standards, the importance of teacher education programs incorporating multiculturalism into all aspects of their programs.

Questionnaires based on the Typology of Multiculturalism model were mailed to 150 randomly selected undergraduate teacher education programs. The dean of the school of education, or his or her designate, was asked to complete the questionnaire and return it to the researcher. Of the disseminated questionnaires, 44% were completed and returned. Preliminary analysis of the data has revealed the following:

(1) Of the responding institutions, 84% scored at the *low end* of Level One. The extent of multiculturalism was the offering of one or two short workshops or seminars and/or one multicultural course during the previous year.

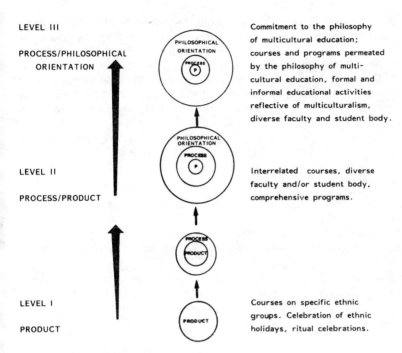

LEVEL III

PROCESS/PHILOSOPHICAL
ORIENTATION

Commitment to the philosophy
of multicultural education;
courses and programs permeated
by the philosophy of multicultural education, formal and
informal educational activities
reflective of multiculturalism,
diverse faculty and student body.

LEVEL II

PROCESS/PRODUCT

Interrelated courses, diverse
faculty and/or student body,
comprehensive programs.

LEVEL I

PRODUCT

Courses on specific ethnic
groups. Celebration of ethnic
holidays, ritual celebrations.

Figure 9.1: Levels of Multiculturalism

(2) Of the responding institutions, 51% had elected not to offer any multicultural courses.

(3) In addition, 29% had not scheduled workshops, seminars, or multicultural courses.

(4) Approximately 11% (10.6%) of the responding institutions were at Level Two. This was accomplished through the restructuring of some education courses to reflect multiculturalism and/or offer a major in multiculturalism. However, a vast majority of multicultural majors were based on just one or two regional multicultural courses.

(5) Of the responding institutions, 10% were at the lower end of Level Three. This was ascertained by an institution having included objectives relevant to multiculturalism within their institutional objectives. However, upon closer scrutiny it was clear that these objectives were not being implemented.

The second study focused on the extent of internalization of multiculturalism within teachers and their opinion as to the extent of it in their classroom instruction and school. The procedure was the following: The typology of multiculturalism was explained to each teacher. The explanation included a complete description of each level including their pertinent characteristics. Examples of school climates and behavioral contexts, classroom instructional strategies and lessons, and teacher behavioral patterns with students, parents, and others were discussed for each level. Then a film of a teacher in demonstrable Levels Two and Three behavioral patterns was shown to each teacher. Each teacher was then given the typology of multiculturalism matrix to complete (see Figure 9.1). This matrix allowed each teacher to determine the multiculturalism level for his or her school, class instruction, him- or herself, and the film.

Preliminary analysis of the responses of 40 teachers indicates the following:

(1) All of the teachers stated that the teacher depicted in the film was operating at Level Three.

(2) Of the teachers, 68% believed that their schools were operating at Level One. The 5% who placed their schools at Level Three did so reluctantly.

(3) Of the teachers, 66% stated that their classroom instruction was at Level Two of multiculturalism and 8% felt they were at Level Three.

(4) Of the teachers, 61% believed that their personal behavior and interaction with students were at Level Two and 28% felt they were at Level Three.

The results cited in the two studies appear to confirm that the internalization of multiculturalism in education, as elsewhere in America, is moving slowly. The writings of the late Ron Edmonds[26] on effective education in urban schools explicitly supports a major underlying principle of multicultural education—promotion of a student's self-esteem and a basic belief that *all* students can learn. During this period of dwindling resources among urban schools, it is very important that we commit ourselves to the sociological concept of cultural pluralism. If the recent celebration of the Statue of Liberty's 100th anniversary is to be more than mere symbolism, then we as a nation must commit ourselves to internalizing multiculturalism in our schools.

NOTES

1. G. Myrdal, *An American Dilemma: The Negro Problem and Modern Democracy* (New York: Harper & Row, 1962).

2. E. Cubberly, *Changing Conceptions of Education* (New York: Riverside Educational Mimeographs, 1909).

3. T. Roosevelt, "Americanism" (speech given in 1909).

4. R. Pratte, *Pluralism in Education* (Springfield, IL: Charles C Thomas, 1979), p. 29.

5. H. Kallen, *Cultural Pluralism and the American Idea* (Philadelphia: University of Philadelphia Press, 1956).

6. *Ibid.*

7. B. Sizemore, "The Politics of Multicultural Education" (Unpublished, 1979).

8. M. Krug, *The Melting of the Ethnics* (Bloomington, IN: Phi Delta Kappa, 1976), pp. 12-13.

9. Pratte, *Pluralism in Education.*

10. M. Novak, *The Rise of the Unmeltable Ethnics* (New York: Macmillan, 1973).

11. *Ibid.*

12. A. Pacheco, "Cultural Pluralism: A Philosophical Analysis," *Journal of Teacher Education* (May-June 1977): 16-20.

13. J. Banks, *Pluralism and the American Teacher* (Washington, DC: AACTE, 1977).

14. M. Ford, "The Development of an Instrument for Assessing Levels of Ethnicity in Public School Teachers" (Doctoral dissertation, University of Houston, 1979).

15. T. G. Green, "Education and Pluralism" (Twenty-sixty Annual T. Richard Street Lecture, School of Education, Syracuse University, 1966).

16. D. Dora-Della et al., eds., *Education for an Open Society* (Washington, DC: ASCD, 1974), p. 3.

17. B. H. Suzuki, "Multicultural Education: What's It All About?" *Integrated Education* 17, 1-2 (1979): 47-48.

18. J. Coleman, *Equality of Educational Opportunity* (Washington, DC: Office of Education, U.S. Department of Health, Education and Welfare, 1966).

19. D. P. Moynihan, *The Negro Family: The Case for National Action* (Washington, DC: U.S. Department of Labor, 1965).

20. A. R. Jensen, "How Much Can We Boost IQ and Scholastic Achievement?" *Harvard Educational Review* 39, 1 (1969): 1-123.

21. O. Gillie, "Did Sir Cyril Burt Fake His Research on Hereditability of Intelligence?" *Phi Delta Kappan* (February 1977): 469:471.

22. C. S. Jencks et al., *Inequality: A Reassessment of the Effect of Family and Schooling in America* (New York: Basic Books, 1972).

23. W. Bennett, "Getting Particular" (U.S. Department of State, 1969).

24. Typology of multiculturalism was first described in H. P. Baptiste, Jr. et al., *Multicultural Teacher Education: Preparing Educators to Provide Educational Equity* (Washington, DC: AACTE, 1980).

25. G. Gay, "Changing Conceptions of Multicultural Education," *Educational Perspectives* (December 1977): 4-9.

26. R. Edmonds, *A Discussion of the Literature and Issues Related to Effective Schooling* (ERIC Clearinghouse Document No. ED.170 394, 1979).

CHAPTER TEN

The Political Economy of Public Schools

WILLIAM LOWE BOYD

Both the current decline in support for the public schools and the organizational-performance problems of schools can be illuminated by the conceptual approach of political economy. This article combines a selective review of the literature with an introduction to this increasingly popular mode of analysis.

American public schools are facing difficult times. Declining enrollments and test scores, soaring costs, and disappointment over the schools' performance in the reform efforts of the past two decades have combined to erode public support for the public schools. A new feature of this latest of a long succession of "crises" over the public schools is an attack on the very concept of the *public* school. With added impetus from the publication of James S. Coleman's controversial study, *Public and Private Schools,* the ideas are gaining popularity that nonpublic schools are doing a better job than public schools and that there no longer may be any compelling civic reasons to patronize and support public schools.[1]

The all too well-publicized performance problems of the public schools have prompted extensive searches for innovative solutions. The rather meager results from a great variety of innovative attempts suggest that the present conceptual cupboards are bare.[2] At the same time, there is a great deal of conceptual confusion among organizational theorists in general and, particularly, when they address themselves to educational organizations.[3] The favorite explanation among scholars today for the peculiar performance of public schools is captured in the concepts and metaphors of "loose coupling" and "organized anarchies."[4] Carried to the extreme, purveyors of these conceptual wares wonder if schools, with all their loose coupling and irrationality, can be called organizations at all.[5] Since public schools obviously are *some kind* of organization, such an extreme position should raise questions about the conceptual perspective being employed.

A conceptual approach that sheds light on both the organizational-performance problems of public schools and the decline in public support of

SOURCE: William Lowe Boyd, "The Political Economy of Public Schools," *Educational Administration Quarterly*, Vol. 18, No. 3, pp. 111-130. Copyright © by The University Council for Educational Administration. Reprinted with permission.

the schools is the subject of this article. Particularly within the past five years, the political economy approach has been applied fruitfully and provocatively to the analysis of the problems of the public schools. Yet, the approach is still rather unfamiliar to many scholars in educational administration, as witnessed by the fact that many authors simply ignore this line of analysis in their discussions of the state of the field.[6]

This article is intended as a brief review of an introduction to the literature and applications of political economy to educational administration. As such, it is selective and illustrative rather than comprehensive in its coverage.

POLITICAL ECONOMY AND INSTITUTIONAL FRAMEWORKS

As Garms, Guthrie, and Pierce have observed, "Organizations can be viewed as a set of opportunities to and restrictions on the ability of people to improve their well being."[7] The problem of organizational design and policy analysis, thus, is "to *identify* institutional frameworks which facilitate [the selection] and enactment of efficient, equitable, and responsive programs."[8]

How well does the institutional framework of public schools meet this standard? One way to answer this question and also to introduce the basic concepts of political economy, is to draw on a recent analysis of issues in organizational theory as applied to public schools.[9]

The starting point for this discussion is a recent article by Daniel Griffiths.[10] In the article, Griffiths directs the attention of theorists in educational administration to Perrow's argument that conventional organizational theories amount to a mystification of reality since they accept the professed goals of human service organizations as the *real* goals and treat as *peripheral* (and sometimes pathological) the various functions these organizations perform for employees, assorted interest groups, and other organizations.[11] Applied to schools, Perrow's insight is reminiscent of Cronin's observation that researchers at Harvard only began to understand the behavior of the Boston school board when they realized that it acted more nearly as the head of an employment agency than an educational organization.[12]

According to Perrow, human service organizations perform three important functions apart from pursuit of their professed goals. First, they regulate the behavior of dependent or "deviant" people. Second, they absorb part of the nation's work force. Third, and most important, they provide resources or benefits for employees, interest groups, and other organizations.[13] As Perrow sees it, it seems to be typical that (a) failure to supply unofficial benefits to the environment (and to employees) will be greatly resisted; (b) the large majority of these benefits are inconsistent with official goals and detract from their realization; but (c) the failure to meet official goals meets with very little resistance because the constituency is poorly organized and/or the goals themselves are recognized as unrealistic.[14]

In sum, Perrow believes that at the center (not periphery) of any realistic theory should be the fact that employees, interest groups, and other organizations "use" human service organizations for their own purposes. The role (and measure of success) of the executive within this view, since professed goals are hard to attain and organizational effectiveness is difficult to measure, is to exploit the environment for resources, maximize the growth and power of the organization, see that unofficial benefits are delivered, and ensure that the organization conforms to environmental expectations, including at least some minimal appearance of meeting (or trying to meet) the professed goals.

Although Griffiths finds Perrow's demystification argument quite convincing, and an improvement over traditional views of human service organizations, he nevertheless remains unsatisfied:

> While traditional organizational theory has taken the executives' statement of goals as central, and Perrow wonders about taking the workers' and other groups' goals as central, both approaches seem wrong to me. Rather, there should be a way of describing organizations that tries to determine, not a priori but in actuality, what the particular organization is attempting to do, and, in particular, what the people in it are attempting to do.[15]

As it happens, the political economy approach does much of what Griffiths wants. This approach, known also as public (or collective) choice, is most germane for the study of public school administration but, because it comes from a tradition foreign to most in educational administration, only recently has begun to be applied systematically to public schools. Public choice is concerned with "the action of individuals when they choose to accomplish purposes collectively rather than individually."[16] Put another way, it is "the economic study of nonmarket decision making."[17] Using the rational choice paradigm from economics, the approach assumes that rational, self-interested individuals try to maximize their own welfare (or benefits) within the context of the institutional or organizational reward structure they face. Alternative institutional arrangements thus need to be evaluated in terms of how variation in the structure of incentives affects behavior. Finally, as Michaelsen notes, "explicit account is taken of the costs of obtaining information, of participating in decision making, of mobilizing political action, and of the entire range of transactions neglected by the older tradition of micro-economic analysis" (and, it might be added, by traditional political science).[18]

In stark contrast to many organizational theories, the public choice approach consists of more than an ad hoc melange of related insights. It provides a deductive theory moving from the behavioral postulates of the rational choice paradigm to the likely consequences for behavior of the specific features of the incentive structure of particular institutions or organizations. While it proceeds from a priori assumptions about human behavior, it generates empirically testable propositions. The specific theories developed out of the public choice approach thus should be evaluated according to how well they predict or explain behavior, *not* according to how well they correspond to humanistic notions of the complexity of humans and of social behavior.

One way to test the utility of this approach is to ask how well it can account for Perrow's conclusions about the behavior of human service organizations—conclusions that Griffiths says accord with his own ob-servations of many educational organizations.[19] Perrow's own explana-tion, such as it is, does little to complete the demystification process he sets for himself. He merely asserts that human service organizations "have more important things to do"—functions to perform and resources to provide—than to meet their announced goals.[20] But why do these matters seem more important, and why do they crowd out attention to the announced goals? The closest Perrow comes to answering these questions is when he notes that failure to provide unofficial benefits will be keenly resisted, but failure to achieve official goals will not. This is because clients are poorly organized and/or official goals are thought to be unrealistic. Still, what accounts for these facts?

One of the virtues of the public choice approach is that the rational choice paradigm immediately calls attention to the difference and tension between the goals of individuals (maximizing their own welfare) and the professed goals of organizations. As a consequence, it provides a rational explanation for much that otherwise appears irrational or pathological in terms of the announced goals of organizations. In the ideal arrange-ment in the profit-seeking, private-sector organization facing competi-tion, the incentive structure of the organization motivates self-interested employees to engage in behaviors convergent with the maximization of profits. This structure necessitates satisfying customers, thereby pre-sumably achieving (or at any rate approaching) the organization's an-nounced goals. In the case of the quasi-monopolistic public schools, the primary announced goal is the production of valued student learning outcomes. But, as Michaelsen and others point out, financial support for the public schools comes through a political process in the form of a tax-supplied budget rather than directly from satisfied clients.[21] Thus, the crucial linkage that ensures consumer sovereignty is broken because of the assurance of a budget *independent* of the degree to which individual consumers are satisfied. Since there are no profits in public bureaus (including public schools) to motivate and reward managers (and teachers' salaries are based on seniority rather than performance), Michaelsen contends that, in place of profits,

> we may assume that bureaucrats, including schoolmen, seek instead to survive, to enlarge the scope of their activities, to gain prestige, to avoid conflict, to control the organization and content of their daily round as much as possible. All these are, as it were, profit in kind. By accepting this theory of motivation, we do not rule out altruism. Administrators and teachers, like entrepreneurs, take pride in their work and strive for excellence. The issue is not whether bureaucrats are altruistic but rather whether there are mechanisms available to harness their self-seeking to the public interest.[22]

In agreement with Niskanen, Michaelsen argues that public bureaus lack such mechanisms, with the consequence that the self-seeking behavior of bureaucrats leads to perverse results.[23] Thus, the public choice approach predicts all the behaviors Perrow vividly reports, but for which he offers no real explanation. First consider the functions of the executive in a public bureau. The public choice prediction is virtually identical with Perrow's account, summarized earlier, of what these executives do.[24] In other words, to maximize the executive's benefits (e.g., power, prestige, salary) requires him or her to maximize the growth, power, and internal stability of the organization (or that portion of it he or she controls). This in turn requires the executive to strike bargains with both employees and external groups in order to insure that he or she can both meet the environment's expectations and exploit it for resources. Thus, a kind of reciprocity with employees and key interest groups is created that, along with the executive's self-interest, tends to foster the maximization of budgets rather than profits (i.e., consumer or client satisfaction).

Second, consider employees. Perrow says that if we were to survey human service organization members in terms of what they really are trying to do, we would ask such questions as:

> Can you minimize the personal costs of working in this place; can you manage to make the work fairly light; can you avoid unpleasant duties or clients . . . can you manage to pick up office supplies or food from the kitchen . . . ? Can you get your friend or relative a job here? Most important of all, can you be sure of having a job here as long as you need it?[25]

Consistent with this line of analysis, Michaelsen concludes that a bargaining process between teachers and their principals and between principals and central office staff results in a generally agreeable arrangement all around: "The needs of teachers and principals for control over their jobs most often take precedence over the needs of individual children and their families." [26] Or, as Mann has observed, "The current procedures for resource allocation at the building level have more to do with the equitability of adult working conditions than with the production of responsive learning environments for children." [27] The propensity for putting employees' interests ahead of students' interests is fostered by the reality that public schools, as "domesticated" organizations, are assured not only of funding but of a largely captive clientele. [28] Moreover, apropos of Perrow's "survey" questions, Cusick found, in a study of two high schools, that the inadequacies of the reward structure, career ladder, and supervision system were such that many teachers not only had second jobs outside of the school day but also used time within the school day to advance these enterprises. [29]

Finally, consider the contest over the official and unofficial goals or benefits of human service organizations. Drawing on Downs' "economic theory of democracy," West and Michaelsen show how public employees stand to gain greater benefits and face lower costs (e.g., lower information, opportunity, and political mobilization costs) in pursuing unofficial benefits from the organization than the lay public stands to gain in seeking to ensure the adequate provision of the official benefits. [30] Downs and Niskanen also show the vulnerability of legislatures (e.g., school boards) to manipulation and lobbying by bureaucratic executives and employees. [31] Furthermore, the exclusivity of unofficial benefits and the non-exclusivity of official benefits create substantial difficulties (especially, the "free-rider" problem) in mobilizing collective action (i.e., in forming and maintaining interest groups) for the public that are not faced by employees or others interested in the unofficial benefits. [32] Taken together, these factors identified by public choice theories provide a comprehensive explanation for the differences Perrow notes in political organization and support for official and unofficial goals.

Each of the foregoing paragraphs compresses a great deal of material. [33] But this discussion should be sufficient to illustrate the economic explanation for the propensity for goal-displacement in public-sector (tax supported, consumer insensitive) organizations, a problem that is exacerbated in public-sector human service organizations because of the ambiguity of their ends and means. Loose coupling theory, of course, springs from a recognition of the ramifications of such ambiguity, and there is no denying that the loose coupling and organized anarchy theories have been rich sources of insights and ideas for research. The public choice approach, however, offers a more succinct and rational explanation for many of the things that are accounted for so colorfully and, sometimes, circuitously by academe's "loose couplers." Significantly, the political economy analysis predicts that loose coupling is likely to be greater in public than in private sector organizations because the former lack the discipline of the marketplace.[34]

The discussion so far also illustrates how the economic approach links up with the concerns of those interested in politics, policy analysis, and organizational behavior in education. If, following Lasswell, politics is defined as "who gets what, when, and how,"[35] then which goals public organization members (including managers) pursue most assiduously—the official or unofficial goals—becomes a subject of politics, policy, and organizational design because this determines what outputs the organization will produce or, put another way, who will benefit and who will lose by the performance of the organization.

Prior to the relatively recent applications of the public choice approach to understanding the behavior of public educational organizations, more traditional economic analysis of the performance of schools already was underway utilizing an input-output focus and anticipating the "school effects" and "policy analysis" movements. Economists have sought a better grasp of the education production function (how inputs are combined to produce outputs). In so doing, they have reminded educators that school administration should be defined broadly to include how resources generally—including, particularly, student and teacher time—are allocated and combined to foster desired outcomes.[36] Some useful concepts to come out of this effort, related to the notion of "opportunity costs," are the concepts of "foregone learning," "foregone teaching," and "foregone schooling."[37] Research findings in this area are staggering and embarrassing. For example, Geske reports studies finding that teachers spent from 40 to 80% of their time on *noninstructional* activities.[38] Wiley and Harnischfeger found that pupils in some public schools in Detroit received more than 50% more exposure to schooling (days and hours of schooling per year) than did students in other public schools in the same system.[39]

Though most of the "school effects" research has been done by scholars outside of educational administration, Erickson and others have called for such an effort by scholars in the field.[40] In so doing, Erickson has raised the question as to why the field of school administration has been so preoccupied with organizational effects on administrators and teachers and, at the same time, so inattentive to research on factors affecting student outcomes.[41] One answer to this question, consistent with the public choice line of analysis, is that the incentive system of public education, abetted by the ambiguity of educational ends and means, produces a setting that is not primarily oriented toward student outcomes or, put another way, toward the official goals.[42] Instead, the focus is process-oriented, role-based rather than goal-based, and strongly inclined toward (official) goal-displacement.[43]

Thus, despite rhetoric about the importance of instructional leadership, research on what school principals actually do has shown that they spend nearly all of their time on organizational maintenance and pupil control activities.[44] Consequently, in terms of attaining the primary (instructional) goals of schools, what may be most important is what school principals *do not* do or do very little: they spend little time on the instructional program and entrepreneurship, and much more time on disturbance handling; they do little by way of external public liaison activity and maintain a pronounced "inside" organizational focus; and their resource allocation activity lacks economic muscle since they have little influence over the reward schedule for teachers. Of course, from the public choice perspective it is no accident that they behave this way: because of the domesticated nature of their organizations, there is little need or reward for doing otherwise.[45]

EXIT, VOICE, AND INEQUALITY

If public schools are so much inclined toward goal displacement, how have they retained as much popular support as they have? The answer, in part, seems to rely on the fact that many public schools, in spite of the systemic deficiencies in their institutional framework, are perceived to perform reasonably well. In some cases, this perception may be well grounded. But in large part, this perception may be explained by Meyer and Rowan's analysis of public schools as institutionalized organizations whose legitimacy with the public is maintained through widely shared myths and a logic of confidence and good faith that accepts the ritualistic classification and certification of students.[46] Still, Meyer and Rowan's emphasis on the societal consensus undergirding these myths ignores the social diversity and concomitant range of opinions and interests within our society.

Recognizing the importance of this diversity, political economy offers another significant part of the answer to questions about the continuation of popular support for public schools or, at any rate, the minimization of popular opposition to the public schools. Yet, paradoxically, the dynamics at work here also help account for the erosion in popular support in recent years.

To begin with, the political aspects of education emerge when individual economic choice is prevented.[47] This happens frequently because, although individuals disagree about education or about the way public schools should be run, they still must agree about a single way of proceeding. Of course, if the goal of "individualizing" instruction could be fully achieved, it might appear that many political problems could be avoided. But an important part of education is that it is a *group* experience, and the norms and values represented in this process inevitably will be contested.

With mandatory taxes and compulsory school attendance laws, compulsory consumption and the political tensions flowing from it are essentially unavoidable: even nonpublic school parents must pay the taxes. In assessing the determinants of local educational expenditures, public choice theory emphasizes that political decisions are the result of individuals rationally pursuing their own self-interest. In school districts with residents whose incomes and preferences vary, each individual may desire a different amount of public educational spending. Assuming a particular tax structure, such as a proportional property tax, individuals will receive different benefits and be subject to different amounts of taxation depending upon the amount of public educational spending. Citizens will weigh these benefits and costs to decide upon their preferred tax rate. Differing demands among individuals are resolved in the voting booth to achieve a single uniform amount of public education. The result is that, with majority rule and certain other conditions, the voter with the median desired amount of educational demand will prevail and that amount of expenditure will be put into effect.

A key implication here is that *most* voter-taxpayers will be at least partially dissatisfied with the level of expenditure chosen.[48] The larger and more socially heterogeneous the population is, the more people there will be who would prefer a higher or lower expenditure level than the one chosen. The opposite is true in smaller, more homogeneous school districts, and this fact makes such units attractive to consumers. Put another way, in larger and more heterogeneous jurisdictions there is a greater probability that people will have negative externalities imposed on them due to political decisions that are not in their interest.

Dissatisfied citizens have two basic options: they may seek satisfaction through the political process by giving *voice* to their grievances or they may choose to *exit* from the school system.[49] Most political studies, such as research on Iannaccone and Lutz's dissatisfaction theory, have focused on the voice (i.e., political action) option, but in many ways the ramifications of the exit option are more important.[50] However, in the final analysis as Hirschman has revealed, one must take account of the significant, and sometimes counterintuitive, consequences of the *interplay* between the exit and voice options.[51]

Because of the severe limitations of the effectiveness of voice, dissatisfied citizens are tempted to "vote with their feet" and exit to other communities (or school districts) that provide a level and mix of public services more to their liking. Consumer mobility thus can provide a check, to some extent, on the monopoly power of a local school district. Indeed, in a classic article, Tiebout proposed that residential mobility between communities provides a means for the efficient provision of local public goods by creating a market for public services.[52] Given this potential mobility, the competition among jurisdictions for desirable residents and commerce is expected to produce a variety of public service offerings or "packages" and a more efficient delivery of public services than will occur in the more monopolistic, consumer-insensitive setting of large area-wide governments.[53]

To the extent that consumers have a choice among a number of jurisdictions and can afford to exercise this choice, mobile consumers will be able to sort themselves out according to their preferences. In many metropolitan areas, this results in the creation and maintenance (through zoning and real estate prices) of small, relatively homogeneous communities and school districts, which can provide well focused educational programs that satisfy many consumers.[54] A significant part of the continuing support for public schools comes from such consumers.

But, because mobility is severely limited for the less affluent and for certain minority groups, this very process of choice and differentiation has created huge inequalities between cities and suburbs and between rich and poor school districts.[55] Moreover, the potential mobility of households and businesses to other communities with more favorable tax and service packages makes it economically and politically difficult for local governments to pursue redistributive policies to reduce such inequities.[56] The dissatisfaction, sense of injustice, and court cases caused by these disparities have brought on a number of much needed reforms in state school finance arrangements. But these disparities and the unrest they have generated also have added to the controversies that color the public's attitude toward the public schools.

A final, seldom noticed feature of the exit option is that it also weakens central city school districts by draining off many of the more articulate and demanding citizens who otherwise might stay and use their voice to fight for the improvement of the school system.[57] As Hirschman notes, employees in large public monopolies may do little to combat such a process (indeed, they may encourage it) since it makes their life easier by ridding them of clients who are articulate "trouble-makers." In the language of political economy, it spares them the "psychic costs" they would incur in dealing with these clients and enables them to enjoy "the best of all monopoly profits . . . a quiet life."[58]

At this point, it might appear that the best thing to do would be to make exit more difficult by creating more metropolitan-wide school districts. There are a number of reasons why this would be an ill-advised step. A great deal of evidence indicates that mammoth school districts are more inefficient and less responsive to consumers than smaller districts.[59] Among other things, the use of voice becomes more costly and (still) less effective as the size of school districts increases and, particularly so, as districts begin to enjoy an almost complete monopoly vis-à-vis consumers. Moreover, the option to exit to nonpublic schools still would exist and would increase in popularity among the affluent if the metropolitan school district was deemed unsatisfactory and unresponsive, as seems likely to be the case. At the same time, less affluent citizens would be left very nearly with Hobson's choice: their only recourse would be through the unpromising channels open for the use of voice.

But why is voice generally so ineffective for citizens in school districts? The obstacles to effective voice are thrown into bold relief by the public choice analysis. As noted earlier, the lay public, as compared to school system employees, stands to gain less and face higher costs (e.g., higher information, opportunity, and political mobilization costs) in seeking the adequate provision of the official benefits of schools than do employees in pursuing unofficial benefits from the organization. Moreover, the exclusivity of unofficial benefits and the nonexclusivity of official benefits create substantial difficulties for the public in mobilizing collective action that are not faced by employees or others interested in the unofficial benefits. The difficulties here revolve around the properties of *separable* or *selective* goods as opposed to *collective* goods.

Briefly, Olson has called attention to the fact that, when certain kinds of goods or benefits are provided to one member of a community, they simultaneously are provided to all members of that community.[60] Such collective benefits as clean air cannot be provided to one person in a given area without being at the same time available to all other persons in the area. Thus, this property of collective benefits causes rational, self-interested persons to realize that it is not to their advantage to contribute to the cost of providing collective goods since they can take a "free ride" and enjoy the benefits at no cost. Of course, in the case of the schools, parents with children in the public schools benefit more than those without children in them. Even among parents using the public schools, however, the great majority are content to enjoy the benefits produced by education-oriented groups, such as the PTA, without contributing to the provision of these benefits. Hence, such groups usually have difficulty maintaining themselves. By contrast, the exclusivity of the personal or selective benefits available from the school organization for employees gives them a keen incentive for maintaining their own mutual benefit organizations (i.e., unions), although even these organizations prefer mandatory membership requirements to avoid "free riders."

Another reason that lay educational groups have difficulty organizing and maintaining themselves is that school authorities tend to follow policies and practices based on bureaucratic norms of equal treatment.[61] Thus, the benefits an educational group may obtain rarely can be restricted to its members, and this inhibits its ability to attract and retain members. Despite the emphasis on equal treatment or universalism, certain accepted educational programs do have some of the properties of selective goods, that is, they benefit certain groups more than they do others (e.g., consider music, vocational, special, and physical education programs). This largely explains the active special interest groups that develop to support these programs. In other words, because the parents of retarded children, for instance, have a disproportionate interest in special education programs, they are willing to incur substantial costs in supporting these programs.

Perhaps of equal importance in overall school politics is the fact that the teacher and professional groups associated with the provision of special programs themselves are inclined to become potent lobbies to protect and enhance their programs. Indeed, as illustrated in the effort to reform special education in Massachusetts, professional groups may provide—and, in fact, may be one of the few sources for—most of the expertise and organizational resources needed for successful campaigns to change educational practices.[62] And, of course, as compared with the usually transient interests of parents in schooling, educators in general—not just those associated with special programs—have an ongoing, important stake in the enterprise and support substantial, ongoing organizations to protect and advance their interests.

The difficulties lay educational organizations face, in trying to secure the resources or selective benefits for members needed to maintain themselves, make them vulnerable to manipulation by the professionals in school systems and other agencies upon whom they may depend, to a greater or lesser extent, for such resources.[63] These problems are well documented in a recent study of sixteen community organizations in three cities: Boston, Atlanta, and Los Angeles.[64] Gittell and her associates found that recent federal policy thrusts, in terms of the mandating of parental involvement (e.g., parent advisory councils for Title I of ESEA) and the funding of community organizations to engage in service delivery, seem to have profoundly influenced the character and behavior of community organizations in poor, minority areas. Not only were they surprised to find "no school-issue-oriented, self-initiated, lower-income organization in any of the three cities," but they also found that the dependency of the organizations they studied on external or school system sources precluded the use of advocacy strategies in pursuit of educational reform.[65] In effect, these organizations appeared to be "toothless tigers." Gittell and her colleagues concluded that, while more affluent populations have the resources to support independent community organizations that thus can pursue advocacy strategies when needed, lower income populations lack this ability. Consequently, the prospects for effective citizen participation are especially dim for lower income populations.[66] One conclusion that can be drawn from this line of analysis is that the "maximum feasible participation" strategy in federal programs, and other reforms instituted at various levels to increase the utility of voice for citizens, actually often may have increased disaffection with the public schools since the expectations raised for citizen input and influence rarely have been realized.[67]

Even if all the foregoing is true, why should the affluent, who enjoy the advantages of the exit option, be showing signs of discontent with the public schools? Part of the answer lies in the fact that residential mobility is a costly and inconvenient activity, even for the affluent, and mobility to nonpublic schools entails "double taxation." Consequently, it is likely that families will exit only in response to substantial deterioration in school quality. At the same time, more desirable alternatives among local public school districts and nonpublic schools are not always available to consumers. Further, even high quality suburban schools often lack sufficient options and flexibility to satisfy consumers. For just one example, consider the usual arbitrariness of the assignment of students in public school districts to particular schools and particular teachers within these schools, and the difficulties parents generally face in obtaining relief from unsatisfactory assignments. The increasing sophistication of the populace in general, which includes a recognition of the strategic importance of high quality education for children, makes it essential for public schools to increase the flexibility and options they provide to meet the needs *and desires* of students and families.[68]

CONCLUSION

There are no simple solutions to the performance and public support problems facing the public schools, but a political economy analysis sharpens an understanding of the sources of the difficulties and of the tradeoffs involved in trying to design solutions. Solutions are elusive precisely because the public desires that the public schools be simultaneously efficient, equitable, and responsive to consumers. But, as this discussion has illustrated, there is a tension among these three values that is highlighted by the public choice analysis.[69]

Although this analysis shows a good part of the reason why public support of public schools has been declining, present demographic and economic trends, in and of themselves, would insure a substantial erosion of support.[70] Moreover, further pressures on public support are caused by the problem of soaring educational costs. The labor intensive character of schooling (about 80% of the school budget is tied up in salaries) and the current tenuous grasp of the educational production function (how inputs are combined to produce outputs) make it difficult to control costs by improving productivity.[71] Finally, there are complex retrenchment problems. The combination of increasing demands for specialized educational services (e.g., special, gifted, and bilingual education) along with the need to maintain regular programs in a time of stable or decreasing enrollments and revenues is forcing painful reassessments of educational programs and priorities. These realities have intensified special interest group activity and contributed to further politicization of education.[72]

In the face of these various considerations, including an increasing recognition of the systemic deficiencies in the institutional framework for public schools, it is no wonder that more than "band-aid" proposals now are being put forward for the reform of education. Of course, considering the perversities of the reward structure and career ladder of public schools, it is remarkable that as many public schools perform as well as they do. That they do is a tribute to dedicated educators who perform well, more or less in spite of the existing reward structure. But would it not be more reasonable to change the structure to one that encourages, rewards, and helps maintain meritorious performance?

Some of the reform proposals now being advanced, such as tuition tax credits and unrestricted voucher plans, appear to threaten the existence of public schools. Although the analysis presented here argues against a sheltered existence (i.e., monopoly) for the public schools, this same kind of analysis supports public finance of education as a *collective* good by showing the dangers of underinvestment and inequity in the financing of education solely as a *private* good. Although the arguments for having *publicly operated* schools are harder to justify from a strictly economic perspective than is public subsidization of education, it appears, from the broader perspective of political economy, that a reliance entirely on private schools would be likely to increase social segregation and inequities within our pluralistic society. The challenging task at present thus is the invention of social arrangements that avoid the dangers of both market failure and nonmarket failure (i.e., the pathologies of public monopolies).[73]

Perhaps the most interesting proposals along this line to emerge from within our profession are two plans suggested by Garms, Guthrie, and Pierce.[74] The first, and more modest plan, is a school site management scheme that would give citizens a significant voice at the school building level through an elected council of parents who would help select the building principal and would collaborate with the building's professional staff in the development of the school's educational program and budget. Following Hirschman's insights, parental voice would be bolstered by the existence of an option to exit to other public schools if parents were dissatisfied with the offerings of their neighborhood school.

The more radical plan Garms, Guthrie, and Pierce propose is a far-reaching combination of basic education in public schools with a voucher-type scheme of educational coupons good for use throughout a person's lifetime. This sweeping plan is full of novel and provocative features and deserves a great deal more attention and discussion than it so far has received. Both plans reflect the insights of public choice analysis and an attempt to strike a more desirable balance in education among the competing values of equality, efficiency, and liberty (or consumer choice).

To conclude, this review and discussion have attempted to show the utility of political economy for understanding contemporary problems in public education. Because of the timely and challenging arguments it presents, scholars in educational administration interested in organizational behavior, policy analysis, and educational finance and politics can scarcely afford to ignore the field of political economy. Research is needed to confirm or refute the predictions derived from political economy. Similarly, if other frameworks or theories, such as loose coupling, actually account better for behavior in public schools, this needs to be demonstrated.

Although the limitations of political economy have not been discussed here, it should be obvious that, like all theories, it involves simplifications and highlights certain dimensions at the expense of others.[75] It is, therefore, but one of a number of worthwhile conceptual approaches or "ways or seeing" the terrain of public school administration, each of which has its own advantages and weaknesses.[76]

The picture political economy reveals of behavior in public schools clearly is narrow, incomplete, and, for some, disturbing. The important question, however, is: how predictive, on the average, is this picture? On this count, evidence is mounting that the political economy approach is beginning to yield, for the first time, a truly *scientific* (i.e., predictive) political science as well as a valuable body of knowledge about practical politics in the "real world."[77] The promise is there, but only the first glimmerings have been seen of the potential payoff for public education.

NOTES

1. J. S. Coleman, T. Hoffer, and S. Kilgore, *Public and Private Schools: A Report to The National Center for Education Statistics by the National Opinion Research Center* (University of Chicago, March 1981).

2. See D. Mann, ed. *Making Change Happen?* (New York: Teachers College Press, 1978).

3. See J. K. Benson, ed., *Organizational Analysis: Critique and Innovation* (Beverly Hills, CA: Sage, 1977); and D. E. Griffiths, "Intellectual Turmoil in Educational Administration," *Educational Administration Quarterly* 15, 3 (Fall 1979): 43-65.

4. K. E. Weick, "Educational Organizations as Loosely Coupled Systems," *Administrative Science Quarterly* 21 (March 1976): 1-19; and J. G. March and J. P. Olsen, *Ambiguity and Choice in Organizations* (Bergen, Norway: Universitetsforlaget, 1976).

5. See the comment to this effect in J. H. Freeman, "The Unit of Analysis in Organizational Research," in *Environments and Organizations*, J. W. Meyer et al., eds. (San Francisco: Jossey-Bass, 1978), p. 335.

6. There actually are two distinctly different approaches to political economy, one from a Marxist orientation and the other from a market orientation. This article deals with the latter approach. Unlike educational scholars in Europe, who have been much concerned with Marxist interpretations, American writers on educational administration have been quite even-handed in regard to the Marxist and market orientations—they usually ignore the political economy of education altogether. On the Marxist interpretation of the political economy of American education, see S. Bowles and H. Gintis, *Schooling in Capitalist America: Educational Reform and the Contradictions of Economic Life* (New York: Basic Books, 1976); and M. Carnoy, ed., *Schooling in a Corporate Society*, 2nd ed. (New York: David McKay, 1975). For the contribution of the market approach to an understanding of the political economy of American public schools, see the following works: J. G. Chambers, "An Economic Analysis of Decision-making in Public School Districts" (Unpublished paper, University of Rochester, 1975); W. I. Garms, J. W. Guthrie, and L. Pierce, *School Finance: The Economics and Politics of Public Education* (Englewood Cliffs, N.J.: Prentice-Hall, 1978); J. B. Michaelsen, "Revision, Bureaucracy, and School Reform," *School Review* 85 (February 1977): 229-246; Idem, "Assessing the Efficacy of Financial Reform in California," *American Journal of Education* 88 (February 1980): 145-178; Idem, "The Political Economy of School District Adminisration," *Educational Administration Quarterly* 17, 3 (Summer 1981): 98-113; Idem, "A Theory of Decision Making in the Public Schools: A Public Choice Approach," in *Organizational Behavior in Schools and School Districts*, S. B. Bacharach, ed. (New York: Praeger, 1981); D. O. Porter, "Responsiveness to Citizen-Consumers in a Federal System," *Publius* 5 (Fall 1975): 51-77; D. O. Porter, *The Politics of Budgeting Federal Aid: Resource Mobilization by Local School Districts* (Beverly Hills, CA: Sage Professional Papers in Administrative Policy Studies 03-003, 1973); T. van Geel, "Parental Preferences and the Politics of Spending Public Educational Funds," *Teachers College Record* 79 (February 1978): 339-363; and E. G. West, "The Political Economy of American Public School Legislation," *Journal of Law and Economics* 10 (October 1967): 101-128. On political economy generally, see N. Frohlich and J. A. Oppenheimer, *Modern Political Economy* (Englewood Cliffs, N.J.: Prentice-Hall, 1978); D. C. Mueller, *Public Choice* (Cambridge, England: Cambridge University Press, 1979); and V. Ostrom and E. Ostrom, "Public Choice: A Different Approach to the Study of Public Administration," *Public Administration Review* 31 (March/April 1971): 203-216.

7. Garms, Guthrie, and Pierce, *School Finance*, p. 76.

8. *Ibid.*, p. 15, emphasis in original.

9. The following discussion, reprinted here with permission from the American Educational Researchers Association, is drawn from W. L. Boyd and R. L. Crowson, "The Changing Conception and Practice of Public School Administration," in *Review of Research in Education*, Vol. 9, D. Berliner, ed. (Washington, DC: A.E.R.A., 1981),

pp. 321-326; 355-356. Copyright 1981, American Educational Research Association, Washington, DC.

10. Griffiths, "Intellectual Turmoil."

11. C. Perrow, "Demystifying Organizations," in *The Management of Human Services*, R. C. Sarri and Y. Hasenfeld, eds. (New York: Columbia University Press, 1978).

12. J. Cronin, "The Boston School District Study" (Presentation at the conference on Big City School District Politics, Pennsylvania State University, October 1970).

13. Perrow, "Demystifying Organizations."

14. *Ibid.*, p. 107.

15. Griffiths, "Intellectual Turmoil," p. 46.

16. J. Buchanan and G. Tullock, *The Calculus of Consent* (Ann Arbor: University of Michigan Press, 1962), p. 13.

17. D. C. Mueller, *Public Choice* (Cambridge, England: Cambridge University Press, 1979), p. 1.

18. Michaelsen, "Assessing Efficacy," p. 156.

19. Griffiths, "Intellectual Turmoil."

20. Perrow, "Demystifying Organizations," p. 106.

21. Michaelsen, "Revision, Bureaucracy"; and Chambers, "An Economic Analysis."

22. Michaelsen, "Revision, Bureaucracy," p. 329. Note that the economic theory of "property rights" provides the point of departure for this line of analysis. See E. Furubotn and S. Pejovich, "Property Rights and Economic Theory: A Survey of Recent Literature," *Journal of Economic Literature* 10 (1972): 1137-1162.

23. W. A. Niskanen, *Bureaucracy and Representative Government* (Chicago: Aldine, 1971); and Michaelsen, "Revision, Bureaucracy."

24. For the public choice predictions, see Chambers, "An Economic Analysis"; and Michaelsen, "Revision, Bureaucracy."

25. Perrow, "Demystifying Organizations," p. 115.

26. Michaelsen, "Revision, Bureaucracy," p. 244.

27. D. Mann, "Education Policy Analysis and the Rent-A-Troika Business" (Paper presented at the American Educational Research Association Annual Meeting, Los Angeles, April 1981), p. 4.

28. R. O. Carlson, "Environmental Constraints and Organizational Consequences," in *Behavioral Science and Educational Administration,* Sixty-third yearbook of the National Society for the Study of Education, Part 2, D. E. Griffiths, ed. (Chicago: University of Chicago Press, 1964).

29. P. A. Cusick, "A Study of Networks Among Professional Staffs in Secondary Schools" (Unpublished paper, Michigan State University, 1980).

30. A. Downs, *An Economic Theory of Democracy* (New York: Harper & Row, 1957); West, "The Political Economy"; and Michaelsen, "Revision, Bureaucracy."

31. Downs, *An Economic Theory;* and Niskanen, *Bureaucracy.*

32. M. Olsen, Jr., *The Logic of Collective Action* (Cambridge, MA: Harvard University Press, 1965); P. E. Peterson, "Community Representation and the 'Free Rider'," *Administrator's Notebook* 22, 8 (1974): 1-4.

33. The bleak picture this analysis presents will strike many people as excessively pessimistic and cynical (and, in some ways, it doubtless is). In the interest of

starting a dialogue on the subject, readers who find the analysis unpleasant or hard to accept are invited to review and rebut this literature, if they can.

34. Obviously, it is in the interest of private sector organizations to minimize the competition they face. When businessmen succeed in so doing, as for example through collusion, the behavior of their organizations becomes less efficient and more inclined toward loose coupling. See H. Leibenstein, "Microeconomics and X-efficiency Theory: If There is No Crisis There Ought to Be,"*The Public Interest,* Special Edition (1980): 97-110; and W. L. Boyd and G. L. Immegart, "Education's Turbulent Environment and Problem-finding," in *Problem-finding in Educational Administration,* G. L. Immegart and W. L. Boyd, eds. (Lexington, MA: D.C. Heath, 1979), pp. 279ff.

35. H. D. Lasswell, *Politics: Who Gets What, When and How?* (New York: McGraw-Hill, 1936).

36. See, for example, B. W. Brown and D. H. Saks, "The Production and Distribution of Cognitive Skills Within Schools," *Journal of Political Economy* 83 (June 1975): 571-594; and J. A. Thomas, *The Productive School* (New York: John Wiley, 1971).

37. Thomas, *The Productive School.*

38. T. G. Geske, "School Administrators Can Make A Difference," *The Executive Review* 1 (January 1981): 1-4.

39. D. E. Wiley and A. Harnischfeger, "Explosion of a Myth: Quantity of Schooling and Exposure to Instruction, Major Educational Vehicles," *Educational Researcher* 3 (1974): 5-12.

40. D. A. Erickson, ed., *Educational Organization and Administration* (Berkeley, CA: McCutchan, 1977); Idem, "Research on Educational Administration: The State-of-the-Art," *Educational Researcher* 8 (March 1979): 9-14; and P. F. Silver, "The Development of a Knowledge Base for the Practice of Educational Administration," *Administrator's Notebook* 29, 1 (1981): 1-4.

41. Erickson, "Research on Educational Administration."

42. Boyd and Immegart, "Education's Turbulent Environment," p. 285.

43. To put the point somewhat differently, since, as Chambers ("An Economic Analysis") argues, the costs of inefficient behavior in public schools (in terms of student outcomes or consumer satisfaction) are low, this in effect creates a "demand for inefficient behavior." For a provocative explanation and application of this kind of analysis (based on the economic "law of demand") to a diverse range of matters, such as the "demand for reckless driving," see R. B. McKenzie and G. Tullock, *The New World of Economics* (Homewood, IL: Irwin, 1975). On the process, rather than outcome orientation of school administration, see W. G. Spady, "The Fundamental Shift from Role Based to Goal Based Organization and Management" (Paper presented at American Educational Research Association Annual Meeting, Los Angeles, April 1981).

44. Boyd and Crowson, "The Changing Conception."

45. For qualifications on this conclusion and a more balanced treatment than space permits of many of the issues covered in this article, see Boyd and Crowson, "The Changing Conception."

46. J. W. Meyer and B. Rowan, "Institutionalized Organizations: Formal Structure as Myth and Ceremony," *American Journal of Sociology* 83 (September 1977): 340-363.

47. I am indebted to Harold Cline of the University of Rochester for assistance in the development of this discussion.

48. Garms, Guthrie, and Pierce, *School Finance*, p. 334.

49. A. O. Hirschman, *Exit, Voice, and Loyalty* (Cambridge, MA: Harvard University Press, 1970).

50. F. W. Lutz and L. Iannaccone, eds., *Public Participation in Local School Districts: The Dissatisfaction Theory of Democracy* (Lexington, MA: D.C. Heath, 1978); and L. Iannaccone and F. Lutz, *Politics, Power and Policy: The Governing of Local School Districts* (Columbus, OH: Charles E. Merrill, 1970).

51. Hirschman, *Exit, Voice*.

52. C. M. Tiebout, "A Pure Theory of Local Expenditures," *Journal of Political Economy* 64 (1956): 416-424.

53. R. L. Bish, *The Public Economy of Metropolitan Areas* (Chicago: Markham Rand McNally, 1971).

54. Cf. Michaelsen, "The Political Economy"; and Idem, "A Theory of Decision Making."

55. For one of many discussions of this problem and data on the disparities that exist in the case of the San Francisco Bay Area, see C. S. Benson, *The Economics of Public Education*, 3rd ed. (Boston: Houghton Mifflin, 1978), pp. 135-179.

56. P. E. Peterson, *City Limits* (Chicago: University of Chicago Press, 1981).

57. Hirschman, *Exit, Voice*.

58. On "psychic costs," see Chambers, "An Economic Analysis"; and John Hicks as quoted in Hirschman, *Exit, Voice*, p. 55.

59. W. L. Boyd, "The Political Economy of Education in Metropolitan Areas: Dilemmas of Reform and Public Choice," *Educational Evaluation and Policy Analysis* 2 (January-February 1980): 53-60.

60. Olson, *The Logic of Collective Action*.

61. J. G. Weeres, "School Politics in Thirty-three of the Local Community Areas within the City of Chicago" (Doctoral dissertation, University of Chicago, 1971).

62. M. Budoff, "Engendering Change in Special Education Practices," *Harvard Educational Review* 45 (1975): 507-526.

63. Peterson, "Community Representation and the 'Free Rider.'"

64. M. Gittell, with B. Hoffacker, E. Rollins, and S. Foster, *Citizen Organizations: Citizen Participation in Educational Decision Making*, Executive Summary (Report prepared by the Institute for Responsive Education for the National Institute of Education, May, 1980).

65. *Ibid.*, p. 7.

66. For a challenge to Gittell's interpretation from the point of view of a school administrator, see D. A. Bennett, "Review of *Limits to Citizen Participation: The Decline of Community Organizations*," *Educational Administration Quarterly* 17, 4 (Fall 1981): 128-132. Although Gittell's work is not noted for its pristine objectivity, Bennett's review suggests that he is not exactly an innocent bystander either.

67. Cf. W. L. Boyd and F. Seldin, "The Politics of School Reform in Rochester, New York," *Education and Urban Society* 7 (August 1975): 439-463.

68. Cf. Benson, *The Economics of Public Education*, pp. 219-235.

69. Garms, Guthrie, and Pierce, *School Finance*.

70. M. Kirst and W. I. Garms, "The Political Environment of School Finance Policy in the 1980s," in *School Finance Policies and Practices—The 1980: A Decade of Conflict*, J. W. Guthrie, ed. (Cambridge, MA: Ballinger, 1980).

71. Cf. W. J. Baumol, "Macroeconomics of Unbalanced Growth: The Anatomy of Urban Crises," *American Economic Review* 57 (June 1967).

72. E. K. Mosher, A. H. Hastings, and J. L. Wagoner, Jr., "Beyond the Breaking Point? A Comparative Analysis of the New Activists for Educational Equality," *Educational Evaluation and Policy Analysis* 3 (January-February 1981): 41-53.

73. C. Wolf, Jr., "A Theory of Non-Market Failures," *The Public Interest* 55 (1979): 114-133; and Porter, "Responsiveness to Citizen-Consumers," p. 77.

74. Garms, Guthrie, and Pierce, *School Finance,* pp. 241-246, 277-294.

75. See, for instance, the criticisms of public choice theory in Boyd and Crowson, "The Changing Conception," pp. 335 and 362; and the discussion in W. L. Boyd, "Local Influences on Education," in *Encyclopedia of Educational Research,* 5th ed., H. Mitzel, ed. (New York: Macmillan, 1982).

76. A way of combating the limitations of individual conceptual models is to employ a combination of models selected to compensate for each other's weaknesses. See G. Allison, *Essence of Decision* (Boston: Little, Brown, 1971); P. E. Peterson, *School Politics Chicago Style* (Chicago: University of Chicago Press, 1976); D. Tyack, "Ways of Seeing: An Essay on the History of Compulsory Schooling," *Harvard Educational Review* 46 (1976): 355-389; and the discussion of this topic in Boyd and Crowson, "The Changing Conception."

77. On the general contribution of political economy to scientific political science with implications for practical politics, see R. Abrams, *Foundations of Political Analysis: An Introduction to the Theory of Collective Choice* (New York: Columbia University Press, 1980); S. J. Brams, *Game Theory and Politics* (New York: Free Press, 1975); B. Bueno de Mesquita, *The War Trap* (New Haven, CT: Yale University Press, 1981); H. Hamberger, *Games as Models of Social Phenomena* (San Francisco: Freeman, 1979); R. D. Luce and H. Raiffa, *Games and Decisions* (New York: John Wiley, 1957); Mueller, *Public Choice;* W. Riker, *The Theory of Political Coalitions* (New Haven, CT: Yale University Press, 1962); and W. Riker and P. Ordeshook, *An Introduction to Positive Political Theory* (Englewood Cliffs, N.J.: Prentice-Hall, 1973). One example of the practical implications for educational politics is found in W. J. Foley, "The Problem of Deciding Without a Majority: The Paradoxes of Choice," *The Executive Review* 2, 2 (1981): 1-4. That a definitive book on practical politics in education has yet to be written is made clear in C. A. Cohn, "Review of Practical Politics for School Administrators," *Politics of Education Bulletin* 10 (Fall 1981): 10-11.

PART THREE

Action Theories and Issues Clarification to Help Leaders Lead

An enduring question is why so much effort is made to blend theory and practice. The ready and realistic answer is that there is nothing more practical than theory.

Without theory the multitudes of administrative decisions which must be made each day may lack unity and purpose. They may be whimsical, responsive to the mood of the moment, and based on liking or disliking individuals who will be affected. Without theory, the leader may appear confused about goals and means to attain them. The leader may portray these characteristics and indeed may feel them and personify them. Struggling with the meaning, significance, and responses on a case to case basis, the administrator understandably can become tired, mentally and physically, and burn out. The lack of undergirding theory to guide practice makes a difficult job an impossible one. There will be little or no physical, emotional, and intellectual energy left over for creative, farsighted leadership. Too much will have been consumed in directing the administrative logistics on a case by case basis.

With a solid theoretical underpinning, the leader will have a difficult *and* do-able job. There is nothing that can make the leader's role simple or easy. There are many demands and tasks for the responsible and responsive leader. The tasks never end. Success in leading in one situation opens up ideas and visions for further actions. The good leader does not look for an easy job. Theory can help to create a milieu in which progress is possible and is the norm.

The norms can be understood by the total staff. All can know the rationale for decisionmaking, participate in it, and maintain a commitment to make participative decisions work. All can participate in evaluation of decisions and to become better decision makers in the future. All staff can interpret decisions to various constituencies to build support and cooperation.

The results that come from the blending of theory and practice more than justify efforts to join them both in the study of education administration and in its practice. (An indispensable third leg, on which administration rests is research, a topic so extensive that it did not fit into the confines of this brief volume. Careful readers in general and varied specialists in particular will wish for other important "legs"!)

This section is composed largely of articles on theory. The current state-of-the-art in educational administration is delineated in the statement by Robert T. Stout. He prepared it as a study document for a national study commission. It is included in this section as a provocative stimulus to those who wish to understand the field and to deal with the issues raised by the author.

CHAPTER ELEVEN

Educational Policy Analysis: The State of the Art

DOUGLAS E. MITCHELL

The author looked at the fact that there were 28,000 ERIC entries on education policy, and he concluded that there was little agreement on methods or goals and few exemplary studies of theoretical perspectives. What evolved was the author's state of the art essay. The analysis found several perspectives: historical, conceptual, subject areas, and methodological. Three conclusions indicate how social science can affect school improvement: document alternative mechanisms available to policy makers, find out the effects of the options on school performance, and connect the effects to alternative social goals or values.

This article was originally intended as a systematic review of the research literature on educational policy. That grand hope was buried quickly, however, under an avalanche of literature citations. A look at the periodical guides to scholarly literature on this topic is enough to sober even the most ambitious potential reviewer. The ERIC system alone contains more than 28,000 entries with both "education(al)" and "policy(ies)" among their key descriptors—more than 2,000 entries a year, every year from 1975 through 1981.[1] In addition, more than 7.3% (2,213) of the 30, 146 new ERIC entries in 1981 used these two key terms. And this is only the top of the proverbial iceberg. Many references in this topical area are found in documents not listed by ERIC. In fact, even the book length treatments of public policy problems and processes have grown too numerous for one person to review intelligently.

How education policy research has changed over the years is pictorially shown in Figure 11.1.[2] As indicated by the broken line in the figure, the proportion (as well as the absolute number) of ERIC entries related to educational policy increased steadily between 1969 and 1981, rising from 3.5% to 7.3% of all new entries. Although entries in the figure prior to 1965 (when ERIC first began operation) are probably not very representative, no clear trend can be seen in the citations prior to 1969. With two exceptions, however, citations in the 1950s were much less likely to

SOURCE: Douglas E. Mitchell, "Educational Policy Analysis: The State of the Art," *Educational Administration Quarterly*, Vol. 20, No. 3, pp. 129-160. Copyright © by The University Council for Educational Administration. Reprinted with permission.

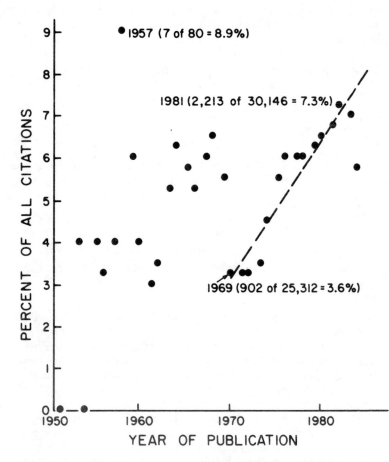

Figure 11.1: Educational Policy Citation Rates in ERIC System

refer directly to policy than were those of the 1960s. The exceptions in this respect are 1957 and 1958, the years right after *Sputnik* was launched.

Disappointingly, the vast literature on the topic of educational policy has produced no standard textbooks, little agreement on the methods or goals of educational policy research, and few "classic" or exemplary studies for defining the area's central thrust or overall theoretical perspective.

Not by choice then, but by necessity, this will be more of a state-of-the-art essay than a comprehensive and detailed review of recent literature.

Four areas of basic questions organize the discussion that follows—each presenting a different analytic perspective on the topic. The questions encompass:

(1) *A Historical Perspective:* Where did all the interest in educational policy research and analysis originate, and why has it become so important in the recent scholarly literature?

(2) *A Conceptual Perspective:* What is meant by the term "educational policy" and how is policy studied?

(3) *A Topical Perspective:* What are the major subject areas covered in educational policy research and analysis?

(4) *A Methodological Perspective:* How are educational policy research and analysis conducted, including what is the relationship between policy research and policy making?

After exploring these four areas, the review article concludes with a postscript on possible new directions in educational policy research and with a discussion of a theoretical framework for relating policy research to the formation, implementation, and evaluation of specific policies.

POLICY ANALYSIS IN HISTORICAL PERSPECTIVE

In education, as in other policy arenas, research and analysis have only recently become *formally* associated with the formulation, implementation, and evaluation of public policy decisions. In the broader domain of public administration, a major step toward formalization of policy analysis appears to have taken place between 1967 and 1974.[3] The earlier date marks the publication of an essay by Yehzekel Dror in the September issue of *Public Administration Review* calling for a "new" professional mission of policy analysis.[4] The latter date reflects the adoption of guidelines identifying policy analysis as a basic topic in the study of public affairs by the National Association of Schools of Public Affairs and Administration (NASPAA). These events, according to Ukeles, mean that "in only seven years, policy analysis moved from propositions to reality, from 'fringe' idea to a central place in official public administration thinking."[5]

Mitchell, following Lambright, linked this major shift in the relationship between social science and public policy with the 1968 congressional reauthorization of the National Science Foundation (NSF).[6] This reauthorization required NSF to develop the Research Addressed to National Needs (RANN) program—a program that shifted the criteria for governmental funding away from the pursuit of scientific knowledge for its own sake toward research aimed at the solution of identified public problems.

The exact date of this shift in the relationship between research and policy action is not too important—and fixing it depends on what one takes to be the decisive change in a broad reorientation of both thought and action that occurred gradually over two or three decades. The important point is that the recent growth in policy oriented research and analysis is part of a very broad reorganization of fundamental beliefs about science and about its value in policy making. This shift can best be understood by examining what Ukeles calls the "theoretical" and the "empirical" roots of modern policy analysis.[7] The theoretical root is primarily *intellectual,* and it involves the development of new ideas about the relationship between science and policy. The empirical root traces changes in the *professional practice* of policy analysis and chronicles the development of new organizations and activities aimed at the incorporation of scientific knowledge into the formation, implementation, and evaluation of policy.

Professional Practice

As a matter of professional practice, the relationship between social science and public policy has a long and fascinating history. In the U.S., it began with an 1832 grant to the Franklin Institute to study the causes of explosions in steamboat boilers.[8] In addition to a report on the causes of these explosions, the researchers involved in that study produced draft legislation aimed at regulating boiler construction.[9]

It took nearly a century, however, for the relationship between researchers and governmental policy makers to become more than a series of haphazard, tentative, and largely isolated activities. The earliest developments took place in the field of agriculture. The Morrill Act (1862), for example, provided a major resource base for agricultural research. That resource base gradually produced a strong relationship between research and public policy in this arena. The first agricultural experiment station began in 1875, a major federal aid program was enacted in 1887, and the massive Cooperative Agricultural Extension Act was passed in 1914.

In the social sciences, it was not until 1929—nearly a century after the Franklin Institute study—that President Hoover established the current pattern of formal involvement by social scientists in federal policy. (See Carey's book, however, for a discussion of the pivotal role played by the American Social Science Association between 1865 and 1915.[10]) It was Hoover's commissioning of the Social Science Research Council to undertake a systematic study of "recent social trends," that solidly established the importance of using scientific data in the analysis of public issues.[11] This landmark study was not matched in education, however, until 1966 when James Coleman and his colleagues produced their watershed study of *Equality of Educational Opportunity* in American schools.[12]

The election of Franklin Roosevelt in 1932 provided a further boost to the legitimacy of scientific policy analysis. His widely respected "brain trust" gave scientific policy study a really good name for perhaps the first time. Under Roosevelt, Charles E. Merriam's leadership permanently altered the role of the use of social research in the executive branch of government. As architect of the 1939 executive reorganization plan, he stimulated the development of a social research staff in nearly every important executive office.[13]

The current period of formalized and highly visible public policy research has been stimulated by three major changes in the operation of the federal government. These changes, arising during the 1950s and early 1960s, included: (1) rapid expansion in the federal courts' reliance on social science evidence in dealing with such highly controversial issues as racial bias, intelligence testing, and special education; (2) adoption of highly publicized rational planning techniques, notably the Planning Programming Budgeting System (PPBS) first introduced into the Pentagon under Robert McNamara and then spread throughout the federal government; and (3) widespread use of scientific program evaluation techniques—especially in response to federal initiatives in education and health care.

Judicial influence. In her review of social science influence on court decisions, Rossell argues that, although many of the key actors do not like to admit it, judicial decision making has been transformed in two important respects by social science evidence.[14] First, beginning with *Sweatt vs. Painter* in 1950—four years before the landmark *Brown* decisions—the courts began to rely on social science evidence to determine whether racial segregation produced significant *harm* among its victims.[15] That is, the courts began to entertain social science evidence in establishing whether there had been a violation of the law or constitution. Secondly, the courts began to seek expert scientific advice on how to discharge their other major function—fashioning a *remedy* in cases where harm had been proven.[16]

The use of general social science knowledge to fashion judicial remedies has been broadly accepted. Using research findings to determine whether legal rights have been abridged is, however, highly controversial. Some observers believe that such use of research reduces legal principles to probabalistic factual questions, making justice depend on the adequacy of the available evidence of science. Rossell is persuasive, however, in her argument that scientific determination of the factual basis of judicial decisions is complementary to, rather than in tension with, legal analysis.[17]

Rational planning. The influence of research on various "scientific" or "rational" planning techniques used by governmental agencies has been widely noted.[18] Ukeles makes a convincing case that the (ultimately unsuccessful) effort to introduce PPBS into the federal bureaucracy during the mid-1960s was a major turning point in this process. He notes that early developments came in foreign affairs and defense, and says that:

> In the domestic arena, post depression and war-time planning and analytic activity were widespread in such areas as price control, scarce resource allocation, etc.; thus the spillover from war planning to domestic planning was substantial. In the post-war era, the increasing scope of the federal government and the increasing complexity of domestic problems led to increased investment in research and analysis in conjunction with the massive federal highway program and the anti-poverty program. In the mid-1960s this effort culminated in the attempt to install a planning-programming-budgeting system in the entire federal governmental system.[19]

Yeakey concurs in the judgment that rational planning processes are a major element in the development of scientific policy analysis. Although she mentions PPBS only in passing, she cites a number of other rational planning techniques as expressions of scientific policy formation.[20]

While legitimacy is the primary issue in the judicial use of social science, ineffectiveness is the major problem in the area of rational planning. For various reasons, many of them first noted in Charles Lindblom's 1959 article on "The Science of Muddling Through," public policy is only marginally influenced by research findings or rational planning processes.[21] Occasional exceptions (like Chicago's widely heralded Burnham Plan) can be found. But these exceptions only serve to make the generally low level of scientific impact on planning more baffling. The most recent studies of the social science-public policy linkage have begun to suggest that research findings contribute more to problem definition and an overall orientation toward decision making than to the identification or evaluation of specific policy proposals.[22]

Program evaluation. Mandated federal program evaluations are the third major source of expanded social science influence on policy. Beginning with post-World War II redevelopment programs, and expanding rapidly during the War on Poverty and Great Society years, federal support for mandated program evaluations covering a broad range of health, education, and welfare policies produced the economic resources needed to support a veritable army of social scientists. These scientific program evaluators have studied (and sometimes manipulated) a broad array of social, psychological, economic, anthropological, and political variables in an effort to determine which, if any, are responsible for the success of a few programs and the failure of many others.[23] McLaughlin's study of Title I of the Elementary and Secondary Education Act (1965), representative of countless other evaluation efforts, carefully documents the existence of intense and frequently intractable problems in the development of social science impact on policy through program evaluation research. She concluded that, "coexisting within the Title I policy arena in 1965 were both a strong interest in the collection of reliable, quantitative data on program effectiveness and powerful incentives not to collect and disseminate these data."[24]

Underlying Issues in Professional Practice

Two basic issues plague the professional practice of scientific policy analysis: appropriateness of *impact* and adequacy of *method*. The impact of science is frequently seen as either very low or as seriously distorted. Patton, for example, reported conclusions from a broad array of social scientists arguing that research and evaluation studies have had little effect on public policy.[25] It is typically argued that, "the little use that has occurred has been fortuitous rather than planned."[26]

Limited utilization of scientific program evaluations, apparent ineffectiveness in rational planning, and controversy over the legitimacy of scientific jurisprudence have combined to produce something of a crisis in the professional practice of scientific policy analysis. Two important strands of the scholarly literature can be traced to this crisis. The first is an intense concern with methodological issues related to policy analysis.[27] Some observers believe that the poor record of scientific policy analysis is largely due to widespread methodological flaws in the design and execution of research studies.[28] A second stream in the literature explores the overall relationship between knowledge generation and policy making and attempts to give a better accounting of when and how scientific evidence can be expected to influence policy.[29] Scholars contributing to this literature believe that the problem is less a matter of inadequate methods and more a question of the lack of knowledge about the limits of scientific inquiry on the part of policy makers and their immediate advisers.

Bias is another aspect of the impact issue. It is widely observed that, on those occasions when scientific evidence is utilized, the utilization of science tends to be biased or inappropriate to the policy decisions under consideration.[30] Policy makers are notoriously more interested in evidence that supports their views, and scientists are frequently charged with succumbing to policy maker biases in gathering or analyzing their data.[31]

These issues of impact and method are examined more fully below.

The Intellectual Roots of Scientific Policy Analysis

During the same general period that the practice of scientific policy analysis was being transformed through court deliberations, social planing techniques, and mandated program evaluations, significant *intellectual* developments in the interpretation and conceptualization of this process were also taking place. Emergence of the idea that policy analysis was a unique scientific discipline took place during a 30-year period bracketed roughly by the 1951 publication of Lerner and Lasswell's *The Policy Sciences* and the 1980 publication of Stuart Nagel's *The Policy-Studies Handbook*.[32] One can find, of course, some earlier examples of a scientific orientation toward policy, and one writer traced it back to 19th century utilitarianism in Great Britain.[33] By some definitions it would even be appropriate to identify Machiavelli's advice to *The Prince*,[34] or even the Biblical account of Joseph's recommendations to the Egyptian Pharoah regarding grain storage and distribution, as points of origin for scientific policy analysis.

Earlier discussions of the technical knowledge base for policy making are distinguished from Lasswell's seminal essay in the 1951 book with Lerner, however, by the latters' vivid and *self-conscious* commitment to policy analysis as a political or administrative discipline. Previous forays into this field focused largely on the policies themselves, rather than on the processes of policy analysis. Lasswell described the shift by saying that:

> A policy orientation has been developing which cuts across the existing specializations. The orientation is twofold. In part, it is directed toward the policy process, and in part toward the intelligence needs of policy. The first task, which is the development of a science of policy forming and execution, uses the methods of social and psychological inquiry. The second task, which is the improving of the content of the information, and the interpretations available to policy makers, typically goes outside the boundaries of social science and psychology.[35]

As the passage quoted here suggests, the emergent policy orientation within the social sciences has two central elements: (1) a growing science *of* the policy process and (2) an increased awareness of science usage *in* the formation of particular policies. Moreover, as Lasswell recognized, a science *of* policy is more easily a true social science—a study of the causes and consequences of identifiable socio-economic, political, or psychological factors on policy decision making, implementation, or outcomes. The uses of science (whether natural or social) *in* policy making is a different matter. Here science becomes a political resource—a weapon or tool for controlling political debate—and, hence, is itself implicated in the process of articulating public values, shaping governmental programs, or controlling the behavior of citizens.[36] The use of science *in* policy formation is both complicated and controversial, and it cannot be properly understood without making some basic assumptions about key theoretical elements in a science *of* the policy making process. It is toward the development of this theoretical framework that the next section of this article is devoted.

A CONCEPTUAL PERSPECTIVE ON POLICY ANALYSIS

Recent attempts to define the term *policy* range from broad and simple statements like, "what governments do and say"[37] to complex lists of characteristics requiring several pages to explain.[38] Several different strategies for defining the term are used. One technique is to simply declare that a particular definition is the one to be used throughout a study or analysis. This approach is illustrated by Dye who begins his book with the declaration that, "Public policy is whatever governments choose to do or not to do."[39] A second popular approach is to take a few paragraphs to summarize earlier definitions and then to offer a revised or expanded definition of one's own.[40] Another approach is to examine dictionary definitions or the philological roots of the term policy.[41] A few theorists even approach the problem through analytical philosophy. Kerr, for example, explores a broad array of philosophical issues on the way to defining policy as "something one undertakes with particular intention and purposes in mind."[42] Numerous authors, of course, offer extended discussions of policy without producing any definition of their central subject at all. A special case of this tendency is found in works by Iannaccone[43] and Coombs who offer detailed discussions of educational *politics*—defining policy as the outcomes of these political processes.

Conceptually, it is fair to say, the term policy is both complicated and subtle. A concise and stable interpretation of its meaning requires more than synthesis of previous usage or a review of dictionary definitions. Definitions used in the most popular works differ in fundamental and irreconcilable ways, but it is difficult to discover exactly why this is so.

Green has suggested a provocative approach to clarifying the meaning of policy.[44] He suggests imagining a situation where no policy is formulated or required and that the term Paradise symbolizes just such a place.

In Paradise, he argues, there is no policy—and none is needed. Whether conceived as a tropical island of endless bliss, a potential but unrealized political utopia, a bygone Garden of Eden, or a transcendental home for the immortal soul, Paradise derives its meaning, as Paradise, from the fact that life there is unencumbered by the constraints and limitations we associate with the notion of policy. It is not that life in Paradise is without order or that the actions of its inhabitants are aimless and random. To the contrary, Paradise is a communal concept, characterized by spontaneous and voluntary organization and cooperation. Social order is sometimes seen as dangerous, but Paradise gains its essential meaning in the human imagination as a place where "the lion and the lamb lie down together" through spontaneous cooperation and shared values. Paradise is Paradise just because it produces community without forcing compromise or limiting self-expression. And Paradise is brought to an end by the formation of explicit policies to guide human actions. The anti-utopian images of Orwell's *1984* and Huxley's *Brave New World* clarify this point by focusing our attention on the image of a world totally dominated by policy.[45] In their literary worlds, all human interests and capacities are captured—often before they are even recognized by the individuals involved—and directed toward the goals of the State.

What is there about this imagined world called Paradise that makes policy unnecessary? It is simply this: in Paradise, *all* values can be pursued simultaneously and without limit. To imagine Paradise is to imagine that resources are infinite (or, equivalently, that goals can be achieved effortlessly) *and* that human conflicts are created entirely by a scarcity of resources rather than fundamental conflicts of interest. Paradise, in short, is destroyed by either of two conditions: (1) inadequate resources or (2) irreconcilable interests or goals. These two conditions— scarcity and conflict—are the origins of both politics and policy. They are the conditions which separate all real, concrete human situations from the imaginary world of Paradise. Thus, the essential meaning of the term "policy" arises from its role in resolving the two fundamental human conditions of scarcity and conflict.

But the analysis is not yet complete. Knowing that policy has its origins in scarcity and conflict does not help much until mechanisms for limiting the effects of these conditions are known. In order to fashion strategies for controlling the pernicious effects of scarcity and conflict, it is necessary to have a socio-political theory which is to be used to explain (and hopefully control) the effects of conflict and scarcity.

It is at this point that the term policy begins to take on multiple, and largely irreconcilable, definitions. The various definitions of policy to be found in the literature can be divided into four generic types. Differences among them arise from that fact that they are rooted in four broad, fundamentally incompatible, social science theories or paradigms.[46] In the space available here, it is not possible to provide a full description of these four basic social science paradigms. A brief review of their essential characteristics will, however, provide the basis for a more adequate understanding of what is meant by educational policy.

Four Social Science Paradigms

A number of theorists, with a broad range of topical interests and diverse disciplinary backgrounds, share the view that there are four basic social science paradigms. Some come to this conclusion "empirically" by reviewing the literature and finding that it falls naturally into four distinguishable clusters—refer, for example, to Iannaccone's summary of alternative political theories or the Brown and Goldin review of definitions of collective action.[47] Other theorists find four paradigms by reflecting on the historical evolution of a particular field of inquiry. Examples of this are found in Kelly's review of organization theory and Mitchell's paper on management metaphors.[48]

In reviewing the paradigms described by these authors, a question naturally arises as to why there should be four paradigms—why not three or five, or twenty-five? A related question also arises: What is the relationship, if any, among the various paradigms identified through these empirical and historical methods? Attempts at answering these questions have led to the publication of several higher level theoretical analyses in recent years. These higher level theories seek to identify specific analytical bases for the different social science paradigms. In various ways, they argue that the basic paradigms express pivotal conceptual or methodological presuppositions that underlie all social science inquiry.

Buckley, for example, traces his version of the basic social science paradigms to conceptions of *causality*.[49] He argues that there are only four alternative theories of social causation and, thus, only four possible social science paradigms. Winter traces the paradigms covered in his analysis to four alternative frameworks for *meaningful* interpretation of the social world.[50] He argues that four unique ways of understanding the forces shaping human action systems have been responsible for the development of four basic social science paradigms. Peterson relates his paradigms to four processes of *decision making* in social systems.[51] Burrell and Morgan focus on the *epistemolotical* and *methodological* underpinnings of social theory building.[52] Turner emphasizes the importance of different ways of accounting for *institutionalization of action* in society as the source of his four distinctive paradigms.[53] Mitchell traces the emergence of four alternative paradigms to the existence of four basic mechanisms of *social control*.[54]

Although space limitations preclude a full discussion here, a close reading of these several higher level theoretical interpretations suggests that they represent alternative approaches to a common reality. They each identify four quite similar social science paradigms, probably because there are just four fundamentally different ways of interpreting social action systems. Divergence in the definitions of terms and concept usage arise from different *perspectives* on social theory construction, rather than from differences in the paradigms themselves. Figure 11.2 presents the critical features of the four social science paradigms that, after making modest allowances for divergent perspectives, confusion, and misunderstanding on the part of various theorists, account for all of the higher level theoretical perspectives cited here. The four paradigms (Structural, Functional, Exchange, and Interaction) are most easily understood in terms of their underlying analogies or generative metaphors.[55] Each generative metaphor suggests a parallel between social behavior and some other important domain of human experience. Structuralist social theories, for example, assert a parallelism between social behavior and the actions of a machine. Functionalism draws upon the self-regulating characteristics of living organisms for the development of its central ideas. Exchange theories seek general principles for analysis in the relationships ordinarily found in the marketplace. And Interaction theories see social action as more like the richly textured spontaneity of human conversations.

Historically, the four basic paradigms can also be traced to the core operations of the four major social institutions that contributed most to the emergence of modernity from the Middle Ages. Modern armies, for example, have emerged as "fighting machines" from the highly individualistic and ultimately ineffective system of combat dominated by medieval knights. The key element in this transformation of military tactics was the development of close-order battle formations based on rigid discipline.[56] Modern military organization emphasizes formal structure, a rigid chain of command, and a carefully planned training program aimed at making every individual and every unit into interchangeable parts. The beliefs and attitudes that make this approach to organization possible lead directly to a vision of society as essentially mechanistic in character. From this structuralist perspective, interest is seen as the motive force for all human action. Individuals, groups, and even nations are conceptualized as "interested parties" whose actions are dictated by the priority they assign to each of their several interests. Social order or equilibrium is maintained through a balance of power (or total domination when one party has overwhelming power resources). Conflict is seen as an endemic characteristic of all human relationships and, therefore, is a central issue in all political theory and action.

	Structural	Functional	Exchange	Interaction
Generative Metaphor	Machine	Organism	Marketplace	Conversation
Historical Origin	Military Tactics	Medieval Church	Bourgeoise Economics	Renaissance Culture
Units of Analysis	Formal Structures	Functional Structures	Rational Agents	Purposive Actors
Dynamics of Action	Conflict of Interest	Cooperative Goal Pursuit	Bargaining Over Scarce Valuables	Creating Symbolic Cultures
Motive Force (Basis of Actions)	Interest (Priority)	Need (Prerequisite)	Desire (Utility)	Meaning (Felt Significance)
Stability Principle	Power Balance	System Homeostasis	Negotiated Contracts	Shared Definition of Situation
Principle of Order	Discipline	Hierarchy	Incentives	Bonding

SOURCE: Adapted from D. E. Mitchell (1982), "Governance of Schools," in H. E. Mitzel (Ed.), *Encyclopedia of Educational Research* (pp. 730-738). New York: The Free Press; and D. E. Mitchell (1983), *Metaphors of Management, or How Far From Outcomes Can You Get?* Paper originally presented at the 1982 Annual Meeting of the American Educational Research Association, New York.

Figure 11.2: Four Alternative Social Science Paradigms

Functionalism, with its organismic analogy, has historical roots less in the military than in the survival of the medieval church. Functionalist theories, like religious bodies, recognize the importance of individual and group beliefs. Within this paradigm, order is generated through widely shared values and a common belief in the sacredness of a hierarchical order which places some individuals in positions of authority over others. Individual as well as collective actions are presumed to be motivated by fundamental needs for homeostatic maintenance of personal and organizational integrity.

Exchange theories have their historical origins in merchantilist bourgeoisie economics. The development of utilitarian philosophy, the establishment of a money economy, the negotiation and enforcement of formal contracts, and, above all, the creation of corporations as "paper persons" provided the underpinnings for modern exchange theories. Exchange-oriented social analysis assumes that social order is created through negotiated contracts that are sustained through the distribution of specific incentives, either tangible or symbolic in nature.

The interactionist paradigm is compatible with the view that modernity sprang from a cultural renaissance, a renaissance with roots in medieval monasticism and given formal expression in the development of universities. Theories rooted in this paradigm presuppose that social action is controlled by the formation of symbolic cultures. They emphasize the importance of social bonding and the creation of shared definitions of the physical and social worlds (i.e., shared knowledge) as the source of stability and order.[57]

Paradigms and Policy Definitions

Each of the four social paradigms shown in Figure 11.2 provides a unique perspective on the problems of conflict and scarcity. As indicated by the column headings in Figure 11.3, two of the four basic paradigms (structuralism and exchange theory) accept scarcity as given and concentrate on the problem of conflict. Conflict is assumed to be amenable to control or elimination through appropriate public or private action. Policy definitions developed within these two paradigms highlight the forces responsible for social conflict and seek to specify mechanisms or processes for controlling them.

The other two paradigms (functionalism and symbolic interactionism) treat scarcity as the central, and at least potentially manageable, problem. Policy definitions developed on the basis of these two paradigms give conflict a less prominent place. They assume that cooperation and consensus are more natural than conflict and that collective actions are rooted in shared values or directed toward common goals.

As suggested by the row labels in Figure 11.3, policy definitions developed within each of the four basic social science paradigms also differ because they tend to treat the problems of conflict and scarcity as either *directly* affected by public decisions or as only *indirectly* affected through the effects of public decisions on private orientations and actions.

Structuralist conceptions of policy emphasize the reduction of conflict through direct regulation of social institutions. A typical structuralist definition of policy is, "what governments do, why they do it, and what difference it makes."[58] The use of governmental policy to regulate is seen as a reflection of how power is (or should be) distributed in society. Whether viewed from the perspective of the "liberal" structuralists who framed the American constitution or from a more "radical" or Marxist

	Presume Scarcity and Try to Manage Conflict	Tackle Scarcity in Order to Reduce Conflict
	Structuralism	Functionalism
Direct Public Control	Regulate Social Institutions, Control Power, Support Equity	Set Course of Collective Action Control Purposes, Support Quality
(Definition of Policy)	("What governments do."— Dye, 1972)	("Proposed course of action . . . to reach a goal"— Freidrick, 1963)
	Exchange Theory	Interactionism
Indirect Public Support for Private Action	Influence over Private Actions, Control Contracts,	Encouragement of Private Expression, Control Problem Definition Support Competence
(Definition of Policy)	("Regulation of private activity" through subsidy, regulation, or manipulation— Ripley, 1966)	("Conscious attempt to find constructive responses" to problems— NAE, 1969)

Figure 11.3: How the Four Social Science Paradigms Approach Problems of Scarcity and Conflict

perspective, structural theories share a commitment to the view that public policies can produce a proper distribution of political power that will lead to the elimination of social conflict, or at least to its just resolution. Hence, structural theories give prominence to equity as a primary social value and see destructive conflict as the result of an inequitable distribution of power. Policy, therefore, is considered primarily as a vehicle for allocating power to individuals or groups with a legitimate right to exercise it and, conversely, for limiting the power of those whose interests are less legitimate.

Functionalism, by contrast, seeks direct control over society by using policy to pursue identifiable public purposes or goals. A typical functional definition of policy is offered by Friedrick:

> A proposed course of action of a person, group, or government within a given environment providing obstacles and opportunities which the policy was proposed to utilize and overcome in an effort to reach a goal or realize an objective or a purpose.[59]

The ability of government to set policy is seen as dependent on its ability to define and articulate public purposes. Hence, functionalists are more concerned with empowering legitimate private interests. Functionalists are much more likely to focus attention on government programs than on the regulation of private actions or social institutions. They see government as "doing something" about the "general welfare," not merely protecting the rights of various individuals or groups. Hence, functionalism gives prominence to quality as a central public value. Whether conceived of as a "liberal" concern with the quality of life available to all citizens or as a "conservative" concern with the quality of performance of public programs and agencies, functionalists tend to prefer quality performance over egalitarian access. Specific policies are, therefore, more often criticized as inadequate solutions to public problems than as the institutionalization of inequality.

Exchange theories conceptualize policy as a vehicle for influencing private choice. By controlling the right to enter into contractual relationships and by enforcing contracts once they are made, exchange policies aim to channel individual and group behavior toward public purposes. A typical exchange view of policy is presented in Ripley's work.[60] He identifies policy with the "regulation of private activity" through governmental "subsidies," "regulations," and/or "manipulation." Theorists who rely on the exchange paradigm tend to focus attention on liberty as the preeminent social value. They believe, with Thomas Jefferson, that the "government that governs best governs least."

The interactionist paradigm conceptualizes policy as a matter of encouraging private citizens to express appropriate beliefs and actions. Interactionists recognize the importance of ideological and symbolic leadership by governmental policy makers. They tend to assume that policy has its effects by controlling how individuals and groups define the problems which they face. The National Academy of Education offers a typically interactionist definition of policy as:

> The conscious attempt of officials, legislators, and interested publics to find constructive responses to the needs and pathologies which they observe in their surrounding culture.[61]

The key elements in this definition are its assertion that policy is an expression of "conscious" action and that this consciousness is concerned with "constructive" responses to problems. These terms imply complex symbolic thought as the basis for policy decision making.

Interactionism tends to identify competence as the preeminent social value. Where functionalists concentrate on the ability of programs to produce results, interaction theorists tend to be less sure of the value of particular outcomes. They are more confident that they know what kind of participation in society is the most desirable. Thus, they measure quality by looking at the performance of individuals or groups rather than at their achievements. A good citizen is not necessarily a successful one—success depends upon imponderable factors beyond individual control. Incompetence, however, is recognizable and should be eliminated. Analysts relying on the interactionist paradigm tend to emphasize the importance of competent and enthusiastic participation on the part of citizens as the basis for successful pursuit of public goals.

MAJOR TOPICS IN EDUCATION POLICY RESEARCH

What do policy analysts typically study? Given the volume of recent work, the apparent answer is, "Everything!" But that does not provide us with a very useful perspective on the central issues or topics of education policy. LaNoue argues that education policy researchers have concentrated on just two basic topics: educational equity and school governance.[62] Other scholars identify a broader array of fundamental policy issues.[63] If the extensive literature on research methodology and science utilization (to be reviewed below) are set aside for the moment and two additional topics (teaching and learning policy and the economics of education) are added to LaNoue's list, his generalization is a convenient starting point for examining the recent literature in this complex and diffuse field.

As indicated in Figure 11.4, each of these four broad topics (equity, governance, teaching and learning, and educational economics) consists of a cluster of loosely related subtopics. Moreover, research and analysis in each topical area can be separated into those concerned with the processes of policy formation or implementation and those concerned with content or the impact of particular policies.

Equity policy is examined in a very large body of research. No single work has, however, matched the impact of the 1966 report by Coleman et al. entitled *Equality of Educational Opportunity*.[64] Race was the early focus of this research, with the nature and effects of decision making related to desegregation of the public schools providing the major theme

	Process Analysis	Content Research
Equity Research Topics:		
1. Race (Segregate/Desegregate)	How decisions to desegregate are made	What effects racial isolation has on children
2. Wealth (Aid/Finance)	Resource generation/ allocation	Categorical program effects
3. Location (Rural/Urban/ Suburban)	Rural/urban tension management	Effects of program differentiation
4. Language/Ethnicity (Bilingual/Multicultural policy)	Mobilization and response to interest groups	How soon should English language be taught
5. Handicap (Special Education)	Political origin of court cases PL-94-142, etc.	Impact of main- streaming, IEPs, test bias, etc.
6. Gender	Politics of EEOC, Title IX, ERA, and affirmative action	Impact of sex dis- crimination on job opportunities and or- ganization processes
School Governance Topics		
1. Authority to act (fed, state, intermed, district, site)	Distribution of powers and re- sponsibilities	Effects of power or level on educational process/outcome
2. Representation/participation (lay/professional; client/ citizen interests)	Who gets access to decisions and how are they made	What difference does it make for educational processes or outcomes
3. Centralization/ decentralization	Community control, vouchers, advisory committees	Implementation of innovations, mandate compliance
4. Collective bargaining	Teacher power, citizen input, impasse resolution	Organizational and teacher work role effects
Governance		
5. Innovation and reform	Resource control, planning, adoption, implementation	Effect of planned variations in program
6. Public/private (parochial/ religious schools)	Politics of aid and accreditation	Quality of private vs. public education

Figure 11.4: Educational Policy Research Topics

(continued)

	Process Analysis	Content Research
Teaching and Learning		
1. Curriculum	Politics of curriculum decisions	Program effects on various students
2. Testing	Adoption, publication, mandates	Construction, bias, interpretation
3. Personnel training and certification	Who trains, what criteria for certification	What effect does training or certification have on performance
4. Instructional processes	Who decides what processes to use	What difference does it make
5. Teacher work roles	Definitions, incentives	Organization and learning effects
6. School effectiveness	Improvement strategies and incentives	Factors: Learning time, leadership, climate
Economics of Education		
1. Manpower forecasting	Responsibility for statistics	Job opportunity and training needs
2. Human capital	Who gets access to advanced training	What are the marginal returns
3. Education production functions	What are the values or goals to be produced	What factors are responsible for results

of most studies.[65] During the mid-1960s wealth replaced race as the key concept in many of the equity studies.[66] There were many reasons for this shift. Among the most important were: (1) the need for documentation of large interdistrict fiscal resource disparities, (2) a growing realization that physical desegregation was not possible for many minority children (hence, equity would have to be reconceptualized as equal resources rather than as integrated school attendance), and (3) the recognition that school achievement problems were more highly correlated with family and community socio-economic status that with race.

Equity policy analysis has also been concerned with problems related to student location.[67] The inequitable effects of school and district attendance boundaries are easily linked to fiscal inequities, but they have other effects as well. Traditional tensions between rural and urban social values have been carried over into policy issues dealing with school size, the creation of regional centers for vocational or special education, and the use of vouchers to permit families to choose among alternative schools.[68]

During the late 1960s and early 1970s, equity policy broadened to include a number of neglected and oppressed population groups. Language and ethnic minority groups, especially Hispanics, were recognized as victims of biased treatment. Substantial attention was focused on sex discrimination in staffing as well as in program implementation by the passage of Title IX of the Education Amendments of 1972. Most recently, children with physical, emotional, and/or learning handicaps were given special recognition in the passage of PL 94-142 (the Education for All Handicapped Law) in 1975.

In contrast with the relatively recent emergence of equity as a major policy topic, school governance problems are as old as public education itself. The distribution of decision-making authority among federal, state, intermediate unit, school district, and school site policy makers has been an ongoing problem for both analysts and reformers. The ebb and flow of policy influence between the state and federal levels has been studied by a number of prominent scholars.[69] Several have pronounced the demise of the local school district as an agency of educational governance, although the evidence on this point is not entirely convincing.[70]

Tensions among the several agencies responsible for governing public schools have received considerable attention. Mechanisms of representation and participation in policy formation have been broadly studied (elections, referenda, advisory councils, influence networks, state education agencies, legislative decision making, and so forth).[71] And, the effects of centralization or decentralization of decision-making authority have been explored in studies of administrative decentralization, client or family choice, state and federal mandates for change, court orders, and the like. At present, representative/participation analysis has led to contradictory conclusions, ranging from declarations of autocratic control over school policy by professional educators and community elites to a fairly vigorous declaration of the vitality of representative elections. Analyses of the centralization/decentralization problem have identified a fundamental dilemma in governance. Decentralized control leads to the neglect of minority interests, but centralization produces serious alienation and resistance among school personnel and local leaders leading to reduced effectiveness of both policy mandates and general school operations.[72]

Three aspects of governance policy are prominent in recent research: (1) collective bargaining for teachers and other school personnel, (2) innovation and reform in school programs, and (3) relationships between public and private or parochial schools. The budgetary and fiscal effects of collective bargaining have received the lion's share of interest, but their impact on the reallocation of authority within the schools is emerging as a major factor in work role definitions and the delivery of educational services.[73] Studies of educational innovation and change by the Rand Corporation remain a watershed in the examination of this crucial governance problem.[74] School reform strategists now recognize that providing proper compliance incentives—not just mandates for appropriate action—are crucial for successful influence over school system operations. The relationship of public and private schools has been dramatically altered by both the equity movement, which stimulated "white flight" and the formation of new private schools, and recent program improvement efforts, which have drawn attention to differences in the organizational characteristics and educational outcomes found in private schools.[75]

Teaching and learning processes were among the earliest topics of educational research and analysis. Only recently, however, have they been recognized as matters of explicit policy.[76] This recognition has led to policy focused studies of how authority over school curricula is distributed and how specific curriculum content decisions are made.[77] Student assessment and testing has probably received the most sophisticated scientific attention, yet it remains a highly controversial area of policy research and action.[78]

Training and certification of school personnel have received major attention by state level policy makers in recent years but that attention is not well supported by research on alternative training strategies. Instructional processes are better researched, but the policy implications of such investigations have been unclear. This is changing rapidly, however, as lesson structures, classroom control processes, classroom climates, and the factors affecting teacher thinking and planning processes become clearer.

Two "hot" topics in recent teaching and learning policy are the effectiveness of individual teachers and the effectiveness of school situation organizations. Exploration of the work role orientations and activities of effective teachers has been undertaken by a large group of research scholars.[79] Although a number of the characteristics of effective teaching can now be confidently identified, it is not certain how policy best supports the development of these attributes. School effectiveness research has become very important in the last five years.[80] As a matter of scientific research, this line of inquiry is plagued with controversy. Nonetheless, school improvement has become the most important topic of debate among state and federal policy makers.[81]

Public interest in the *economics of education* has focused on three broad areas: (1) manpower forecasting (and its attendant contributions to vocational or career education), (2) human capital formation (and its critical appraisal by students of the political economy of education), and

(3) efforts to develop education production functions capable of describing how particular resources contribute to schooling outcomes.[82]

METHODOLOGICAL ISSUES IN POLICY RESEARCH

A number of scholars have concerned themselves with technical issues related to the production and utilization of policy research. Some have examined organizational and funding issues, but most have concentrated on the relationship between research methods and the use of social research by policy makers. The literature dealing with these issues tends to adopt one of two perspective. The first explores issues associated with turning inherently value laden, time constrained, and intensely practical policy issues into scientific research problems. This approach assumes that social research disciplines are fairly well developed and have an identifiable set of performance standards, capable (at least in principle) of producing specific, unequivocal, and universal conclusions about social behavior. Analysts adopting this perspective tend to follow in Lasswell's footsteps seeking to identify points of intersection between policy making and research.[83] This line of inquiry has done much to illuminate problems of scientific knowledge utilization.[84]

A second methodological perspective assumes that social research is an inherently polyphonic enterprise with several essentially different methods for data collection, analysis, and interpretation. Scholars adopting this approach are primarily concerned with delineating the policy relevant characteristics of various research methods and evaluating how each can enhance or detract from the decision-making process. This strand of literature has identified several key problems associated with the application of scientific methods to policy problems.

Two problems trouble both groups of methodologists. The first is *bias.* Both scientists and policy makers have been known to allow personal, political, or cultural biases to influence their judgment. In extreme cases, scientists fake their data or intentionally obfuscate its interpretation.[85] Policy makers usually just ignore unwanted research and adopt non-scientific decision processes when they do not like the available research evidence. Sometimes, however, they devote substantial attention to controlling research priorities or shopping among available studies to find ones that fit their prejudices in order to minimize the likelihood that unwanted policy decisions will be reached.[86]

In addition to outright bias, the problem of *personalized scientific authority,* or the tendency for policy makers to use scien*tists* rather than science in shaping policy, is also widely discussed.[87] This personalization of authority is most often lamented strongly by scholars concerned with refining scientific policy research methods. These scholars tend to feel that personal involvement distracts from the true authority of science—authority derived from the rigorous use of specialized methods for establishing valid and reliable knowledge. The personalization of authority is sometimes defended, however, as the best way to bring abstract scientific findings into the complex, subtle, and value laden processes of political decision making.[88]

Methodological Distortion of Policy Problems

Policy problems are often distorted when they are subjected to scientific analysis. Scientists tend to study what they know how to study, not necessarily what policy makers would like them to study. They also tend to reconceptualize policy problems to fit the conceptual paradigm with which they approach the explanation of social processes and thus fail to examine the problems identified by policy makers. Moreover, on a very practical level, scientific concern with validity and reliability of data frequently leads to a preference for variables with established metrics rather than those which may be interesting but hard to measure.[89]

A more sweeping criticism is made by those who charge social scientists with "abstract empiricism" or the tendency to oversimplify problems to accommodate reified research methods.[90] These critics charge that researchers tend to seek explanations only within existing variations in society and neglect accounting for the reasons why many possible actions never occur.

Social science findings are also distorted because the research is limited in scope.[91] Data collection and analysis are expensive and time consuming as well as intellectually demanding tasks. Social research is, therefore, inevitably time- and circumstance-bound. Research projects conducted in a particular time and place can miss entirely the causal variables needed for general explanations. For practical economic reasons, research studies tend not to be either comparative or longitudinal in character.[92] Most researchers study a single social program or policy problem, and, moreover, even when the research problem is broadly conceived, scientists can measure only a small number of variables over a limited number of cases. It is not surprising, then, that research findings easily become divergent and contradictory, providing limited and uncertain guidance to policy makers.

Recent work has concentrated on two strategies for overcoming the distortions generated by these methodological limitations. One, pioneered by Glass, is "meta-analysis."[93] Meta-analysis seeks greater reliability in research through statistical examination of trends in the findings reported from a large number of comparable studies. A second strategy has been the pursuit of more comprehensive and general theories, such as the paradigms discussed earlier in this article.

Methodological Problems Affecting Utilization

Several problems limit the utility of science policy formation. Foremost among them is the fact that science is only one decision-making resource for policy makers.[94] Political leaders held decision-making responsibilities long before there were any social sciences, and they still have a broad array of non-scientific ways of identifying and selecting policy options. To be usable, therefore, social research must be cost effective—it must be worth more in enhanced decision-making capacity than it costs to find and interpret.

This need for science to be a cost effective resource leads policy makers to be critical of scientists for equivocation and lack of explicit direction. It has also led to the realization that scientists and policy makers tend to operate in two different cultures with different time frames and different levels of need for certainty in their conclusions.[95]

Wirt and Mitchell in a recent essay on this topic suggest that a proper understanding of science utilization is possible only if the policy making process is itself differentiated along two dimensions.[96] First, policy decision making typically passes through four distinct phases or stages which they labeled: issue definition, deliberation of options, authoritative allocation, and oversight. The role of scientific research differs sharply from one stage to the next. Hence, timeliness, although troublesome to scientists, is a crucial factor in science utilization. Second, participants in the policy process play three different roles. One typically small group are advocates for a policy change. Another often equally small group are explicit opponents of the proposed changes. Most policy makers are less active, however. They play a judgmental role, reviewing the arguments advanced by the advocates and opponents to test whether proposed changes will be damaging or beneficial to their interests. The particular methods used to conduct a research study, Wirt and Mitchell suggest, play a major role in determining whether it is likely to be most useful to policy advocates, opponents, or judges.

CONCLUSION: FUTURE DIRECTIONS IN POLICY RESEARCH

The foregoing discussion has explored the literature on educational policy from four different perspective. First, the historical roots of scientific policy analysis were traced to professional activities related to judicial decision making, rational planning, and federal program evalua-tion. Its intellectual roots were found in Lasswell's distinction between the science *of* policy making and the use of science *in* reaching particular policy decisions.[97] Second, it was noted that the definition of policy is conceptually linked to four competing social science paradigms (struc-turalism, functionalism, exchange theory, and symbolic interactionism), which conceptualize the problems of scarcity and conflict in society in unique ways and give primacy to different public values. Third, the major topics of educational policy research were reviewed. It was noted that the bulk of the policy literature deals with four broad clusters of issues: equity, school governance, teaching and learning, and the economics of educa-tion. Finally, several methodological and research utilization problems were identified.

In closing, it is appropriate to speculate on future developments in educational policy research. It takes no crystal ball to predict that policy research in the near future will continue to be conceptually diffuse and politically controversial. The evidence that social science has substantial, although frequently indirect, effects on policy formation is quite convinc-ing. It is not at all clear, however, that the field is moving toward more widely shared or clearly defined conceptions of policy or is establishing common standards for the practice of policy research. Such a state of affairs virtually assures that political conflict will surround discussions of major education policy proposals. Advocates and opponents will con-tinue to challenge the legitimacy of any methods or concepts not congenial to their conceptual paradigms and political interests.

One development which could lead to a significant breakthrough in both the theory and practice of scientific policy analysis would be the development of a stable, empirically grounded, and theoretically sophis-ticated taxonomy of educational policies. A recent paper by Mitchell and Encarnation argues that the appropriate approach to constructing such a taxonomy lies in distinguishing among the fundamental mechanisms available to policy makers to shape the performance of schools and teachers.[98] These authors review several alternative taxonomies and conclude that other approaches are theoretically inadequate because they cannot meet the fundamental criterion for a taxonomy—that categories be exhaustive (covering all alternatives) and mutually exclusive (placing every policy in one and only one category).

Although social values play an important role in stimulating the development of policy proposals, the social structure of the school—both its taken-for-granted cultural form and its material base—determines whether these policies, once adopted, will influence its performance. Policy makers cannot teach students, and they cannot manage school programs unless they change jobs and join the school staff. Hence they must find policy mechanisms that may be used to indirectly restructure the school system through influencing the actions of educators and students by changing the cultural and material environment within which they operate. In order for social science to be effectively used to improve school performance, policy researchers must: (1) document the alternative mechanisms available to policy makers, (2) determine the effects of each mechanism on school performance, and (3) link these effects to alternative social goals or values. However, this knowledge can be generated only if a comprehensive and theoretically meaningful taxonomy of policy alternatives becomes widely accepted as the basis for both policy research and education policy formation.

NOTES

1. The data presented here were garnered from an electronic search of the Educational Research Information Center (ERIC) files conducted in October, 1983.

2. Since it takes from several months to a few years for references to become available through ERIC, the 1982 and 1983 figures are probably less reliable than the years between 1966 and 1981. Before-1966 entries are less reliable because they predate the full operation of ERIC.

3. J. B. Ukeles, "Policy Analysis: Myth or Reality?" *Public Administration Review* 23, 3 (May/June 1977): 221-228.

4. Y. Dror, "Political Analyst: A New Professional Role in Government," *Public Administration Review* 13, 3 (September 1967): 197-203.

5. Ukeles, "Policy Analysis," p. 223.

6. D. E. Mitchell, "Social Science Utilization in State Legislatures," in *Review of Research in Education*, Volume 9, D. C. Berliner, ed. (Washington, DC: American Educational Research Association, 1981); Chapter 6, pp. 257-311; and W. H. Lambright, *Governing Science and Technology* (New York: Oxford University Press, 1976).

7. Ukeles, "Policy Analysis," p. 223.

8. Mitchell, "Social Science Utilization."

9. W. R. Schilling, "Scientists, Foreign Policy, and Power," in *Scientists and National Policy Making*, R. Galpin and C. Wright, eds. (New York: Columbia University Press, 1964).

10. J. T. Carey, *Sociology and Public Affairs* (Beverly Hills, CA: Sage, 1975).

11. Their final report was issued in 1933. See, President's Research Committee on Social Trends, *Recent Social Trends* (New York: McGraw-Hill, 1933).

12. J. S. Coleman, E. Q. Campbell, C. J. Hobson, J. McPartland, A. M. Mood, F. D. Weinfield, and R. O. York, *Equality of Educational Opportunity* (Washington, DC: Government Printing Office, 1965).

13. For a review of this history see Carey, *Sociology and Public Affairs*, or Mitchell, "Social Science Utilization."

14. C. H. Rossell, "Social Science Research in Equity Cases: A Critical Review," in *Review of Research in Education*, Volume 8, D. C. Berliner, ed. (Washington, DC: American Educational Research Association, 1980), Chapter 5, pp. 237-295.

15. Sweatt vs. Painter, 339 U.S. 629; and Brown vs. Board of Education, 98 F. Supp. 797 (1951); 345 U.S. 972 (1953); 347 U.S. 483 (1954).

16. See also R. C. Rist and R. J. Anson, eds. *Education, Social Science, and the Judicial Process* (New York: Teachers College Press, 1977).

17. Rossell, "Social Science Research."

18. See, for example, D. Mann, *Policy Decision Making in Education* (New York: Teachers College Press, 1975); N. Beckman, ed., "Policy Analysis in Government: Alternatives to 'Muddling Through,' " Special Symposium in *Public Administration Review* 27, 3 (May/June 1977): 221-264; S. Nagel, ed. *Handbook of Policy Studies* (Lexington, MA: D. C. Heath, 1980); C. C. Yeakey, "Emerging Policy Research in Educational Research and Decisionmaking," in *Review of Research in Education,* Volume 10, E. W. Gordon, ed. (Washington, DC: American Educational Research Association, 1983), Chapter 7, pp. 225-304.

19. Ukeles, "Policy Analysis," p. 223.

20. Yeakey, "Emerging Policy Research."

21. C. E. Lindblom, "The Science of 'Muddling Through,' " *Public Administration Review 19, 1* (1959): 79-88.

22. See, for example, C. H. Weiss, ed., *Using Social Research in Policy Making* (Lexington, MA: D. C. Heath, 1977); or Mitchell, "Social Science Utilization."

23. See, for example, E. R. House, *Evaluation with Validity* (Beverly Hills, CA: Sage, 1980); or M. Q. Patton, *Utilization Focused Evaluation* (Beverly Hills, CA: Sage, 1978).

24. M. W. McLaughlin, *Evaluation and Reform, Elementary and Secondary Act of 1965, Title I* (Cambridge, MA: Ballinger, 1975), p. 11.

25. Patton, *Utilization Focused Evaluation.*

26. D. R. Weitman, P. Horst, G. M. Taber, and J. S. Whaley, "Design of an Evaluation System for NIMH," *Contract Report 962-7* (Washington, DC: The Urban Institute, 1973).

27. See, for example, D. Dreyfus, "Limitations of Policy Research in Congressional Decision Making," *Policy Studies Journal* 4, 3 (1976): 269-274; M. Timpane, "Into the Maw: The Uses of Policy in Washington," *Phi Delta Kappan* 58, 2 (1976): 177-178; or G. E. Hall and S. F. Loucks, "Bridging the Gap: Policy Research Rooted in Practice," in *Policy Making in Education,* A. Lieberman and M. W. McLaughlin, eds. Eighty-first Yearbook of the National Society for the Study of Education, Part I (Chicago: University of Chicago Press, 1972).

28. See, for example, Weiss, *Using Social Research;* R. F. Elmore, "Complexity and Control: What Legislators and Administrators Can Do about Implementing Public Policy," in *Handbook of Teaching and Policy,* L. Schulman and G. Sykes, eds. (New York: Longman, 1983); or F. M. Wirt and D. E. Mitchell, "Social Science and Educational Reform: The Political Uses of Social Research," *Educational Administration Quarterly* 18, 4 (Fall, 1982): 1-16.

29. See, for example, A. Rivlin, *Systematic Thinking for Social Action* (Washington, DC: Brookings Institution, 1971); or K. Carlson, "Ways in which Research Methodology Distorts Policy Issues," *The Urban Review* 11, 1 (Spring 1979): 3-14.

30. See, for example, F. Harrison, "Educational Evaluation and Public Policy," *Claremont Reading Conference,* 40th Yearbook (Claremont, CA: Claremont Graduate School, 1976).

31. See, for example, H. Morganthau's classic work, *Scientific Man vs. Power Politics* (Chicago: University of Chicago Press, 1946).

32. D. Lerner and H. D. Lasswell, eds., *The Policy Sciences* (Stanford, CA: Stanford University Press, 1951); and Nagel, *Handbook of Policy Studies*.

33. R. Klein, "The Rise and Decline of Policy Analysis: The Strange Case of Health Policymaking in Britain,"*Policy Analysis* 2 (Summer 1976): 458-475.

34. N. Machiavelli, *The Prince and Other Political Writings,* Trans. by Bruce Penman (London: Dent, 1981).

35. H. D. Lasswell, "Introduction," in Lerner and Lasswell, *The Policy Sciences,* p. 3.

36. For an excellent discussion of the relationship between the scientific and ethical aspects of policy, see G. Winter, *Elements for a Social Ethic* (New York: Macmillan, 1966), especially Chapters 7 and 8.

37. M. J. Dubnick and B. A. Bardis, *Thinking About Public Policy: A Problem Solving Approach* (New York: John Wiley, 1983), p. vii.

38. See, for example, the lengthy discussion of policy characteristics in Mann, *Policy Decision Making*.

39. T. R. Dye, *Understanding Public Policy* (Englewood Cliffs, N.J.: Prentice Hall, Inc., 1972).

40. For examples of this approach, see J. M. Rich, *New Directions in Educational Policy* (Lincoln, NE: Professional Educators, 1974); J. E. Andersen, *Public Policy Making* (New York: Praeger, 1975); or Yeakey, "Emerging Policy Research."

41. D. E. Mitchell, *Early Childhood Policy: A Study Guide* (Fort Lauderdale, FL: Nova University, 1978).

42. D. H. Kerr, *Educational Policy: Analysis, Structure and Justification* (New York: David McKay, 1976).

43. L. Iannaccone, *Education Policy Systems* (Fort Lauderdale, FL: Nova University, 1975).

44. This idea was developed briefly in an early draft of Green's chapter in Schulman and Sykes, *Handbook of Teaching*. Unfortunately, it was dropped in the published version.

45. G. Orwell, *1984* (New York: New American Library, 1981); and A. Huxley, *Brave New World* (New York: Harper & Row, 1946).

46. Kuhn's perspective is developed in *The Structure of Scientific Revolutions* (Chicago: University of Chicago Press, 1962). For examples of the use of this term in social science theory, see G. Burrell and G. Morgan, *Sociological Paradigms and Organisational Analysis* (London: Heinemann Educational Books, 1979); or D. E. Mitchell, "Governance of Schools," in *Encyclopedia of Educational Research,* H. E. Mitzel, ed. (New York: Free Press, 1982), Vol. 2, pp. 730-738.

47. Iannaccone, *Education Policy Systems,* p. 34 ff.; M. Brown and A. Goldin, *Collective Behavior* (Pacific Palisades, CA: Goodyear, 1973), p. 172 ff.

48. J. Kelly, *Organizational Behavior* (Homewood, IL: Irwin, 1974, revised ed.); D. E. Mitchell, "Metaphors of Management: or How Far from Outcomes Can You Get?" (Paper presented at the annual meeting of the American Educational Research Association, New York, 1982).

49. W. Buckley, *Sociology and Modern Systems Theory* (Englewood Cliffs, N.J.: Prentice Hall, Inc., 1967).

50. G. Winter, *Elements for a Social Ethic: Scientific Perspective on Social Process* (New York: Macmillan, 1966).

51. P. E. Peterson, *School Politics Chicago Style* (Chicago: University of Chicago Press, 1976).

52. Burrell and Morgan, *Sociological Paradigms.*

53. J. H. Turner, *The Structure of Sociological Theory* (Homewood, IL: Dorsey Press, 1978).

54. Mitchell, "Governance of Schools"; see also, D. E. Mitchell and W. G. Spady, "Authority, Power, and the Legitimation of Social Control," *Educational Administration Quarterly* 19, 1 (Winter 1983): 5-33.

55. See, for example, M. B. Hesse, *Models and Analogies in Science* (Notre Dame, IN: University of Notre Dame Press, 1966); or M. Belth, *The Process of Thinking* (New York: David McKay, 1977).

56. See Max Weber's essay on military discipline in H. H. Gerth and C. W. Mills, trans. and eds., *From Max Weber* (New York: Oxford University Press, 1946), p. 255 ff.

57. Key concepts in each of the works cited above can be classified according to these four paradigms as follows:

	Structural	Functional	Exchange	Interaction
Political Concepts (Iannaccone, 1974)	Structural	Outcome	Process	Ideology
Social Causality (Buckley, 1967)	Efficient	Functional, or Final	Feedback Loop	Mutual Interaction
Institution Origins (Turner, 1978)	Conflict	Functional	Exchange	Interaction
Organization Theories (Kelly, 1974)	Scientific Management	Bureaucratic	Systems Approach	Human Relations
Decision Making (Peterson, 1976)	Ideological Bargaining	Rational	Pluralistic Bargaining	Organizational
Research Paradigms (Burrell & Morgan, 1981)	Radical Structural	Functional	Radical Humanist	Interpretive
Perspective on World (Winter, 1966)	Voluntarist	Functionalist	Behaviorist	Intentionalist

See: Iannaccone, *Education Policy Systems;* Buckley, *Sociology;* Turner, *The Structure;* Kelly, *Organizational Behavior;* Peterson, *School Politics;* Burrell and Morgan, *Sociological Paradigms;* Winter, *Elements for a Social Ethic.*

58. Dye, *Understanding Public Policy,* p. 1.

59. C. J. Freidrick, *Man and His Government: An Empirical Theory of Politics* (New York: McGraw-Hill, 1963).

60. R. B. Ripley, ed., *Public Policies and Their Politics* (New York: W. W. Norton, 1966).

61. National Academy of Education, *Policy Making for American Public Schools* (New York: 1969).

62. G. R. LaNoue, "Political Science," in *Encyclopedia of Educational Research,* H. E. Mitzel, ed. (New York: Free Press, 1982), pp. 1421-1426.

63. See, for example, Nagel, *Handbook of Policy Studies,* p. 48.

64. Coleman et al., *Equality.*

65. See especially, M. Weinberg, *A Chance to Learn: A History of Race and Education in the United States* (Cambridge, England: Cambridge University Press, 1979); W. D. Hawley et al., *Strategies for Effective Desegregation: Lessons from Research* (Lexington, MA: Lexington, 1983); and Rossell, "Social Science Research."

66. See especially, A. E. Wise, *Rich Schools, Poor Schools* (Chicago: University of Chicago Press, 1967). The Ford Foundation played a major role in directing attention to wealth as an entity issue by sponsoring studies of financial inequities in a number of states.

67. The location issue is a very complex one. Attendance boundaries have been attacked in several different ways including the development of "magnet" and "alternative" schools, metropolitan desegregation plans, and so forth. Within school location issues have also come under scrutiny in tracking, drop-out, and special program assignment studies.

68. The voucher argument is presented in detail in J. E. Coons and S. D. Sugarman, *Education by Choice: The Case for Family Control* (Berkeley: University of California Press, 1978).

69. See especially F. M. Wirt and M. Kirst, *Schools in Conflict* (Berkeley, CA: McCutchan, 1982); J. D. Scribner, ed., *The Politics of Education,* The Seventy-sixth Yearbook of the National Society for the Study of Education, Part II (Chicago: University of Chicago Press, 1977); and A. Leiberman and M. W. McLaughlin, eds., *Policy Making in Education,* The Eighty-first Yearbook of the National Society for the Study of Education, Part I (Chicago: University of Chicago Press, 1982).

70. Centralization of authority is described in E. K. Mosher, "Education and American Federalism: Intergovernmental and National Policy Influences," in Scribner, *The Politics of Education,* Chapter 4, pp. 94-113. Analyses of the critical importance of electoral politics in local districts keep being reported, however. Those following the conceptual framework first developed by L. Iannaccone and F. W. Lutz in *Politics, Power and Policy: The Governing of Local Schools* (Columbus, OH: Merrill, 1970) have been most convincing in their documentation of local autonomy.

71. See D. Mann, *The Politics of Administrative Representation* (Lexington, MA: Lexington, 1976).

72. See the Rand Corp. studies of federal change efforts in P. Berman and M. McLaughlin, *Federal Programs Supporting Educational Change,* Eight volumes (Santa Monica, CA: Rand Corporation, 1975-1978). An interesting study of local control over budgetary processes is found in D. O. Porter, D. Warner, and T. Porter, *The Politics of Budgeting Federal Aid: Resource Mobilization by Local School Districts* (Beverly Hills, CA: Sage, 1973). Elmore's study of the limits of federal control is also illuminating, Elmore, "Complexity and Control."

73. See especially D. E. Mitchell, C. T. Kerchner, W. Erck, and G. Pryor, "The Impact of Collective Bargaining on School Management and Governance," *The American Journal of Education* 89, 2 (February 1981): 147-188.

74. Berman and McLaughlin, *Federal Programs.*

75. The controversy surrounding James Coleman's study of private school effectiveness is the most prominent (though perhaps not the most important)

example of this new policy thrust. See, J. S. Coleman, T. Hoffer and S. Kilgore, *High School Achievement: Public, Catholic and Private Schools Compared* (New York: Basic Books, 1982). See also, B. L. Heyns, "Policy Implications of the Public and Private School Debates," *Harvard Education Review* 5 (1981): 519-525.

76. The excellent book by Schulman and Sykes, *Handbook of Teaching,* should go far toward expanding awareness of this policy issue. The series of recent policy analyses identified in note 81, below, all point to the crucial importance of teaching and learning policies.

77. See, for example, T. Van Geel, *Authority to Control the School Program* (Lexington, MA: Lexington, 1979); and W. L. Boyd, "Changing Politics of Curriculum Policy Making for American Schools," *Review of Educational Research* 48 (1979): 577-628.

78. See, for example, P. Lynch, "Public Policy and Competency Testing," *Education and Urban Society* 12 (1979): 65-80.

79. The best work in this area is currently being produced by researchers at the Institute for Research on Teaching at Michigan State University.

80. For divergent views, see H. A. Averch, S. J. Carrol, T. S. Donaldson, H. J. Kiesling, and J. Pincus, *How Effective is Schooling? A Critical Synthesis and Review of Research Findings* (Englewood Cliffs, NJ: Educational Tech., 1974); and G. F. Madaus, P. W. Airasian, and T. Kellaghan, *School Effectiveness: A Reassessment of the Evidence* (New York: McGraw-Hill, 1980).

81. The most important recent policy studies include: National Commission on Excellence, *A Nation at Risk;* Education Commission of the States, *Action for Excellence;* College Entrance Examination Board, *Academic Preparation for College;* The Twentieth Century Fund, *Making the Grade;* The Carnegie Corporation, *Education and Economic Progress;* National Association of Independent Schools, *A Celebration of Teaching: High Schools in the 1980s;* The Carnegie Foundation, *High School: A Report on American Secondary Education;* Institute for Development of Educational Activities (IDEA), *A Study of Schooling in the United States;* and The National Science Foundation, *Educating Americans for the 21st Century.*

82. On manpower forecasting, see P. Doeringer and M. Piore, *Internal Labor Markets and Manpower Training* (Lexington, MA: Lexington, 1971); or F. Harbison and C. Myers, *Education, Manpower, and Economic Growth* (New York: McGraw-Hill, 1964). On human capital development, see, for example, R. L. Johns, E. L. Morphet, and K. Alexander, *The Economics and Financing of Education* (Englewood Cliffs, N.J.: Prentice Hall, Inc., 1983, fourth ed.). On political economy, see S. Bowles and H. Gintis, *Schooling in Capitalist America: Educational Reform and the Contradictions of Economic Life* (New York: Basic Books, 1976); or H. S. Shapiro, "Education and the State in Capitalist Society," *Harvard Education Review* 50 (1980): 321-331. On production function development, see, for example, B. W. Brown and D. H. Saks, "The Microeconomics of Schooling," in *Review of Research in Education,* Volume 9, D. C. Berliner, ed. (Washington, DC: American Educational Research Association, 1981).

83. Lerner and Lasswell, *The Policy Sciences.*

84. For a review of the utilization literature, see Mitchell, "Social Science Utilization."

85. Several stories of blatant bias in educational research are reported in K. Carlson, "Ways in Which Research Methodology Distorts Policy Issues," *The Urban Review* 11, 1 (Spring 1979): 3-14.

86. The tendency for white flight data to be ignored in early desegregation research is reported in J. S. Coleman, "Policy Decisions, Social Science Information and Education," *Sociology of Education* 49, 4 (1976): 304-312.

87. Rossell, "Social Science Research," argues this issue extensively, concluding that "social scientists are no better able to be objective in their criticisms (of policy questions) than are knowledgeable policymakers, lawyers and judges."

88. This point is made explicitly in R. Dworkin, "Social Sciences and Constitutional Rights—the Consequences of Uncertainty," in *Education, Social Science, and the Judicial Process*, R. C. Rist and R. J. Anson, eds. (New York: Teachers College Press, 1977). The important contributions made by senior scholars to school policy are noted in S. Bailey et al., *Schoolmen and Politics* (Syracuse, NY: Syracuse University Press, 1962).

89. See Carlson, "Ways in Which Research"; and Hall and Loucks, "Bridging the Gap."

90. This problem is discussed in Carlson, "Ways in Which Research," and also in Burrell and Morgan, *Sociological Paradigms*.

91. This issue is addressed by Carlson, "Ways in Which Research."

92. Strategies for improving comparative and longitudinal research are suggested in F. M. Wirt, "Comparing Educational Policies: Theory, Units of Analysis, and Research Strategies," *Comparative Education Review* 24, 2 (June 1980): 174-191.

93. G. V. Glass, "Primary, Secondary, and Meta-analysis of Research," *Educational Researcher* 5 (1976): 5-8; Idem, "Integrating Findings: The Meta-analysis of Research," *Review of Research in Education*, Volume 5 (Washington, DC: American Educational Research Association, 1978).

94. See, for example, Wirt and Mitchell, "Social Science and Educational Reform," or Mitchell, "Social Science Utilization."

95. C. P. Snow, *The Two Cultures and A Second Look: An Expanded Version of the Two Cultures and the Scientific Revolution* (London: Cambridge University Press, 1959).

96. See Wirt and Mitchell, "Social Science and Educational Reform." See also, D. E. Mitchell, *Shaping Legislative Decisions: Education Policy and the Social Sciences* (Lexington, MA: D. C. Heath, 1981).

97. Lasswell, "Introduction" in Lerner and Lasswell, *The Policy Sciences*.

98. D. E. Mitchell and D. J. Encarnation, "Alternative State Policy Mechanisms for Influencing School Performance," *Educational Researcher* 13, 5 (1984): 4-11.

CHAPTER TWELVE

A Theoretical Framework and Exploration of Organizational Effectiveness of Schools

WAYNE K. HOY and JUDITH FERGUSON

After the examination of two competing frameworks for the study of organizational effectiveness, a general model of school effectiveness is proposed. This multidimensional perspective was operationalized and explored with data from a sample of secondary schools in a single state. The empirical analysis is supported by the framework, and suggestions for further refinements are made.

Organizational effectiveness remains a complex and difficult problem for both theorists and researchers as well as for practitioners. There is no general agreement on the definition of the concept let alone its measurement; in fact, Goodman and Pennings argue that effectiveness is one of the most pervasive yet least delineated constructs in the study of organizations.[1] Moreover, the current state of the empirical literature is in disarray in large part because of an inadequate theoretical framework.[2]

School effectiveness has emerged as a recent, popular topic among educational researchers. The work of Coleman,[3] Rutter,[4] Brookover,[5] Edmonds,[6] Moos,[7] and Madaus[8] is typical of educational studies on effective schools. However, much of the research has been criticized on measurement, statistical, methodological, and theoretical grounds.[9] It appears that the research on effective schools is limited by the same weaknesses as the research on effective organizations—the absence of both a sound theoretical framework and a careful definition and measurement of the concept.

The question arises as to whether it is possible to develop a definition of effectiveness that is clear, comprehensive, operational, and at the same time fits into a general conceptual framework. The present analysis has three primary objectives: (a) to examine the competing frameworks of organizational effectiveness and to provide a general model for its study, (b) to develop operational criteria for the elements of the model and to

SOURCE: Wayne K. Hoy and Judith Ferguson, "A Theoretical Framework and Exploration of Organizational Effectiveness of Schools," *Educational Administration Quarterly*, Vol. 21, No. 2, pp. 117-134. Copyright © by The University Council for Educational Administration. Reprinted with permission.

measure them in the context of the school, and (c) to explore the relationships between these criteria and two general measures of effectiveness.[10]

CONCEPTUAL PERSPECTIVE

Ascertaining organizational effectiveness is neither simple nor obvious. Scholars now generally agree that effectiveness is a multidimensional rather than a unidimensional construct. For example, Campbell lists 30 criterion measures of organizational effectiveness drawn from the literature; these measures are diverse, overlapping, and vary on a number of dimensions.[11] However, the construct of effectiveness simply does not make sense unless it is placed within a conceptual context. Without a theoretical guide, it is not possible to state that one school is more effective and another is not, or more practically, to plan ways to make schools more effective. There are, nevertheless, two contemporary theoretical models that are potentially useful in making such judgments about effectiveness in schools—the goal model and the systems model.[12]

The Goal Model[13]

The traditional view of effectiveness has been a functional one. That is, an organization is successful to the extent that it achieves its goals. Such a view rests on several assumptions. First, rational decision makers in the organization are guided by a specific set of goals, and second, these goals are both few enough in number and defined clearly enough to be understood and taken on by participants. If these conditions are met, organizational effectiveness can be evaluated by developing measures to determine the extent to which the goals are achieved.

The notion of organizational goals, however, is not simple. Although many scholars accept the general idea that goals are future states of affairs that the organization is attempting to achieve, there are at least three different variants of organizational goals: official, operative, and operational goals.[14] Most organizations in fact have all three types.

Official goals are formal statements of purpose concerning the mission of the organization. They are usually abstract and serve the purpose of securing legitimacy and support from the public rather than guiding behavior. An official goal of schools, for example, is "to educate each student to the best of his or her ability."

Operative goals are the actual intentions of an organization. Such goals guide the actual tasks and activities performed in the schools regardless of official statements. Thus, official goals in schools may or may not be operative ones, depending on the extent to which they accurately reflect actual educational practices. Further, many operative goals are not articulated, e.g., to provide custodial care for students in schools.

Operational goals are even more specific ends defined in terms of criteria and procedures for evaluation. Clearly, these are concrete and measurable goals that the organization can use to evaluate its success. A current school illustration is the goal that "80 percent of the students will pass the minimum basic skills tests in reading and mathematics by the tenth grade." Operational goals are ultimately necessary if an organization is to determine its effectiveness using a goal model.

There are, however, a number of strong criticisms of the goal model.

(1) Organizations typically have multiple goals, many of which are inconsistent, incompatible, and overlooked.

(2) Too often the focus is on an administrator's goals, rather than those set by such other constituencies as subordinates, clients, or the public.

(3) Goals often change as contextual constraints and behavior vary, but goals in the model for evaluation tend to remain static.

(4) Since official goals are often not the operative goals, analysis of their actual operation is complex, difficult, and sometimes misdirected.

(5) Finally, some scholars argue that organizational goals simply do not guide behavior; in this sense, goals are often ex post facto statements that justify existing behavior.

Such pertinent criticisms have led many to conclude that the goal model is inadequate for the study and evaluation of organizational effectiveness.

Systems Model[15]

The systems model postulates that, since the demands placed on organizations are so numerous, complex, and dynamic, it is impossible to define specific goals in any meaningful way; hence the major concerns of organizations are to survive and to grow. This perspective calls attention to the organization's ability to compete and secure essential resources from its environment. Thus, to evaluate the effectiveness of an organization, it is necessary to determine the internal consistency of the organization, the efficiency of use of its resources, the success of its coping mechanisms, and its ability to compete with others for resources, especially scarce ones.[16]

The systems model is typically used by analysts who view the organization as an open system with inputs, transformations, and outputs. It is, therefore, not surprising for their inquiries to dwell on the environment and the capability of the organization to secure an advantageous position over other organizations. In fact, one of the major criticisms of the systems models is that they place too much attention on inputs as opposed to outputs. When an organization becomes consumed with the acquisition of resources from its environment, there is a strong tendency to neglect other functions and the product often suffers.

Critics also argue that increasing inputs is an operative goal; hence, the systems model is actually a goal model concerned chiefly with inputs rather than outputs. Hall has observed: "The acquisition of resources does not just happen. It is based on what the organization is trying to achieve—its goal—but is accomplished through the operative goals."[17] Thus, although the two models of organizational effectiveness discussed emphasize different aspects of organizational life, the approaches are not necessarily incompatible; in fact, Steers has argued that the two perspectives are complementary and that it is possible and desirable to combine both views.[18]

A Synthesis[19]

Both of the above models seem to share a common assumption, namely, "that it is possible, and desirable, to arrive at the single set of evaluative criteria, and thus a single statement of organizational effectiveness."[20] The goal model stresses the successful attainment of specific objectives, while the systems model is more concerned with internal consistency, the ability to adapt, and the optimization of resources. In both cases, however, behavior is explicitly or implicitly goal-directed. From a systems perspective, the goals are more implicit and dynamic; they are not static, ultimate states, but are subject to change as the environment varies. Although the two approaches are different, the general notion of directed organizational behavior represents a common theme. Indeed, a synthesis seems reasonable and possible, but any framework for the analysis of organizational effectiveness should be concerned with at least the following matters: (1) the nature of organization, (2) the definition of effectiveness, (3) the domain of effectiveness, (4) constituencies, and (5) testability.[21]

There is now consensus that modern organizations, including schools, are open systems. Today, few researchers or scholars argue that it is adequate to analyze organizations without reference to their environments; closed-system perspectives are simply insufficient. Schools are open social systems, and any satisfactory definition of organizational effectiveness must recognize that fact.

The definition of effectiveness proposed in this analysis evolves from systems theory. It is assumed that all formal organizations, such as schools, attempt to achieve certain objectives and to develop group products through the manipulation of material and human resources;

hence, the study of effectiveness is concerned with both organizational means and ends. Consequently, organizational effectiveness is defined "as the extent to which any organization as a social system, given certain resources and means, fulfills its objectives without incapacitating its means and resources and without placing undue strain upon its members."[22]

Since a multidimensional definition of effectiveness has been accepted, it becomes necessary to specify the core set of criteria, and to examine interrelationships among the elements, of effectiveness. A useful model to help in determining the criteria of effectiveness has been supplied by Parsons, who postulates that a social system's survival depends on the exercise of four critical functions.[23] All social systems, if they are to develop and survive, must solve four problems:

(1) Adaptation—the problem of accommodating to the environment,

(2) Goal Attainment—the problem of setting and achieving goals,

(3) Integration—the problem of maintaining solidarity among elements of the system, and

(4) Latency—the problem of creating and maintaining the system's motivational and value patterns.

These generic problems are fundamental to resource acquisition, can be considered goals of the organization, and, thus, provide one basis for synthesis.

Using the Parsonian framework, the proposed conceptualization of organizational effectiveness subsumes the following general dimensions: (1) organizational adaptation in the form of successful accommodation to internal and external forces, (2) organizational productivity in terms of the extent to which the organization is successful in setting and accomplishing its internal goals, (3) organizational cohesiveness in the form of the absence of intraorganizational conflict, and (4) organizational commitment in the form of members' motivation and commitment to the organization. These dimensions are concerned with both means and ends; they are consistent with the proposed definition of effectiveness; they are guided by a theoretical framework; and they are concerned with goals as well as system requirements for existence and growth.

Although the general properties of effectiveness have been identified, the problem of the adjudication of it remains. Who or what constituency should determine the specific criteria and level of effectiveness? Relative to schools, should it be students? teachers? administrators? the board of education? or the public at large? Moreover, what time perspective is appropriate in this respect—short term, intermediate, or long-term? Further, since effectiveness criteria often reflect the values and biases of interested groups, it seems appropriate to suggest that such criteria be drawn from a number of perspectives and represent various constituencies.

Eventually, operational measures must link abstraction to activity. Although a model has been developed, the general properties of effectiveness must be converted to operational criteria. Organizational adaptability in the context of the school can be measured in terms of the flexibility and innovativeness of the school as depicted by both administrators and teachers. Goal attainment, most commonly defined in school effectiveness studies as achievement on standardized tests and in organizational studies as production, is probably the most accepted criterion in research on effectiveness and can be used. Notwithstanding its limitations and narrow focus, student achievement remains *one* important goal in virtually all schools. Integration can be evaluated by the cohesiveness of the faculty—the spirit of cooperation and collaboration among faculty and among faculty and administration that contributes to the satisfaction of both individual needs and organizational tasks. Latency deals with the problem of creating and maintaining the motivational and value patterns of the school. As such, it can be measured by the extent to which faculty are committed to the school. The components and measures of this operational model or set of criteria are summarized in Table 12.1.

The proposed model has four distinct dimensions of effectiveness. Each dimension has at least one operational indicator of effectiveness.[24] Moreover, the views of three constituencies—students, teachers, and administrators—are represented in the model. The time perspective, however, as noted is limited solely to the short term. Clearly, the model could be improved by adding more indicators for each dimension, by ensuring that all three constituencies are represented for each dimension, and by including both intermediate and long-term time perspectives. The model is not the ideal, but it provides a realistic beginning.

Although the proposed framework is based on a Parsonian formulation, other schemes might also be used to develop a comprehensive framework of organizational effectiveness. Immegart and Pilecki, for example, developed a four-dimensional scheme for analyzing organizational outcomes.[25] Their model can be used to assess the extent to which productivity, integration, organizational health, and feedback (evaluation) are present in organizational outcomes. Productivity in this format refers to produce and service utility; integration to propensities toward self-actualization, group decision making, and change flexibility; health to adaptability, identity sense, and capacity to test reality; and evaluation to the desirability and penetration of feedback. There is a striking similarity between the Immegart-Pilecki scheme and the proposed model developed above.

TABLE 12.1
A Proposed Model of School Effectiveness

Dimension of Effectiveness	*Indicator*	*Constituency*	*Time Perspective*
Adaptation	Innovation	Administrators Teachers	Short-term
Goal attainment	Academic achievement	Students	Short-term
Integration	Cohesiveness	Teachers	Short-term
Latency	Organizational commitment	Teachers	Short-term

Likewise, Mott developed a multifaceted perspective for measuring organizational effectiveness. He argued that effective organizations "are those that produce more and higher quality outputs and adapt more effectively to environmental and internal problems than do other, similar organizations."[26] To determine the extent to which the organization has mobilized its centers of power for production and adaptation, Mott proposed the following effectiveness criteria: quantity and quality of the product, efficiency of production, and the adaptability and flexibility of the organization. Once again, the conceptual similarity of the Mott perspective and the others is clear. All three frameworks recognize the broad range of organizational outcomes; all are concerned with both environmental and internal problems; and all address both production and adaptation as highly complex processes. The Parsonian perspective, however, provides a theoretical framework evolving directly from the imperative functions of social systems.

EXPLORATION

The approach to analyzing organizational effectiveness developed above was operationalized and explored with data from a sample of schools in a single state. A variety of school settings was sought, but it was also important to ensure that necessary data for all indicators in the effectiveness model could be obtained. In this exploration or "test" of the model, it was deemed advisable to measure operational effectiveness using multiple constituencies, to assess the variation of scores on the measures, to look at the correlations between the measures, and to compare the results of the use of the model with two more general ratings of effectiveness.

As a result, the exploration of the model proceeded as follows.

Sample

Fifty secondary schools were invited to participate in the study from a population of schools that administered a common standardized test of academic achievement, the California Achievement Test. All schools were located in New Jersey and included a diverse cross-section of schools in terms of income, educational and occupational levels of parents, and percent of urban population in the district. Forty of the 50 schools agreed to participate in the study. Unfortunately, although all of the schools initially stated that they administered the California Achievement Tests, 14 of those participating did not have achievement data for their students.

As part of the sampling procedure, all secondary schools from one county were asked to participate. Seven of the nine schools agreed. This subsample enabled an independent panel of experts from the Office of the County Superintendent to assess the organizational effectiveness of these schools.

The sample included responses from teachers and administrators. Ten teachers were selected from each school using a list of random numbers applied to alphabetical listings of staff; 89% of all teachers responded to the instruments. Further, each school principal and all assistant principals were also part of the sample. The *school* was the unit of analysis. Scores obtained by administrators, teachers, or students were aggregated within a school to produce one measure for each school on each variable.

Instruments

A battery of subtests was administered to faculty and administrators in each school, and data on student achievement in mathematics and reading were gathered and summarized from the records in each school. The information obtained from each group was pooled to reflect the properties of the school. Mean scores for each school were computed, and the organizational score for each variable was used in the analyses.

Innovation was measured by the Innovative Experience subtest of the Trouble Shooting Checklist (TSC), which was designed by the Research and Development Center at the University of Texas to measure change potential in school settings.[27] The subtest was selected to measure a school's experience with and attitude toward innovation through staff responses to questions regarding past attempts and present plans for innovation. The scale consisted of 16 Likert-type items; the response to each item was on a five-point scale ranging from very typical to very atypical. Sample items include the following: "Analyses have been made concerning the effects of innovations on the entire school"; "This school is considering innovations that contain easily alterable materials which can meet the demands of varied teaching situations"; and "The school plans for implementation of innovations include systematic procedures for staff education."

Both validity and reliability of the TSC have been supported. Convergent validity for the scale was examined by the developer using Campbell and Fiske's multitrait-multimethod matrix; scores from the subtest correlated (r = .77) with scores from a subjective rating form that asked respondents to indicate their assessment of the school's potential for successfully adopting educational innovations. Reliability coefficients for the scale have been consistently high, ranging from .84 to .92. For the present sample, an alpha coefficient of .84 was obtained.

Achievement was measured by scores on the reading and mathematics tests of the California Achievement Test (CAT). The CAT is a well-known battery of standardized achievement tests used extensively in public schools. Validity and reliability of the scales are well documented, and reliability coefficients consistently range in the .90s.[28]

Cohesiveness was measured by a subtest of the Organizational Climate Description Questionnaire (OCDQ).[29] The scale is a 10-item subtest that reflects the esprit of the faculty—the extent to which the group is enjoying a sense of satisfaction and accomplishment in their job. Teachers were asked to describe the extent to which each statement characterized their school as defined by four categories: rarely occurs, sometime occurs, often occurs, very frequently occurs. Examples of the items include the following: "Teachers at this school show school spirit"; Teachers accomplish their work with great vim, vigor, and pleasure"; and "The morale of teachers is high."

Construct validity of the measure has been supported by Andrews' comprehensive validity study of the OCDQ.[30] Moreover, Halpin and Croft reported a split-half coefficient of reliability of .75 for esprit, and in the present study, an alpha coefficient of .80 was obtained.[31]

Organizational commitment was measured by the Organizational Commitment Questionnaire (OCQ).[32] The 15-item instrument taps the relative strength of employees' identification with and involvement in the organization in terms of their strong belief in and acceptance of the organization's goals and values, their willingness to exert considerable effort on behalf of the organization, and a strong desire to maintain membership in the organization. Responses to each item were measured on a 7-point scale from strongly disagree to strongly agree. Sample items included: "I talk up this organization to my friends as a great organization to work for"; "I find that my values and the organization's values are very similar"; and "I would accept almost any type of job assignment in order to keep working for this organization."

Mowday, Steers, and Porter have provided evidence of both convergent and discriminant validity for the OCQ.[33] In addition, estimates for internal consistency of the scale have range from .82 to .93. An alpha coefficient of reliability of .89 was obtained in the present sample.

Overall school effectiveness was subjectively determined by an Index of Perceived Organizational Effectiveness (IPOE). The IPOE is a derivative of Mott's Index of Organizational Effectiveness that was modified by Miskel and his associates for use in schools.[34] Overall effectiveness of the school is rated along the dimensions of quantity and quality of product, efficiency, adaptability, and flexibility. Respondents select one of five alternatives to assess how well their school achieves eight identified objectives. Sample items include the following: "How good is the quality and the product or services produced by the people you know in your school?" "How good a job do people in your school do in coping with emergencies and disruptions?" and "How informed are the people in your school about innovations that could affect the way they do their work?"

Validity of the Index of Organizational Effectiveness was established by Mott in his ten hospital studies and in a study of the National Aeronautics and Space Administration. The alpha coefficient of reliability for the school version of the index was reported at .89[35] In the present study, the IPOE yielded an alpha coefficient of .87.

Expert Ratings of Effectiveness

Independent ratings of the effectiveness of seven schools in one county were obtained from a panel of expert judges. The county superintendent and his staff were asked to rate the effectiveness of the schools based on overall performance in terms of productivity, adaptability, flexibility, and efficiency. These educators all had first-hand knowledge of the operations of the schools, but none was directly involved in the administration of any of the schools.

EMPIRICAL ANALYSIS

The analytic phase of this exploration was guided by two questions: (1) what are the relationships among the operational criteria of the model, and (2) to what extent is each criterion related to the appraisal of effectiveness by experts and to Mott's overall index of effectiveness. The measures of the effectiveness criteria were expected to be moderately and positively correlated with each other. Moreover, substantial correlations were anticipated between scores on each effectiveness criterion and each independent measure of effectiveness; the extent to which the criterion measures correlated with the independent measures of effectiveness was viewed as providing some indication of the validity of the model.

Operational Criteria

The operational criteria for the four operative goals seem to correlate and vary together reasonably well from the correlations between measures reported in Table 12.2. The coefficient between mathematics achievement and verbal achievement is very strong (r = .97), while the relationship between innovativeness as described by teachers and administrators is only a modest .29. The high correlation between mathematics achievement and verbal achievement for the 26 schools is to be expected, since the schools having high math scores tend to be the same schools that have high verbal scores. Although organizational commitment was strongly related to innovation as perceived by teachers (r = .71) and cohesiveness (r = .72), it was not strongly related to either innovation as perceived by administrators (r = .14) or the achievement measures (r = 14, .10). None of the measures, however, correlated perfectly, and there were no extreme differences in magnitude and sign in the set of correlations.

Each of the criterion measures was related to an independent assessment of organizational effectiveness by the experts for seven schools; in fact, except for the administrators' description of innovativeness, all the indicators were strongly related with the experts' ratings of effectiveness. The results lend some support to the validity of the operational criteria (see Table 12.2).

The final analysis performed, with Mott's subjective index of effectiveness as adapted for use in schools, involved a comparison with each indicator of effectiveness and the effectiveness ratings of the experts. It is demonstrated in Table 12.2 that the subjective index, developed by Mott and adapted by Miskel, has substantial correlations with all of the measures of effectiveness, including a .75 correlation with the expert measure, thus indicating validity of the model explored.

TABLE 12.2

Correlations Among Effectiveness Indicators (with the *school* as the unit of analysis)

	Innovation Administrators (IA)	Innovation Teachers (IT)	Mathematics Achievement (MA)	Reading Achievement (RA)	Cohesiveness Teachers (CT)	Organizational Commitment Teachers (OCT)	Rating by Experts (RE)
IT	.29 (n = 39)*						
MA	.41 (n = 25)*	.29 (n = 26)					
RA	.38 (n = 25)*	.21 (n = 26)	.97 (n = 26)				
CT	.34 (n = 39)*	.74 (n = 40)	.44 (n = 26)	.40 (n = 26)			
OCT	.14 (n = 39)*	.71 (n = 40)	.14 (n = 26)	.10 (n = 26)	.72 (n = 40)		
RE	.26 (n = 7)	.83 (n = 7)	.91 (n = 5)**	.91 (n = 5)**	.75 (n = 7)	.60 (n = 7)	
Mott	.25 (n = 25)*	.71 (n = 40)	.56 (n = 26)	.50 (n = 26)	.74 (n = 40)	.55 (n = 40)	.75 (n = 7)

*Administrators in one school did not respond.

**Two of the schools in the county could not supply achievement data.

Means and Standard Deviations of Indicators:

	X	SD
IA	57.93	7.64
IT	53.44	5.29
MA	58.12	7.44
RA	56.56	8.42

	X	SD
CT	26.09	3.19
OCT	73.04	8.79
RE	4.00	2.16
Mott	28.26	2.38

SUMMARY AND DISCUSSION

Organizational effectiveness is a multidimensional construct. The proposed model of school effectiveness has four general dimensions based on Parsons' system imperatives for growth and survival. These facets of effectiveness are concerned with both means and ends; hence, they provide a framework for analysis directed toward both goals and system requirements. In addition, a set of empirical indicators was specified that included multiple constituencies (students, teachers, and administrators).

The empirical analysis of the model as operationalized in this exploration was reasonably successful. Scores on the measures varied and the operational criteria of the dimensions of effectiveness varied together. Each criterion of effectiveness was also related to an independent standard of effectiveness—the appraisal of effectiveness by an outside panel of experts as well as a subjective index of effectiveness. Moreover, the relationship between the experts' independent judgments and Mott's subjective measure of effectiveness was strong ($r = .75$). The fact that the Mott index was so strongly related to the other measures of effectiveness raises the question as to whether this short, subjective index of effectiveness might be a reasonable index of school effectiveness in subsequent research.

The components of the Mott index are similar to the dimensions of effectiveness in the proposed model. The index is consistent with a multidimensional definition of effectiveness that includes organizational productivity as well as the organization's ability to adapt to both internal and external changes and the absence of strain and conflict within the organization. Accordingly, effective schools should produce higher student achievement, demonstrate more efficient use of resources, adapt better to internal and external constraints, and produce greater satisfaction with school. Mott's perspective fits the proposed synthesis and his index seems to be a useful subjective measure of school effectiveness for both researchers and practitioners. Its advantages are obvious. The index is short, simple, easy, and inexpensive to use.

The exploration of the model of effectiveness developed in this article has been a partial one. The present analysis focused on only six indicators of effectiveness. Other measures of adaptation, goal attainment, integration, and latency should be used in subsequent research. For example, goal attainment was determined by using only the cognitive measures of mathematics and reading achievement; affective student outcomes such as social and emotional development and the self-concepts of students are candidates for inclusion in the model. Similarly, integration and latency were measured using only teachers as respondents; student respondents in these same areas are desirable. Moreover, four of the six indicators were perceptual measures (e.g., administrator and teacher perceptions) rather than more objective indices of the dimensions. More so-called hard criterion measures such as achievement tests and turnover or absenteeism rates need to be included in future evaluations. Finally, the time perspective employed in this evaluation was basically a short-term one; intermediate and long-term time perspectives should also be evaluated in the future.

Notwithstanding the preceding limitations, this exploration of effectiveness has been an important first stop in developing and refining a comprehensive framework for assessing organizational effectiveness in schools. Although Hoy and Miskel proposed such a model a number of years ago, empirical investigations of effectiveness have lagged; there has been no comprehensive test of that model.[36] The model advanced here incorporates the notions that school organizations are natural, open, *and* rational systems.[37] Schools as social systems are concerned with their viability, constrained by their environments, and directed by their instructional goals. Such a framework stresses outcomes and processes—that is, it is concerned with both ends and means.

As subsequent research efforts are directed toward refining and elaborating the model, and as a standard set of operational indicators emerges for the four dimensions, researchers will be able to pursue a programmatic line of inquiry on organizational effectiveness. The current disarray in the effectiveness research should yield to more systematic and cumulative efforts. With refinement comes a multitude of opportunities. Comparative analyses of organizational effectiveness of schools would become feasible. For example, studies designed to examine such determinants of effectiveness as structure, technology, environment, culture, decision making, and leadership would be possible. Although it is presumptuous to suggest that the proposed model will bring order to the chaotic character of research on effectiveness, the framework is a modest first step toward providing theoretical direction for those interested in studying the organizational effectiveness of schools.

NOTES

1. P. S. Goodman and M. Pennings, eds., *New Perspectives on Organizational Effectiveness* (San Francisco: Jossey-Bass, 1977).

2. *Ibid.*, p. 4.

3. J. S. Coleman et al., *Equality of Educational Opportunity* (Washington, DC: U.S. Government Printing Office, 1966).

4. M. M. Rutter et al., *Fifteen Thousand Hours: Secondary Schools and Their Effects on Children* (Cambridge, MA: Harvard University Press, 1979).

5. W. Brookover et al., *School Social Systems and Student Achievement: Schools Can Make a Difference* (New York: Praeger, 1979).

6. R. Edmonds, "Effective Schools for the Urban Poor," *Educational Leadership* 37 (1979): 15-24.

7. R. H. Moos, *Evaluating Educational Environments* (San Francisco: Jossey-Bass, 1979).

8. G. F. Madaus, P. W. Airasian, and T. Kellaghan, *School Effectiveness* (New York: McGraw-Hill, 1980).

9. For example, see E. J. Pedhazur, *Multiple Regression in Behavioral Research: Explanation and Prediction* (New York: Holt, Rinehart and Winston, 1982), pp. 189-199; P. Cuttance, "Reflections on the Rutter Ethos: The Professional Researcher's Response to 'Fifteen Thousand Hours: Secondary Schools and Their Effects on Children,'" *Urban Education* (1982): 483-491; and G. F. Madaus et al., "The Sensitivity of Measures of School Effectiveness," *Harvard Educational Review* 49 (1972): 207-230.

10. For an early, classic attempt at the same task in the industrial sector, see B. S. Georgopoulos and A. S. Tannenbaum, "A Study of Organizational Effectiveness," *American Sociological Review* 22 (1957): 534-540.

11. J. P. Campbell, "On the Nature of Organizational Effectiveness," in Goodman and Pennings, *New Perspectives,* pp. 13-55.

12. *Ibid.,* pp. 19-20. See also, W. K. Hoy and C. G. Miskel, *Educational Administration: Theory, Research and Practice* (New York: Random House, 1982), pp. 319-352.

13. For a more extensive treatment, see Hoy and Miskel, *Educational Administration.*

14. R. M. Steers, *Organizational Effectiveness: A Behavioral View* (Santa Monica, CA: Goodyear, 1977), pp. 23-25.

15. Although others have referred to this perspective as the system resource model, the authors prefer the more generic label of systems model.

16. Campbell, "On the Nature," p. 20.

17. R. H. Hall, *Organizations: Structure and Process* (Englewood Cliffs, N.J.: Prentice-Hall, 1972), p. 100.

18. Steers, *Organizational Effectiveness,* p. 48.

19. For an elaboration of this synthesis, see Hoy and Miskel, *Educational Administration,* pp. 324-341.

20. T. Connolly, J. Conlon, and J. Deutsch, "Organizational Effectiveness: A Multiple-Constituency Approach," *Academy of Management Review* 5 (1980): 212.

21. Goodman and Pennings, *New Perspectives,* p. 5.

22. Georgopoulos and Tannenbaum, "A Study," pp. 536-37.

23. T. Parsons, *Structure and Process in Modern Societies* (New York: Free Press, 1960), pp. 16-19; and T. Parsons, R. F. Bales, and E. A. Shils, *Working Papers in the Theory of Action* (New York: Free Press, 1953), pp. 183-186.

24. Initially the researchers attempted to include several other student indicators of effectiveness, such as student esprit, motivation, and commitment to school; but reliability and validity of the measures were not satisfactory and they were eliminated.

25. G. L. Immegart and F. J. Pilecki, *An Introduction to Systems for the Educational Administrator* (Reading, MA: Addison-Wesley, 1973), pp. 99-141. See

also, G. L. Immegart, "Systems Theory and Taxonomic Inquiry into Organizational Behavior in Education," in *Developing Taxonomies of Organizational Behavior in Educational Administration,* D. E. Griffiths, ed. (Chicago: Rand McNally, 1969).

26. P. Mott, *The Character of Effective Organization* (New York: Harper and Row, 1972), p. 17.

27. B. A. Manning, *The Trouble Shooting Checklist (TSC) for School-Based Settings* (Austin: University of Texas, Research and Development Center, 1976).

28. California Achievement Tests, Forms C and D, *Technical Bulletin* (Monterey, CA: CTB/McGraw-Hill, 1979).

29. A. Halpin and D. Croft, *The Organizational Climate of Schools* (U.S.O.E. Research Project, SAE 543-8639, 1962).

30. J. H. M. Andrews, "School Organizational Climate: Some Validity Studies," *Canadian Education and Research Digest* 5 (1965): 333.

31. Halpin and Croft, *Organizational Climate.*

32. R. T. Mowday, R. M. Steers, and L. W. Porter, "The Management of Organizational Commitment," *Journal of Vocational Behavior* 14 (1979): 224-247.

33. *Ibid.*

34. Mott, *The Character;* and C. Miskel, D. McDonald, and S. Bloom, "Structural and Expectancy Linkages within Schools and Organizational Effectiveness," *Educational Administration Quarterly* 19 (1983): 49-82.

35. R. Fevurly, C. Miskel, and J. Stewart, "Organizational Structure and Processes, Perceived School Effectiveness, Loyalty, and Job Satisfaction," *Educational Administration Quarterly* 15 (1979): 97-118.

36. Hoy and Miskel, *Educational Administration,* pp. 319-352.

37. For an excellent review of natural, open, and rational systems, see W. R. Scott, *Organizations: Rational, Natural, and Open Systems* (Englewood Cliffs, NJ: Prentice-Hall, 1981).

CHAPTER THIRTEEN

Using Bureaucratic and Cultural Linkages to Improve Instruction: The Principal's Contribution

WILLIAM A. FIRESTONE and BRUCE L. WILSON

Principals can influence instruction by working through the linkages that govern teacher behavior. What these linkages are, how they affect instruction, and the impact of the principal on them are the focus of this article. Two kinds of linkages are distinguished: bureaucratic and cultural. Past research has attended extensively to bureaucratic linkages without analyzing cultural linkages. It is argued that the principals have access to weak linkages of both kinds. The task for the principal is to consistently employ the full range of linkages through a multitude of major and minor actions to generate a common purpose and effect in the school.

How do principals influence the instructional work of their schools? Remarkably little attention has been given to this topic.[2] Generally, studies of administrators examine their attitudes and traits with little attention to showing how those factors, or others, influence the outcomes of schooling.[3] A long tradition of organizational research suggests that schools are loosely linked organizations that provide limited means for principals to influence teachers' work.[4] However, recent research on effective schools suggests that in some cases the principal can make an important contribution to instruction.[5]

The contradictions between these two bodies of research are resolvable by attending to a broader array of linkage mechanisms in schools. Linkages are those mechanisms in schools that serve to coordinate the activity of people who work there.[6] It is argued in this article that principals can identify linkages to or among teachers that are tight or can be tightened and can use them to influence instruction. While agreeing that schools are loosely linked organizations, it is suggested that principals have a wider range of linkage mechanisms available to them than has been recognized in the past. These include not only the more

SOURCE: William A. Firestone and Bruce L. Wilson, "Using Bureaucratic and Cultural Linkages to Improve Instruction: The Principal's Contribution," *Educational Administration Quarterly*, Vol. 21, No. 2, pp. 7-30. Copyright © by The University Council for Educational Administration. Reprinted with permission.

commonly recognized bureaucratic linkages, but also a set of cultural linkages.

The concept of linkage in schools is first described in this article. Then it is argued that previous studies have attended too much to bureaucratic linkages and too little to cultural ones. Next, how bureaucratic and cultural linkages work and how they can be manipulated by principals are discussed. Bureaucratic linkages have their effects by creating or limiting opportunities for certain kinds of action; as such, they can be modified through formal decisions. Cultural linkages affect the way teachers (and students) think about their work. Such linkages are changed by the principal's symbolic activity. Sometimes the same principal activity can have implications for both bureaucratic and cultural linkages. In the third section of the article, the problems of using linkages to change instruction are assessed and it is suggested that the challenge is to coordinate many small actions as much as it is to make a few dramatic ones. Implications for research are drawn in the concluding section.

SCHOOL LINKAGES

Weick[7] provides the most complete discussion of the concept of linkage or coupling, and he offers a range of definitions of coupling or linkage. Generally, these have to do with the coordination of individuals in organizations.[8] In the simplest form, linkages are tight when the activity of person A leads to some kind of activity by person B. Here linkage has a connotation of responsiveness. Such linkages come as a result of communication, persuasion, the use of sanctions, or simply the passing of a part down an assembly line. They are short term and direct. In other situations, linkage may have the connotation of predictability. That is, person A has considerable assurance that person B will behave in a certain way. Schedules, rules, norms, values, and goals all promote this kind of linkage. In these cases, the time between the action and the linked response may be longer and the connection may be less direct, but the shaping of response can last for a longer time.

There is general consensus that, in comparison to other organizations, schools are loosely linked. Although there is some ambiguity about what the full range of relevant linkage mechanisms might be, most commentators have focused on the lack of strong bureaucratic ties, especially through the weak formal hierarchy in schools.[9] For instance, Meyer and Rowan[10] described how schools are designed so the instructional enterprise is decoupled from the formal structure. Bidwell[11] spoke of the structural looseness of schools, meaning that teachers not only work in isolated classrooms hidden from superiors, but also from colleagues. They are "behind the classroom door," as Goodlad and Klein have put it.[12] Lortie[13] provided an insightful analysis of how such a design creates a zoning of control that gives teachers control over day-to-day, in-class instructional decisions and principals control over long-term decisions affecting resource allocation and related matters.[14]

Bureaucratic and Cultural Linkages

The challenge offered by Weick[15] in his discussion of loose coupling was to identify the range of linkage mechanisms that integrate and coordinate activity in organizations. That requires moving beyond just a focus on bureaucratic linkages to include cultural ones as well. The differences between these linkages are outlined in this section.

Bureaucratic linkages are the formal, enduring arrangements that allow an organization to operate. These include the roles, rules, procedures, and authority relations that Ranson, Hinings, and Greenwood refer to as the "prescribed framework" of the organization.[16] These linkages control the behavior of organizational members. Attention to the prescribed framework alone, however, offers a limited, static view of the organization that ignores a great deal of the activity in organizations that shapes how individuals in the organization interact. The prescribed framework must be periodically renegotiated.[17] It is frequently violated, sometimes for the organization's own good,[18] and it is intentionally recreated on occasion through reorganizations that cannot be understood simply with reference to that framework alone.[19]

Behavior in an organization is also patterned by its culture. Culture refers to the subjective side of the organization.[20] More specifically, a culture is the system of publicly accepted meanings for the activities of a group of people.[21] Analysis of organizational culture focuses on three areas: its content, which refers to the meanings that are shared; the means of denoting the culture through symbols, stories, and rituals; and the influence of the principal on communication networks that allow for the negotiation of shared characteristics that are most appropriately viewed as bureaucratic linkages. There has been a recent growth in interest in the cultural side of organizations in organizational studies.[22] Culture can be an important linkage mechanism. Deal and Kennedy[23] speak of it as the glue that holds organizations together, but other commentators note that organizational subcultures can create problems for internal coordination.[24]

Because cultures often arise naturally in organizations, they may not be considered as one of the linkage mechanisms at the disposal of managers such as principals. However, one view of the manager's leadership responsibility is that his or her main task is to create coherence between the organization's basic purposes and its culture.[25] Strong cultures with appropriate content can promote school effectiveness, and principals can contribute to such cultures.

There have been a few studies of the cultures of schools, but these have attended more to the subcultures of students than those of staff.[26] In any case, at least two school characteristics make it difficult to create strong professional subcultures in these organizations. First, schools have basic purposes that are ambiguous and poorly specified. They also suffer from an overload of purposes that are difficult to prioritize.[27] As a result, it is difficult to develop a culture with strong beliefs about what should be accomplished in schools. Second, teachers are isolated, not only from administrators, but also from each other. They get most of their work satisfaction from students rather than peers.[28] For that reason, it may be difficult for teachers to develop a strong, binding culture. These observations suggest that cultural linkages, like bureaucratic ones, will be weak in schools. However, they do not reveal how much a school's culture can be influenced by the principal.

LINKAGES, INSTRUCTION, AND THE PRINCIPAL

The relationships between linkages and instruction work in a variety of ways. Generally, bureaucratic linkages establish constraints on and opportunities for how teachers teach. Cultural linkages shape what teachers want to do or how they take advantage of those constraints. Both make direct effects on what students learn. The following sections examine how each kind of linkage relates to instruction and how each can be manipulated. Principals face a further difficulty because the same action can affect bureaucratic and cultural linkages differently. The third section illustrates this point.

Bureaucratic Linkages

Daft identifies five bureaucratic linkage mechanisms; hierarchical referral and supervision, rules and procedures, plans and schedules, adding positions, and vertical information systems.[29] Principals are commonly thought to impact instruction primarily through supervision and evaluation. Supervision is attractive because it seems so direct: one person helps or directs another person to do something. There is, as a result, a strong belief that principals ought to supervise assertively. The effective schools literature contributes to this belief,[30] and a variety of professional associations, state education agencies, and other groups are now developing ways to tighten the supervisory linkage.

Yet, past experience suggests that while supervision can be improved, it is not likely to become *the* master linkage through which principals make massive modification in teachers' classroom or instructional behavior.[31] For supervision to be effective, it has to be employed frequently.[32] The old adage "more is better" applies here. However, there is ample evidence indicating that supervision is *not* a frequent activity in schools.[33] Traditionally, there have been few incentives for principals to supervise seriously. Except in a few school systems that have operated on a merit-pay system for many years,[34] there are few rewards—or punishments—for principals to make supervision a top priority.

Although most of the literature on educational administration pays homage to the importance of supervision, most principals have had little experience in working with constructive supervision programs. This problem is even more acute in secondary schools where content specialization means that principals may not have the expertise to evaluate adequately performance in some areas and where their authority to do so is often questioned. As Natriello and Dornbusch further point out,[35] for supervision to be effective, recommendations in an evaluation must be followed up. Just pointing out weaknesses creates insecurity and resentment. Time must be committed to follow-up activities in order to help teachers overcome weaknesses.

If the effectiveness of supervision has been overrated, there is an equal tendency to underrate another linkage mechanism: plans and schedules. These devices shape behavior indirectly in ways that affect how teachers carry out their work and interact with others as well as their attitudes towards their work.[36] Four planning devices deserve special attention as means to shape instruction:

(1) *Schedules*—Daily, weekly, and annual schedules have a substantial impact on the time available for instruction, a potent variable affecting student learning. The flexibility in scheduling for inservice and staff development time, as well as the way available time is used, affect teachers' ability to upgrade their skills and their attitudes toward their work.[37]

(2) *Allocation of students to classrooms*—The number of students a teacher is responsible for and the range of their abilities shape the instructional strategies used. Recent analysis suggests that both factors influence student achievement.[38]

(3) *Budgets*—At issue here are the small discretionary funds that most principals control. Their judicious distribution can greatly enhance innovative instructional activities and create additional learning oppor-

tunities. The way these funds are distributed can also have a disproportionate influence on teachers' attitudes towards their work.

(4) *Curriculum*—Students will experience success and learn more
when they are taught lessons that match their previous learning. Ar-
ticulation of curriculum across grade levels makes optimum use of
instructional time and facilitates the match to student knowledge. Finally, alignment of curriculum and testing programs ensures that tests
accurately reflect what students learn.[39]

Less attention may be given to the principal's contribution in these areas
because control is often shared with the district administrators and
supervisors. Nevertheless, an integrated approach that attends to both
supervisory and planning mechanisms is likely to have a greater impact
on instruction than any effort that attends to only one of those areas.

Cultural Linkages

Although bureaucratic linkages serve to coordinate action through the
"organization's prescribed framework" by shaping opportunities to act in
certain ways, cultural linkages work directly on people's consciousness
to influence how they think about what they do. Cultural linkages affect
at least two aspects of thought. The first is the individual's definitions of
the task. The school's organizational culture provides answers to such
questions as: What does it mean to teach? What should be accomplished
by teaching? What techniques or approaches are available? What are the
children like who are being taught? and so forth. The second aspect of
thought is the individual's commitment to the task. Commitment refers
to the individual's willingness to devote energy and loyalty to the organization and the attachment of that person to the organization. It
includes a willingness to keep working in the school (continuance commitment), emotional bonds to the school (cohesion commitment), and a
willingness to follow the rules and norms governing behavior (control
commitment).[40]

Specification of task definitions is important because in education, as
in many people-processing fields, there are few clear answers to the
questions of what is to be done or how it should be accomplished.[41]
Moreover, teachers' expectations for students have direct effects on what
they learn.[42] Commitment is an issue because education is a low-commit-
ment occupation, where people often have strong conflicting attachments
to family or other jobs.[43] Often, the improvement of instruction requires
more effort as well as a different kind.

A focus on cultural linkages raises three questions. First, what is the
content of the culture that promotes successful instruction? What kinds

of task definitions and commitments are desirable? Second, how is that culture denoted? What forms, symbols, or stories carry the desired content? Third, how and to what extent can the principal influence the school's culture?

Cultural content. One can derive the appropriate culture for successful instruction from a number of sources. One is to look at the culture of successful institutions. There have been few if any attempts to study effective schools from this perspective, but studies in other organizations may also provide some suggestions about what might be found. For instance, Berman and McLaughlin found that especially innovative school districts had cultures with the following characteristics:[44]

- an emphasis on diversity in services delivered.
- the primacy of improved educational service over "bureaucratic or political" concerns,
- open boundaries to the environment which allowed for learning about new approaches and new resources, and
- norms of mutual trust and encouragement for risk taking.

Studies of large corporations also indicate that a strong culture separates the high performers from the low in any market sector.[45] Peters and Waterman concluded that the content of those cultures includes the following:[46]

- a bias for action by trying things rather than elaborate planning,
- norms encouraging the employee to stay close to customers and try out new ideas on them,
- a respect for individual autonomy and enterpreneurship combined with a belief that productivity comes through people,
- strong definitions of what the company stands for and the kinds of products in which it deals, and
- a commitment to developing high-quality products.

There is a significant amount of overlap between the kinds of cultures identified by Peters and Waterman and by Berman and McLaughlin. Both emphasize a commitment to quality service, a willingness to take risks, a setting where individuals can experiment and take initiative, and close ties to the outside world that is a source of ideas as well as political and financial support. A study of excellent schools is likely to find that similar values are stressed.

The study of successful institutions in other spheres helps address the problem of commitment and that part of the task definition issue related to how people should relate to each other. It does not address the more central question of task definition, however, which is how should the craft of effective teaching be defined? Advances in this area can be made by synthesizing the existing research on teaching and deriving from it some themes that one might hope to find in the professional culture of schools.[47]

Cultural denotation. The study of cultures frequently separates the contents of a culture from its expressions. The latter refer to the ways those contents are communicated to members of the organization. Typically, the major themes in a culture are expressed redundantly through a variety of symbol systems.[48] In fact, the repetitions of a theme is what convinces the analyst of its importance. The analysis of symbols is complex because effective symbols are inherently ambiguous. The power of symbols comes from the way in which they combine particularistic elements of the specific situation with more universalistic issues or concerns of humankind. Moreover, the relationship among these particularistic and universalistic elements may shift with the situation, and the most powerful symbols may combine a number of such elements.[49]

Three symbol systems communicate the contents of an organization's culture: stories, icons, and rituals. Stories include myths and legends as well as true events. The true event takes on much of its meaning as it is interpreted in the telling. Usually stories are about individuals and are interpreted to indicate positively or negatively valued traits or the likely consequences of certain sorts of action.[50] Deal and Kennedy emphasize that stories are often about heroes, but who a hero is may vary.[51] Sometimes it is a now mythical figure like the founder of a company (Thomas Watson of IBM) or the person who gives a school a new mission (Arthur Morgan of Antioch College). At other times it is a representative of "the common worker," like the assembly line worker who made the company president put on safety glasses while touring his or her area. Stories have been collected in both business and higher education settings, but not to the same extent in schools. It would be useful to find out what stories exist among school staffs (and students), and what they are about.

Icons and rituals also communicate culture. Icons are the physical manifestations (logos, mottoes, and trophies) while rituals are ceremonial activities. Barley has shown how the culture of undertakers can be constructed from an examination of the symbolic value of such artifacts and activities as the decor of funeral parlors, the way the face of the corpse is arranged, and even the way removals from the home are handled.[52] A great deal can be learned about schools through similar analyses of assemblies, teachers' meetings, community functions, report cards, awards and trophies, lesson plans, and the furnishing of classrooms and work spaces among other things.

In addition to symbol systems, the study of cultures must examine communications patterns. Stories and symbols carry their meaning through an ongoing flow of communications among organizational members. The amount of internal communications probably varies among different types of organizations. Although opportunities to share are limited in education, it is still useful to look at variation in communications among schools or to explore the way that networks work. In business, Deal and Kennedy have identified special roles that facilitate internal communications, including priests, whisperers, gossips, and secretarial sources among others.[53] Similar specialized roles may serve important functions that are as yet undiscovered.

Culture and the principal. The third question about cultural linkages is how can they be influenced by the principal? The new management literature on organizational cultures is rather optimistic about the ability of managers to shape cultures.[54] However, earlier studies took a natural systems perspective that assumed that an organization's culture developed incrementally and largely outside of anyone's conscious control.[55] Until there have been more studies of the professional cultures of schools, judgment must be withheld about how susceptible they are to administrative influence. Nonetheless, it is useful to suggest a number of hypotheses about how principals could influence the cultures of their schools that reflect the different ways that organizational cultures are denoted symbolically and communicated interpersonally.

First, principals can manage the flow of stories and other information in their schools. Metz describes a principal who actively shaped the culture of his school in the mid-1960s by controlling the circulation of stories.[56] During a time when many people defined the frequent disruptive events in all schools in the district as part of a collective action that reflected injustice in the larger society, this principal tried to maintain a definition that discipline problems were rare individual outbursts that teachers could handle with patience and skill. He frequently told stories such as the following that reinforced his own view:

> I saw this done beautifully in a classroom with the kids. "I ain't going to study today, 'cause I don't feel like it." And the teacher just grinned at him. And she said "Well, I'm going to give you a book just in case you change your mind." In five minutes he was studying.[57]

Spreading stories is a positive approach to shaping a school's culture. In addition, this principal actively suppressed viewpoints different from the one he projected. For instance, he limited discussion at faculty meetings and was able to minimize knowledge of black students' collective walkout of an after-school dance. In other instances, a principal may influence the spread of stories by adjusting schedules and physical spaces in ways that facilitate or inhibit communications among teachers. Thus, the principal may be in a position to both initiate and reduce the spread of certain stories.

Second, the principal can create and manipulate symbols and rituals. These might include academic pep assemblies or symbolic rewards for especially effective teachers. In some cases, the principal may actually become a symbol as happened in an all-black school in Atlanta. This ghetto school was considered one of the worst in the system until the new principal turned things around. Through his own deportment, he came to symbolize a new assertive order that took education more seriously and required an orderly atmosphere for instruction:

> He dominated the school. Hogans [the principal] is a man of great energy. He moves about the campus in perpetual motion, looking severe and deter- mined, always carrying his walkie-talkie. Hogans does not want to be out of touch with any part of his sphere. . . . His requests sound like commands. There is an immediacy about him, and unwillingness to wait or be held back.[58]

Moreover, by being a black person who had come up from the ghetto by getting an education, he became a symbol to his own students of what was possible with hard work.

Third, the principal can be an active communicator of the culture. Principals typically communicate a great deal with their staffs. Recent time-and-motion studies of principals indicate that they spend a phe- nomenal amount of time in unscheduled, impromptu conversations with teachers and students.[59] The sheer frequency of interaction suggests that principals practice what Peters and Waterman admiringly called "man- agement by wandering around."[60] Yet, these studies tell us very little about what is discussed. More research like Gronn's is needed that examines the content and sequence of the frequent, disconnected conver- sations of principals to see how they are used to influence events and accomplish administrative work.[61] Existing research leads to the con- clusion that for the principal to shape a school's culture, considerable consistency must be maintained across hundreds of interactions. Metz summarized the work of the principal she observed as follows:

> Mr. Brandt's style of running the school . . . made it hard to define. It resembled an impressionist painting. Seen from up close, where the faculty and students were, his style had a soft, diffuse, blurred appearance. But seen from the distance perspective of comparison with [another school] it was sharp, clear, and vivid. Like an impressionist painting, too, it was made up of a myriad of little touches, each seemingly meaningless, but taken together forming a sharp image.[62]

She describes how the principal paid lip service to almost every educational philosophy imaginable while constantly returning to his own preferred solution to the problem of order. This principal had the effect he desired by constantly coming back to his main theme without crystallizing opposition to it.

Finally, principals must have high energy levels and considerable self-consciousness to influence the cultures of their schools. Principals generally spend long hours at their work.[63] Case studies of principals who seem to shape their schools' cultures lead to the suspicion that even more time, energy, and initiative may be required to do this. In fact, it may be that this work cannot be done by one person alone. The study of Hogans, the Atlanta principal, indicates that he is supported by a "kitchen cabinet" consisting of a vice-principal, a department head, and the school's registrar.[64] This same phenomenon has been seen in some more effective middle schools in Philadelphia.[65] Still, high energy and help are not enough. As Metz's case analysis indicates, the principal must be able to subtly work the major themes that are deemed important into interactions with others.

Simultaneous Effects of Principal Action

Although bureaucratic and culture linkages in a school are conceptually distinct, the actions of a principal may influence both simultaneously. This can work for the principal if effects on both linkages are complementary, but it will be counterproductive if those effects are contradictory. A few examples will illustrate this issue. Consider first the problem of ability grouping in the classroom. Grouping to minimize variation in ability allows classes with faster students to move more quickly through the curriculum and get to enrichment material or to address more complex topics while classes with less intelligent students proceed more slowly and cover material more intensively until the material is learned. Thus, from a pure management perspective, there seems to be some advantage to ability grouping.[66] However, grouping also labels students and creates differential expectations for what they will learn. Lowered teacher expectations (a part of the school culture) can seriously impair the education of less intelligent students.[67]

School discipline policy (which Daft would call linkage through rules) is another area that can have differential effects through bureaucratic and cultural linkages. Discipline policies that effectively maintain order will increase time for instruction. However, if this discipline is accompanied by what Metz calls an incorporative view of education that views the child as an empty vessel who must be taught a curriculum defined by adults and to follow rules established by adult authority, opportunities

for higher order cognitive thinking and more advanced social development will be limited.[68] Metz argues that, if discipline is grounded in a
more developmental view of education that views students as active
learners, more opportunities for advanced learning will occur. At the most
authoritarian extreme, excessive emphasis on discipline and order can
actually create a culture that impairs learning. In this case, the same
bureaucratic linkage can have very different impacts depending on what
cultural meaning is imposed on it.

Manipulation of bureaucratic linkages can as well reinforce cultural
content. Resource allocation is the best example of this possibility. Allocation of discretionary funds in a school in a manner that is fair and that
provides extensive support for instruction can promote commitment
among teachers and signal that instructional priorities are more important than is often the case. As these examples indicate, an important task
for both the researcher and the school administrator is to ensure that
bureaucratic and cultural linkages are mutually reinforcing.

THE PROBLEMS OF WORKING THROUGH LINKAGES

The principal can shape both the bureaucratic and the cultural linkages in a school. However, none of these linkages alone is a powerful
means for influencing instruction. The principal's contribution comes
through the orchestration of a variety of actions working through a range
of linkages to have a consistent impact on what is taught and how. Why
this is so becomes apparent when one considers the separate effects of a
principal's efforts to use each linkage mechanism as a means of improving
instruction.

The difficulty with employing bureaucratic linkages is that the principal's opportunities to exert influence are constrained. Limits to the
principal's authority reduce the utility of supervision as a strategy. There
are also two major constraints to the use of plans to shape teachers'
opportunities to teach. First, principals' options are severely constrained
by external policies. The major design decisions about the school program
have been in place since early in this century and are codified in state
law or board policy.[69] The principal may have some say at the margins of
the program over whether the school day has six periods or seven.[70]
However, more basic decisions about whether there will be a counseling
department, a sports program, or a social studies department are already
decided. Similarly, curriculum and grouping decisions are often constrained by district policies, disciplinary actions by court decisions, and
the distribution of discretionary resources by the fact that those resources
are quite small when compared with the overall budget of the school, most

of which is committed to personnel. Second, even when a decision is to be made, the principal rarely makes it alone. There is substantial agreement that the principal's role is highly interactive, requiring discussions with teachers, district office staff, and—in high schools—department heads.[71] The nature of this interaction is not so clear, however; some people stress the reactive nature of the principal's role[72] and others the proactive.[73] Still, major decisions are often delegated, made by committees, or guided by formulae in ways that limit the principal's discretion to shape teaching conditions.

What increases opportunities for the principal to shape the bureaucratic linkages governing teachers is the ambiguity surrounding both that role and the organization of the school.[74] The resulting policies need to be clarified and are sometimes contradictory. By interpreting policy, the principal gains authority to shape instruction.[75] For instance, one principal used a little known state law to buttress a decision on pledge of allegiance ceremonies when district policies were going against him. He even sought support from the local district attorney when his interpretation was challenged.[76]

The use of cultural linkages to shape instruction depends on another kind of ambiguity—that governing the principal-teacher relationship. McPherson points to the real ambivalence that teachers have for principals. It is as if they say: "Leave me alone. Don't interfere in my classroom. Don't tell me how to teach. Protect me from all who challenge me. Support my decisions. *And* show you care about and appreciate me."[77] Teachers look to their principals for certain kinds of support. They want to know that the principal will maintain an orderly climate in the school and back them when they have discipline problems. Too, they want protection from parents and community groups who challenge their decisions. Finally, they look to the principal for moral support, for a word of praise after spending almost all their working day with no adult contact. At the same time, they want autonomy to teach the way they want and often what they want.[78] Usually, they do not see that their wants may require some sort of trade-off; they want it all.

This ambiguity stems from three characteristics of teaching.[79] First, neither criteria for success nor means of achieving it are clear. Even when the results come out right, teachers find it hard to know if they can take credit. This ambiguity leads to the second problem: vulnerability. Teachers are sensitive to infringements on their authority and autonomy from both the public and students. Third, teaching is a lonely occupation with little chance to talk about one's work with others who can appreciate what one has done.

These conditions give teachers a great stake in viewing the principal as a powerful, wise individual whose praise is meaningful and protection is sure. The principal is in the right place to become a reference point and to establish norms because he or she is close, has relevant expertise, and is in a position of authority. As a result, teachers invest a good deal of affect in their view of the principal; the office is a symbolic one that can be used to manipulate the stories and rituals that interpret teachers' work. Nevertheless, when the principal cannot meet teachers' standards or when things go wrong that no one can control, there is a strong tendency to scapegoat and blame the principal.[80] This, too, is a cultural phenomenon, one that can victimize the principal rather than being used to advantage.

Although principals are well placed to affect the school's culture, it is not clear how well that culture can influence instruction. One observer of principals suggests that when a principal "turns around" a school, the change is usually in the student climate and the discipline situation, especially at the high school level.[81] In the study of the effective high school in Atlanta mentioned above, the observers noted that, while the climate of the school and motivation of students and staff had improved, instruction had not.[82] However, it is also clear that the principal did not place a high priority on trying to shape instructional practice. This lack of attention to instruction seems to be typical. In many schools principals seem overly ready to leave instruction to teachers and not to try to shape thinking about what should be taught and how. Thus, even though results have been less than impressive in the past, it seems likely that the potential for influence is there, but to date, it is largely unrealized.

In sum, the conclusion of this analysis is not that emphasis on any one kind of linkage will provide a magic wand to give the principal great influence over a school's instructional program. Rather, the principal has a number of weak means of control or coordination available. These are employed through countless interactions with teachers over the course of the school day and year. A few interactions result in strategic decisions affecting major time and resource allocations (bureaucratic linkages) or the school's culture, but most are quite minor. These interactions can become so numerous that the principal is more reactive than proactive. The principal's task and challenge is to develop a clear vision of the purposes of the school that gives primacy to instruction and to carry it through consistently during those countless interactions. By doing so, the principal uses bureaucratic linkages to create opportunities for teachers to follow that vision and minimizes chances to operate in different ways. At the same time, the principal uses cultural linkages to communicate that vision so that, to a greater or lesser extent, it becomes the teachers' own culture. The initiative for carrying out instructional work then rests with teachers, but they are much more likely to incorporate the principal's perspective. This approach to the job is similar to the task of leaders of many kinds of organizations.[83]

RESEARCH IMPLICATIONS

This discussion has provided details about the complex nature of schools, how loose the linkages are between teachers and administrators, and the difficulties a principal confronts in using linkages to improve instruction. However, the argument has been largely speculative and has raised issues that require additional research. First, it is important to clarify further the nature of linkages in schools. The research in this area has been uneven. Studies have been conducted on the distribution of authority and influence,[84] on supervision by principals[85] and on communication patterns.[86] Research has also been conducted on other bureaucratic linkages like the allocation of students, and still other linkages like scheduling practices and resource flows should be relatively straightforward to document. The most problematic tasks facing researchers are (1) to identify the nature of organizational cultures and (2) to develop means for comparing them in terms of content, means of denotation, and effectiveness as sources of social constraint or obligation on individual behavior. These tasks may require borrowing conceptualizations and techniques from disciplines or areas of inquiry not usually relied on in the study of schools.

The second issue arising from the discussion is that of clarifying the impact of school linkages on instruction. To address this issue, it will be necessary to identify the areas of instruction that vary among teachers and schools. There seem to be many teaching activities, such as lecturing and recitation, that occur quite uniformly across schools and time.[87] Other important attitudes and activities, like teacher expectations for student performance or their allocation of time in class, do vary among individual teachers and schools in ways that influence instruction.[88] These should be the focus of attention for future research. What has yet to be done is to identify whether tight linkages affect the distribution of these attitudes and activities.

Finally, it is important to explore how principals use linkages to change instructional practice. Too much research on principals has focused on how personal attitudes and traits affect behavior.[89] Little attention has been paid to the opportunities and constraints on principal behavior created by the organizational setting in which they work. Research in this area should identify the organizational linkages that are most susceptible to adjustments by the principal. For instance, it may be that certain norms of the professional culture are established by teachers and cannot be influenced by the principal. Yet, principals may be able to modify other linkages easily. It will also be important to learn more about how principals change these linkages. Modifying organizational culture is rarely a straightforward task. Changing schedules or allocations of students also requires negotiations with a variety of people. Finally, research should examine how the multiple weak linkages accumulate, either canceling out or reinforcing each other, and how principals can manipulate these linkages.

These issues have methodological as well as conceptual implications. A full understanding of school linkages, the impact of linkages on instruction, and the role of the principal in using linkages to change instructional practices requires a more intensive study of American schools. The research effort needs to move beyond the cross-sectional survey approach that has dominated research on school administration.[90] While there will be a place for such studies in the future, researchers now need to spend considerably more time in schools. A number of approaches—including observational, ethnographic, qualitative, or interpretative procedures—can be adopted as the means to focus attention on learning first-hand what is happening in schools. These approaches allow for ample exposure to school activities. Furthermore, research time should be devoted to learning more about linkages, instructional practices, and the impact of the principal on them. Three specific methodological implications need further elaboration.

First, there is the need for more thick description of what life is like in schools and how principals create or maintain some order and direction in that life. As Geertz points out, it may be fairly simple to describe the concrete actions that are present.[91] What is not as simple is identifying the meanings that are given to actions by the various participants. Those meanings help determine both the cultural and bureaucratic linkages in a school. A fuller understanding of the potential impact of the principal will be gained by intensively studying events and behaviors and trying to understand how principals, teachers, and students interpret them.

Second, linkage patterns and instructional practices in schools do not just happen; they evolve over time. Consequently, some studies should employ a historical perspective. Such a perspective allows one to follow the development of both linkages and instructional practices and to unravel the relationship between them. For example, there are a number of ways that cultural linkages can develop in schools.[92] The school may have been established "de novo" with a clear purpose in mind. The creation of magnet schools that focus on specific subject areas are an example of this. Cultural linkages may also evolve out of a crisis over a key event. A school may be floundering because of a lack of direction. A consequent collapse or common rallying point may be sufficient to focus and redirect the efforts of the school. Yet another alternative is that a strong leader takes charge and gradually tightens the cultural linkages in the school. In all three cases, a look at current conditions would show evidence of tight cultural linkages. However, without understanding the historical context, the detailed relationship between the cultural linkages and instructional practices would be missing. Research strategies need to emphasize the exploration of past events and patterns of leadership in order to determine their impact on present school conditions. Historical analysis to uncover the development of cultural linkages in schools has been almost entirely overlooked. Describing and interpreting past events will clarify current situations and facilitate analysis of the role that linkage mechanisms play.

Finally, research design must also be considered since design features influence what is studied and how long it is studied. Here one can learn a great deal from the shortcomings of the effective schools research. Those research designs have been faulted on a number of grounds,[93] but two criticisms are salient. The first is the vexing problem of causal ordering among variables. Do linkage mechanisms affect instruction or does instruction affect linkage patterns? Designs must be developed that disentangle that question. Intensive observation over long periods of time, something missing from much of the effective schools research, is one solution. Another way to address the causal ordering is through a historical understanding of the people and events leading to present conditions. As Rowan et al. suggest,[94] it would also be instructive to develop a design that focuses on schools in transition, i.e., those currently in the process of moving from loose to tight linkages. By following the changes in linkage patterns over time, one can clearly assess their effects on instruction and the impact of the principal.

An equally troubling design problem concerns generalization. Much of the effective schools research has focused on the characteristics of a narrow sample of unusually effective schools. The assumption has been made that those findings can be applied to other kinds of schools. Similarly, if tight linkages are associated with uniformity of instruction, can it also be argued that schools with loose linkages can change instruction solely by working on linkage mechanisms? There may be some other factors that are affecting instruction in these schools. The problem has a two part solution. First, it is necessary to understand what is important about tight linkages in schools. Are they associated with uniformity of instruction? This can best be done by learning from intensive observation in a small number of schools where tight linkages exist. Once the relationship has been established, it may well be useful to use a survey approach to test wider applicability of the findings to different types of schools. The effective schools research moved to prescription without considering the second step while the research proposed in this article has yet to fully address the first step.

CONCLUSION

Research on effective schools has promoted the view that schools can be organized to improve instruction and that principals have a key role to play. Still, that optimism must be tempered by the knowledge that schools are loosely linked organizations where the impact of principals on instruction is limited. The argument of this article has been that cultural and bureaucratic linkages independently and interactively influence the quality of instruction. Ways in which the principal can effect these linkage patterns have also been explored. An adequate understanding of the contribution of the principal to the quality of instruction rests in a careful analysis of cultural linkages and how they interact with bureaucratic ones.

NOTES

1. Appreciation is acknowledged for helpful comments offered by Dick Corbett, Tom Corcoran, Ken Duckworth, and Gretchen Rossman, as well as an anonymous reviewer. The preparation of this report was supported by funds from the Center for Educational Policy and Management (CEPM) at the University of Oregon, Eugene, Oregon, and the National Institute of Education (NIE), Department of Education. Additional support was provided by Research for Better Schools, Inc. (RBS). The opinions expressed do not necessarily reflect the position or policy of CEPM, RBS, or NIE, and no official endorsement should be inferred. Each author made an equal contribution to this article.

2. W. D. Greenfield, *Research on Public School Principals: A Review and Recommendations* (Paper prepared for the National Institute of Education, 1982).

3. E. M. Bridges, "Research on the School Administrator: The State of the Art, 1967-80," *Educational Administration Quarterly* 18, 3 (Summer 1982): 12-33.

4. C. E. Bidwell, "The School as a Formal Organization," in *Handbook of Organizations,* J. G. March, ed. (Skokie, IL: Rand-McNally, 1965); and K. E. Weick, "Educational Organizations as Loosely Coupled Systems," *Administrative Science Quarterly* 21 (1976): 1-19.

5. W. Brookover, C. Beady, P. Flood, J. Schweitzer, and J. Wisenbacker, *School Social Systems and Student Achievement: Schools Can Make A Difference* (New York: Praeger, 1979); and J. B. Wellisch, A. H. MacQueen, R. A. Carriere, and G. A. Duck, "School Management and Organization in Successful Schools (ESAA in-depth study schools)," *Sociology of Education* 51 (1978): 211-227.

6. R. L. Daft, *Organization Theory and Design* (St. Paul, MN: West Publishing, 1983).

7. Weick, "Educational Organizations."

8. S. Rosenblum and K. S. Louis, *Stability and Change* (New York: Plenum, 1981): 85-104.

9. M. B. Miles, "Mapping the Common Properties of Schools," in *Improving Schools: Using What We Know,* R. Lehming and M. Kane, eds. (Beverly Hills, CA: Sage, 1981).

10. J. W. Meyer and B. Rowan, "The Structure of Educational Organizations," in *Environments and Organizations: Theoretical and Empirical Perspective,* M. Meyer and Associates, eds. (San Francisco: Jossey Bass, 1978).

11. Bidwell, "The School as a Formal Organization."

12. J. I. Goodlad and M. F. Klein, *Behind the Classroom Door* (Worthington: C. A. Jones, 1970).

13. D. C. Lortie, "The Balance of Control and Autonomy in Elementary School Teaching," in *The Semiprofessions and Their Organization,* A. Etzioni, ed. (New York: Free Press, 1969).

14. Some of these "related matters" may actually be decided outside the school altogether as, for instance, when curriculum and textbook decisions are made in the district office. For a discussion of how principals cope with district influence, see V. Morris, R. L. Crowson, E. Hurwitz, and C. Porter-Gehrie, *The Urban Principal: Discretionary Decision-Making in a Large Educational Organization* (Chicago: College of Education, University of Illinois at Chicago Circle, 1981).

15. Weick, "Educational Organizations."

16. S. Ranson, B. Hinings, and R. Greenwood, "The Structuring of Organizational Structures," *Administrative Science Quarterly* 25, 1 (1980): 1-17.

17. A. Strauss, *Negotiations* (San Francisco: Jossey-Bass, 1979).

18. M. Dalton, *Men Who Manage* (New York: John Wiley, 1959).

19. Ranson, Hinings, and Greenwood, "The Structuring of Organizational Structures."

20. L. Smircich, "Concepts of Culture and Organizational Analysis," *Administrative Science Quarterly* 28, 1 (1983): 339-358.

21. Culture has been used in a number of ways in organizational studies. Smircich in "Concepts of Culture," distinguishes between uses of the concept as a variable and as a root metaphor. The first approach views the organization as a system and culture as simply a part of the organization or its environment. This approach is easiest to reconcile with existing organizational research. In the second approach, culture replaces system as the guiding metaphor, and organizations are viewed as expressive forms rather than in economic or material terms. This second approach has a number of variants reflecting different conceptions of culture in anthropology. While it is closer in some ways to the major traditions of the study of culture, the second approach is more difficult to incorporate with existing organizational research. By treating culture as an internal characteristic of the organization, this paper is more closely allied with the first approach. A more detailed explanation of this approach may be found in A. M. Pettigrew, "On Studies in Organizational Cultures," *Administrative Science Quarterly* 24, 4 (1979): 570-581.

22. Smircich, "Concepts of Culture."

23. T. E. Deal and A. Kennedy, *Corporate Cultures: The Rites and Rituals of Corporate Life* (Reading, MA: Addison-Wesley, 1982).

24. K. L. Gregory, "Native-View Paradigms: Multiple Cultures and Culture Conflicts in Organizations," *Administrative Science Quarterly* 28, 3 (1983): 359-376; P. Riley, "A Structurationist Account of Political Cultures," *Administrative Science Quarterly* 28, 3 (1983): 414-437.

25. P. Selznick, *Leadership in Administration* (New York: Harper & Row, 1957).

26. C. W. Gordon, *The Social System of the High School* (Glencoe, IL: Free Press, 1957); and P. A. Cusick, *Inside High-School* (New York: Holt, 1973). Two recent studies that help fill the void in work on professional cultures include S. L. Lightfoot, *The Good High School: Portraits of Character and Culture* (New York: Basic Books, 1983); and P. A. Cusick, *The Egalitarian Ideal and the American High School: Studies of Three Schools* (New York: Longman, 1983).

27. Miles, "Mapping the Common Properties of Schools."

28. D. Lortie, *Schoolteacher* (Chicago: University of Chicago Press, 1975).

29. Daft, *Organization Theory.*

30. Wellisch et al., "School Management."

31. R. G. Corwin, "Patterns of Organizational Control and Teacher Militancy: Theoretical Continuities in the Idea of 'Loose Coupling,'" in *Research in Sociology of Education and Socialization,* Vol. 2, A. C. Kerchoff and R. G. Corwin, eds. (Greenwich, CT: JAI Press, 1981).

32. S. M. Dornbusch and W. R. Scott, *Evaluation and the Exercise of Authority* (San Francisco: Jossey-Bass, 1975).

33. Morris et al., "The Urban Principal"; and N. A. Newberg and A. G. Glatthorn, *Instructional Leadership: Four Ethnographic Studies on Junior High School Principals* (Final report of grant number NIE G-81-0088, 1983).

34. G. Natriello and M. Cohn, *The Evolution of a Merit Pay System* (Unpublished manuscript, Washington University, 1983).

35. G. Natriello and S. Dornbusch, "Pitfalls in the Evaluation of Teachers by Principals," *Administrator's Notebook* 29, 6 (1980-81): 1-4.

36. For a discussion of indirect shaping of behavior, see S. T. Bossert, *Tasks and Social Relationships in Classrooms* (New York: Cambridge University Press, 1979).

37. D. E. Wiley and A. Harnischfeger, "Explosion of Myth: Quantity of Schooling and Exposure to Instruction, Major Educational Vehicles," *Educational Researcher* 3 (1974): 7-12; and H. D. Corbett, J. L. Dawson and W. A. Firestone, *School Context and School Change* (New York: Teachers College Press, 1984).

38. G. V. Glass and M. L. Smith, "Meta-Analysis of Research on Class Size and Achievement," *Educational Evaluation and Policy Analysis* 1 (1981): 2-16; N. N. Filby, L. Cohen, G. McCutchen, and D. Kyle, *What Happens in Smaller Classes* (San Francisco: Far West Laboratory, 1980); T. Beckerman and T. L. Good, "The Classroom Ratio of High- and Low-Aptitude Students and Its Effects on Achievement," *American Educational Research Journal* 18 (1981): 317-327; and Bossert, *Tasks and Social Relationships.*

39. B. S. Bloom, "The 2 Sigma Problem: The Search for Methods of Group Instruction as Effective as One-to-One Teaching," *Educational Leadership* 13, 6 (1984): 4-16; and W. W. Cooley and G. Leinhardt, "The Instructional Dimensions Study," *Educational Evaluation and Policy Analysis* 2 (1980): 7-25.

40. R. M. Kanter, "Commitment and Social Organizations: A Study of Commitment Mechanisms in Utopian Communities," *American Sociological Review* 33 (1968): 499-517.

41. C. Perrow, "Hospitals: Technology, Structure and Goals," in *Handbook of Organizations,* J. G. March, ed. (Chicago: Rand-McNally, 1965).

42. Brookover et al., "School Social Systems."

43. Lortie, *Schoolteacher;* and P. A. Cusick, "A Study of Networks among Professional Staffs of Secondary Schools," *Educational Administration Quarterly* 17, 3 (Summer 1981): 114-138.

44. P. E. Berman and M. W. McLaughlin, *An Exploratory Study of School District Adaptation* (Santa Monica, CA: Rand Corporation, 1979).

45. Deal and Kennedy, *Corporate Cultures.*

46. T. J. Peters and R. H. Waterman, *In Search of Excellence: Lessons from America's Best Run Companies* (New York: Harper & Row, 1982).

47. For one such synthesis, see D. A. Squires, W. G. Huitt, and J. K. Segars, *Effective Schools and Classrooms: A Research-Based Perspective* (Alexandria: ASCD, 1983).

48. S. R. Barley, "Semiotics and the Study of Occupational and Organizational Cultures," *Administrative Science Quarterly* 28, 3 (1983): 393-413.

49. A. Cohen, "Political Symbolism," *Annual Review of Anthropology* 8 (1979): 87-113.

50. J. Martin, M. S. Feldman, M. S. Hutch, and S. D. Sitkin, "The Uniqueness Paradox in Organization Stories," *Administrative Science Quarterly* 28, 3 (1983): 359-376.

51. Deal and Kennedy, *Corporate Cultures.*

52. Barley, "Semiotics."

53. Deal and Kennedy, *Corporate Cultures.*

54. Deal and Kennedy, *Corporate Cultures;* and Peters and Waterman, *In Search of Excellence.*

55. A. W. Gouldner, "Organizational Analysis," in *Sociology Today: Problems and Prospects,* R. K. Merton, L. Broom, and L. S. Cottrell, eds. (New York: Basic Books, 1959).

56. M. H. Metz, *Classrooms and Corridors: The Crisis of Authority in Desegregated Schools* (Berkeley: University of California Press, 1978).

57. *Ibid.,* pp. 195-196.

58. S. L. Lightfoot, "Portraits of Exemplary Secondary Schools: George Washington Carver Comprehensive High School," *Daedalus* 110, 4 (1981): 20.

59. W. J. Martin and D. J. Willower, "The Managerial Behavior of High School Principals," *Educational Administration Quarterly* 17, 1 (Winter 1981): 69-98; and J. T. Kmetz and D. J. Willower, "Elementary School Principals' Work Behavior," *Educational Administration Quarterly* 18, 4 (Fall 1982): 62-78.

60. Peters and Waterman, *In Search of Excellence.*

61. P. C. Gronn, "Talk as the Work: The Accomplishment of School Administration," *Administrative Science Quarterly* 23, 1 (1983): 1-21.

62. Metz, *Classrooms and Corridors,* p. 190.

63. H. F. Wolcott, *The Man in the Principal's Office: An Ethnography* (New York: Holt, Rinehart, Winston, 1973).

64. Lightfoot, "Portraits."

65. Newberg and Glatthorn, *Instructional Leadership.*

66. R. Calfee and R. Brown, "Grouping Students for Instruction," *Classroom Management: The Seventy-Eighth Yearbook of the National Society for the Study of Education,* Part II (Chicago: University of Chicago Press, 1979).

67. Brookover et al., *School Social Systems.*

68. Metz, *Classrooms and Corridors.*

69. D. K. Cohen and B. Neufeld, "The Failure of High Schools and the Progress of Education," *Daedalus* 110, 3 (1981): 69-90; and L. Cuban, "Persistent Instruction: The High School Classroom, 1900-1980," *Phi Delta Kappan* 64, 2 (1982): 113-118.

70. E. L. Boyer, *High School: A Report on Secondary Education in America* (New York: Harper & Row, 1983).

71. Greenfield, *Research on Public School Principals.*

72. Wolcott, *The Man in the Principal's Office.*

73. R. Edmonds, "Effective Schools for the Urban Poor," *Educational Leadership* 37, 1 (1979): 15-23.

74. Greenfield, *Research on Public School Principals.*

75. R. L. Crowson and C. Porter-Gehrie, "The Discretionary Behavior of Principals in Large City Schools," *Educational Administration Quarterly* 16, 1 (Winter 1980): 45-69.

76. Metz, *Classrooms and Corridors.*

77. G. H. McPherson, "What Principals Should Know About Teachers," in *The Principal in Metropolitan Schools*, D. A. Erickson and T. R. Relker, eds. (Berkeley, CA: McCutchan, 1979), p. 241.

78. Cusick, "A Study of Networks."

79. McPherson, "What Principals Should Know About Teachers."

80. *Ibid.*

81. G. L. McAndrew, "The High School Principal: Man in the Middle," *Daedalus* 110, 3 (1981): 105-118.

82. Lightfoot, "Portrait."

83. Selznick, *Leadership in Administration;* and Peters and Waterman, *In Search of Excellence.*

84. R. G. Corwin, *Militant Professionalism: A Study of Bureaucratic Conflict in High Schools* (New York: Appleton-Century Crofts, 1970); and Weick, "Educational Organizations."

85. Dornbusch and Scott, *Evaluation and the Exercise of Authority.*

86. Lortie, *Schoolteacher;* and J. W. Little, "Norms of Collegiality and Experimentation: Workplace Conditions of School Success," *American Educational Research Journal* 19 (1982): 325-340.

87. K. A. Sirotnik, "What You See is What You Get: Consistency, Persistency, and Mediocrity in the Classroom," *Harvard Education Review* 53, 1 (1983): 16-31; and Cuban, "Persistent Instruction."

88. Brookover et al., *School Social Systems.*

89. Bridges, "Research on the School Administrator."

90. *Ibid.*

91. C. Geertz, *The Interpretation of Cultures: Selected Essays* (New York: Basic Books, 1973).

92. B. R. Clark, *The Distinctive College: Antioch, Reed, and Swarthmore* (Chicago: Aldine, 1970).

93. R. Rowan, S. T. Bossert, and D. C. Dwyer, "Research on Effective Schools: A Cautionary Note," *Educational Researcher* 12, 4 (1983): 24-31; and J. H. Ralph and J. Fennessey, "Science or Reform: Some Questions About the Effective Schools Model," *Phi Delta Kappan* 64, 10 (1983): 689-694.

94. Rowan et al., "Research on Effective Schools."

CHAPTER FOURTEEN

An Analysis of the Metaphorical Perspectives of School Principals

PAUL V. BREDESON

In this study, the investigator sought to identify the metaphors for administration of school principals as evidenced in the current literature and to describe the images that currently exist in the statements, beliefs, values, and daily routines of five school principals. Three metaphors of purpose—maintenance, survival, and vision—that characterize the ethos of the principalship are explored. These metaphors appear to have significant implications for schools, for school administrators, and for administrator preparation programs.

Are there any differences in administrative behaviors and organizational priorities if a school principal views schooling and its attendant activities as well-oiled, efficient production lines, as nurtured organic systems, or as garbage cans with loosely coupled handles? This question was posed to the graduate students in introductory courses in educational administration. From the ensuing discussion of metaphors and creative imagery, the questions addressed in this article emerged.

Metaphors are useful linguistic structures that have helped theorists and practitioners generate ideas, concepts, models, and theories for describing, examining, and understanding phenomena in education. Whether metaphors are verbalized openly, expressed symbolically, or hidden in the organizational structures of school and administrative behavior patterns, these images reveal a great deal about how school principals interpret their organizational role, how they conceptualize schooling, and how they put their beliefs and values into practice. The investigator sought in this study to identify the metaphors of administration for principals as evidenced in current literature; to describe the images that currently exist in the statements, beliefs, values, and daily routines of five school principals; and to examine the implications of these metaphorical perspectives for the role of the school principal.

SOURCE: Paul V. Bredeson, "An Analysis of the Metaphorical Perspectives of School Principals," *Educational Administration Quarterly*, Vol. 21, No. 1, pp. 29-50. Copyright © by The University Council for Educational Administration. Reprinted with permission.

All languages have deeply embedded metaphorical structures that are reflective of and influential in the meaning of "reality."[1] However, as Embler has pointed out: "What is important is not the originality of the metaphors . . . but the relationship which these figures of speech bear to their times."[2] Metaphors then become vehicles of vernacular for expressing one's understanding of one's environment within a specific cultural, historic context. The utility and durability of the metaphor is its ability to draw attention to and assent for the "minutiae of correspondences, analogies, and contrastive 'opposites' on which our world depends. Like language itself, metaphor thus binds the culture together in a rough unity of experience."[3]

Rooted in sociohistoric contexts, metaphors are links between the "real" world and a scientific language that attempts to explain the perceived phenomenon. Although metaphors, like language itself, are attempts to provide a unity of experience and understanding for a field of study, practice—or even an entire culture, the very words and analogies used—may limit the view that one has of phenomena and the world. As Embler has stated: "More often than not, our thoughts do not select the words we use."[4] Rather, behavior often becomes a function of the words we use and, indeed, may even determine the thoughts we have.

Social systems theory suggests that one of the most important analytic units is that of *role*. Role within this framework is thought of as "structural or normative elements defining the behavior expected of role incumbents or actors, that is, their mutual inputs and obligations," within a particular social system.[5] Parsons and Shils have defined role as: "That organized sector of an actor's orientation which institutes and defines his participation in the interactive process. It involves a set of complementary expectations concerning his own activities and those of others with whom he interacts."[6] Blumberg and Greenfield have expanded this notion of role by stating that: "Principals daily face pressures of competing images about what their role should be."[7] The alternative images the principal holds are affected to varying degrees and are constrained by the various role expectations principals have within the school setting. Miklos has indicated that role definition should not be seen as a static condition but, rather, as a dynamic and creative process—with notions of change, situational accommodation, and endless variety—characterizing one's administrative role.[8]

Although this study does not address the issue of "effective schools," the findings and conclusions from such studies are relevant to the focus of this investigation, the role of the school principal. From this research, two major conclusions continue to be emphasized. The first is that the "behavior of the school principal is the single most important factor supporting high quality educational programs."[9] The second conclusion is that "while schools make a difference in what students learn, principals make a difference in schools."[10]

METHODOLOGY

Paradox is often the genesis of research questions. Based on a clearly stated research problem statement and purpose, the researcher must select an appropriate investigatory approach and tools. However, the determination of research methodology does not always follow this pattern. Too often researchers are already heavily armed with research approaches and tools, ready to do work on any phenomenon regardless of the nature of the problem. This dilemma posed two critical problems for the investigator. The first dealt with the notion that if the investigator did not know what he was looking for, how would he ever know if he had found it? The impulses for rational hypothesis testing were influential in the conceptualization of this study. On the intuitive side, however, the researcher was aware that if one already knew what one was looking for, was there not a danger that it most certainly would be found? In this sense, sooner or later the researcher might force the observations of principals into preconceived notions or a previously structured perspective.

The middle ground methodologically was a formative, qualitative study that combined a determined empirical focus with naturalistic methods of inquiry. Similar to Wolcott's participant-as-observer role, the investigator's presence was obviously known to all, but he was able to be present and was allowed to observe as opposed to being expected to perform as other participants in the events were expected to do.[11] This role became much more natural for the researcher, the principals, and their staffs as the research progressed. In fact, if anything was surprising, it was the ease with which each principal and others were able to accept the investigator's role, explain it to others, and then go about their daily routines. Even sensitive teacher evaluation conferences, parent conferences, and student disciplinary actions did not appear to be affected by the researcher's presence. In the ten days of shadowing the principals in this study, the investigator was asked to step outside the principal's office on only four separate occasions for less than a total of 90 minutes. After these private sessions, the principals shared the nature and purpose of all of the private meetings. This was an agreed upon procedure established at the outset of the investigation.

Five principals, three secondary and two elementary, participated in the study. The five districts from which the principals were selected represented a variety of local communities, school types, and socioeconomic characteristics in a large midwestern state. The schools had student populations that ranged from 320 to 1650 average daily membership. The two women and three men principal subjects had a total of 35 years of experience as principals, and their terms of experience ranged from 2 to 12 years. They had an average of 6.4 years of teaching experience prior to their initial appointment as principals. Superintendents, spouses, and university professors were mentioned by them as key influentials in their individual decisions to become principals.

Although unclear about particular career timeliness, only one of the principals expected to be a principal five years from the time of the study. Projecting ten years into the future, even this principal reported that he "hated to become an institution." When asked why they had become principals, three indicated that their entry into the principalship was a "fluke" or they had "backed into it." The other two were able to articulate clear reasons in this regard. One principal had worked in a quasi-administrative capacity in another agency and saw the need for principals who could positively influence programs in their buildings. Besides wanting to have more input and influence on new school programs, the other principal cited more pay and the belief that he could do a better job than a former principal with whom he had worked as the major factors affecting his decision to become an administrator. None of the principals was radically deviant from the principal's role described in most textbooks on school administration. However, each principal had appeared effectively to adapt and mold the role of principal to help his or her school and satisfy his or her personal and professional career expectations.

Data were collected over a five-month period and included five visits to each of the five principals. Three visits were for the purpose of intensive interviews. The other two days were spent in shadowing the principals. In-depth interviews, informal discussions of particular activities and events, participant observations, shadowing, document analysis, and the examination of physical environmental factors were all used to gather the case study data.

All data were recorded using a combination of researcher shorthand and field notes that were later transcribed. (The use of mechanical recording devices was not seen as appropriate for the investigation.) The combination of the above techniques into what could be described as topically oriented naturalistic inquiry was particularly appropriate because such a methodology permitted the researcher to examine the metaphors of administrative practice of school principals as well as to identify the underlying meanings of these images and the organizational and social structures engendered by them. As Wilson has stressed, a research design that takes the actors out of their naturalistic settings may negate those forces and obscure the understanding of the phenomenon.[12]

FINDINGS

Before reporting the findings of this investigation, the literature relating to metaphors of the school principalship will be briefly discussed.

A Review of the Literature

There is a rich tapestry of metaphors of the principalship. An historical overview reveals that the images associated with a principal's role definition have primarily been dominated by a functionalist view that has prescribed sets of administrative responsibilities. From the "principal teacher" role of the late 1880s to the notion of the "building administrators," Blumberg and Greenfield have listed three critical and enduring functions of the principalship that have evolved: the organization and general management of the school, the supervision of instruction and staff development, and the interpretation of the work of the school to the immediate school community.[13] But, has the principalship evolved beyond these three critical functions into a new role? And, if so, what effect do such potentially competing images have on schools?

Knezevich quite appropriately has described the principalship as a "constellation of positions."[14] The school principal also has been characterized as a consummate manager using Mintzberg's typology as employed by Kmetz and Willower[15] and by Martin and Willower;[16] a combination administrator-manager and educational leader by Roe and Drake;[17] a leader with technical, human, and conceptual skills that are practiced in five major functional areas—the instructional program, staff personnel services, student personnel services, financial-physical resources, and school community relations—by Lipham and Hoeh;[18] an organizational change agent by Small;[19] a synthesis of applied philosopher, school manager, and behavioral scientist by Wayson;[20] a politician and facilitator by Miklos;[21] and a wide variety of other characterizations including broker, negotiator, gamesman, missionary, social person, and thermostatic person by still others.

In the study of schools and their administration, metaphors become image games that are useful for suggesting hypotheses, presenting alternative lenses for the study and practice of administration, offering means to schematize and organize insights, providing labels for data and observations, and providing a basis for formal theory. Sergiovanni, Burlingame, Coombs, and Thurston[22] have suggested that metaphors go beyond mere theory and practice. The metaphors that may have spawned the theory to which a building principal ascribes his or her major activities and priorities are also the vehicles that get from the "fact" of an organization and its administration, as tenuous as they may be, to "value" in the form of beliefs and opinions. Sergiovanni et al. identified three major views of educational administration and the generative metaphors of these predominant concerns: *Efficiency* (the rational mechanistic), *the person* (the organic), and *political decision making* (bargaining).[23] These views are useful for examining the focus and the emphasis in the development of theory in administration and for analyzing the current practices of school principals. What effect do these metaphors, and others associated with them, have on how principals interpret their role in the school and how they express these values and beliefs through their administrative priorities and their daily routines?

The principal, as a consummate manager guided by the efficiency model, views the organization, operation, and administration of the school primarily as an attempt to match efficient practices and procedures with the desired goals of the organization. Steeped in the principles of scientific management as espoused by Frederick Taylor and brought to education by advocates like Franklin Bobbitt, the efficiency model has contributed a long list of metaphors that provide a particular lens through which schools can be examined. The rational mechanistic metaphor of a well-oiled machine epitomizes the notion of efficiency in education. Metaphors of the educational engineer designing operational blueprints for precise machining in an assembly line of educational processes can help theorists and practitioners in administration look at the principles and fundamentals of "good management" that are already known from the industrial sector. Bureaucratic theory of formal organizations based on Weberian characteristics of the bureaucracy represent a theoretical exemplar of this intellectual strand. Whether these metaphors are good or bad is, however, not the point. The concern centers on whether or not they contribute to theory and ultimately to a better understanding of administration in education. The custodial management functions of schools—the scheduling of classes, the business operations, the classification of jobs and differentiation of positions—are all products of such efficiency metaphors. Although somewhat deemphasized now in research and theory construction, the notion of achieving organizational outputs with maximum efficiency has not completely lost its appeal. Witness only the emergence of performance objectives, competency testing, management by objectives (MBO), management information systems (MIS), and planning, programming, budgeting systems (PPBS)—all of which are accompanied by the efficiency model's reliance on "norms of rationality as it pursues accountability, control, and efficiency."[24]

The humanistically oriented principal, guided by organic metaphors and concern for the human side of the person in the organization, views schools and the people in them as biological organisms capable of growth and feeling. The school and the people in them also may be afflicted with ill health if they are not properly nurtured. Two broad areas are generally given attention: the human relations side, which sees the social needs of the people within the school, and the human resources view, which recognizes the inherent conflict between organizational needs and individual needs but focuses on integrating the two conflicting areas of need into a mutually beneficial system through shared decision making, joint planning, and common goal setting. Getzels and Guba's "social systems model" provides a two-dimensional way of combining the concern for efficiency, the nomothetic, with the needs of the individual, the idiographic.[25] The strength of this model lies partly in its mix of concern for efficiency with a concern for the person and, to a great extent, in the contribution of a rich diversity of new metaphors, concepts, and hypotheses for both research and practice in administration. Images of an administrator as the missionary tending to the needs of the individual within the hostile dimensions of the organization or the gardener carefully nurturing the plant by watering and fertilizing it and being concerned with climatic conditions, as suggested by Halpin and Croft, and by Likert,[26] provide a great diversity of possibilities for research and practice. School structures and practices that emphasize meaningful human relations activities, maintenance of positive school climates and highly affective environments for learning, working, and social interaction; stickers with smiley faces; the reliance on psychic rewards; and personalized gifts distributed in staff lounges and mailboxes are all used to support the metaphorical concern for the person in school organizations.

The third generative metaphor is that of the principal as gamesman, politician, and broker. This represents a clear shift from the concerns for efficiency and for the person, both of which emphasized "internal-to-the-organization" issues. This newer metaphor sees the school and the role of the administrator as dynamically linked to the external environment. Conflict is a natural and necessary part of the processes of politics and decision making. The more traditional image of rationality as assumed in the efficiency and person oriented strands have been replaced in this view by the satisficing image of man and organization.[27] The metaphors in this sense envision the individual and organization as players and actors in a game, bounded by rules, with divergent stakes and interests in the outcome of decisions that are made as the "game" is played. Bargaining and negotiating for solutions that satisfy the competing demands are the metaphorical milieu of this strand. Theories of conflict resolution, decision making theory, the garbage can model as described by Cohen, March, and Olsen,[28] and loosely coupled systems as discussed by Weick[29] are the frameworks to be used in examining administration. Metaphors such as coalitions, trade-offs, gamesmanship, and the thermostatic person are also used to describe the phenomena of education as they relate to the science of school administration. The concern for politics and decision making is evidenced in notions of school principals who, as organizational change agents, assume a variety of roles including those of ombudsman, advocate, orchestrator, persuader, and mediator and principals who are portrayed as consummate decision makers, value-based jugglers, brokers, catalysts for action, and politicians.[30]

A Study of Five Principals

This section includes the introduction and discussion of a typology of three metaphorical themes that predominate the practices and role priorities of the five principals studied. Within this typology the principals will be described in terms of how each personalized the role of principal to meet individual personality and professional needs. In the discussion section that follows, the predominant themes and role adaptations will be discussed in terms of their implications for principals, for the schools in which they work, and for professional administrative preparation programs.

As already noted, numerous metaphors have been used to characterize administrative practices and beliefs. A limitation of previous studies that have characterized principals as politicians, value jugglers, helpers, brokers, humanists, catalysts, and rationalists[31] is that these images only represent differences in leadership styles and individual role interpretations. Although useful in the initial stage of analysis, these typologies proved to be inadequate as this investigation progressed. It became increasingly apparent that there were broader and more encompassing themes that cut across the practices and perspectives of the principals. Using the typology developed by Sergiovanni et al., each principal in the study exhibited behaviors and beliefs reflective of the three major views or generative metaphors.[32] Each principal blended notions of efficiency, humanism, and political bargaining into a workable administrative approach to the role of the principalship. Although each principal could be characterized by an affinity to one of these views, it seems more beneficial to examine the blending of these images and how this composite imagery appeared to affect the principal and the school environment. A researcher who attempts to define a principal's administrative role by any one image or dominant metaphor might well risk oversimplification and distortion of the role within the context of the total organization. It is also important to look beyond the apparent images to metaphors of purpose, which are much more deeply embedded in the principalship.

In assessing the metaphorical perspectives of the five principals, it became apparent that two forces were simultaneously at work. The first was the degree to which organizational role expectations, school structures, tradition, and community standards engendered the perspective each principal had of their administrative position. The second was that of the individual trying to make sense of the world of the principalship. Each of the principals came into the role with differing backgrounds, experiences, and values that became perceptual screens for interpreting the administrative role and how it related to the school. Based on personal values, each of the principals projected a highly individualized leadership style in their role as principal. The effect that personal role adaptation had upon daily routine and priorities in their work was obvious. The principal who envisioned the role as that of a chief executive officer carried out the responsibilities from the main office and functioned from behind a desk, much like the common conceptualization of a command center. The disciplinarian differed in that he involved himself in almost every aspect of school operations and decision making in which student discipline could possibly be an issue. Even though cognizant of other duties, he was quick to admit that discipline was "unfortunately number one." The principal who emphasized the fact that principals are teachers too, spent time in various ways supporting, organizing, and actively participating in the instructional program. One characteristic of the principal's role is that unlike the classroom teacher, the role is not necessarily restricted to one room, location, or even a single role. The affective or person-oriented principal spent as little time as possible in the office and reported that: "My place is with the students and the staff." Paper work and routine duties that confined him to the office were seen as negative aspects of his job. The counselor as principal chose to use all the skills of a seasoned guidance counselor in order to work one on one with staff and students, and to "keep the doors opened and process going" while at the same time "providing an atmosphere conducive to education." Each of these individualized interpretations of the role of the principal satisfied individual needs and played on the personal and professional strengths of each of the administrators.

A fundamental assumption in this analysis is that metaphor is more than just a nice linguistic device. The metaphors of principals—whether expressed verbally or hidden in values, behavior patterns, or administrative structures—reveal a great deal about the shared cultural associations of the principals as well as provide a profile of individual creativity and adaptability to the role of principal. Although each of the principals studied maintained degrees of individuality and idiosyncratic styles of leadership, each practiced the craft of the principalship within the parameters of three broad metaphors of purpose. The analysis of interview data, documents, and records as well as the daily activities of the five principals revealed that, regardless of individual role adaptations and definitions or priorities, three metaphors of purpose characterized the ethos of the principalship. Perhaps because the investigator tends to be visually oriented, the typology of metaphors that follows assumes a

pictorial semblance of the bell-shaped curve. The major purpose metaphorical theme for the principalship was that of *maintenance*. Tailing off
from this bulge was the purpose metaphor of *survival* on one end of the
continuum and that of *vision* at the other.

The metaphor of maintenance. In the *American Heritage Dictionary*,
maintenance is defined as "the action of continuing, carrying on, and
preserving."[33] Without a doubt, the major activities in which each of the
principals was involved and their individual senses of administrative
priorities and responsibilities supported the metaphorical theme of maintenance. In response to questions about what they saw as their major
responsibilities as principals, maintenance was clearly the intended
purpose. Regardless of personal leadership style, 89% of the principals'
total number of daily activities were intended to "keep the school doors
open and the process going." Whether the school was likened to a
governmental bureaucracy, a well-oiled truck, a business enterprise, a
social service agency, or a hospital, the major responsibilities of the
principal were seen as all encompassing. Three of the principals said their
major responsibilities were everything that happened on school grounds
and all of the students that come to them daily. This sense of "total"
responsibility took on the connotation of the caretaker or overseer of a
large estate. More specifically, the principals listed writing up job descriptions, disciplining and maintaining a rein on students, supervising curriculum, purchasing and ordering supplies, providing resources and other
supports to the curriculum, communicating and disseminating information, and providing an atmosphere conducive for learning within the
school as their most important responsibilities.

An interesting professional dilemma existed for four of the five principals. Based on the rhetoric of the profession, of administration preparation programs, and of a great deal of extant literature, one of the major
responsibilities advanced for the school principal has been that of curriculum leadership. Two comments typified the principals' collective
sense of guilt about not fulfilling this particular role expectation: "I should
be a curriculum leader but I'm not," and "I feel curriculum development
is one of the most important things I should do, but I don't do it."

With maintenance as the predominant concern of their organizational
role, the principals saw communications skills as one of the most important factors for success in their job. To be knowledgeable was necessary,
but it was not sufficient. Each principal maintained formal communication networks through periodic faculty meetings, daily announcements,
weekly bulletins, and sundry memoranda. Accompanying these formal
networks were highly personalized touches in the form of thank you notes
to teachers for jobs that were well done, notes with smiley faces, notes on
blackboards, candy in teachers' mailboxes, and any number of face-to-face

encounters on a daily basis. Communication was seen as the lubricant to help things run smoothly and to help provide and maintain a sense of security and a positive situation for learning.

The five principals saw few substantive changes in what was currently going on in their schools. When asked what changes they would make in their schools if they were unrestricted by legislative mandates, dollars, or local bargaining agreements, the status quo and the action of continuing on was clear. One principal stated, "I'm happy where we are and with what we're doing." Another listed his educational priorities as being pretty much in line with what is currently being done: "We'll continue on the path we're currently on." The most free-wheeling response for unrestricted change related to getting rid of a few teachers who were reported to be weak links in the systems. All five principals saw the security of a few incompetent teachers as debilitating to their schools and their programs. Other than firing these incompetents and hiring exceptionally good people, few suggestions were offered in terms of dealing with this kind of problem with staff personnel. Giving more money to those doing the job was seen as one way of differentiating the rewards for teachers in the school. However, the idea of being able to distinguish grades of teacher performance and then apply available rewards was not articulated by the principals. Buying computers for each room in the school and increasing the number of course offerings and classrooms were specific items listed as desirable factors toward change, but unrestricted change was seen by the principals only in terms of change in the number or quality of factors currently *in* the school. Unrestricted change to these five principals clearly did not mean changing the factors themselves. The system and its continuing operational process were accepted as givens.

Daily routines and activities also revealed the predominant maintenance role of the school principal. Recent studies by Kmetz and Willower and by Martin and Willower[34] have provided useful analytical frameworks for examining the daily tasks of school principals. As a result of adapting the frameworks and definitions of tasks, combined with analysis of purpose of the activities in which each principal was engaged, it is revealed in Table 14.1 that 51.7% of the major activities of the principals collectively was for purposes of maintenance. When the pupil control category (12.1%) and extracurricular activities category (12.7%) are added to the maintenance tasks, 76.5% of the major daily tasks are accounted for and are clearly related to the purpose of overall organizational maintenance.

Of particular interest in relation to this analysis were the differences between individual principals. The principal who spent 42.1% of his daily activities on maintenance also spent 17.3% of his time on pupil control tasks and 21.5% of his time on extracurricular activities. The principal who spent the highest percentage of work activity on maintenance tasks

TABLE 14.1
Analysis of the Purpose of Daily Activities of the Principals

	Average Percentage	Percentage Range Among Principals	
Maintenance	51.7	42.1	60.0
School academic program	16.1	11.3	20.4
Pupil control	12.1	6.2	17.3
Extracurricular activities	12.7	5.7	21.5
Personal	7.4	4.1	11.8

per se (60.9%) was in the largest school. However, with five administrative support staff members, that principal was released from major responsibilities in the areas of pupil control (9.0%) and extracurricular activities (8.3%).

The data were, however, analyzed primarily to address the issue of metaphor and its implications to the administrative practices of school principals. Other studies by Kmetz and Willower, Martin and Willower, and Wolcott[35] have described in richer detail the work behaviors and the nature of the school principalship. Of most interest in this investigation was the fact that an analysis of the purpose of activities of the five principals yielded similar descriptive data in terms of daily routines and tasks: (1) Maintenance tasks accounted for 51.5% of the principals' activities (compared to 53.9% for Martin and Willower; and compared to 53.7% for Kmetz and Willower); and (2) School academic program tasks, that is, non-routine curricular matters, accounted for 16.1% of the principals' activities (compared to 12.3% for Kmetz and Willower).

An additional analysis that describes the activities in which the five principals were primarily engaged is provided in Table 14.2.

That these five principals were heavily involved in maintenance activities in their schools was not all that surprising. Sergiovanni et al. list four major responsibilities typically vested in administrators in schools: goal attainment, internal maintenance, maintenance of the school's cultural patterns, and external adaptation.[36] If the principal is to assume these four responsibilities, then the relationship of the three predominant purpose metaphors to daily practice is an important consideration. If the maintenance metaphor dominates daily worktime and tasks as it did in this study, then one needs to explore the degree to which principals are meeting the responsibilities of external adaptation and goal attainment.

The metaphor of survival. Although overlapping images of maintenance, the metaphor of survival can be distinguished in that, beyond a mere

TABLE 14.2
Daily Tasks

Type of Activity	Average Percentage of Total Number of Activities
Unscheduled meetings	22.0
Exchanges (Interactions with parents, teachers, and others of less than 1-minute duration)	19.6
Telephone calls	16.2
Desk work	11.7
Scheduled meetings	8.5
Monitoring	5.4
Tours	4.7
Processing	4.3
Other activities	7.6

sense of continuance and preserving what is, the survival image must deal with the threat of not continuing on or threat to the very existence of an enterprise. The emphasis on survival for principals and for the schools in which they operate is one that focuses on meeting immediate needs and the mustering of the most vital resources available for continued existence. The immediacy of crisis-based management is characterized by: short-range planning; the need for dramatic, often harsh and autocratic, actions; an environment that is likely to be stressful; educational priorities and time, resources, and energy allocations skewed toward the present; and little attention to long-range outcomes or to the implications of activity for the schools and the people in them.

The survival metaphor is engendered in part by the socioeconomic conditions that are now prevalent in, for example, a heavily industrialized midwestern state. High unemployment, a diminished tax base, and the restructuring of local economies have affected the school districts in which the five principals in this study worked. In addition, state funding formulaes and statutory restrictions on local school district budget increases for operating and capital expenditures have added to the fiscal ambiguity within which daily educational decisions must be made and actions taken. Planning on a yearly basis does go on, but with almost certainty that state aid and local tax revenues will not match the projected budget and expenditures. Within this economic malaise, principals at times become leaders of bands of seasoned professional survivors who begin each fall somewhat optimistically but who, through the next 180 school days, must barter for supplies, compromise instructional programs and plans, delay purchases, and defer all but emergency repairs on buildings and equipment.

Perhaps the most revealing images of survival came in response to a question about what changes the principals would make in their schools if they were not restricted by money, legislation, or local contracts. Three of the principals immediately answered that they would build "a new building." One principal summed up his frustration saying: "We need a new financing method for schools. Property taxes and the need to pass local levies are ridiculous." He indicated that the lack of dollars was affecting his choice of educational priorities. The last nine local tax levies had been defeated in his district, and he added: "Conditions in education now are not good. I can't identify one single important thing to do." The need for more dollars to operate existing programs was reflected in all of the principals' responses. More money for new facilities, for needed supplies and equipment, and for salaries were viewed as necessary, at least to help meet some of the most immediate concerns. Financial survival was a powerful influence on the principals' priorities and activities.

In all, 5½% of the principals' daily tasks were related to the survival metaphor. From collecting candy money to fixing broken locks and paper cutters, bartering for supplies over the telephone, filling soda machines, negotiating product purchases at favorable discounts, and coordinating and managing raffles and bazaars, each principal to varying degrees was conscious of the necessity to carry on such survival types of activities.

The metaphor of vision. Although located at opposite ends of the metaphor continuum, survival and vision are interrelated. Less affected directly by the survival activities listed above, one principal permitted a wide range of these activities within her school, but they were carried on by others. Her role in this regard was mainly in making certain that policy guidelines and fiscal mandates were followed. Her sense of survival went beyond the immediacy of making enough money to repair or replace a few sets of curtains in classrooms. Reflecting a personal style of corporate management, she said: "If public education is to survive, it needs to show the value of its product to the consumers of these products." This interpretation of survival represented her sense of vision for the school and for the major activities and programs with which the school was involved.

Broadly conceived, vision is the principal's ability to holistically view the present, to reinterpret the mission of the school to all its constituents, and to use imagination and perceptual skills to think beyond accepted notions of what is practical and what is of immediate application in present situations to speculative ideas and to, preferably, possible futures.

Tasks of this nature accounted for 5½% of the principals' total number of daily tasks.

Similar to research findings about why teachers enjoy teaching, each principal exhibited a sense of vision and satisfaction in the effects they could have on the lives of children and members of their staffs. One principal stated: "I want to be able to communicate that I am an approachable person and that, as a principal, I have a clear vision of what we're doing and why we're doing it." The ability to communicate within and beyond the school to parents and community members was seen as a key task for each of the principals.

The involvement of parents in the educational process was seen as very important, but it was also viewed as a source of frustration for each principal. The potential of becoming embroiled in any of an array of domestic problems involving parents who were "irrational" and who "do not understand the whole school, the total picture," who are "unsupportive parents," who "do not give a . . . about the education of their kids," and parents who "will not support new taxes because education is not their priority (their own economic survival is more important)" are reflective comments expressing the five principals' frustration with parents and their relationship to their children's education.

Parent involvement in a formal sense was limited to these principals' schools. Only in one school were parents (over 100 volunteers) actively participating in the educational process at school. The other principals viewed parent involvement as supportive of the school's work but not intricately tied either to daily school programs or to activities. In fact, one principal indicated that there were problems in having parents in the schools because they often do not understand many things that are occurring. Therefore, parent involvement was more often viewed as supportive and tangential as opposed to a rich source of expertise and knowledge. Participation in bake sales, involvement with band and athletic booster clubs, supervision at extracurricular functions, and consumption of any number of products sold for school fund raising purposes were all accepted areas of parental participation. This is not to suggest an insensitivity to parents on the part of the principals. When asked what kind of reputation they wanted to have with parents, the principals mentioned the words: approachable, fair, empathetic, honest, and available. Additionally, the principals wanted parents to know that they cared about their children, that they could be trusted to do things for the education of children, that they were advocates for children, and that they focused the curriculum on community-perceived needs and provided valuable learning experiences.

DISCUSSION

The three metaphorical themes of maintenance, survival, and vision have significant implications for the daily practices of principals and for administrative preparation programs. Each principal in this study performed similar tasks, had similar daily routines, and differed little from the others despite very clear differences in their administrative images of leadership style and action. Individual personalities and favored activities in the principalship might tempt one to characterize the principals as Blumberg and Greenfield did in describing eight principals.[37] Nonetheless, the overwhelming dedication to continuance of the current processes in their schools was less a matter of personal choice or characterization and more a matter of community, organizational, and professional role expectations. Little evidence existed from these five principals that the principal should be anything other than that of the ultimate director, the facilitator, the keeper, the maintenance manager, or the person in the organization who sees and understands the total process and is responsible for everything that goes on. The principal was responsible for keeping the process going. All five principals shared a common culturally standardized image of the principalship. Although it was made more colorful by individual variations, to a large degree the parameters of role expectations were set by teachers, administrators, students, parents, and professional training institutions, and they determined the maintenance metaphor. Significant deviations from these expectations created serious role conflicts for the principals, the like of which are typically resolved by reemployment in other settings or positions.

In some respects, the survival and vision images can be seen as mutually exclusive perspectives. Further, the more time and energy individual principals spent on the immediacy of existence, the less time there was for looking beyond the issues and crises of the present. Rather than look at preferably possible futures, the reality of insufficient funds for buying even rudimentary supplies for classroom activities or repairing needed equipment and facilities required delicate negotiations, bartering, and a variety of creative activities simply to make it to the end of the day, week, or school year.

Each of the principals expressed frustration at the discrepancy between what the professional literature espoused and what he or she was confronted with on a daily basis. Curricular leadership was recognized as one of the most important responsibilities of their jobs, but none of them was able to spend time or devote the necessary resources to fulfill even conservative expectations for curricular leadership.

In many respects, there is evidence in this investigation that the principalship has become the dumping ground for all of the maintenance responsibilities in the school. This is due in part to the evolution of the principalship from principal-teacher to a manager and facilitator of any and all events within the school. More and more complexity has been added to schools and, consequently, their administration. Increased responsibility for the totality of school operations, for meeting state curriculum standards, and for meeting the special educational needs of all children have added to this role complexity. In addition, the increasingly litigious nature of schools, the assumption of responsibilities and activities previously assumed by other agencies and institutions in society, the expansion of extracurricular programs, the professionalization and credentialism of school staffs, and proliferation of mandates that cause schools to try to ameliorate many social and cultural problems, which the larger society has not been able to resolve, have all added to the burden of the constellation of role expectations for the school principal. With no clear sense of who should assume all of these responsibilities, the principalship has become a catch-all for all of the tasks not accepted by other administrators, by teachers, or by the community.

In part, the acceptance of the maintenance metaphor for the principal is a conscious decision to take hold of some of the more tangible "nuts and bolts" aspects of the position. There is security, and to a certain degree status, in being able to define one's major responsibilities as a facilitator, resource person, and provider who watches over everything in the school and keeps the process going. It is often easier to assume tedious tasks in the cafeteria, in parking lots, or at athletic events because what one does and who one is as principal are apparent, quite recognizable, and expected by most constituents than to engage in long-range planning, the assessment of educational needs, or massive curricular change. The latter simply do not provide immediate results or gratification, and they may not even be equally valued.

The program components, the instructional delivery modes, and the core curriculum of graduate programs for preparing school administrators also can be examined using the survival, maintenance, and vision typology. To be sure, most graduate programs for preparing educational administrators include a wide range of activities and experiences for students. There is recognition of the need for developing broad conceptual skills for administrators, but this is tempered by students who are usually teachers working in schools and who have various expectations as to the types of administrative skills and competencies they need for being effective principals. As a result, there is the demand for highly specific vocational or technical skills such as those related to class scheduling, personnel hiring and evaluation, or curriculum management that are necessary maintenance and survival skills for keeping the novice principal in his or her job. This does not, however, reduce the need for encouraging and nurturing notions of leadership and vision that cut across the major functional tasks of administration and that permit broader interpretation of educational issues and administrative responsibilities. Students do need to develop and practice these skills in courses and in internship experiences. As well, the relationship of knowledges, skills, attitudes, and values that characterize educational administration programs to the metaphors of survival, maintenance, and vision ought to be explored. Finally, the degree to which administrator preparation programs create, foster, and maintain a culturally standardized image of the school principalship merits serious consideration.

CONCLUSION

To survive is commendable. It is even the stuff of great literature. However, the inevitable question in this regard is: At what price? With survival as a metaphor, the principalship assumes a necessarily reactive posture and one characterized by crisis-based management and satisficing, decision making with little or no thought of the future in terms of the broader issues of education, such as the nature and purposes of schools and their organizational and curricular structures.

With maintenance as the predominant metaphor, there is some sense of the future although it is inexorably linked closely to the acceptance and continuance of what is. The initiation of significant changes in the school itself or in its primary purpose meets powerful forces of resistance in people, in structures, in traditions, and in policies that are protected and, in some cases, reified so that no one questions their legitimacy. The purpose of maintenance is to preserve and to keep things running as efficiently and effectively as possible; it is not to create new structures, functions, or purposes.

The metaphor of vision offers the most hope of the principalship, but it is also the most problematic. Although each principal in this study aspired to broader views of educating children and to the ability to look beyond present issues and conceptualizations of schooling, each was frustrated by the frenetic pace of their work. Also there is the natural tendency to become personally involved in the most current and pressing situations. The realities of politics, career mobility, salary increases, and an endless number of system constraints all conspire to rob even the most earnest visionary of devoting significant blocks of time, resources, and energy to creative possibilities for the future. Yet, the greatest hope for the further evolution of the principalship lies beyond the image of that of overseer of the internal maintenance of curriculum, staff and student personnel systems, and facilities and finances.

Besides making personal adaptations to their administrative role, principals need to help in redefining the nature of their role and its attendant responsibilities. Not only has the role of principal become stagnant, but also it has become a repository for any and all activities not delegated or assumed by others in the school or in the community.

One principal in a rural consolidated school district was asked on several occasions by the local sheriff's deputy to discipline students for reckless driving away from the school grounds. The principal refused and indicated that a better idea was for the deputy to issue some traffic citations with fines. This is but a simple illustration of how principals need continually to contribute to the definition of their roles. Perhaps by indicating very clearly those activities and responsibilities they will not assume, a role definition of the school principalship will emerge that will leave time for envisioning and for interpreting the work of the school for various educational stakeholders in the community.

To spend more time and energy under the metaphorical rubric of vision does not mean abandoning maintenance or survival tasks and activities. What is necessary is a redistribution of role emphasis among these three metaphorical themes. It would be impossible to deal solely with the future with no concern for past history or the problems and issues of the present. The challenge for principals is to examine their daily routines, their priorities, and their resources and see how they might best function through being knowledgeable of the past, remaining well grounded in the present, and continually looking to the future.

NOTES

1. T. Hawkes, *Metaphor* (London: Metheun and Co., Ltd., 1972).

2. W. Embler, "Metaphor and Social Belief," in *E.T.C. A Review of General Semantic* 82 (1951): 82-93.

3. Hawkes, *Metaphor.*

4. Embler, "Metaphor and Social Belief."

5. A thorough discussion of social systems theory is presented by J. W. Getzels, J. M. Lipham, and R. F. Campbell, *Educational Administration as a Social Process: Theory, Research and Practice* (New York: Harper & Row, 1968).

6. T. Parsons and E. A. Shils, *Toward a General Theory of Action* (Cambridge, MA: Harvard University Press, 1951).

7. For an overview of the principalship and competing images in administration, see A. Blumberg and W. Greenfield, *The Effective Principal: Perspectives of School Leadership* (Boston: Allyn & Bacon, 1980).

8. E. Miklos, "Alternative Images of the Administrator," *The Canadian Administrator* 22, 7 (1983).

9. For a discussion dealing with the first conclusion, see the following sources: G. R. Austen, "Exemplary School and the Search for Effectiveness," *Educational Leadership* 37, 1 (1979): 10-14; M. Rutter, B. Maughan, P. Mortimore, and J. Outson, *Fifteen Thousand Hours: Secondary Schools and Their Effects on Children* (Cam-

bridge, MA: Harvard University Press, 1979); and R. Edmonds, "Making Public Schools Effective," *Social Policy* 12 (1981): 56-60.

10. J. Lipham, *Effective Principal, Effective School* (Reston, VA: National Association of Secondary School Principals, 1981), p. 1.

11. H. E. Wolcott, *The Man in the Principal's Office: An Ethnography* (New York: Holt, Rinehart and Winston, 1973).

12. S. Wilson, "The Use of Ethnographic Techniques in Educational Research," *Review of Educational Research* 47, 2 (1977): 245-265.

13. Blumberg and Greenfield, *The Effective Principal.*

14. S. J. Knezevich, *Administration of Public Education* (New York: Harper & Row, 1975).

15. For a more detailed discussion of the characterizations of the school principal's (administrator's) role, see the following sources: J. T. Kmetz and D. J. Willower, "Elementary School Principal's Work Behavior," *Educational Administration Quarterly* 18, 4 (1982): 62-78.

16. W. J. Martin and D. J. Willower, "The Managerial Behavior of High School Principals," *Educational Administration Quarterly* 17, 1 (1981): 69-90.

17. W. H. Roe and T. L. Drake, *The Principalship* (New York: Macmillan, 1974).

18. J. M. Lipham and J. A. Hoeh, Jr., *The Principalship: Foundations and Functions* (New York: Harper & Row, 1974).

19. J. F. Small, "Initiating and Responding to Social Change," in *Performance Objectives for School Principals: Concepts and Instruments,* J. A. Culbertson, C. Henson, and R. Morrison, eds. (Berkeley, CA: McCutchan, 1974).

20. W. W. Wayson, "A New Kind of Principal," *The National Elementary Principal* 50, 4 (1971): 9-19.

21. Miklos, "Alternative Images of the Administrator."

22. T. J. Sergiovanni, M. Burlingame, F. D. Coombs, and P. W. Thurston, *Educational Governance and Administration* (Englewood Cliffs, N.J.: Prentice-Hall, 1980).

23. *Ibid.*

24. *Ibid.*

25. J. W. Getzels, "Administration as a Social Process," in *Administrative Theory in Education,* Andrew Halpin, ed. (Chicago: Midwest Administration Center, The University of Chicago, 1958).

26. A. W. Halpin and D. B. Croft, *The Organizational Climate of Schools* (Washington, DC: U.S. Office of Education Research Project, 1962); and R. Likert, *The Human Organization: Its Management and Value* (New York: McGraw-Hill, 1967).

27. Sergiovanni, Burlingame, Coombs, and Thurston, *Educational Governance and Administration.*

28. M. D. Cohen, J. G. March, and J. Olsen, "A Garbage Can Model of Organizational Choice," *Administrative Science Quarterly* 17, 1 (1972).

29. K. E. Weick, "Educational Organizations as Loosely Coupled Systems," *Administrative Science Quarterly* 21 (1976): 1-19.

30. The following provide discussions of these metaphors: J. F. Small, "Initiating and Responding to Social Change"; and Blumberg and Greenfield, *The Effective Principal.*

32. Sergiovanni, Burlingame, Coombs, and Thurston, *Educational Governance and Administration.*

33. *American Heritage Dictionary of the English Language* (New York: American Heritage, Inc., 1971).

34. Kmetz and Willower, "Elementary School Principal's Work Behavior"; and Martin and Willower, "The Managerial Behavior of High School Principals."

35. *Ibid.;* and Wolcott, *Man in the Principal's Office.*

36. Sergiovanni, Burlingame, Coombs, and Thurston, *Educational Governance and Administration.*

37. Blumberg and Greenfield, *The Effective Principal.*

CHAPTER FIFTEEN

Toward a Comprehensive Theory of Communications: A Review of Selected Contributions

JEROME P. LYSAUGHT

The author notes administrators' desire for an organizational formula that can guide them in solving communications problems. Such problems are depicted as extremely important, persistent, and ever-present. The author reviewed the pertinent literature on the state of the art in communications theory to find theories that have withstood the test of time and permit readers to understand and control future communications.

If one were to appoint a "Patron Philosopher" of communications theory, a logical candidate might be that ancient Ephesian, Heraclitus, who argued that the only constant is change and that "one never steps into the same river twice." Certainly, as the long history of the study of language and communications is examined, change in concepts and meanings is ever constant and ever present.

If one were to look at an appropriate starting point for the discussion of communications theory, it might be in the words of the ancient Athenian, Socrates, who said in the beginning of Book II of *The Republic:*

> With these words, I was thinking that I had made an end of the discussion; but the end, in truth, proved to be only a beginning.

The concept of change is central to the study of communications. Words, over time, alter their meaning. Concepts, over time, vary their interpretation. Media, over time, are transformed by technology. And yet, just as Heraclitus' river, there is an elemental constancy in the very midst of change. What Greek philosophers said about language and meaning can be understood. What early scientific studies have documented in such fields as semantics, social psychology and organizational behavior concerning words and their communication can be understood. So there is

SOURCE: Jerome P. Lysaught, "Toward a Comprehensive Theory of Communications: A Review of Selected Contributions," *Educational Administration Quarterly*, Vol. 20, No. 3, pp. 101-127. Copyright © by The University Council for Educational Administration. Reprinted with permission.

the ultimate paradox of the old philosopher, that change ultimately leads full circle, not to the precise starting point, but to an enlarged understanding of where it all began. Those studying language and communications, then, must confront an ever-expanding pattern of growth which also continually reaches back to its varied sources of explanation, enrichment, and entries into new study and advancement.

Similarly, the words of Socrates are reminders that we are far from a conclusive understanding of either the phenomena or the processes of communications. The growth of knowledge in this field is characterized by a form of accretion, not permutation. The conceptual framework of communications theory consists of many bits of information gathered from widely distributed sources that are slowly fashioned into a more and more meaningful whole.

Too many administrators—and not just those in education—rebel at this frustrating state of affairs and seek some formula, some panacea, which can guide them in solving the problems of interpersonal and organizational communications. This desire is understandable because they recognize that problems of language, and meaning, and their transmission are among their most important, persistent, and ubiquitous organizational difficulties. More frequently than not, failures in communication lie at the heart of problems in organization, goal setting, productivity, and evaluation.

Unfortunately, the search for some new device, technique, or formulation for conducting organizational communications carries within itself twin dangers of self-delusion. It can lead, on the one hand, to the neglect of that which is "known" (Type I Error), simply because proven processes and admonitions seem prosaic and limited. On the other hand, an overwhelming desire for "new" approaches to communications can lead to the acceptance of unsubstantiated rhetoric and claims (Type II Error) on the basis of specious argument or spurious face validity.

It is the purpose of this review to portray the current state of the art in communications theory and to suggest certain selected contributions to the understanding of these processes which have stood the tests of time and which add to the ability to comprehend, predict, and control organizational communications in the future.

TOWARD A DEFINITION

As vital as communications is to all human behavior, there is no single, commonly accepted definition of the process or its key elements. Dance has compiled a collection of almost one hundred attempts to define the term, and he, himself, has settled for a helical model of the process which suggests that the most pervasive characteristics of communications are a constant movement both forward and backward along an enlarging orbital pathway which (shades of Heraclitus!) keeps passing over its starting point but at greatly expanded content levels which press onward toward infinity.[1]

If this model seems a bit breath-taking, one might settle at the operational level for the more behavioral, and pedestrian, formulation of Herbert Lasswell which suggests the importance of Five W's: "Who, says What, to Whom, in Which channel, with What effect?"[2] This approach emphasizes several particular elements in the process of communications: a transmitter, a receiver, a message, a medium, and a result or outcome. As Severin and Tankard point out, however, even these reference points are not universally accepted.[3] Those authors suggest that the many approaches to defining communications have so few points in common that one can only classify the consensual agreements in the following ways:

(1) Those definitions which stress the sharing of meaning.

(2) Those definitions which stress intentional influence toward a response or effect.

(3) Those definitions which stress a response or effect even without particularized intentions.

In their abbreviated taxonomy, it is possible to see that many definitions which stress meaning without concern for explicit outcomes are unacceptable to those who emphasize results, while even the latter differ in important ways depending on the specificity of the outcomes obtained. What one theorist defines as a form of communications might be viewed by another as an exercise in information transmission simply because there are no definable results obtained. Similarly, what might be defined by one observer as a failure in communications because intended outcomes were not realized might be seen as successful by another due to the occurrence of unintended responses not anticipated by the speaker. These differences are very real and emphasize how far the field is from a common concept of interpersonal or organizational communications.

TOWARD A MODEL

If there is a lack in terms of an agreed definition of communications, there is, nonetheless, movement in the direction of better understanding of models for portraying the elements and the relationships that take place in the dynamics of communication. This can be developed in a form of sequential growth.

Figure 15.1: Naturalistic Model of Communications

In terms of a naturalistic model based on observation, the elements for communication included a speaker, a listener, and a message. This can be simply diagrammed as in Figure 15.1.

Lasswell added two elements to this basic model.[4] The first concept was that the message is transmitted by way of a medium or channel which is, itself, an important element of communications (that is, the message may be conveyed by face-to-face dialogue, through a newspaper, in a personal letter, etc.). The second of Lasswell's concepts, which is not universally accepted, had to do with results. For the sake of simplicity and agreement, only the first of these two elements are added to the basic model as in Figure 15.2.

Shannon and Weaver in their information theory approach added the concepts of source, destination, and noise to the developing model as portrayed in Figure 15.3.[5] The source of the information or material to be communicated may be outside the transmitter; similarly, the intended destination of the message may be beyond or outside the receiver. Noise represents both the natural static within the communication lines and processes as well as competing signals and variant information transmissions.

Modifications to the basic Information Theory model, including the work of Weiner[6] and Berlo,[7] suggest still other essential elements: encoding, decoding, and feedback as represented in Figure 15.4. Encoding is more than the selection of a medium; it is the choice of a "language" together with a selection of cognate and affective referents to delineate a "feeling" as well as a literal rendition of the message. Similarly, the process of decoding presumes the feelings and perceptions of the receiver as he or she transforms the language and the affect of the message picked up, and, in turn, renders these into an idea or translation. Feedback is the completion of the communications "loop" and conveys in the concepts of systems theory the capability of interactive modification and control processes that permit the original receiver to become the transmitter in order to verify, enlarge, or correct the message proper.

For purposes of completeness, the experimental context factors identified by such theorists as Andersen[8] and Schramm[9] can be added to the model. These might be postulated as in Figure 15.5. Andersen suggests that there is a specific setting which impacts on the communications process together with a much broader, binding context that might be described in some interpretations as a cultural surround. Schramm

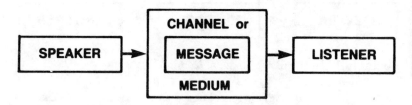

Figure 15.2: Modified Lasswell Model of Communications

proposes further that the individuals also bring their own idiographic fields of experience to bear on the communications situation so that, in a sense, there is a three factor contextual model similar to the Getzels-Guba-Thelen[10] formulation for organizational behaviors: the idiographic field of the participants, the nomothetic field of the specific organization or institution, and the general cultural or societal context in which both the individuals and the organization are to be found and within which they must function.

This enlarged model of the communications process, while perhaps still incomplete, is largely functional and operates to provide defined categories for research and analysis. In the balance of this paper, four particular aspects of the model will be examined: the language of communications, the elements of interpersonal communications, factors in organizational communications, and the growing body of analytical tools formulated to study dynamic processes of communications.

THE LANGUAGE OF COMMUNICATIONS

In his volume on *Administrative Behavior,* Simon has placed his argument simply, "Without communication there can be no organization." [11] Just as simply, and even more fundamentally, Sargent and Williamson point out that ". . . without language there is no true culture; moreover, language is fundamental to human nature as we know it." [12] Concepts of language, then, are vital to an understanding of communications—and its models—as well as to any effort to improve its processes. From a voluminous literature on language and communications, the following theoretical approaches seem to be particularly useful.

The Sapir-Whorf Theory. Anthropologists and early folk psychologists discovered there were important links among language, culture, and behavior. While the English language, for instance, has several words to describe frozen water, Eskimos have an elaborate repertoire of several

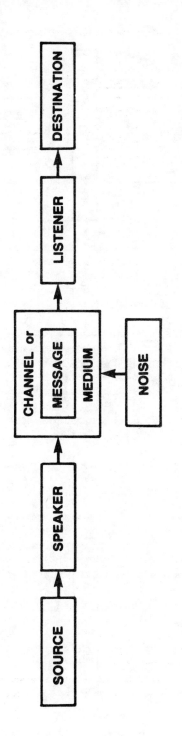

Figure 15.3 Modified Shannon-Weaver Model of Communications

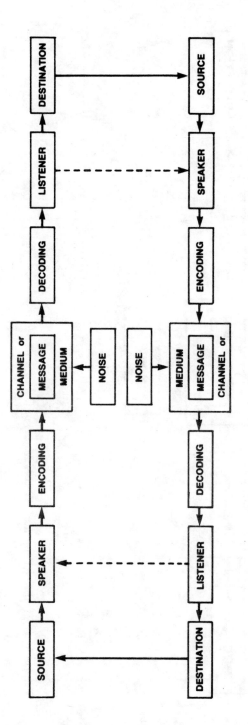

Figure 15.4 Modified Weiner/Berlo Model of Communications

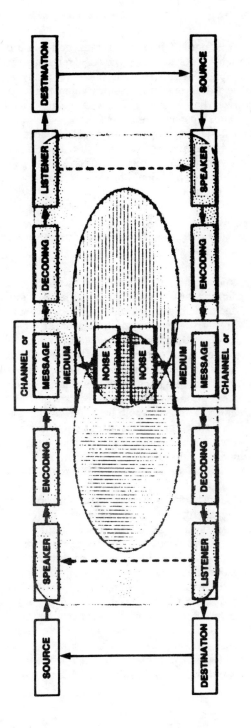

Figure 15.5 Completed Model of Communications

dozen terms to distinguish the various states and conditions of this same element.[13] Klineberg has described the basic relationship in the Chinese language between its lack of distinctive forms for many conceptual terms and the blurring of differences in classifications of philosophy and thought that characterize that culture as viewed through Western eyes and translated through Western language.[14]

From a multitude of examples drawn from a variety of cultures, it is valid to deduce that a language reflects those aspects of a culture which are deemed most important—most necessary to be talked about. The work of Edward Sapir[15] and Benjamin Whorf,[16] however, raises an even greater issue. In the words of the latter,

> . . . the linguistic system . . . is not merely a reproducing instrument for voicing ideas, but rather is itself the shaper of ideas, the program guide for the individual's mental activity . . .[17]

Thus, language not only provides a documentary record of what is important to communicate, it also determines in large measure what will be communicated, how it will be communicated, and why. Language, to a great extent, constructs the culture's view of the world and organizes its categories for describing space, time, causality, and relatedness.

While there is no absolute acceptance of the Sapir-Whorf theory, there is substantial agreement on the operational importance of the interactive effects of culture and language, such that facile attending to words without careful attention to their cultural context and specific setting can be most misleading. The distinction between "democratic processes" as practiced in the Soviet Union and in most western republics may be apparent; it may be less easily recognized that such terms may mask important behavioral differences as practiced in the United States, Great Britain, and Australia—countries which, in a real sense, are "separated" by a common language.

Because social institutions and organizations represent separate and, frequently, distinct cultures, it is essential that one "digs into" the operative language system in order to understand the communications which take place. To the extent that Sapir-Whorf are correct, the language of a school or corporation not only reflects the cultural and belief systems of that organization, but tends, in fact, to shape the way that collectivity views ideas, mores, expectations, and, indeed, "truth." This approach to language understanding suggests that many an organization's communications processes are essentially telelogical in their construction—finding their cause in their expression and their expression, ultimately, in a primal cause. In this light, Swift's portrayal of the fundamental disagreement between Lilliput and Blefescu over the "right" end of an egg to crack assumes the tallest satiric heights he meant to portray. To organizational protagonists of any given view, there may arise an elemental credo which affects all other relationships and understandings. Witness the recent disclosure of a United States Information Agency "blacklist" of unacceptable speakers to portray the American view of freedom of speech.

If one is to comprehend interpersonal and organizational communications, one must learn to "think" in the operative language—not just "speak." Likewise, if one wants to change behavior, it is essential that both language and culture be influenced. This concept was understood by some as long ago as in Elizabethan England. Stanyhurst urged that the law, culture, and language of Ireland be directed into the English model because ". . . if any of these lack, doubtless the conquest limpeth."[18] He saw clearly that independence of language or customs would perpetuate independence of behavior and sentiment. His observations were borne out. In the twentieth century, the rebirth of the Irish language preceded and helped to precipitate the uprisings which led to the establishment of the Irish Republic. In less dramatic terms, Sapir-Whorf instruct one to learn the language and the customs of any organization in order to understand its behavior.

Implicit in their concept is the need for time—time to live with an organization, time to learn its verbal and non-verbal patterns of language, and time to discover the cultural components which Andersen[19] and Schramm[20] have emphasized as providing the context for communications.

Korzybski and General Semantics. To understand the relationship of language and culture in a given organization is a matter of identifying the systems of thought and speech which prevail within the society or the wider culture. To Alfred Korzybski, however, every language system further contains a broad set of silent assumptions and premises which are so fundamental and pervasive that they represent a foundational orientation to life itself. In his concepts of general semantics, Korzybski illustrates his point by discussing the general, but silent, assumptions that our language system contains—and fosters.[21] While few may have taken formal courses in logic or rhetoric, our grammar and our language, built on the cultural components of Western thought processes, contain a variety of primitive premises and silent assertions which include unarticulated elements of Aristotelian logic and Nichomachean ethics. To Korzybski, of course, the major problem lies in the unrecognized structures of the language; once it is known how our thought processes are affected, they can be studied and accepted or modified as experience suggests. Until, however, these assumptions have been identified and articulated, we are powerless to understand or to change our behavior.

In the case of Aristotelian logic, for example, Korzybski suggests that language and culture combine to assert as "givens" three fundamental laws for structuring thought patterns:[22]

(1) *The Law of Identity*—A is A, a man is a man, a woman is a woman, a school is a school.

(2) *The Law of Contraction*—A cannot be both B and not B, a man cannot be both young and old, a woman cannot be both beautiful and ugly, a school cannot be both effective and ineffective.

(3) *The Law of the Excluded Middle*—A must be either B or not B, a person must be either a woman or a man, a man must be either liberal or conservative, a school must be either effective or ineffective.

These belief patterns materially affect individual and group behavior and generally result in what is called *Two-valued Thinking.* A school budget must be supported or defeated. A superintendent is either doing a proper job or not. A textbook is either obscene or it is not. And these are often the ways in which issues concerning organizations and society are framed.

Korzybski proposes that society would be much better served by using a different form of language system, a relativistic approach which would avoid the faults and disorders inherent in the over-application of the Aristotelian structure.[23] (Note that Korzybski would agree that there are times when Two-valued systems are appropriate—as in the development of a truth table based on Aristotelian logic. It is when this system is extended beyond its natural limits to the entirety of the culture that difficulties are encountered.)

As a substitute for the three Aristotelian laws, general semantics would postulate three premises which differ in both language and thought patterns.[24] These could be stated as follows:

(1) Premise 1. A *map* is not the territory. What I say is not the same as the person or the object I am talking about.

(2) Premise 2. A map is *not all* the territory. I never say everything that could be said about a person or an object. I select, abstract, or emphasize certain aspects depending on my purpose, breadth of knowledge, and time constraints.

(3) Premise 3. A map is *self-reflexive.* We can talk about talking about. Having abstracted one quality or aspect of a person, we can, then, discuss this quality apart from the person himself and get farther and farther away from the reality of the territory we set out to describe.

Korzybski goes on to suggest that each of these premises, even though they contain their own *caveats,* should be subjected to empirical testing and should not be allowed to construct structural assumptions about the world or nature of reality beyond that which can be validated by experiential data.

In short, general semantics is a methodological system for determining the silent assumptions of any language, for exposing the structural and grammatic features which determine thought patterns and generalizations, and for reeducating and reorienting language users into a more useful form of communications that will improve understanding and more closely reflect the reality of the organization and its culture.

One need not go beyond the realm of sexual and racial stereotypes with which our culture has contended to recognize the existence of primitive Two-value assumptions underlying our language and thought patterns. Korzybski would argue that these phenomena are more than likely only the surface manifestations of even more elemental beliefs which are so deeply embedded that we must work to discover them and the effects they have on our thoughts and behaviors.

Operational Semantics and Communications. To many individuals, Korzybski's general system, and his related work in areas like non-Euclidean mathematics, was overwhelming in its portrayal of concepts and processes. Chase,[25] Hayakawa,[26] Johnson,[27] and others, however, have been instrumental in developing operational principles to enhance the accuracy and relevance of communications at both the interpersonal and organizational levels without requiring the full, in-depth understanding of the responsible-orientation process anticipated by general semantics.

Hayakawa, for example, has proposed six specific guides to thinking and speaking that embody principles of semantics.[28] These include:

(1) *Indexing.* The use of indexes or subscripts to remind us that Republican$_1$ is not the same as Republican$_2$ or Republican$_n$. General labels obscure important details and differences in our verbal maps.

(2) *Dating.* People, institutions, and beliefs change over time. The Supreme Court (1904) was not the Supreme Court of 1954, or that of 1984. You and I are not the same as we were ten years ago. It is important that we date our "maps" since territories change markedly over time.

(3) *Et cetera.* All statements should carry an explicit "etc." since all maps are incomplete and fail to contain information that may be very relevant to some listeners or viewers.

(4) *Quotation Marks.* Many terms have multiple references and contain their own structural implications. Mentally setting quotation marks around terms like "affirmative action," "civil rights," "nuclear deterrence," should remind us that these are inexact and have reference to widely disparate cognate and affective systems of belief.

(5) *Hyphens.* Language arbitrarily separates verbally things which cannot truly be divided. The use of real or implicit hyphens in maternal-child care, psycho-somatic medicine, or preparatory-continuing education reminds us that the arbitrariness of terms should not divide that which exists on a range or continuum of reality.

(6) *Is of Identity.* This is a general admonition to avoid confusing terms with their referent reality. Many terms are deliberately used to affect the emotions—pinkos, fascists, wasps, and wetbacks are labels intended to short-circuit thinking and to elicit broad generalizations in the minds of listeners.

These particular devices can and should be used in the analysis of interpersonal and organizational communications. They help to avoid two of the most common problems experienced in the uncritical use of language—the mechanism of projection and the unlimited application of inference. On the one hand, projection places undue emphasis upon the words spoken rather than in seeking out the intent of the speaker or the context in which the discussion takes place. Projection neglects indexing or dating or any of the other operational semantic devices and fastens on the internalized system of meanings adopted by the individual. Inference, on the other hand, goes beyond the words and the message to attach interpretations and judgments far beyond the reality of the fact or event which caused communications to take place in the first instance. Inference cultivates its own facts and organizes them into a system of generalizations and interpretations which can become unrecognizable to those outside the world of the interpreter.

For administrators, and for their organizations, then, it is essential that operational semantic devices be utilized to provide reality tests for communication content and processes. Projection and inference are but two elements in the construction of a concept of "allness" which causes people to behave as though they had said it "all" or heard it "all" when, in fact, there is no such thing as an instruction, or statement, or question that cannot be misunderstood. The contribution of operational semantics is both to alert people to the problems and to provide remedial behaviors that can lead to better, more factual, more emphatic communications.

The Misuse of Language.   In the work of Sapir-Whorf, Korzybski, and the later semantic writers, there is an effort to develop a concept of truth in language—a truth, indeed, that overcomes the implicit errors and mis-directions which arise from the influence of cultural miasmas and unex-amined assumptions. The suggestion to the institution or the organiza-tion is that, if proper study and analysis is given to language, then clarity and consensus can result. This is all well and good when the intent of communications is to inform correctly or to seek truth. There has, of course, been a long history of the use of language to hide, distort, or to reconstruct truth, and an appreciation for the misuse of language is essential to be understanding of interpersonal and organizational communication.

Distortion and dissemblance have as lengthy a history as their opposites, but it was perhaps only with the propaganda efforts of the First World War that scientific analysis was given to the intended and unintended consequences of systematic efforts to misuse language for the benefit of the communicator.[29] The general examination of propaganda is beyond the scope of this paper, but there are elements of language misuse in terms of interpersonal and organizational communications which are important. Three phenomena deserve particular mention:

(1) *Calculated Euphemism.* The literature of propaganda is replete with the development of "glittering generalities" to clothe what we wish to sustain and "defamatory labels" to destroy that which we wish to oppose. What is less obvious is the development of a new language of euphemism to obscure the intent of communications. Orwell originated the term "Newspeak" which aptly describes our present predeliction for describing job firings as "outplacement" or military campaigns as "pacification measures."

(2) *Selective Attention.* The constant emphasis on, and return to, a theme which focuses attention on specific details rather than whole pictures. In American education, one could be pardoned if merit pay and prayer were seen as the only "issues" worthy of attention and discussion. They have been treated so at the very highest levels of public debate.

(3) *Selective Retention.* Closely related to, and in part a consequence of, the first two elements is the continuing perception of primacy and causality that causes distortion in memory and recollection. As Orwell indicates, those who control the present also control the past and can selectively rewrite history—including the events and chronicles of a school district or a school administrator. One need not even write an untruth; it is sometimes sufficient to ignore part of the truth or simply to present those aspects of truth which are in agreement with the intended recall of events.

These aspects of the misuse of language are inherent in the nomothetic and idiographic dimensions of organizations. Their dangers in concealing and redirecting truth, however, are significant. The old maxim applies here: those who fail to learn from history are doomed to relive it. In the case of those from whom history is withheld or distorted, there is even more probability that lessons will remain unlearned.

From the standpoint of the administrator and the organization, it is important that there be a search for truth. Communications demand acceptance of the concept that there may exist simultaneously "many truths" and alternative interpretations. By exploring these, and by seeking common elements, one senses the probability of generalized accuracy. It may be that only through the selected perceptions of administrators, teachers, parents, students, and dispassionate observers can any general picture of "truth" emerge about a given school. The operational answer may lie—as in the proposals of Korzybski—in developing a probabilistic, nondogmatic approach to truth discernment which rests less on a "belief" system than on empirical testing and continuing readjustment to data, experience, and perceptual evidence.

INTERPERSONAL COMMUNICATIONS

In his preface to the volume entitled, *Interpersonal Communication, Essays in Phenomenology and Hermeneutics,* Pilotta makes the point that an understanding of interpersonal communications begins with the concrete research of sociologists and other scientists, but it is grounded in a concept of mutuality such that:

> Seeing, experiencing, and hearing are not contained in isolated subjects but I see and hear with the sensibilities of the other and the other with mine. . . . One looks from "there" and I look from "here" and the relationship institutes a mutual tuning-in where one and the other's sensibilities intersect.[30]

This concern, and its attendant research, goes beyond the traditional model of information theory to an understanding of those elements which stimulate interpersonal communications, modulate its interactions, and elevate the depth of understanding afforded by its processes. In terms of small group and organizational behavior, the work of the "group dynamics" researchers including Lewin,[31] Lippitt,[32] and Haire[33] has contributed enormously to the understanding of communication processes. To be selective is, of course, to be exclusionary, but three particular contributions to interpersonal communications seem to be especially helpful for efforts to improved organizational effectiveness.

Festinger and Cognitive Dissonance. Leon Festinger has developed a series of hypotheses concerning the needs and purposes of communications within groups, factors which affect the stimuli for interpersonal communications.[34] Grouped collectively under the concept of cognitive dissonance, these hypotheses suggest that there is a pressure on members of a group to communicate that increases in intensity according to the perception of discrepancy in opinion regarding an "item x" among members of the group. The more relevant "item x" is to the purposes and activities of the group, the greater the pressure to develop uniformity and rule out discrepancy or dissonance concerning the matter.

From this starting point, Festinger and Newcomb, whose related work is frequently referred to as the "symmetry model" for communications,[35] develop a pattern of expectancies concerning interpersonal exchange. The more cohesive the group, the greater the pressure toward discussion; the need to communicate to a particular member of the group is directly related to the perceived discrepancy of his opinion or behavior—there is a need to make the deviate more consonant in relation to the group as a whole.

On one hand, some perceptions will stimulate further, more intense communications—if, for example, there is some evidence that the dissonant member is willing or about to change his opinion about the "item x." On the other hand, there are perceptions which will tend to reduce communications—if, for example, the deviate is perceived as a marginal or unwanted member of the group. At some point, continued dissonance on important items or issues will result in pressure of the intractable deviate.

These and other formulations from the literature of cognitive dissonance and symmetry modeling provide a significant focus for the analysis of actual small group and organizational communications. They explain the intolerable frustrations that many groups experience when they find disagreement over goals and activities, and they provide predictable directions for the ways in which uniformity pressures are brought to bear on those individuals who profess less than complete acceptance of group standards and beliefs.

Response Elements in Interpersonal Communications. While Newcomb and Festinger emphasized the stimulus aspects of communications, the work of Sherif[36] and Asch[37] has probed the shaping of response behavior in communication situations. In early experiments on the impact of group presence on individual behavior, Sherif found that individuals tended to initiate "group norm constructs" even in the case when they were essentially placed together as an aggregate rather than a purposively organized grouping. The group norm effect even carried over when the persons were separated and returned to individual behavior modes.[38]

Asch, over a series of experiments with varied control conditions, reported that individual response behavior could be modified or controlled in a large number of cases. Given a relatively simple judgment task, he found that individuals tended to modify their response behavior (and accuracy) when faced with the fact that other members participating in the experiment were given different and unanimous responses. Over three-quarters of the subjects gave in to some extent to group pressure, while over one-third of the total responses were incorrect given the pressure of group conformity.[39]

In succeeding trials, Asch found that the presence of only one supporter could effectively marshal resistance to the group pressure while the withdrawal of that single "ally" could have a devastating effect on some respondents. The size of the group exercising pressure toward conformity did not seem to have great importance—three concerted members had about the same swaying effect as twelve to fifteen. There did appear to be some cultural variations when the experiments were conducted in different countries, but there was still general evidence that group behavior seriously affects individual response behavior—even when there is gross discrepancy between what the group is saying and what the individual is seeing.[40]

The significance of these findings relative to response patterning becomes greater when one recognizes that most institutions and organizations have much stronger nomothetic and superordinate dimensions than any of the experimental groups mounted by Sherif, Asch, or other social researchers. As Severin and Tankard[41] suggest, there is a multiplicative factor in group pressures in "real" organizations that causes the members to accept and adopt measures that, perhaps, none of the persons operating as individuals might countenance or practice. The combination of stimulus imitation and response conformity can cause great problems in both interpersonal and organizational communications. Only proactive recognition and overt efforts to combat these phenomena can reduce the harmful effects of pressure and conformity behavior on communications.

Levels of Interpersonal Communications. Over recent years, there has been a considerable growth in the literature of interpersonal communications analysis. Berne, for example, has developed a system of transactional analysis to explicate the relationships which are fostered by stylistic approaches to conversation.[42] Karpman has proposed an analytic approach to the discrimination of appropriate and inappropriate communication strategies.[43] In related work, Johnson has attempted to fashion a conceptual framework for the enhancement of interpersonal feedback to improve the quality of both cognitive and affective elements of communications.[44] Perhaps, however, the work of Powell is of even greater consequence to the enhancement of interpersonal communications in the sense of his distinction between "subject-object" communications and that form of dialogue which he terms an "encounter."[45]

Powell proposes an inverse ordering of five levels of interpersonal communications as follows:[46]

(1) Level Five: *Cliche Conversation*. This is the superficial and conventional level of speaking. "Hello! How are you?" "Fine, thank you."

(2) Level Four: *Reporting Facts about Others*. We offer nothing of ourselves, but we do provide information or narrate accounts of events.

(3) Level Three: *My Ideas and Judgments*. I am willing to tell you some of my feelings and ideas though generally at a somewhat guarded level.

(4) Level Two: *My Emotions and Gut Feeling*. I am willing to be more honest—and vulnerable—about my feelings, my personal concerns, and beliefs.

(5) Level One: *Peak Communication*. A degree of absolute openness and honesty in which authentic thoughts, feelings, needs, and beliefs are exposed and shared.

Perhaps a clearer understanding of Powell's concern for high and, therefore, more honest and open forms of communication can be gained from considering how Likert characterized the highly effective work group. Among the points which he feels are most related to high productivity and high morale are:

(1) Members have a high degree of confidence and trust in each other.

(2) There exists an unusually open exchange of information.

(3) Constructive criticisms are freely exchanged.

(4) Decisions are reached through consensus after members freely exercise their influence.[47]

Each of these aspects of affective work group behavior represents interpersonal communications at the third or higher levels. None of them fall at the cliche or dispassionate reportorial level. Relatedly, Argyris argued that conditions for effective organizational behavior must include a high tolerance for deviancy from existing norms[48]—note that both Festinger and Asch would argue that most "traditional" group behavior tends to reduce deviancy unconsciously if not consciously. Argyris further proposed that there must be a high degree of inter-relatedness both among individuals and between individuals and the group in such ways that Powell's higher level formulations of communication expression obviously must be invoked.

Powell concluded that "gut level" communications are the only possible way that individuals (and, by extension, organizations) can establish a true "authentic" relationship, and that this will, in turn, foster emotional and intellectual growth on the part of all concerned, and, finally, evoke responsive honesty and openness from all the relevant others.[49] Indeed, much of the work of the applied group dynamics school, embodied in the experience of T-groups, lay in fostering a willingness to expose one's self through gut level communication so that significant others could respond freely and with confidence.

ORGANIZATIONAL COMMUNICATIONS

From the earliest formal studies of organizations and their behavior, communications has taken a central focus. The "functional" arrangement proposed by Frederick Taylor, for example, was designed so that each worker would have eight specialized "bosses" to provide information on job functions, speed, quality, and other details of the shop.[50] Developers of bureaucratic theory stressed the need for detailed communications—usually in writing—so that there would be no doubt or confusion regarding the elements or the limitations of a position. The more recent work, however, of Barnard, Simon, and Likert deserves to be singled out in terms of organizational communications.

Communications and the Executive. In *The Functions of the Executive,* Chester Barnard defined the first responsibility of the leader in terms of providing for a system of communications.[51] The attributes of such a system were carefully explained. The communications network must be known, including both formal and informal exchange patterns. Information to be distributed throughout the system must be definite so that ambiguity and inferential processes are reduced to a minimum. The messages should characteristically be direct and short, and couched in the simplest possible language. Each transmission should be complete in itself so that understanding and compliance are enhanced. Finally, Barnard sketched out the need for "circuitous" communications by which he meant a system that provided a closed loop feedback—a concept of essential proportions to later information theorists working with mathematical and cybernetic models of communications.

Barnard defined an organization as that kind of cooperation among men which is conscious, deliberate, and purposeful, and he saw the success or failure of the organization directly related to the success of communications in establishing and maintaining the processes for cooperation. In order to become effective and efficient, organizations had to deal continually and successfully with their individuals and groups in such ways that a mutuality of goals is perceived and attained. As simple as this concept may be, Barnard argued that successful cooperation in most organizations is short-lived and often terminated in frenetic failure.[52]

To overcome these problems of cooperation, Barnard emphasized the centrality of communications in developing healthy interactions between and among the individuals and groups which comprise the organization. He rejected the mechanistic approaches of classical bureaucratic theory and constructed a concept of the individual as the prime actor in bringing harmony into focus within the organization. He argued that coercion is self-defeating and that persuasion through rational processes is the only guarantee of continuing cooperation. Contrary to the proposals of many of his contemporaries, Barnard saw the informal organization as a vital and positive force for cooperation, and he urged the executive to learn and to utilize this network in order to enhance communications.[53]

Organizational Models and Communications. Herbert Simon went even further than Barnard in rejecting classical administrative theory based in large part on the limitations of those formulations in treating motivational considerations and information processes.[54] In Simon's own approach to administrative theory, communications, influence, and coordination are basic elements which undergird the entire structure. Communications become the bridge between individual participation and group identification.

The unique contribution of Simon to communications theory lies in his development of models for adaptive behavior which permit the generation of probabilistic statements concerning the impact of various forms and processes of interaction. In the analysis of the intended and unintended consequences of using general and impersonal rules (March and Simon[55]), for example, he argued that what is intended simply to convey the organizational power relationships may also provide the workers with knowledge about minimally acceptable behavior, which tends to exacerbate the differences between the organizational goals and individual achievement levels. Analyzing the model facilitates the development of alternative processes and networks to provide a closer realization of intended consequences while avoiding the most problematic of the unintended results.

In arriving at his formulation of "bounded rationality," Simon sought through communications processes to look for satisfactory choices rather than optimal ones, to replace global goals with tangible and measurable subgoals, and to divide up decision making among many specialists by means of a structure of communications and authority relationships. By concentrating on the boundaries of the possible rather than the unknowns of the ideal, intractable problems can be reduced to tractable proportions. In this process, communications becomes the key to organizational decision making and problem solving.[56]

Participation and the Linking-Pin. As Barnard rejected the mechanistic approaches of classical administration theory in favor of a dynamic consciousness of the communications process central to cooperation, so

Simon emphasized the need to use communications to reduce problems and decisions into a manageable form. To these important insights, Rensis Likert proposed a new foundational concept, that of participation, and a new formulation of the executive/administrative role, the link-pin concept.[57] Taken together, these two propositions magnify both the importance and the contributory effects of organizational communications.

The consequences of participation in decision making through the communications process is seen by Likert not only to be important in terms of the idiographic dimension and to the outcomes for individual and group morale, but also as essential, moreover, in attaining the nomothetic goals of the organization in terms of outcomes and effectiveness. In addition, there is a natural growth process in which deeper and deeper involvement in the communications-participation interaction is not only desirable, but, in Likert's opinion, also necessary for continuing cooperation and adjustment. In this respect, his work is closely aligned with that of Argyris[58] and Maslow[59] in terms of personality, motivation, and organizational growth. All three of these theorists see individual growth and organizational development as closely intertwined in such ways that greater "adulthood" in individual decision making, communications, and time perspective can lead to greater organizational effectiveness, efficiency, and cooperation. To Likert, participation is essentially a continuum with a natural growth from lesser involvement and lesser communications to greater involvement and greater communications with no necessary cut-off point. To Maslow, the concept of Eupsychian Management is essentially a process of letting the organization as well as its people reach the meta-needs of belongingness, esteem, and self-actualization by a combination of participation and goal-achievement. For Argyris, the only effective organization is that which listens to the maturational needs of its people. In all three instances, organizational and individual communications are essential to motivation, activation, and accomplishment.

The second of Likert's proposals for administrative theory, the link-pin concept, is also essentially derived from his studies of communications. Noting that Barnard and others had observed the difficulties of achieving both upward and downward networks that would provide undistorted communication channels, Likert advanced the need for group processes that will overcome the natural obstacles to single superordinate-subordinate relationships and offer alternative ways in which participation is encouraged within the sub-groups of the organization. The supervisors and administrators represent the linkage of their subordinate groups with their peers and their supervisor. Essentially, this means that no administrator customarily deals with a single subordinate—rather, each administrator deals with a group of subordinates whose combined perspective and persuasive powers can offset the natural imbalance of the traditional organizational power relationships. Likert argues that the link-pin concept will legitimate the participation process and reduce the possibility of pseudo-invocation of two-way communications.[60]

TOWARD A CONCEPTUAL UNDERSTANDING

Although it is correct and proper to ascribe the beginnings of language and communications study to the pre-Christian era, it is also accurate and important to recognize that most systematic inquiry into communications is less than 70 years old and that much of the work to date is of a probing rather than a probative nature. Faced with the facts that there is no common definition of communications and that there is a variety of models of communications from which to choose, it seems important that the next round of investigations seek to expand the conceptual understandings before more generalizations are hazarded. The following analytic approaches would seem to be particularly salutary in terms of deepening understanding of essential elements of communications.

Content Analysis—Getting at the "What" of Communications. Berelson has described content analysis as the "objective, systematic, and quantitative description of communication content."[61] Much of the effort in such analysis to date has been in the area of mass communications and the treatment of political, racial, and sexual stereotypes. From the work of linguists and semanticists, however, it is recognized that organizations and institutions have their own *patois* and language patterns which must be understood in order to effect measurement and effective change procedures. The work of content analysis can be shifted from the macro to the micro level in order to discover the parlance and the positioning of communications patterns and networking at the institutional unit of observation and analysis.

This approach could provide a much richer knowledge of what is important to be talked about and in what ways these "important subjects" are treated. In gross ways, it is known that school systems have ceased to speak of expansion and now talk of decline and retrenchment. What impact and what behavioral consequences can be drawn from the communications practiced in such a period of change? Similarly, it is known that there are differences in viewer perceptions of school administrator capacity, authenticity, and effectiveness. Content analysis might move us a long way toward understanding the relationship of communications to the judgmental processes exercised by teachers, students, board members, and the public.

Communications Surveys—Getting at the "How" of Communications. A second analytic technology that promises to develop better insight into organizational communications is the "communications survey." As described by Severin and Tankard,[62] these surveys have generally been conducted on large media samples to determine the accuracy and contagion of certain news stories or releases. In sociometric group studies, however, there is companion work on small group communications analysis that has influenced the use of communications surveys in individual corporations and institutions for the purpose of determining what the actual patterns and networks are for information passage, and, then, an analysis of ways of improving that system.[63]

Institutions have used a variety of sampling and communications log techniques[64] to collect information on individual and group communication processes. These can then be combined and portrayed in a sociometric pattern display to picture both formal and informal interaction processes. As in the case of sociograms, both "stars" and "isolates" sometimes emerge in ways which might not be at all expected from a perusal of the institution's organization charts or job descriptions.

By better documentation and understanding of the actualities of institutional communications, it is possible to utilize better the insights of Barnard, Simon, and Likert in providing planned editorial or alternative patterns and routes to improve the participative processes and enhance the flow (and accuracy) of both upward and downward communications within the organization.

Attitude Surveys—Getting the "Outcomes" of Communications. While Halpin and Croft have made the "Organizational Climate" survey[65] a household term in American schools, there is growing interest in all manner of organizations and institutions to develop a periodic, continuing process of surveying to determine attitudes, opinions, and organizational norms for such dimensions as: goal focus, communications adequacy, relationships with peers and supervisors, status and recognition, and identification with the institution.

In the past, attitude surveys too often have been viewed as one-shot, or at best, occasional exercises to provide an overview of organizational "health." In this context, it can be seen how important repeated sampling and cumulative data-gathering is to diagnosis. It is only when sound data bases have been established that it can be known whether, in a given individual situation, a weight loss or a cholesterol gain is significant or unimportant. Moreover, for any two patients, the vital health indicators may not be the same. The diagnosis of institutional health is also situation specific. Change and directionality may be much more important than mean levels of response to any given item on a single administration of an attitude survey.

For executives and administrators, the accumulation of accurate organizational feelings on important institutional dimensions can provide the soundest possible guide for needed changes in communications and authority relations in order to achieve the best outcomes. In the absence of "real" information, change or improvement efforts may not only be of limited utility, but may also even be dysfunctional.

Toward the Future

Even in the still emergent field of study that characterizes communications theory, there are sound injunctions and suggestions for the educational administrator to ponder. First, there is a common (if not unanimously accepted) model for communications that proceeds from information theory which can detail essential elements for understanding communications. The processes of encoding, media selection, transmission, and provision for feedback are open to administrative amelioration currently. In addition, the following approaches can be utilized:

(1) An examination of the language-culture interface within the institution or organization based on the insights of linguists and semantics. The applied school of general semanticists offers a concrete set of guides for the clarification of communications.

(2) The enhancement of interpersonal communications through the insights of the group dynamics and the transactional analyses approaches to improve the quality of communications stimuli, response, and "level" of understanding and empathy.

(3) The improvement of organizational concepts using the insights and the evidence of theorists who have advocated the fundamental contribution of communications to organizational cooperation, effectiveness, and growth.

(4) The application and redirection of analytic tools such as content analysis, communications surveys, and attitude surveys to organizational units of observation and analysis.

In short, much more has already been learned about organizational communications than is frequently put into practice. The primary emphasis for the near future should be on specific organizational and institutional inquiry which can form the basis for the generation of new hypotheses for more general and systematic propositions and parameters for societal research.

NOTES

1. F. E. X. Dance, "The 'Concept' of Communications." *Journal of Communication* 20 (1970): 201-210.

2. H. D. Lasswell, "The Structure and Function of Communication in Society," in *The Communication of Ideas,* Lyman Bryson, ed. (New York: Harper & Bros., 1948).

3. W. J. Severin and J. W. Tankard, Jr., *Communication Theories* (New York: Hastings House, 1979).

4. Lasswell, "The Structure and Function."

5. C. Shannon and W. Weaver, *The Mathematical Theory of Communication* (Urbana: University of Illinois Press, 1949).

6. N. Weiner, *Cybernetics* (New York: John Wiley, 1948).

7. D. Berlo, *The Process of Communication: An Introduction to Theory and Practice* (San Francisco: Rinehart, 1960).

8. K. E. Andersen, *Persuasion Theory and Practice* (Boston: Allyn & Bacon, 1971).

9. W. Schramm, ed., *The Process and Effects of Mass Communications* (Urbana: University of Illinois Press, 1954).

10. J. W. Getzels and H. A. Thelen, "The Classroom Group as a Unique Social System," in *The Dynamics of Instructional Groups,* A. B. Henry, ed. (Chicago: National Society for the Study of Education, 1960).

11. H. A. Simon, *Administrative Behavior,* 2nd ed. (New York: Free Press, 1957).

12. S. S. Sargent and R. C. Williamson, *Social Psychology,* 2nd ed. (New York: Ronald Press, 1958).

13. F. Boas, *General Anthropology* (Boston: D. C. Heath, 1938).

14. O. Klineberg, *Social Psychology,* rev. ed. (New York: Harper & Row, 1926).

15. E. Sapir, *Language: An Introduction to the Study of Speech* (New York: Harcourt, Brace, and Co., 1921).

16. B. L. Whorf, *Language, Thought and Reality* (New York: John Wiley, 1956).

17. *Ibid.*

18. D. B. Quinn, ed., *The Elizabethans and the Irish* (Ithaca, CA: Cornell University Press, 1960).

19. Andersen, *Persuasion Theory and Practice.*

20. Schramm, *The Process and Effects.*

21. A. Korzybski, *Science and Sanity* (Lancaster, PA: Science Press, 1933).

22. *Ibid.*

23. *Ibid.*

24. *Ibid.*

25. S. Chase, *The Power of Words* (New York: Harcourt, Brace & Co., 1953).

26. S. I. Hayakawa, *Language and Thought in Action* (New York: Harper & Bros., 1946).

27. W. Johnson, *People in Quandaries* (New York: Harper & Bros., 1946).

28. Hayakawa, *Language in Thought and Action.*

29. Sargent and Williamson, *Social Psychology.*

30. J. J. Pilotta, ed., *Interpersonal Communication* (Washington, DC: Center for Advanced Research in Phenomenology and University Press of America, 1982).

31. K. Lewin, *Field Theory in Social Science* (New York: Harper, 1951).

32. R. Lippitt, "An Experimental Study of Authoritarian and Democratic Group Atmospheres," *University of Iowa Studies in Child Welfare* 16, 3 (1940): 143-195.

33. M. Haire, "Group Dynamics in the Industrial Situation," in *Industrial Conflict*, A. Kornhauser, R. Dubin, and A. M. Ross, eds. (New York: McGraw-Hill, 1954).

34. L. Festinger, "Informal Social Communication," *Psychological Review* 57 (1950): 271-282.

35. T. M. Newcomb, "An Approach to the Study of Communicative Acts," *Psychological Review* 60 (1953): 393-404.

36. M. Sherif, *The Psychology of Group Norms* (New York: Harper & Bros., 1936).

37. S. E. Asch, "Studies of Independence and Conformity: I. A Minority of One Against a Unanimous Majority," *Psychological Monographs* 70, 9 (1956): 1-70.

38. Sherif, *The Psychology of Group Norms.*

39. Asch, "Studies of Independence and Conformity."

40. *Ibid.*

41. Severin and Tankard, *Communication Theories.*

42. E. Berne, *Games People Play: The Psychology of Human Relationships* (New York: Grove, 1964).

43. S. Karpman, "Fairy Tales and Script Drama Analysis," *Transactional Analysis Bulletin* 7, 26 (1968): 39-43.

44. D. W. Johnson, *Reaching Out: Interpersonal Effectiveness and Self-Actualization* (Englewood Cliffs, NJ: Prentice-Hall, 1972).

45. J. Powell, *Why Am I Afraid to Tell You Who I Am?* (Niles, IL: Argus Communications, 1969).

46. *Ibid.*

47. R. Likert, *The Human Organization: Its Management and Value* (New York: McGraw-Hill, 1967).

48. C. Argyris, *Personality and Organizations* (New York: Harper & Row, 1957).

49. Powell, *Why Am I Afraid to Tell You Who I Am?*

50. F. W. Taylor, *The Principles of Scientific Management* (New York: Harper & Bros., 1923).

51. C. I. Barnard, *The Functions of the Executive* (Cambridge, MA: Harvard University Press, 1938).

52. *Ibid.*

53. *Ibid.*

54. Simon, *Administrative Behavior.*

55. J. G. March and H. A. Simon, *Organizations* (New York: John Wiley, 1958).

56. Simon, *Administrative Behavior.*

57. R. Likert, *New Patterns of Management* (New York: McGraw-Hill, 1961).

58. Argyris, *Personality and Organizations.*

59. A. H. Maslow, *Eupsydian Management* (Homewood, IL: Irwin, 1965).

60. Likert, *New Patterns of Management.*

61. R. T. Budd and L. Donohew, *Content Analysis of Communications* (New York: Macmillan, 1967).

62. Severin and Tankard, *Communication Theories.*

63. M. E. Shaw, *Group Dynamics: The Psychology of Small Group Behavior,* 3rd ed. (New York: McGraw-Hill, 1981).

64. J. P. Lysaught, "Notes on the Communication Survey in an Industrial Setting" (Unpublished manuscript. University of Rochester, 1984).

65. A. W. Halpin and D. B. Croft, *The Organizational Climate of Schools* (Washington, DC: U.S. Office of Education, Research Project, Contract #SAE 543-8639, August 1962).

CHAPTER SIXTEEN

The Aesthetics of Leadership

DANIEL L. DUKE

The author conducts a brief analysis of contemporary approaches to understanding leadership. New approaches to the study of leadership are joined with a theory of aesthetics in developing an aesthetic-based leadership model. Four aesthetic properties of leadership are proposed along with ways these properties became manifest.

Recent years have witnessed the publication of numerous studies of leadership. As scholarship accumulates in this area, however, we seem to grow less clear about the nature of leadership. For the moment, the present perspective is likely to add to this general confusion. It is hoped, though, that confusion eventually will yield to clarity, as awareness builds that leadership may best be understood as an aesthetic phenomenon.

Of what value is the concept "leadership"? For scholars it serves a variety of purposes. Leadership is used as a general description of what leaders do. It is employed as an independent variable, to help account for organizational success or failure, and as a dependent variable, when the goal is to better understand how to train leaders or how to create organizational conditions conducive to leadership. Related to leadership's utility as an independent variable is its current popularity as an attribution. Overall the uses to which scholars put leadership tend to concern characteristics of persons in executive and managerial roles or characteristics of organizations. Certain people are found to manifest or not to manifest behaviors associated with leadership. Certain organizations are characterized by the presence or absence of leadership.

Reflecting on the bulk of this scholarship on leadership leaves one with a feeling akin to that which follows a feast in a Chinese restaurant. An hour after consuming these informative accounts, one wonders whether he really has acquired any greater understanding of leadership. This perspective contends that current appreciation of the nature of leadership will be incomplete as long as the term is used solely to characterize leaders and organizations. Leadership may also be thought of as an aesthetic quality, like beauty. Situations in which leadership is perceived to be

SOURCE: Daniel L. Duke, "The Aesthetics of Leadership," *Educational Administration Quarterly*, Vol. 22, No. 1, pp. 7-27. Copyright © by The University Council for Educational Administration. Reprinted with permission.

present or absent tell something about those who observe leadership and the cultural context in which they live. It is leadership's value as a source of knowledge concerning social meaning that serves as the central focus of the present work.

First a brief analysis of some of the limitations of contemporary approaches to understanding leadership will be conducted. This will be followed by a discussion of several promising developments in the study of leadership. Based on key themes in these new approaches as well as work in the theory of aesthetics, a case will be made for regarding leadership as an aesthetic phenomenon. An aesthetics-based "model" of the leadership experience is proposed and its potential benefits assessed. This perspective will conclude with a discussion of four aesthetic properties of contemporary leadership and several ways by which these properties become manifest.

CONVENTIONAL EFFORTS TO UNDERSTAND LEADERSHIP

Scholarly fascination with leaders and leadership dates back to at least the work of Plato, who regarded statecraft as a member of the same general class of human endeavors as the fine arts.[2] Machiavelli prided himself on being a connoisseur of leaders. His classic manual for leaders— *The Prince*—opened with a letter to his patron, Lorenzo de Medici, in which he stated, "I have not found among my belongings anything as dear to metaphor or that I value as much as my understanding of the deeds of great men."[3]

Understanding the "deeds of great men" has become an increasingly great challenge over the years since 1514. As the world in which leaders function has grown in complexity, so too has the study of leadership. The concern of modern social science with the relationship between means and ends (as well as inputs and outcomes, independent and dependent variables, etc.) has fostered a variety of paradigms which focus on how leaders behave and what they accomplish. The world of the leader often is portrayed as a rational one in which goals are set, resources are mobilized, plans are implemented, and problems are solved. The behaviors of leaders are presented as occurring in patterns, which permit certain generalizations to be made across leaders. Contemporary studies of leadership examine phenomena such as the exchange relations between leaders and subordinates, the types of leader behavior associated with certain predictable situations, and the characteristics of leaders of successful organizations.[4] The state of scholarship on leadership, from a conventional perspective, is ably captured in the following paragraph:

Definitions of leadership abound. There is no clearcut agreement on the meaning of leadership for all circumstances. Leadership can probably best be understood by submitting specific behaviors and roles to careful study. Management of functional and nonfunctional behavior play an important role in achievement of authority, power, and effectiveness of leaders.[5]

Conventional efforts to understand leadership have provided important contributions to an awareness of how leaders are selected, spend their time, and impact events. In spite of these contributions, leadership remains an elusive phenomenon. Limitations can be found with at least three of the prevailing conceptions of leadership: leadership as role, leadership as control or influence, and leadership as behavior.

Leadership as Role. Leadership is frequently treated as if it is synonymous with the role of leader. A tautology results in which leadership is conceptualized as that which leaders do or are expected to do. Leadership therefore becomes a value-neutral term used strictly for descriptive purposes. Such a conception seems to preclude the possibility that leadership, particularly as used in common parlance, conveys social meaning or value. It is known though, that in the late 1960s in the United States, leadership frequently connoted exclusion, suspicion, and oppression. Fifteen years later the term has become associated with very positive feelings of hope and recovery.

A further limitation with role-based conceptions of leadership concerns the nature of executive work. It seems reasonable to maintain that not all of what a leader does represents leadership. Much of the work is routine administration. In some cases, a particular leader may not be engaged in any activity worthy of the label leadership. In other instances, a person who does not occupy an executive role may seem to possess leadership qualities. Role-based conceptions of leadership simply are too restrictive.

Leadership as Control or Influence. Leadership is often associated with organizational control—especially control of resources—and influence.[6] While these conceptions may have been useful in earlier times, they seem too simplistic for today's circumstances. For one thing, they overlook the reciprocal relationships between leaders and followers.[7] Such conceptions also minimize the numerous constraints on the behavior of leaders.[8] Finally, control and influence-based notions of leadership too easily become focused on the tangible accomplishments of leaders. What is missed are those instances when leaders serve symbolic purposes. Pfeffer and Salancik[9] suggest, in fact, that the symbolic dimension of leadership may become crucial when the constraints on leaders prevent them from achieving major objectives.

Leadership as Behavior. One of the most popular ways to think about leadership is to conceive of it as a set of behaviors or activities.[10] Mintzberg,[11] for example, considers leadership behavior to be one of nine subsets of managerial behavior. Unlike role-based conceptions, these notions allow for the possibilities that non-leaders may exhibit leadership and that only a fraction of a leader's work may actually involve leadership activities.

Unfortunately there is little evidence that most people think of leadership as a batch of discrete behaviors. When a complaint is heard about a lack of leadership, it is unlikely that it refers to the absence of a particular set of behaviors. What is perceived to be missing is not so easily observed or described. Furthermore, it is conceivable that there are individuals who manifest all the behaviors associated with leadership, yet fail to embody leadership. Those who attempt to "train" leaders long have recognized this problem. Some students master all the necessary operations—from planning to decision making—but they do not convey the impression of leadership.

Leadership seems to be a *gestalt* phenomenon, greater than the sum of its behavioral parts. Neustadt[12] recognized this quality of leadership in his work on presidential power. He noted that the impression the President makes "depends not only on the content of his action but on the events surrounding it, as these events are understood by men who watch him work."[13] Neustadt's work reminds us that we are unlikely fully to understand leadership as long as we try to construct boundaries around it. Making sense of leadership entails understanding what it means when people apply the term, not stipulating what it is and what it is not. Leadership is, first and foremost, a perception invested with social meaning and value.

Promising Directions

Despite the general trends in scholarship on leadership, a small number of thinkers have insisted on seeking alternative understandings of the phenomenon. Among the first to challenge prevailing conceptions of leadership were those who recognized its symbolic functions. Symbols have been characterized as "signs which express much more than their intrinsic content" and "significations which embody and represent some wider pattern of meaning."[14] Symbolic functions have typically been associated more with public needs than leader intentions. As Klapp maintained:

The pure symbolic leader may "act" in a dramatic sense, but it is quite possible for him to be otherwise inert and passive. He does not actually lead; the public uses him. Even in action he is a vehicle. Such a leader does not ride his following as though it were a horse; rather, the horse, it might be said, rides him.[15]

Much of the scholarship on the symbolic dimensions of leadership derives from the work of anthropologists and communication theorists. Geertz,[16] for example, notes the capacity of traditional societies to invest in leaders and their accouterment of office, certain key beliefs and sentiments. Elder and Cobb observe, however, that the "symbolism that supports power arises not only from the trappings of position but also from the gestures and behaviors of officeholders."[17] They go on to contend that the public perception of leadership is closely linked to a leader's ability to "engage in actions that symbolize for followers responsible coping behavior." These actions are likely to change over time and from one culture to another.

Recently theorists have begun to apply the concept of symbolism to understanding organizational behavior. Leaders, as well as other members of organizations, are "able to use language, can exhibit insight, produce and interpret metaphors, are able to vest meaning in events, behavior, and objects, seek meaning in their lives—in short, can act symbolically."[18]

Compatible with notions of symbolic leadership is the work of interaction theorists, who contend that leadership is an "interactional phenomenon arising when group formation takes place."[19] Even when Mintzberg[20] focuses on leadership behavior, he is careful to stress the relational behavior between leaders and subordinates. Leadership, to interactionists, cannot be understood solely as a set of behaviors by individuals in executive roles, but must be studied in terms of the reciprocal influences exerted by leaders on followers and vice versa. Interactionist ideas owe a debt to Parsons and his distinctions between the cognitive perceptions of people engaged in interactions. He pointed out that people perceive each other in three distinct ways

(1) cognitive perception and conceptualization, the answer to the question, *what the object is,* and (2) cathexis—attachment or aversion—the answer to the question of *what the object means* in an emotional sense. The third (3) mode by which a person orients himself to an object is by evaluation—the integration of cognitive and cathectic meanings of the object to form a system, including the stability of such a system over time.[21]

During the past decade organization theorists have increasingly applied the concepts of cognitive psychology to the study of leadership.

Cognitive psychology focuses on such matters as the influence of schemata on expectations and the role of meaning in perception.[22] Eoyang[23] provides a useful bridge between the older work on symbolic leadership and more recent applications of cognitive theories. Symbolic meaning is characterized, not as an independent attribute of the symbol (in this case, the leader), but as an attribute of the interaction of the symbol and the perceiver's previous experience and knowledge. For the most part the symbols people encounter are congruent with established beliefs. Occasionally, however, symbolic transformations occur, the effect being to produce dramatic changes in cognitive systems. Burns[24] links this process with a particular variety of leadership.

Pfeffer draws heavily on cognitive psychology in this treatment of leadership as an attribution. Citing Kelley's[25] contention that attribution processes serve as means by which individuals try to control as well as understand their world, Pfeffer states that "the emphasis on leadership derives partially from a desire to believe in the effectiveness and importance of individual action."[26] Salancik and Meindl[27] recently have used attribution theory to analyze the annual reports of major corporate executives. They contend that executives are apt to take responsibility for corporate problems, as well as successes, in order to foster the impression that leadership matters.

Applications of cognitive psychology to the study of leadership stress the structures of meaning associated with the exercise of authority. Meaning is also a theme in the work of Pondy. Taking up his own challenge to think more creatively about the nature of leadership, Pondy proposes that leadership is a language game. Language becomes a vehicle through which meaning is conveyed. The effectiveness of a leader

> lies in his ability to make activity meaningful for those in his role set—not to change behavior but to give others a sense of understanding what they are doing, and especially to articulate it so they can communicate about the meaning of their behavior.[28]

This new thinking about leadership conveys a considerable distance from the classical conceptions of command and decision. Leadership is portrayed as a less straightforward, more subtle phenomenon, involving more than what meets the eye. There is acknowledgment that leadership is a perception. As such, it reflects the structures of meaning of the perceiver and the culture and times in which the perceiver lives. The new scholarship therefore is concerned about those who look at leaders as well as the leaders themselves. How do people make sense of what leaders do? What do leaders' actions mean? At what point is a leader perceived to be exercising leadership? How is this impression of leadership created? Such questions suggest that leadership may best be understood as an aesthetic phenomenon.

UNDERSTANDING LEADERSHIP AESTHETICALLY

What does it mean to view a phenomenon aesthetically? Hospers maintains:

> The aesthetic attitude, or the "aesthetic way of looking at the world," is most commonly opposed to the *practical* attitude, which is concerned only with the utility of the object in question.[29]

Rather than riveting attention to what leaders achieve, an aesthetic perspective on leadership would be concerned with the meaning attached to leaders and what they do. *Leadership, in fact, helps bring meaning to the relationships between individuals and greater entities—communities, organizations, nations.* Leaders may engage in numerous activities, but without leadership their actions are likely to lack meaning for those around them. Meaning often results less from achieved objectives, rational planning, and the manipulation of power than from dramatic performances, inspiring expressions of public concerns, and creative responses to unforeseen occurrences. Consider the case of John F. Kennedy, a president credited with impressive leadership whose actual accomplishments were dwarfed by those of other presidents. While Lyndon Johnson and Richard Nixon may have accomplished more, they were perceived to embody less leadership than Kennedy, in part because of what the Kennedy presidency meant to so many people. In his words, style, and public performance, Kennedy symbolized youth, vigor, hope, and social commitment—all qualities that captured the imagination of Americans.

Would "the Kennedy magic" have worked immediately after World War II or in 1980? Probably not to the extent it did in the early 1960s, when the "baby boomers" came of age and the nation hungered for youthful leadership. Timing is a critical dimension of leadership. Timing is, in part, a function of the "fit" between a leader and the historical and cultural context in which he leads.

The salience of issues like meaning, timing, and fit suggest that leadership is rooted in experience—an active rather than a static phenomenon. Child's[30] schematic representation of the subject matter of aesthetics (see Figure 16.1) may be useful in conceptualizing leadership as an aesthetic experience.

Child proposes that a work of art—an aesthetic creation—derives from human behavior. Therefore he posits the existence of an artist or artists.

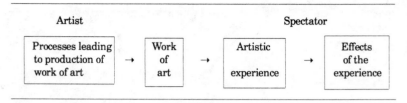

Figure 16.1: Child's Model of Aesthetics

While the artist produces a work of art, that product has no meaning of its own. Meaning is generated as a result of artistic experience or the perception with which the observer responds to the work of art. Experiencing a work of art has the potential to exert more than a momentary impact on the observer. Child contends that artistic experience may influence personal understanding and morality, among other things.

Adapting Child's model to the specific case of leadership, a picture begins to emerge of how leadership might be understood aesthetically. Figure 16.2 shows the behaviors of a leader to be the original source of stimuli. Only a portion of these behaviors, however, may be intended to foster the impression of leadership. These are referred to as "acts of leading" and correspond to an artist's works of art. Acts of leading constitute a form of artistry and may involve a variety of creative endeavors, including dramatics, design, and orchestration. As those who observe leaders are exposed to creative acts of leading, they may begin to experience leadership. This experience becomes meaningful to the extent that it evokes certain feelings that are valued by the observer. These feelings are associated with identifiable *properties of leadership*. Properties are aesthetic in nature and linked closely to a cultural and temporal context. Examples of aesthetic properties of contemporary leadership include direction, engagement, fit, and originality.

The aesthetic model of leadership draws heavily on cognitive psychology in that it acknowledges that the behavior of a leader does not constitute leadership until it is perceived to do so by an observer. Hence, a leader's personal proclamation of leadership is of little direct significance. For the perception of leadership to occur, an observer must find something about a leader meaningful. Meaning may derive from what a leader does or what a leader does not do. Meaning may also be attached to certain abstract qualities symbolized by the leader. While a leader may consciously seek to create meaningful impressions, ultimately the determination of meaning resides with the observer, who in turn is subject to the influence of his present beliefs and past experiences, as well as the cultural context in which he lives. To better understand the relationship

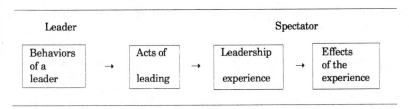

Leader				Spectator		
Behaviors of a leader	→	Acts of leading	→	Leadership experience	→	Effects of the experience

Figure 16.2: Aesthetic Model of Leadership

between leadership and meaning, it may be useful to examine more closely a few aesthetic properties of leadership.

Aesthetic Properties of Leadership

Personal appreciation for the properties associated with leadership builds gradually, as people are socialized at school, home, and business. Just as there is probably no one moment when a person is conscious of learning the properties of beauty, so there is unlikely to be a precise instant when the elements of leadership are first understood. Instead, perceptions of leadership become more sophisticated and individual as experience with leaders accumulates.

The four aesthetic properties of leadership below are not intended as a complete set of conditions nor do they necessarily represent universally acknowledged criteria. They simply seem to be some properties of leadership currently valued in Western industrial nations.

Direction. In the presence of leadership the individual senses direction. Direction is more than a course to follow. It is a path *together* with a reason for traveling it. Direction presumes meaning. Furthermore, with direction the elements of uncertainty and surprise are minimized. An analogy may be drawn between leadership and literature. Direction is felt when starting a great novel. While the specific conclusion remains unknown until the final chapter, the skilled author is able to introduce signals foreshadowing the ending. While great leaders hardly are capable of controlling events the way a novelist does, they still are able to convey a sufficient sense of certainty about the course of events to allay paralytic anxieties and permit energies to be mobilized productively. Franklin Roosevelt comes to mind. Even in the darkest moments of World War II, he was able to project a feeling that, in time, the Allies would prevail.

Churchill's leadership during the Second World War also could be characterized by direction. In a recent analysis of Churchill's world view, Thompson distinguishes between the Prime Minister's statesmanlike capacity to lead public opinion and the current tendency of many leaders to be led by public opinion:

> The concept of the leader in modern democratic societies is epitomized in the sensitive yet half-tragic figure of the present-day "practical politician" who takes soundings of the swift-running tides of public opinion in order to discover whither he is going to lead the people. What such a conception of popular leadership gains in responsiveness to rapid shifts in public opinion, it can lose in the quality of bold and creative leadership.[31]

Direction does not require a complicated content analysis of press releases and speeches to be identified. Nor does it depend on polls or surveys. Direction—as a property of leadership—is apparent, felt, part of the whole, inseparable from the leader. To think of Lincoln is to think of the unflagging commitment to preserving the union. To think of Gandhi is to be aware of his total dedication to liberating India through nonviolent means. Such a sense of direction appeals more to people's values and ideals than to their concerns for rewards and sanctions. It compels people to commit to causes greater than themselves.

Weick notes that direction should be a particularly vital concern of leaders in loosely coupled systems:

> The effective administrator in a loosely coupled system makes full use of symbol management to tie the system together. People need to be part of sensible projects. Their action becomes richer, more confident, and more satisfying when it is linked with important underlying themes, values, and movements. It is precisely this linking that is made possible when administrators articulate general directions.[32]

The sense of direction upon which the leader capitalizes is typically not an exclusive product of his own imagination, but a partial outgrowth of forces greater than himself—the values of a culture, a social movement, an idea "whose time has come." In his work on the inner experience of power, McClelland characterizes how successful leaders express direction:

> His message is not so much: "Do as I say because I am strong and know best. You are children with no wills of your own and must follow me because I know better," but rather, "Here are the goals which are true and right and which we share. Here is how we can reach them. You are strong and capable. You can accomplish these goals."[33]

Engagement. An old adage goes, "Things are managed, but people are led." Where there are people, there are feelings, thoughts, and aspirations. Leadership is distinguishable from management in part because of the extent to which it is capable of engaging these feelings, thoughts, and aspirations. An analogy can be made with art and its capacity to absorb the attention of the viewer or listener. In a good dramatic production, the playwright and actors are able to involve the audience. Yalom[34] notes that involvement leads to meaning rather than the reverse. In other words, meaning is a byproduct of the act of becoming engaged in activity. Unflagging loyalty may be the reward for leaders able to engage the hearts and minds of followers.

Loyalty traditionally has been associated with battlefield leadership. The example of Henry V at Agincourt comes to mind. The words Shakespeare attributes to Henry epitomize the capacity of an extraordinary leader to command more than routine involvement:

> From this day to the ending of the world,
> But we in it shall be remembered—
> We few, we happy few, we band of brothers;
> For he today that sheds his blood with me
> Shall be my brother.[35]

Many empirical studies of leadership fail to capture the aesthetic quality of engagement. The willingness to lay down one's life for a leader cannot necessarily be understood as a rational decision or the result of sheer coercive power. There is a quality to human behavior under exceptional circumstances that itself is exceptional.

Leadership has traditionally been a term used by male observers to describe the actions of male leaders. With the growth of scholarly inquiry concerning issues of gender, conceptions of leadership have been subjected to serious reexamination. Lightfoot,[36] in a series of case studies of high schools, comments on masculine and feminine qualities of leadership among high school principals. She notes that a feminine model of leadership finds leaders expressing a need for partnership and nurturance. Furthermore, relationships and affiliations come to be regarded as central dimensions of the exercise of power. Engagement, therefore, may be more than a component of heroic action in the service of some greater cause. It may be necessary to the personal well-being of the leader.

Fit. Could the "Kennedy magic," referred to earlier, have worked equally well at a time other than the early sixties? It is unlikely. To some extent such properties as direction and engagement are dependent on the relationship between a leader and his times. No leader fully controls such a relationship. Recent studies of charismatic leadership stress the importance of accordance between the perceptions of followers and the actions of leaders.[37] A continuing interaction takes place between the leader, his followers, and the culture in which they exist. As the leader attempts to give direction to his followers and engage their attention, so too do his followers strive to influence him and attract his commitment. For leadership to exist under such circumstances, general agreement must exist on the meanings attributed to various aspects of the culture, including its guiding values.

In an essay on organizational effectiveness, Lotto[38] refers to such general agreement as *congruence*. She characterizes the ineffective organization as one in which such congruence—or "collective reality"—fails to supplant the centrifugal tendency of people and groups to harbor competing interpretations of cultural phenomena.

A slightly different conception of fit is provided by Kupfer:

> In aesthetic experience, we respond to what is presented to us by discriminating among its constituents so as to integrate them into a unified whole. The whole is formed out of the interaction among its parts. While these parts are distinct, making distinctive contributions, their relations with one another and their place in the whole is decisive for their meaning and value. In the aesthetic ideal, they enhance and deepen each other's significance.[39]

Neisser[40] notes a growing appreciation of the importance of fit by psychologists. He gives some of the credit for the recognition that context and meaning play a crucial role in cognition to the work of Goffman. Goffman's[41] conception of frames forces us to consider what observers are thinking as they watch the performances of others. The meaning of these thoughts cannot be understood without also understanding the setting in which the performance occurs.

The cognitive perception that leadership exists may be regarded as recognition that a carefully framed situation exists in which the actions of a leader, the actions of his followers, and the traditions of their culture are mutually reinforcing and correspondingly meaningful. Such a situation characterized the educational leadership of Leonard Covello. In an inspiring case study of this New York high school principal of Italian heritage, Tyack and Hansot[42] try to account for Covello's remarkable success at East Harlem's Benjamin Franklin High School. Covello did not ignore the ethnic and racial backgrounds of his students as he attempted to provide them with the skills and knowledge needed to "make it" in America. He defined diversity as an opportunity rather than a problem. Franklin High was transformed from "an outpost" of the district office into a community. Covello recognized that the most important function of his school, given its location, was "to mobilize neighborhood people to bring about social justice" rather than raise test scores or increase college admissions. The essence of Covello's leadership was his refusal to impose a conventional model of schooling on a community for which cultural continuity and social cohesion were ultimately more critical to survival than curriculum and instruction.

Confirmation of the importance to leaders of fit comes from recent studies of Japanese corporations. Note has been taken of those aspects of Japanese culture which subtly influence corporate operations and which may confound efforts by Americans to import Japanese organizational models. Pascale, for example, stresses the constructive role played by ambiguity in Japanese organizational leadership. Unlike Western business leaders who often take pride in clarity and directness, Japanese counterparts may avoid explicit communication in an effort to minimize confrontations and embarrassment that could undermine continuing relations. Fear also exists that the premature rush to resolve a problem may "freeze things into rigidity."[43]

Originality. Having stressed the vital link between leadership and context, it is also necessary to point out the critical role played by originality. Some observers discuss this quality in terms of leadership style, but originality will be used in this context to avoid confusion with more narrowly defined constructs. Originality refers to the capacity of a leader to capture the public's imagination through uniqueness—in ideas, behavior, programs, and so on. Goffman[44] might have referred to such a property in terms of "reframing" or the discovery of new ways to interpret experience. Those who slavishly emulate a predecessor's model or seek cues on how to behave from opinion polls generally are perceived to lack authenticity and leadership, at least in cultures that value individuality.

The importance of originality to popular perceptions of leadership may be one reason why many social scientists experience difficulty defining leadership. Concern for generalizability and predictability cause them to hunt for similarities among leaders and to develop conceptions of leadership consisting of common denominators. Leadership, almost by nature, however, defies generalizability and predictability. No "one best" style of leadership exists any more than "one best" conception of beauty does. Each set of circumstances is unique—with a special ethos, a different configuration of actors, and a meaning all its own. Students of leadership, therefore, should not be surprised when, just as they feel they have identified the essence of leadership, an exception arises to defy their efforts.

It is probably safe to assume that most leaders strive to be original. They do not always succeed, however. In the first place, originality is more than mere novelty. Novelty is uniqueness without meaning—newness for the sake of newness. A thin line separates originality from eccentricity. Second, there is no manual which those aspiring to leadership can study with reasonable assurance of success. As soon as a leader begins to rely on such training material, leadership arrogates to the trainer. A leader who is not his own boss—who listens too much to the advice of others—discovers major questions being raised about his leadership. Adverse publicity surrounding Richard Nixon's and Ronald Reagan's advisers is a case in point.

A wellspring of originality for contemporary leaders has been the increase of women in top-level positions. Traditional conceptions of leadership have been based largely on masculine notions of what is meaningful—military courage, athletic prowess, fatherly control.[45] Women leaders are demonstrating that leadership may also embrace styles based on such values as nurturance and cooperation. Furthermore, Gandhi's leadership proved that these values may characterize the actions of male as well as female leaders.[46]

The Artistry of Leadership

In the preceding discussion several contemporary aesthetic properties of leadership were identified. A case was made that properties such as these are associated with the meanings that people bring to leadership experiences. The question that remains to be addressed below is, "how are people made aware of these abstract properties of leadership?" The model presented earlier suggests that awareness results in large part from the creative public acts of leaders. These creative acts are to be distinguished from other activities of a leader—routine tasks, managerial duties, private acts inaccessible to the public. A critical concern for the leader, as for the artist, is getting the attention of others—capturing their imagination. How attention is attracted becomes a central concern in the aesthetics of leadership. The artistry of leadership encompasses leaders' purposeful efforts to foster the impression of leadership. Three categories of artistry are briefly explored in this section—dramatics, design, and orchestration.

Dramatics. Leadership is a realm of ritual, ceremony, and dramatic performance. Leaders speak of feeling as if they were always "on stage." Memorable performances by leaders help overcome the problem of public recognition and serve to evoke the feelings that are necessary for action. There are several important dimensions of the dramatics of leadership, including image, voice, setting, and timing.

Before the advent of still and motion photography, relatively few people could partake firsthand of a leader's performances. As a result, a leader had a greater need to be a skilled rhetorician or spellbinding orator. If he had but one chance to impress an audience, he had better succeed. Today, a leader with access to the media can reach many more people and more frequently. A poor performance can often be corrected by an improved sequel. Editing of videotape may even eliminate some poor performances altogether. Even when a leader is not physically present, photographs may lock impressions of leadership into the public consciousness. Images immediately come to mind of a pensive John F. Kennedy on a Cape Cod beach, a confident Franklin Roosevelt with jaw jutting upward, and a determined Winston Churchill flashing a "victory" sign.

While images are important, the leader's world is still largely a verbal one.[47] The skill with which words are delivered and the nonverbal gestures that accompany delivery often carry as much weight as the substance of the words themselves. For this reason, some observers urge great caution in assessing the public appearances of leaders.[48] Every speech, every invocation, every official welcome provides a leader with an opportunity to communicate leadership.

One leader who took great advantage of oratory was Woodrow Wilson. Barber has said of Wilson,

> The core of Woodrow Wilson's Presidential style was rhetoric—especially "oratory"—and he excelled in that beyond any of his near predecessors or followers. Again and again he met opposition and turned to speech-making as the way out. Would the wily European leaders try to bamboozle him? Then he would take his case to the people of Europe, "over the heads" of their supposed representatives.[49]

Martin Luther King was another leader whose oratorical gifts contributed to his leadership image. Of King's prowess Pondy[50] has noted that it was not only his dream, but his capacity to describe it, to make it accessible to millions of people, that gave him such enormous leverage. To understand King's leadership is to appreciate his ability to put very profound ideas in very simple language.

Leaders for whom oratory is most successful are able to establish a "voice"—a manner of expressing themselves that is authentic, unforced, and clear. The voice may be folksy and plain like Truman's or elegant and educated like JFK's. What the voice may not be, though, is copied. When Gary Hart adopted too much of the Kennedy voice in the 1984 Democratic primaries, he drew heavy criticism for lack of originality.

Setting is another important dimension of dramatic performance. For FDR the "fireside chat" was an effective mode of communication. John Kennedy thrived in the give-and-take of the press conference, where his humor and spontaneity captivated listeners. When other leaders, such as Nixon and Carter, tried to take advantage of similar settings, their impact was far less great.

One further component of performance is timing. Leaders who are able to use public performances to greatest advantage understand when the delivery of a message or the evocation of a feeling will have the greatest effect. Timing may be related to a leader's capacity to apprehend the entirety of a situation instantaneously.[51]

Design. Leadership is not only dramatic performance. It also entails the transformation of vision into reality. This process is essentially a creative one. Langer[52] has distinguished between creation and manufacture. The latter calls for mass production and involves no vision, once the initial conception of the product is developed. When a leader brings forth a new program or organization, the result is unique and typically unreplicable. Such an effort may be compared to that of a designer or architect whose task is to blend imagination and familiarity with resources in the creative act of translating inchoate ideas into constructive action. Horace Mann's common school and Woodrow Wilson's League of Nations may be considered acts of creation in the same basic sense as a Frank Lloyd Wright structure.

Sometimes the leader's creation is not quite as tangible as a new program. Selman and Dibianca note the artistry involved in developing an organizational ethos,

> Building a new organizational context is essentially an abstract task of creating something where nothing existed before—like an artist about to paint on a blank canvas. There are no models or theorems or proven texts for guidance; the discoveries . . . come from their [leaders'] seeing things as they are and in their intention to bring their vision into existence.[53]

Selznick sees the creativity of leadership manifested in institution-building, by which he means "the reworking of human and technological materials to fashion an organism that embodies new and enduring values."[54] Institution-building relies on a leader's capacity for infusing day-to-day behavior with meaning and purpose. One technique for accomplishing this task is "the elaboration of socially integrating myths." Such myths are idealistic expressions of what is distinctive about a particular enterprise. Selznick concludes,

> For creative leadership, it is not the communication of a myth that counts; rather, creativity depends on having the will and the insight to see the necessity of the myth, to discover a successful formulation, and above all to create the organizational conditions that will sustain the ideals expressed.[55]

Orchestration. Leaders frequently are called upon to bring together individuals for the sake of accomplishing goals. When they are successful in coordinating the energies of an assortment of people with different abilities, their efforts can be likened to those of a gifted conductor blending together elements of sound to produce an integrated piece of music. If a leader misjudges what a person is capable of doing or if he fails to keep in mind the overall impact he hopes to achieve, the result may be comparable to a poorly orchestrated musical composition. It will not sound right when performed. The meaning of the aesthetic experience will be diminished.

Levinson is one organization theorist who regards orchestration as a critical dimension of leadership. He opens his book *Executive*[56] with a quote from Jean-Jacques Servan-Schreiber in which the work of top administrators is characterized as the organization of talent. Throughout his analysis, Levinson reiterates the need for leader awareness of what people do well and what talents are needed to get the job done. George Marshall provides a good illustration of skilled orchestration. In his biography of Marshall, Mosley writes of certain officers with whom the Chief of Staff had to work:

> He [Marshall] knew one of them, General George Patton, to be a profane braggart, a bully, and a brute, and another, General Terry Allen, to be a riproaring drunk; but he nurtured both of them, covered up for them, protected them, because he knew they were splendid officers likely to prove brave, resourceful leaders of men on the battlefield.[57]

Recognizing that a person like Patton was essential to the overall outcome he sought to achieve, Marshall retained him, while blending in the talents of officers like Omar Bradley to offset the negative attributes of the tempestuous Patton. The quest for balance and harmony is as critical to the leader as it is to the conductor.

There is also another sense in which the analogy between orchestration and leadership may be appropriate. A piece of music must be heard in its entirety for its overall impact—or meaning—to be fully appreciated. In a similar sense, people are likely to reserve judgment on leadership until the completion of a set of events. To this extent, the perception that leadership exists can never be totally divorced from outcomes. Had the Allies been defeated by the Germans in France, Marshall's orchestration is likely to have been judged discordant.

CONCLUSION

The quest for a richer understanding of the concept of leadership prompted this examination of aesthetics. Building on recent applications of cognitive psychology to the study of leadership, an argument was made that leadership is perceived as well as exercised. In other words, leaders act, but observers judge whether or not the actions constitute leadership. Judgments derive from a variety of factors, including the artistry of the leader, the prior experiences of the observer, and the cultural context in which the observer lives. The perception of leadership at any point in time is associated with a set of aesthetic properties, some examples of which are discussed in this perspective. These properties represent sources of meaning for observers. Leadership, therefore, may be conceptualized as that which helps bring meaning to the relationships between individuals and greater entities, such as organizations, communities, and nations.

What are the implications of such an aesthetics-based model of leadership? First, it suggests that the study of leadership may provide valuable information about cultures and their inhabitants as well as about specific leaders and their organizations. By identifying the properties associated with leadership, an understanding may be gained of prevailing structures of social meaning. How people make sense of leadership can tell us a great deal about how they regard themselves, their society, and the future.

A second implication involves the interaction of leaders and observers. How, exactly, do people experience leadership? What is the link between the actions of leaders and the formation of impressions or schemata concerning leadership? If leadership is primarily a matter of visual and aural perception, does a person who is both deaf and blind experience leadership? How do leaders transmit qualities such as direction, engagement, fit, and originality? These and other questions await a new generation of leadership studies. As Pondy[58] has suggested, we need to investigate how non-leaders come to invoke categories such as leadership as a means of making sense of their experience.

For those involved in preparing leaders, implications also exist. As leadership has become more professionalized, the preparation of leaders has entailed increasing amounts of skill-based training.[59] If leadership is concerned as much with meaning and values as it is with budget decisions and policy, then prospective leaders may derive great benefit from a classical liberal arts education. Such an education strives to cultivate a sensitivity to the richness of human experience and an appreciation for all the senses. Leadership, in the present model, is not only a matter of what a leader does, but how he makes people feel.

Besides its value as an alternative perspective for research and educators, an aesthetics-based model of leadership provides a framework for the appreciation of leadership. Like beauty, leadership deserves to be enjoyed for its own sake, apart from ideologies and tangible accomplishments. A citizenry made up of connoisseurs of leadership might foster a set of leader expectations that is so lofty that the likelihood of inadequate performance in high places would be substantially reduced. Of such stuff the pursuit of excellence is made.

NOTES

1. The author would like to express his appreciation to Elliot Eisner, William Rottschaefer, and the reviewers of this article for their very helpful suggestions.

2. M. C. Beardsley, "History of Aesthetics," in *The Encyclopedia of Philosophy,* Vol. I, Paul Edwards, ed. (New York: Macmillan and Free Press, 1967), p. 19.

3. N. Machiavelli, *The Prince* (New York: Penguin, 1961), p. 29.

4. T. J. Peters and R. H. Waterman, *In Search of Excellence* (New York: Harper & Row, 1982); and G. A. Yukl, *Leadership in Organizations* (Englewood Cliffs, NJ: Prentice-Hall, 1981).

5. W. R. Lassey, "Dimensions of Leadership," in *Leadership and Social Change,* W. R. Lassey and R. R. Fernandez, eds. (La Jolla, CA: University Associates, 1976), p. 15.

6. C. A. Gibb, "Leadership," in *The Handbook of Social Psychology,* Vol. 4, 2nd ed. (Reading, MA: Addison-Wesley, 1969), p. 212.

7. *Ibid.,* pp. 268-271.

8. J. Pfeffer, "The Ambiguity of Leadership," in *Leadership: Where Else Can We Go?* M. W. McCall, Jr., and M. M. Lombardo, eds. (Durham, NC: Duke University Press, 1978); and J. Pfeffer and G. R. Salancik, *The External Control of Organizations* (New York: Harper & Row, 1978).

9. *Ibid.,* p. 17.

10. D. D. Dill, "The Nature of Administrative Behavior in Higher Education," *Educational Administration Quarterly* 20 (Summer 1984): 69-100, pp. 78-80; and Gibb, "Leadership," pp. 214-215; and R. M. Stogdill, *Handbook of Leadership* (New York: Free Press, 1974).

11. H. Mintzberg, *The Nature of Managerial Work* (New York: Harper & Row, 1973).

12. R. E. Neustadt, *Presidential Power: The Politics of Leadership* (New York: John Wiley, 1960).

13. *Ibid.,* p. 81.

14. G. Morgan, P. J. Frost, and L. R. Pondy, "Organizational Symbolism," in *Organizational Symbolism,* L. R. Pondy, P. J. Frost, G. Morgan, and T. C. Dandridge, eds. (Greenwich, CT: JAI, 1983), p. 5.

15. O. E. Klapp, *Symbolic Leaders: Public Dramas and Public Men* (Chicago: Aldine, 1964), pp. 42, 43.

16. C. Geertz, *Local Knowledge* (New York: Basic Books, 1983), p. 124.

17. C. D. Elder and R. W. Cobb, *The Political Uses of Symbols* (New York: Longman, 1983), p. 19.

18. Morgan, Frost, and Pondy, "Organizational Symbolism," p. 4.

19. Gibb, "Leadership," p. 268.

20. Mintzberg, *The Nature of Managerial Work.*

21. T. Parsons, "The Super-ego and the Theory of Social Systems," in *Working Papers in the Theory of Action,* T. Parsons, R. F. Bales, and E. Shils, eds. (Glencoe, IL: Free Press, 1953), p. 16.

22. U. Neisser, *Cognition and Reality: Principles and Implications of Cognitive Psychology* (San Francisco: Freeman, 1976).

23. C. K. Eoyang, "Symbolic Transformation of Belief Systems," in *Organizational Symbolism*, L. R. Pondy, J. Frost, G. Morgan, and C. Dandridge, eds. (Greenwich, CT: JAI, 1983), p. 115.

24. J. M. Burns, *Leadership* (New York: Harper & Row, 1978).

25. H. H. Kelley, *Attribution in Social Interaction* (Morristown, NJ: General Learning Press, 1971).

26. Pfeffer, "The Ambiguity of Leadership," p. 28.

27. G. R. Salancik and J. R. Meindl, "Corporate Attributions as Strategic Illusions of Management Control," *Administrative Science Quarterly* 29 (June 1984): 238-254.

28. L. R. Pondy, "Leadership Is a Language Game," in *Leadership: Where Else Can We Go?* M. W. McCall, Jr., and M. M. Lombardo, eds. (Durham, NC: Duke University Press, 1978), p. 94.

29. J. Hospers, "Problems of Aesthetics," in *The Encyclopedia of Philosophy*, Vol. I, P. Edwards, ed. (New York: Macmillan and Free Press, 1967), p. 36.

30. L. L. Child, "Esthetics," in *The Handbook of Social Psychology*, Vol. III, 2nd ed., G. Lindzey and E. Aronson, eds. (Reading, MA: Addison-Wesley, 1969), p. 855.

31. K. W. Thompson, *Winston Churchill's World View: Statesmanship and Power* (Baton Rouge, LA: Louisiana State University Press, 1983), pp. 114, 115.

32. K. E. Weick, *The Social Psychology of Organizing*, 2nd ed. (Reading, MA: Addison-Wesley, 1979), p. 75.

33. D. C. McClelland, *Power: The Inner Experience* (New York: Irvington, 1975), p. 260.

34. I. D. Yalom, *Existential Psychotherapy* (New York: Basic Books, 1980).

35. W. Shakespeare, *Henry V* (New York: Pocket Books, 1960), Act IV, Sc. III.

36. S. L. Lightfoot, *The Good High School* (New York: Basic Books, 1983), pp. 323-333.

37. I. Schiffer, *Charisma: A Psychoanalytic Look at Mass Society* (New York: Free Press, 1973); and A. R. Willner, *The Spellbinders* (New Haven, CT: Yale University Press, 1978).

38. L. S. Lotto, "Revising the Role of Organizational Effectiveness in Educational Evaluation," *Educational Evaluation and Policy Analysis* 5 (Fall 1983): 367-378, p. 374.

39. J. H. Kupfer, *Experience as Art: Aesthetics in Everyday Life* (Albany: State University of New York Press, 1983), p. 4.

40. Neisser, *Cognition and Reality*, pp. 57, 58.

41. E. Goffman, *Frame Analysis* (Cambridge, MA: Harvard University Press, 1974).

42. D. Tyack and E. Hansot, *Managers of Virtue* (New York: Basic Books, 1982), pp. 207-211.

43. R. T. Pascale, "Zen and the Art of Management," in *Executive Success*, E. G. Collins, ed. (New York: John Wiley, 1983), p. 515.

44. Goffman, *Frame Analysis*.

45. Lightfoot, *The Good High School*, pp. 323-333.

46. S. H. Rudolph and L. I. Rudolph, *Gandhi: The Traditional Roots of Charisma* (Chicago: University of Chicago Press, 1967), p. 94.

47. A. W. Halpin, "Muted Language," *The School Review* 68 (Spring 1960): 85-104.

48. R. D. Brown, "Where Have All the Great Men Gone?" *American Heritage* 35 (February/March 1984): 12-19; and C. Krauthammer, "Lights, Camera, . . . Politics," *The New Republic* (November 22, 1982): 19-22.

49. J. Barber, *Presidential Character: Predicting Performance in the White House* (Englewood Cliffs, NJ: Prentice-Hall, 1972), p. 58.

50. Pondy, "Leadership Is a Language Game," p. 95.

51. R. D. H. Siu, "Chinese Baseball and Public Administration," *Administration Review* (November/December 1975): 636-640.

52. S. K. Langer, *Problems of Art* (New York: Scribner, 1957), p. 27.

53. J. Selman and D. F. Dibianca, "Contextual Management: Applying the Art of Dealing Creatively with Change," *Management Review* 72 (September 1983): 13-19, p. 14.

54. P. Selznick, *Leadership in Administration: A Sociological Interpretation* (New York: Harper & Row, 1957), pp. 52, 53.

55. *Ibid.,* p. 151.

56. H. Levinson, *Executive* (Cambridge, MA: Harvard University Press, 1981).

57. L. Mosley, *Marshall: Hero for Our Times* (New York: Hearst Books, 1982), p. 216.

58. L. R. Pondy and I. I. Mitroff, "Beyond Open System Models of Organization," in *Research in Organizational Behavior,* Vol. I, B. M. Staw, ed. (Greenwich, CT: JAI, 1979), p. 28.

59. C. Hodgkinson, *The Philosophy of Leadership* (Oxford: Basil Blackwell, 1983), p. 102.

CHAPTER SEVENTEEN

The Instrumental Value of the Humanities in Administrative Preparation

SAMUEL H. POPPER

This selection from a 1987 UCEA monograph advocates the use of the humanities in preparation programs for administrators. The author would have administrators gain insights on their field through a study of such fields as language, literature, history, philosophy, and archaeology. The selection demonstrates the instrumental values of the humanities in administration and ways to incorporate humanities content into preparation programs. The presumed consequence would be a significant shift from coercive administrative controls to the practice of leadership. Through gained emphatic insight, leaders would be better able to gain multiple insights into the human situation in formal organizations. The author claims instrumental—clinical—value for the study of selected humanities content by administrators.

The appointment in 1905 of George D. Strayer and Elwood P. Cubberly as professors in Educational Administration marked the beginning of professional preparation for school administration in the United States. Academic offerings before then typically were little more than an extension of the teacher-education program. Columbia University, in its Teachers College catalogue of 1899-1901, announced administrative preparation as, "A graduate course leading to the Higher Diploma for research and investigation in any field of education, and for the highest professional training of teachers in colleges and normal schools, and of superintendents, principals and supervisors of public schools."

Discrete programs for school administration did evolve eventually. They were clinically based for the most part and they stayed much the same until after World War II. Cognitive content stressed techniques of the "practical," it was atheoretical and, as Daniel Griffiths summarized administrative preparation during the first half of the twentieth century,

SOURCE: Samuel H. Popper, "The Instrumental Value of the Humanities in Administrative Preparation," *Pathways to the Humanities in Educational Administration*. (Tempe, Arizona: University Council for Educational Administration, 1987), pp. 80-109. Copyright © by The University Council for Educational Administration. Reprinted with permission.

"School administration had generally lacked a unifying theory around which to solidify. It had lacked a way of looking at itself."[1]

Things changed in the early 1950s. Educational administration turned to the social and behavioral sciences in search of usable knowledge for the conceptual enrichment of its preparation programs. It was the beginning of a so-called "theory movement" in the field which, in 1966, brought into existence the University Council for Educational Administration (UCEA).

Initiatives for the instrumental use of academic disciplines came from three organized efforts. Two of these already were on line by the time UCEA was founded as a membership organization of Ph.D.-granting universities: The National Conference of Professors of Educational Administration, organized in 1947, and the Cooperative Program in Educational Administration, which came on the scene in 1950 with generous support from the W. K. Kellogg Foundation.[2] By and large, however, these two efforts had but a modest impact on program sophistication by the time UCEA had received its charter. An assessment by Andrew Halpin of their developmental impact is informative:

> The National Conference of Professors of Educational Administration . . . was aware of some of the developments in the social sciences. Yet when the Cooperative Program in Educational Administration . . . began in 1950, its initial projects paid little heed to the new approach to administration; they tended to ignore the role of theory in research.[3]

UCEA program initiatives, on the other hand, did accelerate the pace of theoretic sophistication. In its first year, UCEA joined with Teachers College and the Educational Testing Service in a theory-based research project which, among other outcomes, generated the empirical data for the Whitman School simulation. The second year saw the Career Development Seminar launched; a program which has as its purpose, still, to take professors of UCEA member universities to the frontiers of new ideas and trends.

Altogether, the UCEA agenda was to enrich the intellectual content of preparation programs, to help them break with their atheoretical antecedents, and otherwise to provide leadership in the advancement of Educational Administration as a field of scholarship and practice. Donald Willower, the then UCEA president, assessed the UCEA performance record in 1974 and concluded, "At its best, UCEA has been able to stimulate vision, raise sights, and foster excellence in Educational Administration."[4] In the years following Willower's assessment, and to this day, the UCEA presence in Educational Administration has been the point of forward movement in the field. Select UCEA task-force groups of professors have periodically revitalized simulation materials and have produced literature in such diverse areas as Special Education and Futurology.[5] In time, UCEA also published two refereed journals in educational administration, each with an independent editorial board.

THE UCEA INITIATIVE IN THE HUMANITIES

The foregoing narrative of UCEA efforts to enrich the cognitive content of preparation programs by use of the social and behavioral sciences provides a facilitating contrast for its only so-so success with a like effort in the humanities. The following statement from a UCEA "Annual Report" is a revealing assessment of the UCEA humanities effort:

> Concentrating specifically upon the preparation of educational adminis-
> trators, the University Council for Educational Administration in 1963
> established a task force charged with exploring the feasibility of incorporat-
> ing humanities content into preparatory programs. This resulted in a 1963
> career development seminar at the University of Oklahoma at which the
> relationships between philosophy and educational administration were ex-
> plored in a series of papers, and in a 1965 Humanities Task Force meeting
> at the University of Virginia during which participants reacted to a position
> paper, supporting the use of humanities content in administrator prepara-
> tion programs. . . . Significant program changes, however, have not resulted
> from the work of this task force, and those innovations which have occurred
> comprise a variety of isolated attempts by individual professors with excep-
> tionally strong commitment to the idea of the Humanities Task Force.[6]

Notwithstanding this bleak self-assessment, UCEA did not abandon its quest of usable content in the humanities. UCEA plenary-session discussions to set the agenda for the 1974-79 program period included a reconsideration of the humanities as a source of knowledge utilization in preparation programs.[7] Once again, alas, there was little to show at the end of that five-year UCEA program period. And, to this day, there is still a marked diffidence in preparation programs toward the humanities. What accounts for this attitude? Two explanations come to mind.

First, the pervasive attitude seems to be that the humanities as *high culture* are of *consummatory* value only for school administrators. Every-one, in whatever societal role, ought to be sensitized by aesthetic richness in the humanities and this, by specialization in academia, is the task of a humanities faculty.[8] But in an applied field, such as educational administration and its self-affirmed preoccupation with the *practical*, one also has to lay out in clear view the *instrumental* value of the humanities to practice in the field. How, specifically, will preparation programs in school administration, already laden with courses in personnel management, school law, plant development, statistics, and the like, gain in practicality from encounters with the humanities?[9]

Second, advocates of the humanities in educational administration have not presented ways-and-means models of how humanities content might be integrated with other components of preparation programs. It is one thing to say "yes" to the humanities, but quite another to find instrumental applications for their content in program contexts.

If, indeed, these explanations summarize the pervasive attitude in the field, then the first is flawed by a hidden assumption which seems to equate the "human-relations model" with "the human-resources model" in management process. But the qualitative difference that sets these models apart is important to specify.

The human-relations model is anchored in civilizing assumptions and objectives, whereas the human-resources model is anchored in assumptions and objectives of administrative transactions between idiographic and nomothetic tensions in formal organization. It is a qualitative difference of importance to the management process.

The former is the quintessential and universal "golden-rule" model, whereas the latter is a model, to use Norbert Weiner's language, for "the human use of human beings." More specifically, it is a guide for administrative transactions between role and personality in formal organization. Members of the organization, in both of these models, have to be respected as human beings and made to feel wanted. However, and this is the critical differentiating value, the sociological significance of the human-resources model is informed by its instrumental orientation. People as role-incumbents contribute with a heightened motivation to the attainment of organizational goals when administrative decisions are attuned to their idiographic need-disposition.[10]

The twofold task ahead, then, is to demonstrate the instrumental value of the humanities to administrative practice and to suggest feasible instructional methods of integrating their content with practice-oriented objectives in administrative preparation programs.

LEADERSHIP AND FOLLOWERSHIP

All preparation programs in school administration have in common the goal of training for leadership. But what is *leadership*? How is one to distinguish a leader from the nonleader in an administrative role? These are researchable questions and, indeed, there is extant a considerable literature which addresses the multitude of variables in administrative relations which inform these questions. For the task at hand, however, it is enough to state that administrative control that obtains compliance to management decisions by means of a *coercive* capacity; that is, the enforcement of bureaucratic rules and regulations, is by no stretch of the imagination an exercise of leadership. The *sine qua non* of leadership is followership; a condition that is not there when, in a formal interactive relationship, A controls the role-behavior of B not because B is persuaded by the leadership *influence* of A, but rather because A has an implicitly acknowledged right from B to use *authority* and, therefore, B grants compliance to administrative directives from A.[11]

Here exactly is the rub! The skill to shift from a reliance on a coercive capacity in administrative control to a reliance on leadership influence is in large part idiographic. It is a skill derived from multiple insights into the human situation in formal organization. And one such is what psychologists call *emphatic* insight.

A constituent element in administrative leadership is an ability to *know* empathically the role strain human beings encounter in complex systems of organization. The humanities, it is urged now, are preeminently equipped aesthetically to sharpen emphatic insight by means of its own way of *knowing*. John Ciardi, poet and literary critic, thinks of this type of knowing as "esthetic wisdom." Here is his vivid illustration of "esthetic wisdom:"

> Years ago, the psychiatrist Frederick Wertham spent many hours interviewing a young man charged with matricide. The young man was nearly illiterate; yet, as Wertham listened, he began to feel that he had heard it all before. He eventually turned to *Hamlet* and then to Aeschylus' *Oresteia*. In these plays, Wertham found much of what he had just heard from the young man he had been interviewing—not exactly the same words, but the same feelings stated in the same order.
>
> Wertham need not have felt surprise. He had located in the plays that ability to project oneself vicariously into an emotional situation, which is exactly what we expect of great artists and is what lesser artists try to achieve.
>
> Aeschylus and Shakespeare were not matricides. They were special men capable of understanding what is human. When the human thing turned out to be a matricide, they imagined themselves in that situation (sent out their nerve nets) and brought back exactly the reactions and the order of reactions the clinician will eventually parse out of the actual matricide.
>
> I don't like the word "wisdom." It tends to sit a bit sententiously in my vocabulary. Yet every word will find its exact place in time, and here no other will do. That body of knowledge and experience that senses the world as Aeschylus and Shakespeare sensed it is Esthetic Wisdom. Art is not its ornament but its way of knowing. It is what Robert Frost called "a thought-felt thing." It is the essential human act and the consequence of good art. It is what Vergil represents in the *Divine Comedy*—not Human Reason, and not antireason, but reasoning that leads to a way of seeing, recognizing, reacting, and giving order to.[12]

Ciardi's definition of "esthetic wisdom" as a special type of enlightenment is well taken, as is his illustration of its usefulness to a clinical process. Wertham's *déjà vu* was triggered by what F. S. C. Northrop thinks of as "the aesthetic component of reality."[13] It enabled him to relate with a heightened empathy to the significant other in a professional encounter. Aesthetic enlightenment likewise can be useful to the clinical process of administration.

It comes to this: If a program objective in administrative preparation is to lay a foundation for leadership behavior which will be sensitive to the idiographic in formal organization, then Ciardi's "esthetic wisdom" is a useful source for the cultivation of emphatic skill. It is a type of skill which enables one to know by means of intuitive and appreciative perception the emotional state of another. Theodor Lipps, a German phenomonologist of the nineteenth century, had called this type of knowing *Einfühlung*. Psychology, as was noted earlier, calls it empathy.

Emphatic skill can be of considerable clinical—say instrumental—value to administrative processes in the all-important leadership task of fusing informal organization with formal organization. When the tactical objective is to keep in low profile the power dimension of administrative office and to maximize idiographic opportunities in the organization to raise system efficiency, then empathy-based perceptions of formal organization are an asset indeed to administrative leadership.

Psychological science can, and does, provide a cognitive foundation for empathic insight into the human situation. Wertham, the psychiatrist, had no doubt learned how to use empathic skill in medical training. It is an everyday tool in psychiatric diagnosis and treatment. However, as John Ciardi has demonstrated, "esthetic wisdom" in the humanities sharpens this skill with an enlightenment of its own. Moreover, and especially as it relates to institution-building skill, this type of enlightenment has still other uses in administrative preparation. A glance back in time is helpful again now.

INSTITUTIONAL LEADERSHIP

The School of Scientific Management, of which Frederick Winslow Taylor was a founding figure, had provided the generic model of administrative preparation to the end of World War II. Then, the sustained impact of two connected interventions broke its hold on administrative preparation in the United States. One of these was the publication of Chester Barnard's *The Functions of the Executive,* the other was a critical need in *post-bellum* American society of institutional leadership in the management of organizations. A dynamic self-revitalization movement was under way and organizations had to be equipped by means of strategic planning with renewed adaptive capabilities.

Barnard's *The Functions of the Executive,* published in 1938, was a landmark work. It brought fresh theoretical insight to the management of organized human enterprise. It laid a conceptual base, drawn largely from the earlier Hawthorne Studies, for a human-resource model in administration and, more directly to what was needed in the *post-bellum* period, it provided a handbook for institutional leadership. Its impact upon administrative preparation in the United States, at first put off by the war, was immediate after the war.

Preparation programs in educational administration, nurtured now by the "theory movement," also were responsive. Institutional leadership in school administration was made the guiding ideal of preparation. Then, when UCEA came on line, Barnard's *The Functions of the Executive* became, and is still, a standard reference in the field.

The definition of "organization purpose," one of the three "functions of the executive," was for Barnard an unending administrative task in raising levels of transcendence in bureaucratic organization. Skill in purpose definition is by Barnard's light the hallmark which sets institutional leadership apart from mere management. At the foundation of this skill is what Barnard has called "moral creativeness." He acknowledged the importance of "technological proficiency" in administrative leadership, but as he put it, "The strategic factor in the dynamic expression of leadership is moral creativeness, which precedes, but is in turn dependent upon, technological proficiency and the development of techniques in relation to it."[14]

Both the idea and the ideal of transcendence were not entirely new to the literature of educational administration. Jesse Newlon, as one example, was of one mind with Barnard in urging institutional leadership in administration. In a book published in 1934, he wrote:

> The need for efficiency in education cannot be questioned. But what is efficiency? Efficiency involves more than thorough applications of techniques in the mechanical aspects of administration—finance, buildings, equipment, child accounting, supervision, and the like. It involves the employment of broad social methods for the accomplishment of social purposes.[15]

Newlon, of course, was striking at the "cult of efficiency" which then had school administration in its grip.[16] But its source, the School of Scientific Management, was at the time still the dominant influence in administrative preparation. After the war, with a society in dynamic transition, institutional leadership was an idea whose time had come.

Barnard the business executive and Newlon the school executive-turned-academician, each out of a different field in administration, saw eye-to-eye the central task of institutional leadership: to harmonize mundane goals of formal organization with transcendent definitions of "organization purpose." All of which means that institutional leadership has to generate moral creativeness with which to transmogrify bureaucratic rules and regulations into the language of social values.

Their shared view of institutional leadership was before long reinforced by a flowering literature in the sociology of formal organization. Philip Selznick, whose *Leadership in Administration* was one of the first in this new literature, eloquently stated the Newlon-Barnard idea of institutional leadership in one capsulated sentence: "The executive becomes a statesman as he makes the transition from administrative management to institutional leadership."[17]

Eventually, the centrality of institutional leadership in administration also became a major theme in UCEA publications. "Administrators who head viable organizations," wrote Jack Culbertson soon after he had become executive director of UCEA, "must be concerned with much more than administrative process; the policy and purposes toward which these processes are directed are of equal, if not greater significance."[18] Clearly, Culbertson had in mind transcendent purpose definition in relation to the ubiquitous problem of goal displacement.

Goal displacement by a reversal of ends and means values is an ever-present prospect in formal organization. The research literature has confirmed its reality by many studies. Culturally grounded and value-sensitive administrative action is the only viable defense. It is precisely for this reason that Selznick has fixed "the maintenance of institutional integrity" as a central task of administrative leadership.[19] It is also, to repeat, the referent in Barnard's pithy "moral creativeness." All of which provides a conceptual setting for the instrumental value of the humanities in the training for institutional leadership.

The humanities provide an aesthetic structure to knowledge and have a rich variety of material with which to *reinforce* grounding in both interpersonal and institutional leadership preparation. Cognitive content in most preparation programs is formed, by and large, around a configuration of three skills. Students are trained in technical-management skill to deal with school organization as a formal system, to cope with clinical problems of bureaucratic effectiveness. They are trained in social-psychological skill to deal with school organization as a personality system, to cope with clinical problems of motivation and efficiency. Last, and most illusive, they are trained in conceptualization skill to deal with school organization as a cultural system, to cope with problems of institutional leadership.

Institutional leadership is society's sobriquet for the best in administrative practice. Selznick, and others, have equated skill in institution building with administrative statesmanship. But in the tri-skills configuration of administrative preparation, skill in institution building holds the greatest challenge for training.

Skill in institution building, at the least, requires insight into the way organization-based mythology motivates goal attainment.[20] Such insight, moreover, has to be coupled with insight into universal dilemmas in the human situation; of how, for example, humankind has been groping over the ages to discover its transcendental purpose, and of how it has been frustrated in this by an ascending domination of rational conventions in human enterprise.[21] And nowhere is this insight more useful to administrative process than in strategic planning.

Formal organization has to attend periodically to a category of *recurring* problems which are generated by what Max Weber has called "the problem of meaning." Attention to this pattern-maintenance function—to use Talcott Parsons' language—is where strategic planning begins; most usually with a declaration of the organization's mission. It is at this stage that institutional leadership is in greatest need of a humanistic foundation in order to be effective.[22]

To summarize: The foremost requisite of institutional leadership in education is "moral creativeness" in the form of a purpose-defining skill which, when fused with bureaucratic and social-psychological skills, facilitates the administrative integration of school organization as a formal system of differentiated roles, as a personality system of individuals whose psychological motivation in roles continually has to be reinforced by an optimum balance of burdens and gratifications, and as a cultural system whose dominant orientation in the social division of labor is to the socialization needs of society; Parsons' pattern-maintenance. Purpose-defining skill includes: (1) the art of valuing in administrative decision-making, (2) cultural insight into the collective idealism of society and its relation to both genesis and charter myths, (3) knowing emphatically of the nonrational in human enterprise, (4) aesthetic awareness of the egocentric predicament in administrative behavior, and (5) a humanistically grounded perspective of the omnipresent *Gemeinschaft-Gesellschaft* dilemma in formal organization. The "esthetic wisdom" in the humanities is available to be used, just as the social and behavioral sciences are used already to enrich the training for institutional leadership.

FEASIBLE PATHWAYS

Several already familiar instructional methods are available for using the humanities in educational administration. Method selection, as a tactical decision, will be affected by which pathway to the humanities is taken and by whether it is entirely a departmental initiative or taken in collaboration with other faculty; say faculties in philosophy, art history, humanities, or classics.

One familiar method which seems to lend itself readily to the blending of humanities content with administrative preparation is case analysis. The so-called case method, of course, has been used in university instruction at least since the Harvard Law School of the 1870s. Harvard Graduate School of Business Administration has been identified with case-method instruction from about 1919. By the late 1950s, case method was brought to educational administration first by Cyril Sargent and Eugene Belisle and then by Jack Culbertson and Daniel Griffiths.

Griffiths, especially, made an inventive application of the method by using social and behavioral science concepts and models—Selznick and Gouldner models—as tools for analyzing case material which had been prepared for educational administration; *The Jackson County Story* for example.[23] He appeared frequently on UCEA programs to demonstrate his way of analyzing case material, and, in quick-time, the Griffiths' style had a wide diffusion in the field.[24]

UCEA case-material preparation followed Paul Lawrence's maxim, "A good case is the vehicle by which a chunk of reality is brought into the classroom."[25] If "reality" is the controlling instructional value in "a good case," and it ought to be, then the humanities have a boundless quantity of engaging and ready-made "good case" material waiting to be used. Reality in human experience, after all, has been given a variety of ontological definitions, and are not artistic depictions of human experience—Northrop's "aesthetic component of reality"—the very essence of the humanities? Terence's *homo sum: humani nil a me alienum puto* has been for centuries the universal attitude of the humanities.[26]

The fine point is that ready-made case material in the humanities, the novel and even more so tragedy written for theater, lends itself exceedingly well to case-method analysis with the frequently used concepts and models in Educational Administration as tools. *Mutiny on the Bounty,* an historical novel, is illustrative.

To establish authority for administrative transactions between nomothetic and idiographic values in the management of formal organization—in Chester Barnard's sense between formal and informal organization—is a primary administrative role-expectation. It is this role-expectation, precisely, which informs the theoretic usefulness of the role-personality model which Jacob Getzels and Egon Guba have adapted from Parsonian theory and introduced to preparation programs in Educational Administration.[27] The following episode in *Mutiny on the Bounty* lights up this complex idea with aesthetic realism.

First is this exchange between Captain Bligh and Master-Mate Fletcher Christian before the mutiny:

> Bligh: La-di-da, Mr. Christian! On my word, you should apply for a place as master of a young ladies' seminary! Kindness, indeed! Well, I'm damned. . . . A fine captain you'll make if you don't heave overboard such ridiculous notions. Kindness! Our seamen understand kindness as well as they understand Greek! Fear is what they do understand! Without that, mutiny and piracy would be rife on the high seas!
>
> Christian: I cannot agree. Our seamen do not differ from other Englishmen. Some must be ruled by fear, it is true, but there are other, and finer men, who will follow a kind, just, and fearless officer to the death.

After the mutiny, Fletcher Christian now in command of the Bounty, addresses the crew to instruct them in the basics of reciprocal role-expectations:

> There is one matter we will decide once for all . . . and that is who is to be captain of this ship. I have taken her with your help, in order to be rid of a tyrant who has made life a burden to all of us. . . . In our situation a leader is essential, one whose will is to be obeyed without question. It should be needless to tell British seamen that no ship, whether manned by mutineers or not, can be handled without discipline. If I am to command the Bounty I mean to be obeyed. There shall be no injustice here. I shall punish no man without good cause, but I will have no man question my authority.[28]

Mutiny on the Bounty portrays dramatically certain structurally induced tensions in formal organization, but in the role-personality model these are depicted as abstractions. By joining the two in a case analysis, one has here a method of using the humanities and whose instrumental value will be acknowledged readily by most professors who are challenged to blend the abstractness of theory with empirical equivalents in formal organization.

Because case material from the humanities cannot be expected to have the sharp clinical focus of say *The Jackson County Story,* whose content was drawn from actual events in school-community relations, some may see in this a debilitating condition. For this reason, exactly, material from the humanities has to be selected with care so it will correspond with the objectives of instruction. Perfect artistic equivalents are rarities for much the same reason that social science theories rarely have perfect empirical equivalents. Another illustration.

Clifford Dowdey's *Death of a Nation* is a near-perfect case for the study of leadership. Although it is a fictional account of the chance encounter in 1863 between the armies of Generals George G. Mead and Robert E. Lee at Gettysburg, it is nonetheless a fertile setting for the conceptually prepared student to contemplate nuances of leadership and the limitations of leadership capacity in altered situations. Confederate generals who were quite competent at division-level command proved themselves failures when, by the constraints of altered field conditions, they were elevated by General Lee to corps command.[29]

Still other case material is available in artistic depictions of human aberration in the pursuit of ideal-driven ends which lead to disaster. In these depictions lie embedded usable models and antimodels for students in administration as they sharpen insight into the pervasive problem of value reversal in human enterprise.

Ciardi, earlier, informed his definition of "esthetic wisdom" with a recital of how Frederic Wertham's clinical psychoanalytic insight was enlarged by Shakespeare's *Hamlet* and Aeschylus' *Oresteia*. Ciardi could have elaborated further with the now-defunct Students for a Democratic Society—SDS.

When the organization of SDS was formed in 1962, at Port Huron, a manifesto was adopted which read in part.

> We regard *men* as infinitely precious and possessed of unfulfilled capacities for reason, freedom, and love. . . . Men have unrealized potential for self-cultivation, self-direction, self-understanding, and creativity. . . . The goals of men and society should be human independence: a concern with . . . finding a meaning of life that is personally authentic . . . one which has full, spontaneous access to present and past experiences. *Human relationships* should involve fraternity and honesty.[30]

Many of those who had signed this statement of student idealism were within a few years, in the words of James Wilson, "attacking universities, harassing those who disagreed with them, demanding political obedience, and engaging in deliberate terrorism."[31] Social psychology, no doubt, has a cogent clinical explanation for this incident of the nonrational in human behavior, and it is of value to have it, but Fyodor Dostoyevsky's *Crime and Punishment*, in the student Raskolnikov who commits two brutal murders to gain his own ideal-motivated ends, provides "esthetic wisdom" for the imagination to grasp its larger universal meaning in the human situation.[32]

And who has endowed belletristic literature with more variants of what is universal in the human situation than William Shakespeare? No one, not in antiquity or in modernity! His depictions of the human predicament are as contemporary to this time as they were to the age of Elizabeth. Available demonstrations of their contemporaneity are legion, as are demonstrations of their usefulness for the infusion of "esthetic wisdom" in the content of administrative preparation. An episode of sexual harassment in Shakespeare's *Measure for Measure* (II, iv) will have to do for now as a demonstration.

Angelo is selected by the Duke of Vienna to rule in his absence while abroad because:

If any in Vienna be of worth
To undergo such ample grace and honor,
It is Lord Angelo.

But straight-as-an-arrow Angelo is soon corrupted by his newly bestowed
authority and gives free rein to lust when Isabella stands before him to
plead for the life of her condemned brother. Shakespeare shows here that
this type of harassment in a hierarchically unequal relationship is
universal both in form and its denial. How all-too contemporary is the
following exchange between Isabella and Angelo once she is on to what
he has in mind.

Isabella: Sign me a present pardon for my brother,
           Or with an outstretched throat I'll tell the world aloud
           What man thou art.
Angelo: Who will believe thee, Isabel?
           My unsoiled name, th'austereness of my life
           My vouch against you, and my place i' th' state,
           Will so your accusation overweigh,
           That you shall stifle in your own report,
           And smell of calumny. I have begun;
           And now I give my sensual race the rein;
           Fit thy consent to my sharp appetite;
           Lay by all nicety and prolixious blushes,
           That banish what they sue for; redeem thy brother
           By yielding up the body to my will;
           Or else he must not only die the death,
           But thy unkindness shall his death draw out
           To ling'ring sufferance. Answer me tomorrow,
           Or, by thy affection that now guides me most,
           I'll prove a tyrant to him. As for you,
           Say what you can, my false o'erweighs your true.

And it is altogether useful in administrative preparation that students
in Educational Administration be disabused of the notion that Max Weber
was the inventor of bureaucracy. By their immersion in Edward Gibbon's
The Decline and Fall of the Roman Empire, Chapter 3, they will find in
the distant past, not in perfect situational correspondence to be sure, a
model of Robert Merton's "bureaucratic virtuoso" in the person of Em-
peror Caesar Augustus.[33]

Through administrative manipulations of power, and a cunning conformity to republican conventions, Augustus had transformed the Roman
Republic into a monarchy. Also, from reading of the *Cursus Honorum,* the
civil service code-manual of the Empire, they will discover how the
Romans socialized to bureaucratic roles during the period of *Pax Romana.*

Comparative analysis is another method of using the humanities and, like case method, it is also an instructional tool already familiar to educational administration. The most troublesome program objective in administrative preparation, and this holds for all fields of administration, is training in managerial ethics or, and they are related, in Barnard's "moral creativeness."[34]

Such instruction, if it is to be at all effective, has to begin with a lesson which Emile Durkheim had taught his students at the Sorbonne, where he held professorial chairs in both sociology and education. He pressed upon his students in one lecture that:

> Educational practices are not phenomena that are isolated from one another; rather, for a given society, they are bound up in the same system all parts of which contribute toward the same end: it is the system of education suitable to this country and to this time. Each people has its own, as it has its own moral, religious, economic system, etc.[35]

Moral practice, following Durkheim, is not possible *in vacuo*. The practice of private banking in the United States is moral, in the Soviet Union it is immoral. Instruction in administrative ethics, therefore, without some axiological grounding is futile. Cultural sensitivity to the institutionalized value system of society, once again Parsons' pattern-maintenance system, is its essential stuff.

The acquisition of cultural sensitivity in administrative preparation, however, is no light task. Theoretical literature in the social and behavioral sciences can generate it cognitively, but the humanities will nurture it also aesthetically. Comparative analysis is an ideal instructional tool for joining the two in a learning experience. Not only is cultural sensitivity sharpened by such an exercise in comparative analysis, but so is the scholarly imagination.

Comparative analysis toward this end works best when it is set in concept-specific frames. Authority to use power in normative order, as an example, is a subject which is central in Sophocles' *Antigone,* Machiavelli's *The Prince,* and Chester Barnard's *The Functions of the Executive.* A comparative analysis of the three can generate an informative cross-reference to the legitimation of power in cultures separated by time and values. All that is needed is a concept-specific frame, scholarly imagination, and the right questions to sort out their commonalities and differences within the structure of a taxonomy.[36] A brief comment on these three works is helpful here.

Barnard's *The Functions of the Executive,* as has been noted earlier, is a standard reference in the literature of educational administration. His ideas, however, are jarring for most students in a first encounter; this is especially so upon first encountering his concepts of "authority" and its subsumed "zone of indifference," "moral creativeness," "executive responsibility," and the like.

Sophocles' *Antigone* is a play out of Greek classical antiquity with layers of meaning. At one level is the universal egocentric predicament in the use of authority. Another level is focused on a reversal of ends and means values. Still another level throws aesthetic light on the importance of moral constraint in executive-level decisions.

Machiavelli's *The Prince* was written specifically as a guide to the practice of executive-level statecraft in sixteenth-century Florentine society. It is, in point of fact, a sixteenth-century version of *The Functions of the Executive*. Machiavelli himself was a major figure of the Italian Renaissance. The imprint of his influence on Shakespeare's English chronicle plays, especially the Henriad, is itself an aesthetic revelation of how multi-faceted are the problems of responsibility and morality in governance.

Another concept-specific frame in comparative analysis, to illustrate further, might be the centrality of values and valuing in institutional leadership. These inform the ethical and the nonethical in administrative behavior. Philosophy, and most especially axiology, lays the cognitive foundation for thinking about values and valuing. Here too, however, the humanities can provide aesthetic reinforcement. A slight digression will help.

It is quite correct to say, at a general level of discourse, that moral philosophy has produced two basic theories in ethics: cognitivist and noncognitivist. The former is associated in American philosophical scholarship with the antinominalist pragmatism of Charles Sanders Pierce, whereas the latter is associated with the eighteen-century nominalist idealism of George Berkeley and David Hume. Beyond this level of background structuring, one has to reach back to fourteenth-century scholasticism and the nominalism and antinominalism, respectively, of William of Ockham and John Duns Scotus.[37]

Most programs in professional education seldom provide such a learning experience in philosophy. Through the humanities, however, students in school administration can experience encounters with these ethical theories in moral philosophy; that is, the philosophical face of ethics, either as *relativistic moral realism* or as *intuitionistic moral realism*.

Relativistic moral realism is to be found in a plentiful variety of literary works. Examples are Amos Hawley's *Executive Suite*, a novel which deals with the tensions of corporate infighting for executive succession, and in Robert Browning's *My Last Duchess;* a dramatic poem which, among other things, is a caricature of situational ethics. T. S. Eliot, likewise, fires moral imagination with *Choruses from "The Rock."*

Intuitionistic moral realism is to be found in George Bernard Shaw's *Man and Superman,* a play whose creative inspiration was Henri Bergson's moral philosophy. *Don Juan in Hell,* a dramatic reading for four characters, is an extended Act 3 of *Man and Superman* whose central theme is Bergson's concept of a "life force"—*élan vital.* Then there is Albert Camus' *The Fall,* also a dramatic work whose inspiration was existentialist moral philosophy.

These representative works in the humanities are ready-made aesthetic settings for speculative thinking about the values-ethics nexus within concrete contexts of the moral dilemma. Their depiction of the human predicament straightaway leads to moral philosophy, theories in ethics, and questions about moral behavior. What better way is there to illuminate moral issues and of cultivating what John Dewey has called "the habit of reflective thought?"[38]

In all, both case-method and comparative analysis are especially attractive as instructional methods of using the humanities. But others, also familiar to instruction in educational administration, should be considered. The following are suggestive:

(1) Shakespeare's *Hamlet* provides the clue for how future UCEA simulations of reality could include material from the humanities. *Hamlet* is an Elizabethan model of the play-within-a-play and which by now is a familiar *genre* in theater. Why not do future UCEA simulations with a scenario that includes a logical story-line rationale for, say, a showing of *Antigone?* Jean Anouilh's adaptation of *Antigone* has been performed in modern dress on educational television, with a distinguished company of actors headed by Fritz Weaver, and it should be available, therefore, in video-tape. Educational television has other such video-tape gems out of the humanities available to be used in the same way.

(2) UCEA simulation also brings to mind "The Conference," a filmed case produced by UCEA and in much use with UCEA simulation of the 1960s. "The Conference" can stand as a production model for a theme-specific mini art lecture in color video-tape. Such a lecture would bring the humanistic discipline of art-historical scholarship into administrative preparation for the purpose of reinforcement in instruction. "The Ambassadors" by Hans Holbein the Younger, the National Gallery in London, will illustrate the idea of a theme-specific art lecture.

The egocentric predicament is an occupational hazard in all formal relationships wherein one person is authorized, through legitimation, to use power over another. Much has been written about the corruptive headiness of power. Hans Holbein the Younger, of the German Renaissance and after 1536 court painter to Henry VIII of England, chose the symbolism of a *memento mori*—a reminder of inevitable death—to caution viewers of "The Ambassadors" about the egocentric predicament in power.

Artists and writers of all periods have used the symbolism of a *memento mori* to state that "A last day is reserved to all of us."[39] "The Ambassadors," shows the *memento mori* as a skull in trick perspective set against symbols of formal office and the opulence of sixteenth-century mercantile capitalism. The artist does not preach nor lecture; these are left to churchmen and academicians, but he does provide aesthetic illumination for their subject matter. In this instance, it is the theme of an egocentric predicament in high-status office.

(3) Still another method would have to be organized in collaboration with faculty in the humanities and in other fields of administrative preparation. Program initiatives of this kind will not be easy to implement, given the ingrained reticence toward interdisciplinary collaboration in academia, but the promise of attractive rewards makes the investment of effort well worth the risk.

Administrative preparation in all fields—business, education, social work, penology, and so forth—are in need of like aesthetic reinforcement in instruction. Now the tactical challenge is in how to join these diverse faculty interests in a binding collaboration for the attainment of shared program objectives. Negotiated Investment Strategy—NIS—suggests itself as one negotiating technique that might be tried.[40]

NIS was developed with support from the Charles F. Kettering Foundation of Dayton, Ohio. It is an instrument for negotiating the commitment of resources among parties-in-interest in a joint enterprise. NIS has been tested in several cities, and with good results, wherein human-service organizations were brought together to negotiate a collaboration in the delivery of community services. More directly to the point, NIS is an adaptable instrument and should be tested also in the academic community.

A negotiation with interdisciplinary faculty might aim at the following collaboration:

(a) a seminar by a humanities faculty which has been prepared especially for students in all administrative fields,

(b) a regularly scheduled cross-listed catalogue offering between educational administration and some department in the humanities group, and/or

(c) a short-term, but time intensive humanities institute, on or away from campus, modelled after the Executive Development Program at Harvard, Columbia, and other universities.

CONCLUSION

To conclude, there are any number of pathways to the humanities and a variety of methods of using their content instrumentally in administrative preparation. Several of these pathways have been discovered already by inventive scholars in the social sciences. Alvin Gouldner in sociology and Anthony Podlecki in political science, as examples, have demonstrated that belletristic works of Greek classical antiquity can be of instrumental value to the generation of fresh intellectual insight in the social sciences. Lewis Coser has discovered the availability of enlightening sociological insights in fiction literature. He holds:

> Fiction is not a substitute for systematically accumulated, certified knowledge. But it provides the social scientist with a wealth of sociologically relevant material. . . . The creative imagination of the literary artist often has achieved insights into social processes which have remained unexplored in social science.[41]

Faculties in education administration, likewise, once they take pathways to the humanities, will find much that is useful to administrative preparation programs.

But there is yet one other instrumental value in the humanities which, by itself, is deserving of an essay-length commentary. It turns on the mental-health consequences of a consuming preoccupation with the *practical* in administration. John Ciardi eloquently addressed this occupational hazard in a talk to executives, "An Ulcer, Gentlemen, is an Unwritten Poem," who had come together for in-service professional development through the humanities. In it, he distinguished between the two worlds of practicality and of creative imagination as follows:

> The poet enters his world as an *as if:* he writes *as if* he were analyzing a real man seated before him. . . . The practical man has no such large freedom. He enters a world called *is*. When he is at work, he is plowing a field, he *is* assembling chemical apparatus, he *is* interviewing an actual man whose name appears on the census listing and who *is* offering his services in return for real and taxable wages. . . . There is no poetry for the practical man. There is poetry only for the mankind of the man who spends a certain amount of his life turning the mechanical wheel. But let him spend too much of his life at the mechanics of practicality and either he must become something less than a man, or his very mechanical efficiency will become impaired by the frustrations stored up in his irrational human personality. An ulcer, gentlemen, is an unkissed imagination taking its revenge for having been jilted. It is an unwritten poem, a neglected music, an unpainted watercolor, an undanced dance. It is a declaration from the mankind of the man that a clear

spring of joy has not been tapped, and that it must break through, muddily, on its own.[42]

And John Ciardi's remarks provide just the right closure for this introduction. Now, on to the pathways!

NOTES

1. D. E. Griffiths, *Human Relations in School Administration* (New York: Appleton-Century-Crofts, 1956), p. 4; see also A. W. Halpin, ed., *Administrative Theory in Education* (Chicago: Midwest Administration Center, 1958), "Editor's Introduction." This volume contains the papers read at the first UCEA Career Development Seminar, cosponsored with the University of Chicago Midwest Administration Center, in 1957.

2. For a panoptic account of this developmental turn in educational administration, see J. A. Culbertson, "Trends and Issues in the Development of a Science of Administration," in *Perspectives on Educational Administration and the Behavioral Sciences* (Eugene: The Center for the Advanced Study of Educational Administration, University of Oregon, 1965). Culbertson served UCEA with distinction as its executive director for 22 years. Halpin, a social psychologist, came to educational administration in the mid-1950s and soon thereafter was established as a major figure in its "theory movement."

3. Halpin, *Administrative Theory in Education,* p. xi. The Cooperative Program in Educational Administration—CPEA—is no more, but the National Conference of Professors of Educational Administration is still active. Its most enduring literary contribution to the field was published the year after UCEA was organized as a multi-authored work. See, R. F. Campbell and R. T. Gregg, eds., *Administrative Behavior in Education* (New York: Harper Brothers, 1957). For more on the CPEA, see H. A. Moore, Jr., *Studies in School Administration* (Washington, DC: American Association of School Administrators, 1957).

4. D. J. Willower, "Educational Administration and the Uses of Knowledge," 1974 Presidential Address, in W. G. Monahan, *Theoretical Dimensions of Educational Administration* (New York: Macmillan, 1975), p. 457.

5. One such early task force was the Interdisciplinary Content Task Force. It brought forth these two works: L. Downey and F. Enns, eds., *The Social Sciences in Educational Administration* (Edmonton, Alberta: Division of Educational Administration, University of Alberta and the University Council for Educational Administration, 1963); and K. Goldhammer, *The Social Sciences and the Preparation of Educational Administrators* (Edmonton, Alberta: Division of Educational Administration, University of Alberta and the University Council for Educational Administration, 1963).

6. *Annual Report,* 1966-67 (Columbus, OH: The University Council for Educational Administration), p. 3. See also, R. H. Farquhar, *The Humanities in Preparing Educational Administrators,* Educational Administrators (Eugene: ERIC Monograph, University of Oregon, 1970). Out of the University of Oklahoma—UCEA

Career Development Seminar came R. E. Ohm and W. G. Monahan, eds., *Educational Administration: Philosophy in Action* (Norman: College of Education, The University of Oklahoma, 1965). For representative "isolated attempts at the humanities by individual professors," see W. R. Lane and P. T. West, "If You Can't Pretend, You Can't be King," *Phi Delta Kappan* 53 (June 1972); R. O. Gibson and M. Stetar, "Trends in Research Related to Educational Administration," *UCEA Review* 16 (July 1975); and S. H. Popper, "An Advocate's Case for the Humanities in Preparation Programs for School Administration," *The Journal of Educational Administration* 20 (Winter 1982).

7. See, S. H. Popper, "The Continuing Quest of Applied Knowledge," *UCEA Newsletter* 14 (January 1973).

8. For a well-crafted introduction to the aesthetic richness in the humanities, see *Articulating the Ineffable: Approaches to the Teaching of Humanities* (St. Paul: Minnesota State Department of Education, Division of Instruction, 1979); especially Chapter I, J. Reedy, "From Socrates to Solzhenitsyn: An Overview of the Humanities," pp. 9-29.

9. The term "humanities," as defined programmatically by the National Endowment for the Humanities, "includes, but is not limited to, the study of the following: language, both modern and classic; linguistics; literature; history; jurisprudence; philosophy; archaeology; the history, criticism, theory, and practice of the arts; and those aspects of the social sciences which have humanistic content and employ humanistic methods." Quoted in *Ibid.*, p. 12.

10. For good textbook treatments of qualitative differences between "human relations" and "human resources" models, see F. Carver and T. Sergiovanni, *The New School Executive: A Theory of Administration* (Cambridge: Harvard University Press, 1975); and R. G. Owens, *Organizational Behavior in Education* (Englewood Cliffs, NJ: Prentice-Hall, 1981), Chapter 10, "Emerging Perspectives on Organizational Behavior." At the core of a differentiation between these two models is Chester Barnard's concept of an "economy of incentives" in work motivation and in the reward system of formal organization. A penetrating analysis of the latter concept has been provided by Douglas E. Mitchell in a paper presented at the April, 1986 annual meeting of the American Educational Research Association, "Inducement, Incentive and Cooperation: Barnard's Concept of Work Motivation." For "the human use of human beings," see N. Weiner, *The Human Use of Human Beings: Cybernetics and Society* (New York: Doubleday Anchor, 1954).

11. Ideas central to this statement have been drawn from T. Parsons, "On the Concept of Influence," *Public Opinion Quarterly* 27 (Spring 1963); T. Parsons, "On the Concept of Political Power," *Proceedings of the American Philosophical Society* 107 (June 1963); and C. I. Barnard, *The Functions of the Executive* (Cambridge, MA: Harvard University Press, 1971).

12. John Ciardi, "Manner of Speaking," *Saturday Review* 55 (8 April 1972): 22.

13. F. S. C. Northrop, *The Logic of the Sciences and the Humanities* (New York: World, 1963), p. 175.

14. Barnard, *The Functions of the Executive*, p. 288. One illustration of "moral creativeness," or of "transcendence," has been provided by George Bernard Shaw in the following exchange between Captain Robert de Baudricourt and Joan in the play *Saint Joan* (I, i). Robert tells Joan the more devil a soldier is the better he will fight, "That is why the goddams [the English] will take Orleans. And you cannot

stop them, nor ten thousand like you." And Joan, inspired by voices of saints she claims to hear, responds, "One thousand like me can stop them. Ten like me can stop them with God on our side. You do not understand, squire. Our soldiers are always beaten because they are fighting only to save their skins; and the shortest way to save your skin is to run away. Our knights are thinking only of money they will make in ransoms: it is not kill or be killed with them, but pay or be paid. But I will teach them all to fight that the will of God may be done in France; and then they will drive the poor goddams before them like sheep. You and Polly [Monsieur de Poulengey] will live to see the day when there will be but one king there: not the fuedal English king, but God's French one." Further elaboration of Barnard's statement is in Part II.

15. Jesse H. Newlon, *Educational Administration as Social Policy* (New York: Scribner, 1974), p. 237.

16. For more on the "cult of efficiency" in school administration, see R. E. Callahan, *Education and the Cult of Efficiency: A Study of Social Forces that have Shaped the Administration of the Public Schools* (Chicago: University of Chicago Press, 1962).

17. P. Selznick, *Leadership in Administration: A Sociological Interpretation* (Evanston: Row, Peterson and Company, 1957), p. 4.

18. J. A. Culbertson, "New Perspectives: Implications for Program Change," in *Preparing Administrators: New Perspectives,* J. A. Culbertson and S. P. Hencley, eds. (Columbus, OH: University Council for Educational Administration, 1962), p. 162. In the same publication, J. G. Harlow, then Dean of the College of Education, University of Oklahoma, elaborated on Culbertson's statement in Chapter IV, "Purposing-Defining: The Central Function of the School Administrator."

19. Selznick, *Administrative Leadership,* p. 138. Selznick himself has done a frequently cited study of goal displacement in formal organization. See, P. Selznick, *TVA and the Grass Roots* (Berkeley: University of California Press, 1949).

20. For more on the social function of organizational mythology, see the section, "Creative Leadership," in Selznick *Leadership in Administration,* pp. 149-54. The integrative value of organizational mythology is dealt with in textbook literature of other fields under a variety of headings. One such work, as example, uses "organizational saga" as a subhead and its authors state, "We use the concept of *organizational saga* to include the shared group fantasies, the rhetorical visions, and the narratives of achievements, events, and the future vision of dreams of the entire organization." E. Bormann, W. S. Howell, R. G. Nichols, and G. L. Shapiro, *Interpersonal Communication in the Modern Organization* (Englewood Cliffs, NJ: Prentice-Hall, 1982).

21. An instructive elaboration on this theme will be found in F. Tonnies, *Community and Society,* translated by C. P. Loomis (East Lansing: Michigan State University Press, 1957). For a humanist's statement of this ubiquitous dilemma in a contemporary idiom, see A. MacLeish, "The Revolt of the Diminished Man," *Saturday Review* 52 (7 June 1969).

22. For a recently published work which affirms the validity of this thesis, see G. Keller, *Academic Strategy: The Management Revolution in American Higher Education* (Baltimore: The Johns Hopkins Press, 1983).

23. The Selznick and Gouldner models were adaptations of models depicting a variety of sociological and behavioral concepts. They were taken from J. G. March

and H. A. Simon, *Organizations* (New York: John Wiley, 1968). K. Goldhammer and F. Farner, *The Jackson County Story* (Eugene, OR: The Center for Advanced Study of Educational Administration, 1969).

24. Perhaps the single publication which best illustrates the Griffiths' style is Griffiths, *Human Relations in School Administration.* Culbertson's identification with the case method in educational administration dates from his faculty days at the University of Oregon and before his appointment as Executive Director of the University Council for Educational Administration. See J. A. Culbertson, P. P. Jacobson, and T. L. Reller, *Administrative Relationships* (Englewood Cliffs, NJ: Prentice-Hall, 1960). See also, C. G. Sargent and E. L. Belisle, *Educational Administration: Cases and Concepts* (Boston: Houghton Mifflin, 1955).

25. Quoted in G. L. Immegart, *Guides for the Preparation of Instructional Case Material in Educational Administration* (Columbus, OH: University Council for Educational Administration, 1967), p. 1.

26. A line spoken by a character in one of the six comedies by Terence that have survived. "I am a man: nothing human is alien to me."

27. See Getzels's acknowledgment in J. W. Getzels, "Conflict and Role Behavior in the Educational Setting," in *Readings in the Social Psychology of Education,* W. W. Charters, Jr., and N. L. Gage, eds. (Boston: Little, Brown and Co., 1932), p. 310.

28. C. Nordhoff and J. N. Hall, *Mutiny on the Bounty* (Boston: Little, Brown, 1960), pp. 38, 145-46.

29. Clifford Dowdey, *Death of a Nation* (New York: Alfred A. Knopf, 1967). Another example in literature of a near-perfect case, now for the study of obedience to orders—Barnard's three zonal responses to directives from a superior—is Stephen Crane's *Red Badge of Courage,* most especially in the protagonist, Henry. In the vault of some film library is a movie version of *Red Badge of Courage,* directed by John Huston and Audie Murphy in the role of Henry. It is a short film, little remembered, but one of Huston's masterpieces.

30. J. Q. Wilson, "Liberalism versus Liberal Education," *Commentary* 53 (June 1972), p. 54.

31. *Ibid.,* p. 54.

32. A similar anti-model is available in the character of Colonel Nicholson in *The Bridge on the River Kwai.*

33. The concept of "bureaucratic virtuoso" is in R. K. Merton, *Social Theory and Social Structure* (New York: Free Press, 1968), p. 239.

34. It is instructive to call attention at this juncture to a paper R. Farquhar had prepared for a UCEA-University of Alberta Career Development Seminar in 1979, "Ethics in Administration." In it, Farquhar dealt with the problem of training for ethical behavior in administration. He suggested five approaches to the problem and one of them is through the humanities. He wrote, "It involves having recourse to the study of problems in values and moral dilemmas." Robin H. Farquhar, "Preparing Administrators for Ethical Practice," unpublished paper, p. 18.

35. Emile Durkheim, *Sociology and Education,* translated by S. D. Fox (New York: Free Press, 1956), p. 95.

36. There is a plentiful literature in the journals of administration to facilitate the use of Barnard's concepts as tools of analysis. One such is D. Mechanic's "Sources of Power of Lower Participants in Complex Organizations," *Administrative Science Quarterly* 7 (December 1962). Mechanic defines high-ranking positions and, in turn,

lower-stationed participants, in this way: "One might ask what characterizes high-ranking positions within organizations? What is most evident, perhaps, is that lower participants recognize the right of higher-ranking participants to exercise power, and yield without difficulty to demands they regard as legitimate." He defines power as "any force that results in behavior that would not have occurred if the force had not been present." *Ibid.,* pp. 350-51. For ways of taxonomy construction, see D. E. Griffiths, ed., *Developing Taxonomies of Organizational Behavior* (Chicago: Rand-McNally, 1969). Also useful is B. McKelvey, *Organizational Systematics: Taxonomy, Evaluation, Classification* (Berkeley: University of California Press, 1982).

37. In his *Treatise Concerning the Principles of Human Knowledge,* 1710, Berkeley held that particular qualities of objects are known only in the mind, and that they do not exist except as they are perceived by the mind. This nominalist philosophical attitude later was refined in the thoroughgoing skepticism of David Hume. A philosophically grounded treatment of cognitivism and noncognitivism in moral philosophy is to be found in S. Lovibond, *Realism and Imagination in Ethics* (Minneapolis: University of Minnesota Press, 1983). For an especially rewarding venture into philosophical attitudes of Hume and Berkeley in belletristic literature, see "A New Refutation of Time" in J. L. Borgess, *A Personal Anthology* (New York: Grove Press, 1967).

38. Jack Culbertson has stated the same conviction early in his UCEA service. See J. Culbertson, "The Preparation of Administrators," in D. E. Griffiths, ed., *Behavioral Science and Educational Administration* (Chicago: National Society of the Study of Education, Sixty-Third Yearbook, 1964).

39. A line spoken by Oedipus at the end of Sophocles' play, *Oedipus the King.* A memento mori in Shakespeare is contained in the following exchange, *Hamlet* (IV, iii), between the King and Hamlet.

> Hamlet: A man may fish with the worm that hath eat of a king, and eat of the fish that hath fed on that worm.
>
> King: What does thou mean by this?
>
> Hamlet: Nothing but to show you how a king may go a progress through the guts of a beggar.

40. The Kettering Foundation has printed literature which provides procedural details in the use of NIS.

41. See A. W. Gouldner, *The Hellenic World: A Sociological Analysis,* in 2 volumes (New York: Basic Books, 1965); A. J. Podlecki, *The Political Background of Aeschvlean Tragedy* (Ann Arbor: The University of Michigan Press, 1966); and L. A. Coser, ed., *Sociology Through Literature* (Englewood Cliffs, NJ: Prentice-Hall, 1963), p. 3. In a sentiment kindred to Coser's, M. M. Kessler, a student of information systems in science, has stated, "Even the masterpieces of scientific literature will in time become worthless except for historical reasons. This is a basic difference between the scientific and belletristic literature. It is inconceivable for a serious student of English literature, for example, not to have read Shakespeare, Milton, and Scott. A serious student of physics, on the other hand, can safely ignore the original writings of Newton, Faraday, and Maxwell." Quoted in Merton, *Social Theory and Social Structure,* p. 28.

42. J. Ciardi, "An Ulcer, Gentlemen, is an Unwritten Poem," in R. A. Goldwin, *Toward the Liberally Educated Executive* (White Plains: The Fund for Adult Education, 1957), p. 52.

CHAPTER EIGHTEEN

A Review of Criticisms of Educational Administration: The State of the Art

ROBERT T. STOUT

The author developed a statement on the current status of educational administration to stimulate discussion at regional seminars of the National Commission on Excellence in Educational Administration, Feb. 18–May 8, 1987. He reviewed the literature which criticized the field—training, selection, placement, and career development of administrators. He created "clusters" of criticisms to guide his analysis of the literature. The clusters include alleged low academic standards of training programs, ineffectiveness of administrators in establishing effective schools, administrators' "high handedness," the teacher pool from which administrators are drawn, the relative absence of data for administrators selection procedures, and the mismatch of job requirements and candidate skills. He critiqued the criticisms in an orderly fashion which is helpful to the reader who is interested in thinking through the state of the art in educational administration.

During the last few years, almost all of the reports of national commissions have called for renewed strength of educational leadership. School administrators have been admonished that necessary reforms in America's schools depend, in large measure, on forward-looking administrators who will establish the conditions for improvement. Unfortunately, the reports are devoid of elaboration on this theme.

However, the national literature has not been devoid of criticisms of school administrators. Perhaps it is not an overstatement to say that school administrators have been criticized routinely in this century. Nonetheless, in the past five years or so the criticisms have been extensive, focused and harsh. This paper is an effort to review the recent

SOURCE: Robert T. Stout, "A Review of Criticisms of Educational Administration: The State of the Art" (Statement prepared for discussion purposes at regional seminars of the UCEA National Commission on Excellence in Educational Administration, Feb. 18–May 8, 1986). Copyright © by The University Council for Educational Administration. Reprinted with permission.

criticisms in order to build a context for the work of the National Commission on Excellence in Educational Administration.

Criticisms of school administrators (and by inference their training, selection, placement, and career development) occur in the context of larger questions about school effectiveness. This paper will first be a discussion of some of those larger questions and then be a synthesis of critiques of administrators and their careers, including more particularly, their preparation.

Although modern critics of public schools are neither in agreement about the nature of the problems nor in agreement about remedy, there has been general agreement among citizens and influentials that something is amiss in the public school system of the United States. Risking oversimplification, the 20 or so major reports, books, and monographs appearing since 1982 can be categorized as being in one or the other of two ideological clusters.

In one cluster are arguments to the effect that academic standards and expectations are too low, that academic work is not sufficiently rigorous, that the core academic activity of a school must supersede other activity and that schools are best construed as arenas of academic competition. These reports have as historical and intellectual antecedents the recommendations of the Committee of Ten chaired by President Eliot of Harvard in 1894.

In the other cluster are those current reports that reflect the assumptions that underlay *The Cardinal Principles of Education* published in 1918. These assumptions are that the education of productive citizens in a modern democracy requires more than an academic emphasis. Public schools, in this view, have a responsibility to offer a wide array of experiences in order to accommodate and capitalize on differences in human capacity and interest.

While these clusters represent (and have represented) long-standing disagreements among policymakers, current reform efforts seem more driven by the former cluster than the latter. State and federal policy are being devised to raise standards, to focus schooling on academic matters and to orient students, parents, and educators to the serious business of academic rigor. The dominant mood of policymakers is to foster higher standards, more rigor and more academic substance.

Contemporaneously with publication of reports calling for reform of public schools has been publication of a growing body of studies generally called "research on effective schools." Researchers are attempting to explain why it is that student achievement (defined as scores on an achievement test) in some schools is unusually high or higher than could be predicted by such common indicators as student social class, dollars spent per pupil or student ethnicity. While the findings are far from unequivocal, reflecting the state of much social science research, responsible scholars and policymakers give them credence. In broad outline, "effective" schools are argued to differ from "ineffective" schools in a number of systematic ways.

In effective schools, parents, students, and teachers share a common understanding that the mission of the school is to foster academic achievement. Teachers and parents have high expectations for student achievement and make these expectations explicit. The school is an orderly, purposive place in which students are serious about academic matters. Academic achievement is recognized and celebrated. Teachers are colleagues, sharing ideas and instructional techniques with one another, and participating actively in decisions about school matters. Inside classrooms, students are actively engaged in carefully designed learning activities grounded in an overall curriculum which is systematic and cumulative. Out of class, students are expected to complete homework. Leadership of this enterprise is by someone or some group (generally, the school principal is discovered to be the leader) who has a clear focus, a good understanding of effective instructional techniques, views the principalship as an influential position, actively intervenes in classroom instruction by observing and critiquing teachers, and rather forcefully captures the attention of teachers, students, and parents and focuses it on the academic mission of the school. An effective school is described as one in which all participants share and work diligently toward academic achievement without forsaking other important goals. Effective leadership is leadership that produces a school with these characteristics.

Contemporary criticisms of public school administrators are, for the most part, that they do not produce effective schools. Although the "effective schools research" literature posits the necessity for strong leadership, what such leadership comprises is not fully articulated. It is possible to make some inferences about effectiveness by examining literature that describes a "typical" school administrator's work. If one uses as a standard some of the current literature on effective top leadership, school superintendents are thought to be wanting. Superintendents are criticized for being conservative, timid, concerned about short-term matters, isolated from the technical cores of the enterprise (teaching and learning), worried more about noninstructional matters than instructional issues and generally inadequate to the task of building a purpose-driven, adaptable organization. School superintendents are said to spend their energies on maintaining the status quo and defending the organization from outside influences. Because of the lack of long-range planning and of their systems for sensing environments, designing, and evaluating programs and adjusting the organization to changes in environments, school districts are viewed as closed political systems in which change, when it occurs, is cataclysmic rather than gradual.

Descriptions of the work of typical school building principals offer another set of criticisms by inference. The general picture which emerges is of (typically) a harried man interacting in short episodes over trivial (or at least noninstructional) matters. In the course of a day, a school principal might be engaged in 150 or so different and disparate activities. These activities are divided among dealing with disruptive students, smoothing interpersonal conflict, placating parents, defending the school from intrusions either from the community or from "central office" staff, seeing to the physical appearance of the school, and filling out forms demanded by central administration. Principals infrequently engage in activities that directly promote academic excellence.

Other, more direct, criticisms are not uncommon. Superintendents are criticized by school board members for high-handedness and failure to keep them adequately informed. Teacher groups criticize superintendents for shoddy personnel practices and for arbitrary decision making. Citizens criticize school superintendents for failure to respond to their demands in such matters as program emphases, treatment of students with special needs, and the efficient expenditure of public funds. State policymakers criticize superintendents for general intractability and, occasionally, for subverting state mandates.

School principals are generally most criticized for their lack of technical competence and for their arbitrariness in decision making. Principals, it is argued, cannot be instructional leaders because they do not have knowledge of instructional techniques and strategies. Such principals cannot assess instructional programs and cannot evaluate teaching. Their decision making is criticized as arbitrary, more frequently responsive to political pressure than to program integrity. Parents criticize principals for protecting incompetent teachers, while teachers assert that principals cave in to unreasonable parent demands. The general criticism is that principals engage in unimportant activity and are ineffective even in that.

While it may be argued that such criticisms are unjust, inaccurate or applicable to only a few administrators, the general call for reforms in administrator behavior has been substantial. State and local policymakers have acted and are acting as though the criticisms are valid.

Whatever the actual state of affairs, perceived problems with administrators have been grouped into six general areas: recruitment, selection, placement, ongoing training, career progress, and preparation.

RECRUITMENT

The pool of potential school administrators is the teaching force of the country's public schools. This is said to be a difficulty because of characteristics of the group. Teachers are among the least academically able college students and have had below standard intellectual experiences as college students because of their majors in education. Thus the intellectual and academic qualities of administrators are suspect, even if administrators were the most able in the pool.

In addition, the academic capital of the pool is said to diminish through selective attrition from the profession. In any given year of the tenure of a cadre of teachers, the most academically able are the most likely to exit the profession. Because the practical pool of potential administrators is of those who have taught five to seven years, the presumption is that the persisters are among the less intellectually able of the original pool.

The difficulty has been exacerbated in the last several years by dramatic changes in social forces. The pool of teachers (and thus of potential administrators) is declining overall, with selectively worse declines in the number of particularly able women and ethnic minorities. These able people have chosen other occupations as discrimination in those occupations has diminished. The potential for real harm is heightened by what are believed to be impending large-scale retirements among teachers and administrators.

A less obvious, but perhaps more powerful, mechanism further restricts the pool of exceptional future administrators. Informal systems of sponsored mobility exist in most school districts. While the mechanisms vary, typically a sitting principal will spot and tap a favorite. The person so chosen will be encouraged to think about "getting into administration," will be counseled about appropriate steps and will be given opportunities to become known to other administrators and to demonstrate leadership potential. Without such sponsorship, a teacher who aspires to administration is disadvantaged. There is some evidence that the systems of sponsored mobility work to weed out change-oriented teachers, women, ethnic minorities, and all those who represent a threat to the status quo. Assertiveness, independence of thought, and considered skepticism are said to be undesirable characteristics, while passivity, willingness to go along, and enthusiasm for current modes of operation are favored. These systems of sponsored mobility further homogenize the pool of potential administrators.

SELECTION

Unlike many organizations, schools are relatively undifferentiated administratively. A typical school district may have only five or six line administrative titles: assistant principal, principal, director, assistant superintendent, superintendent, with some elaboration of titles in support functions. One consequence is to limit the opportunities for practice in anticipation of selection or for building an administrative record. Unlike organizations with multiple administrative layers and relatively fine gradations of administrative work, school district administrative functions are substantially dissimilar. For example, the work of assistant principals (typically student discipline and support services) does not provide many opportunities to practice the presumed work of the principalship (instructional leadership). In more formal terms, the work roles among levels are discontinuous.

One consequence is to reduce the amount of evidence available for making rational selection decisions. Since past performance records are accumulated in dissimilar positions, the process depends on high levels of inference. Will a sponsored teacher make a good assistant principal? Will an assistant principal who is a good student disciplinarian make a good principal, in which role adult-to-adult interactions are critical? Lacking low inference predictors, school district selection procedures typically rest on less objective criteria. While many districts have begun to use administrator assessment center technologies, most do not. The more general pattern rests on having an influential sponsor, or making a good showing in an interview, or having good letters of reference, or having legitimation from the local preparation institution and/or gaining the endorsement of a superior that the candidate will "fit in." This latter criterion is thought to be important because school systems have relatively weak mechanisms for controlling the performance of incumbents. For example, school principals can behave with high degrees of autonomy. Thus having determined that a candidate will "fit in" or be of the "right sort" is critical in the absence of controls once the person is selected. "Being of the right sort" is often enough translated in practice to mean "being like the superordinate."

Two other characteristics of selection are criticized. The first is that selection is generally parochial in nature. Positions are advertised within the district (if they are advertised at all) or in the immediate vicinity. This has the consequence of further restricting the pool of applicants.

The second is the general lack of specificity in expected performance requirements. For example, few school boards engage a systematic process of assessing the district and projecting future directions prior to selecting a superintendent. Consequently, mismatches often occur in which the new superintendent's strengths and biases for action and direction are inappropriate in that setting. Superintendents who are let go after short tenure are not necessarily incompetent. Often they are simply mismatched to the requirements of that particular district. At lower levels, as well, the lack of clarity about the work to be done produces mismatches between candidate skills and the requirements for successful performance.

PLACEMENT

If the argument holds that job requirements and candidate skills are often mismatched at the point of employment, much the same argument holds with respect to placement. If job requirements are poorly defined and if candidate skills are only known superficially, then placement becomes problematic. At one extreme placement becomes almost random. This randomlike activity may be seen in rotation schemes in which principals are moved from one school to another on some fixed schedule. The expressed rationale for such schemes is often that "it's good to shake up things a bit" or "new principals bring new ideas." Sometimes the private rationale is a reflection of the other end of the placement continuum; that which asserts that influential principals are able to choose good schools. In practice, principals who have built powerful political bases in a school neighborhood may be invulnerable to incursions by the superintendent or staff.

Certainly examples exist of careful placement. Such placements are serious attempts to match an administrator's skills to someone's decision about what tasks must be accomplished in the setting. But we assert that these examples do not represent predominant organization practices.

CONTINUED TRAINING

Among the most frequently criticized areas of administrative life is the provision for continuing education. Although major efforts are made by professional associations, universities, and school districts, school administrators seem to be caught in a continuing game of catch up. That is, changes in demands on schools appear to happen more quickly or more unpredictably than the system of continuing training can accommodate. Consequently, school administrators appear routinely to be unprepared to implement the new demands. In part this may be a function of the size of the occupation group, in part a function of rapidity of new demands, in part a function of inadequate delivery systems or in part a function of the generally low priority for continuing education in the profession. However caused, school administrators are routinely criticized for technological backwardness. Competent evaluation of teachers, installation and use of computers, and lack of implementation of findings from the effective schools research are only current examples of such criticisms.

CAREER DEVELOPMENT

The criticisms in this area are, perhaps, of a different sort. They parallel the current criticisms of incompetence among teachers. The relatively thin administrative structure of schools combines with other factors to make administrator removal a painful process. The public ouster of school superintendents masks the multiple cases of organizational immobility concerning nonperforming lower-level administrators. In part this reflects the lack of good evaluation procedures and in part the difficulty of action. Until recently state retirement systems provided little opportunity for exit. Unlike university administrators, former school administrators may not find graceful exit by returning to the professoriate. Unlike the situation in many businesses, school districts may have no nooks and crannies in which to hide formerly productive administrators. School districts often are faced with enduring (or attempting to obscure) the poor performance or engaging a painful process of terminating a formerly valuable employee.

CAREER PREPARATION

Of all the areas which may contribute to the current state of criticism of school administrators, the area of career preparation is our major focus. Criticism and disagreement abound in this area, although the quality of data available for assessing the state of affairs is quite poor. In general, university professors do not know in any valid sense the effects of their efforts. This section, then, rests mostly on considered judgments of experienced participants. Much of the process of preparation can be described or mapped. The effects of differences in preparation are less easily discussed. We must avoid the temptation to attribute to preparation programs either more or less fault for the current state of practice in school administration.

THE STRUCTURE OF PREPARATION

Preparation for educational administration is different in structure from preparation for other professions or near professions. In the latter cases, preparation is usually continuous, requiring full-time commitment by candidates, undertaken immediately or soon after college, begun and finished in the same institution, and sequenced for a cadre who move together through defined stages. None of these conditions prevails in the preparation of school administrators. Preparation in educational administration is discontinuous and part-time. Candidates work on degrees and certificates while employed full-time as teachers or administrators. Most often progress consists of taking one course a semester, one or two courses in the summer, and enrolling in one intense period of residency (usually a semester, sometimes an academic year). Preparation normally is begun five to eight years after college graduation and may extend, in the case of doctorates, 20 or more years including long periods of hiatus. Only in rare cases will students finish a degree at the institution of first graduate enrollment. Under such conditions, course sequencing and cadre identification are difficult. In structure, then, preparation in educational administration is unlike preparation for other professions.

STUDENT CHARACTERISTICS

Students in educational administration are older, score less well on standard measures of intellectual capability (the Graduate Record Examination or the Miller Analogies Test), and have weaker undergraduate records than do candidates in most other fields. They are as likely to be women as men and are likely to attend part-time at an institution close to their current employment. For the most part they are quite pragmatic in outlook, treating the degree as a "ticket" for upward mobility.

RECRUITMENT AND SELECTION

With minor exception it may be said that recruitment into preparation programs is informal, local, intermittent, and as much in the hands of practicing school administrators as of university faculty. Faculty rely on these arrangements to produce a pool of applicants, most of whom are admitted. While more deliberate and careful procedures exist, they are not usual. Admission to master's degree and certificate programs is more perfunctory than admission to doctoral programs. There is little systematic recruitment beyond state lines or across territorial lines within states.

Criteria for selection reflect both disagreement and confusion. Disagreement arises over the relative weights to be given academic indicators and measures of potential leadership. The disagreements exist within departments and between departments and other academic units in the university. Confusion derives from the lack of clarity about purpose in most programs. For example, faculty disagree about such issues as whether a select number of carefully chosen and prepared students is preferable to offering opportunities on a more equalitarian basis. The lack of clarity over purpose results in the inability to choose from a wide array of predictors of success.

Once admitted, few students are let go from programs. Persistence seems sufficient for eventual completion. In sum, standards for recruitment, admission, and retention are criticized as too low and, more telling perhaps, beside the point.

ISSUES OF PEDAGOGY

Criticisms of the processes of instruction come from faculty members and students and are of two types; that the processes are wrong and that they are so in spite of knowledge of better ways. A typical program is some mixture (either systematic or not) of formal didactic classwork, simulations and case studies, field work (either directed or supervised), perhaps an internship, written and oral exams, perhaps a residency, some of which can be fulfilled while working full-time, and a dissertation that has been characterized as having little to do with the core problems of educational administration. These processes are said to be incapable of building occupational commitment, collegiality, commitment to professional norms, or a serious commitment to analysis and synthesis as the bases for solving educational problems.

Since accommodation is made to a part-time student body, classes are held at night or on weekends, assignments to field experiences are made as much for mutual convenience as for learning value and learning experiences are modified to fit into two- to three-hour chunks once a week. Typically, instruction is faculty dominated in the definition of both what is to be learned and how it is to be learned. Faculty are perceived by students as out of touch with the important issues of school life and as not current in the general fields of study.

Criticisms of these processes take several forms. Field experiences are criticized for being haphazard or unsupervised or irrelevant to the course of study. Examination practices are criticized for being irrelevant to the

practice of school administration. Faculty dominance is seen as dysfunctional for preparing leaders. Dissertations are criticized as unrelated to
the use of analysis and synthesis usually associated with executive
positions. In sum, the processes of training are said to provide little or no
opportunity to learn and practice the necessary skills of educational
leadership.

Perhaps the most interesting criticism with respect to instructional
processes is that a sufficient knowledge base exists to permit better design
in programs. The possibility of redesign is being ignored.

THE CONTENT OF PREPARATION

Little if any agreement exists concerning the appropriate content of
preparation for educational administration. Similarly, there exists little
consistency in the criticisms. However, it is possible to synthesize them.
Before doing so, it is useful to describe typical content, with the caveat
that no typical content may exist in fact. Generally, programs have four
content emphases. The first is content that is driven by state certification
requirements, often encompassing technical matters such as school law,
school budgets, school buildings, and others. Second is content in educational research tools such as statistics, research design, and data-gathering techniques. A third content emphasis is in such supporting fields as
educational psychology, educational philosophy, educational history, and
curriculum design. The fourth general content focus might be called
theory or theories of educational administration. This content may
emphasize organization design and management, research on leadership, education politics, economics of education, or other topics thought
to be interesting or useful.

Criticisms of content are directed at all of these areas. In a more
abstract way, disagreement exists over the appropriate mix of content
drawn from theories or research and content drawn from practice. Some
argue that preparation is too theoretical or abstract, having no direct
connection to the practice of administration. Others argue that the typical
content is too mechanical or technical to provide students with conceptual
skills necessary for solving complex problems in variable settings. The
disagreement produces criticisms of both approaches.

A second general criticism is that there is confusion over what might
be called the philosophy of content. This criticism asserts that confusion
exists over whether preparation should focus on administration as craft,
art, science; knowable or ultimately unknowable. Perhaps the clearest
indication of the confusion is seen in the lack of differentiation between
a professional degree (Ed.D. or Doctor of Education) and a research

degree (Ph.D. or Doctor of Philosophy). In concept, the two degrees should differ sharply: the professional degree (Ed.D.) as appropriate for those who intend to practice the profession—that is, become school principals or superintendents—as is true for other professional degrees such as the D.D.S. or the J.D. or the MBA; the research degree (Ph.D.) as appropriate for those who intend to become university professors or full-time research workers. In practice, little if any differentiation exists. Those who aspire to become school administrators complete programs that differ neither in content nor process from programs for those who intend substantially different careers. The confusion over the assumptions that underlie the practice of administration creates a more general confusion over what should be the nature of preparation.

A third overarching criticism is that preparation content is undifferentiated with respect to student career progress. It is asserted that no analogue exists in education for the advanced training provided in other executive occupations. Other executives are provided with sophisticated training as they move up the executive ranks. The content of education administration programs is nonlinear and noncumulative, with novices receiving essentially the same content as more experienced students.

A fourth general criticism is that the content of both theory and technique is wrong content. Admitting that technique is necessary, critics assert such technical skills as budget making are less important than skills in small group leadership or public speaking or memo writing.

Criticism of the theory-related content exists as well. Critics assert that the theories most commonly used in preparation programs are wrong on two counts. The first is that they are so limited in scope that they are virtually useless for understanding the complex, hurly-burly nature of the real world of educational administrators. The second criticism is that theory makers view schools as serving basically desirable ends. These critics argue that our understanding of schools as organizations would be more complete if we made explicit the characteristics and structures which contribute to harm for those who work and study in them.

A fifth criticism is that much important content is simply missing from the preparations of school administrators. Although the list of absent content is long, some illustrative suggestions should be noted. Few students receive extensive preparation in strategies and techniques for program design, implementation, evaluation, and redesign. It is said that such skills as strategic planning and cost effectiveness analysis are missing. Few students receive training in group processes (working with groups as decisions are developed, chairing or participating in meetings, using groups to bring about organizational changes). Other missing content is the study of values and ethics, the study of alternative futures, and systematic study of the core activities of the school, teaching, and learning.

In sum, criticisms of content reveal the absence of agreement about what administration is, what administrators do, what they should do, and how what happens to them in university programs is related to any of the other issues. As one critic has said,

> There is no assurance, however, the persons who emerge from educational administrator programs have leadership skills commensurate with the requirements of the future.

PART FOUR

Visions to Help Leaders Move Forward

George Counts's powerful question of the 1930s remains: Dare
we build a new society? In today's rather conservative times, there
is a related question: Do we *want* to rebuild society and *should*
we? The alternative futurists ask: Granted the inevitability of
dramatic, rapid changes, how can we develop the will and the
capability to invent the kind of desirable future we want?

If educative institutions are to bridge for learners the wisdom
of the past, the realities of the present, and the probable alternatives of future times, education leaders should understand futuristic issues and incorporate such thinking into their strategic planning. The rapidity and complexity of social and technological
changes require leaders who are proactive in their attitudes and
practices.

There is a juggling act required of leaders: How to be proactive
and concurrently to maintain traditional, sustaining values and
practices. In the 1987 Alabama school book case, a federal judge
expressed alarm about what was included in the contested textbooks and also what was left out (for example, neglected topics
such as the role of the Puritans and early religious evangelists).

What should be read into educated conjectures about future
alternatives will be a function of several values—moral, political,
and economic. The World Future Society takes no position on what
it reports as alternative futures. Education leaders do not have
that option. They must select what to include in and exclude from
the curriculum. They should select instructional strategies and
leadership styles that are compatible with the kind of democratic,
effective society preferred by our people. They should have the
leadership skills that are essential in helping society to identify
and implement its goals. The students in the schools today should

be taught in ways that will prepare them for effective living in the society that today is being planned for the coming times, which for them will include living in two centuries.

Our democratic society should respond dynamically to probable future options. It can look with favor on some likely directions. It can favor certain probabilities with selected revisions. It can largely reject selected alternatives and take actions necessary to redirect likely events and conditions. The schools can be laboratories in which the ways of thinking critically and proactively are taught and practiced. The wisdom of the past and the experiences of the present provide some guidelines for futuristic invention of the kind of world we seek.

Educators have to be exceedingly well educated in order to help students—also adult citizens—to bridge past, present, and future. Education leaders have to be conservers of the best of what built the nation at its best and vision builders of what can be. (At the same time, education administrators must deal with day-to-day issues!) This section addresses the alternative futures aspect of education leadership.

CHAPTER NINETEEN

A Futuristic Cognitive View of Leadership

G. BARRY MORRIS

The concept of leadership is a major issue in Western society. In education, new directions to the study of leadership are apparent. This article proposes a reconceptualization that focuses on the individual, on future consciousness, and on outcome behaviors. The psychotherapeutic model of Rational-Emotive Theory is presented as a basis for identifying new strategies for effective leadership in the future. An application of this reconceptualization is made to leadership training programs in education.

The study of the concept of leadership has generated numerous definitions, conceptualizations, and formulations. Analyses have yielded countless traits, an array of behaviors, and a multitude of leadership styles deemed necessary for effectiveness. Although well-documented, the concept of leadership has recently come under a great deal of scrutiny in Western society. In keeping with this general trend, those in education are pursuing new directions in the study of leadership.

This article proposes a reconceptualization of leadership by examining three major areas: the individual, futures thinking, and outcome behaviors. The individual component comprises the rational/irrational dimensions of cognitive functioning as reflected in the leader's psychological health. Futures thinking is viewed in terms of identifying new beliefs required for leadership success in the decades ahead. The behavioral outcomes category is a consequence of the integration of the individual and futures thinking components and takes the form of a unique pattern of behaviors. An application of this conceptualization is then made to leadership training programs. A brief overview of current perceptions of leadership is presented prior to the reconceptualization.

THE STUDY OF LEADERSHIP

Defining the concept of leadership has been a challenging and major task for educators and social scientists in general. The literature is replete with varied and sometimes conflicting definitions. For instance, Lipham defines leadership "as the initiation of a new structure or procedure for accomplishing an organization's goals and objectives."[1] Cunningham describes this concept as "a curious blending of leading and following, provoking and calming, disturbing and stabilizing . . . generating new strength and capability along the way."[2] Leadership, according to Sergiovanni, "involves introducing something new or helping to improve present conditions."[3] Burns believes that leaders should "induce new, more activist tendencies in their followers; arouse in them hopes, and aspirations and expectations."[4] A simplified definition by Halpin describes the leader as "the outstanding member of a class."[5] Still others identify leadership in terms of the attainment of group goals, the fulfillment of designated responsibilities, or the process of problem solving.[6] Focusing on the nature of the individual, Scott, Hickcox, and Ryan believe that the educational leader needs to be a "practicing psychologist, a sociologist, a person knowledgeable in public finance, and a skilled politician."[7] Perhaps it was this multiplicity of definitions that prompted Spikes to conclude "that there appears to be no universally accepted definition of this concept which has stood the test of time and inquiry."[8]

The study of leadership, according to Lipham, has evolved through four major stages of development. First, the concept was examined from the "great men" approach. Second, the importance of describing the traits and characteristics of leaders was emphasized. Third, investigations consisted of determining and identifying those situational factors that affected the leader. And fourth, leadership was studied through the observation of the behaviors of individuals.[9]

The extensive literature on leadership, however, is not readily categorized into the above developmental stages. The problem is due to the interrelatedness of the stages. For instance, in reviewing the "great men" approach, relevant traits and characteristics are often described and reported. Similarly, determining the influence of situational factors involves observing the leader's behaviors and, accordingly, identifying specific traits and attributes. In this article, a small effort at categorization is made; however, certain modifications and combinations are required of Lipham's stages.

The "great men" and "observation of the behaviors of leaders" are closely related stages, revealing a number of leadership styles. For instance, Weber distinguishes differences among the legal, traditional, and charismatic styles of leadership.[10] Havighurst places great leaders into one of three categories: (a) the prophet, (b) the scholar-scientist, and

(c) the social engineer.[11] Democratic and authoritarian leadership are contrasted by Halpin,[12] while job-centered and employee-centered styles are compared by Likert.[13] The theoretical formulations and research unfolding from these approaches to the study of leadership identify, compare, and determine the effectiveness of differing behavioral styles of leaders.

The "traits" stage provides another focus for the study of leadership. In a review of those traits generally attributed to successful leaders, Abrell concludes that the following appear to be the most significant: (a) active participation, (b) creating a facilitating climate, (c) providing inspiration, (d) providing justice and fairness, (e) resisting unnecessary demands, (f) recognizing talent, and (g) practicing ethical integrity.[14] Others report similar traits.[15] In addition, the leader should be creative,[16] be aware of organizational structure,[17] and use teamsmanship.[18] Perhaps Berg best describes those characteristics necessary for effective leadership:

> Effective educational leaders should have a clear understanding of their functions; a desire for and a knowledge of group dynamics; be academically and professionally honest; have a desire to cut red tape; be understanding, patient, imaginative, and innovative; . . . must exhibit the virtues of honesty, integrity, cooperation, and concern for others; . . . and must be adaptable.[19]

Another stage of development in the study of leadership is the "analysis of situational factors."[20] This approach, according to Saville, views leadership "as a process of structuring, organizing, and guiding a situation so that all members of a group can achieve common goals with maximum economy and minimum time and effort."[21] Sergiovanni and Carver point out that situational analysis emphasizes the process or interaction between the leader and the group and identifies the "it depends" variables in relation to the leader's characteristics or orientation.[22] Matching leadership style to existing situational factors should create a degree of congruence, thereby enhancing the likelihood of success.

A new focus of studies of leadership, one attracting numerous advocates, is the leader's awareness of the future. Goodlad provides a reason for this interest and suggests alternatives in the following statement:

> We have yielded to the pressures and temptations of becoming experts in fiscal and personnel management, public relations, collective bargaining, and the political process. . . . It is now time to put the right things at the center again. And the right things have to do with assuring comprehensive, quality educational programs in each and every school.[23]

Quality education in the future is dependent upon "good" leaders and effective leadership approaches. One such approach, proposed by Spady, Bell, and D'Angelo is *Zeitgeist Communication.* An awareness by all individuals of the influence of socio-politico-economic developments on education is the most significant aspect of this position. The process involves the establishment of a forum among all individuals of the organization. Information giving, communication, and interaction among the members generates ideas and opinions about important educational issues:

> In this way the Zeitgeist—the prevailing system of beliefs and opinions of a specific group of people at a point in time—is revealed, and it begins to allow everyone to provide leadership and help direct the organization toward its goals.[24]

The leader's understanding of the "spirit of the times" is increasingly being recognized as a critical determinant of success.[25] Goldman contends that "leaders must be students of society and educators must be able to understand the interplay of both."[26] According to Wenrich, the leader must "live ahead" of others, and this involves the development of new behavioral strategies and mechanisms.[27] Van Avery supports this contention and suggests that "new leadership skills in the future will need to include a tolerance for multiple interpretations and the ability to explore and create alternatives."[28] If this is the case, then an essential trait of educational leaders today is an awareness of tomorrow.

Thus a review of the literature on the study of leadership supports the three major categories suggested as the framework for the reconceptualization proposed in this article: the individual, futures thinking, and behavioral outcomes. The proponents of the individual category place value on investigating leadership traits, behaviors, and styles. The importance of leaders attaining an awareness of the influence of societal trends on educational practice characterizes the futures thinking approach. The interaction between the leader and situational contingencies is examined in terms of outcome behaviors.

New perspectives on the study of leadership emerge, however, if one logically extrapolates from and extends the boundaries of the above categories. For instance, the "individual" component, with emphasis on desired leadership traits and characteristics, can be perceived as the leader's level of human functioning with a particular emphasis on psychological health. The "futures thinking" dimension can be interpreted as the leader's ability to recognize and develop specific strategies and coping mechanisms for effectiveness in a rapidly changing society. The integration of the individual and futures thinking components results in the outcome behaviors of the leader. A reconceptualization, based on new perceptions of the traditional dimensions associated with the study of leadership, requires, first, a description, definition, and orientation of each category.

INDIVIDUAL

Fiedler provides direction to an attempt to delineate the "individual" component of leadership. According to his position, psychological factors are the primary motivating forces influencing the leader's behavior. The leadership variable of significance in Fiedler's view is the leader's perception of the events, situations, and others, and not the behavior itself.[29] In other words, the "mental set" or inner nature of the leader is the predominant factor determining behavior and, hence, effective management.

The inner state of the leader is the key concept for Kimbrough, Fogel, and Farquhar and is viewed in terms of individual serenity, level of maturity, and positive relations with others.[30] Thom points out that leaders should "cultivate a continual inner calmness and serenity in the midst of a hectic milieu with all the stress factors."[31] Inner calmness is cultivated by relaxation, self-talk, and adhering to certain principles. The objective of this activity is to enhance the leader's emotional stability.

Psychotherapeutic models such as Transactional Analysis, Transcendental Meditation, yoga, biofeedback, and human relations training are used by leaders in pursuit of personal growth.[32] These systems of therapy, however, deal largely with behaviors and not the inner state or underlying dynamics of the individual. Combs believes that "an adequate understanding of human beings requires understanding of the causes of behavior that lie in the inner lives of individuals."[33] This goal may be achieved by considering specific aspects of the leader's cognitive functioning—in particular, beliefs about self, others, and society.

These beliefs, and their effect on the inner lives of individuals, are best viewed from the theoretical perspective of Rational-Emotive Therapy (RET) as postulated by Ellis. The focal point of RET is that man is uniquely rational as well as irrational and that emotional or psychological disturbances result from irrational or illogical thinking.[34] When a person bases a decision about himself, others, and/or his environment on a learned irrational belief, it results in disturbed behavior. Ellis has, accordingly, identified eleven irrational beliefs:

(1) The idea that it is a dire necessity for an adult human being to be loved or approved by virtually every significant other person in his community.

(2) The idea that one should be thoroughly competent, adequate, and achieving in all possible respects if one is to consider oneself worthwhile.

(3) The idea that certain people are bad, wicked, or villainous and that they should be severely blamed and punished for their villainy.

(4) The idea that it is awful and catastrophic when things are not the way one would very much like them to be.

(5) The idea that human unhappiness is externally caused and that people have little or no ability to control their sorrows and disturbances.

(6) The idea that if something is or may be dangerous or fearsome one should be terribly concerned about it and should keep dwelling on the possibility of its occurring.

(7) The idea that it is easier to avoid than to face certain life difficulties and self responsibilities.

(8) The idea that one should be dependent on others and needs someone stronger than oneself on whom to rely.

(9) The idea that one's past history is an all-important determiner of one's present behavior and that, because something strongly affected one's life, it should indefinitely have a similar effect.

(10) The idea that one should become quite upset over other people's problems and disturbances.

(11) The idea that there is invariably a right, precise, and perfect solution to human problems and that it is catastrophic if this perfect solution is not found.

Ellis firmly believes that these self-defeating thoughts are conditioned within the individual and become the roots of emotions and behaviors. Individuals learn irrational thinking from parents, church, television, peers, reading, and school. The goal of rational thinking involves replacing the illogical belief with an appropriate thought that leads to emotional stability. A simple A-B-C approach is used in identifying those beliefs that determine thought patterns and lead to pathological behavior.

In the Rational-Emotive approach to understanding human behavior, the significant factor is the individual's perception or interpretation of the event or situation. Thus, A represents the event affecting the individual; B is the thought or belief resulting from the interpretation of the event; and C is the consequence or action taken by the individual. In this case, B influences the behavior adopted by the individual in reacting to the situation. Analyzing behavior in this manner isolates self-defeating thought patterns that can then be replaced with logical beliefs.

In addition to the eleven irrational beliefs, other operating principles also lead to negative emotion. For instance, sustained negative emotion occurs when individuals function from such absolutes and "shoulds and should nots," or "oughts and ought nots." Disturbed behavior also results from faulty logic or functioning from false assumptions (i.e., assumptions that lack data and supporting evidence). Moreover, neurotic tendencies in individuals develop from an inability to discriminate between "needs and wants." According to the model, "needs" are biologically determined and "wants" are socially conditioned. Individuals often confuse this dichotomy and truly believe they "need" when, in actual fact, they "want." Unproductive behavior is avoided if individuals consciously examine their beliefs and other principles leading to irrational thinking. Learning to think rationally in this vein leads to psychological health.

FUTURES THINKING

The individual section of this article equated the inner state of the leader with cognitive functioning and, specifically, personal integration with rational thinking. The assumption was made that the psychological health of the leader, a prerequisite to effectiveness, is achieved through rational thought processes. The beliefs associated with Rational-Emotive Theory, however, may be temporarily relative to the societal context in which they were postulated and, thus, restricted to human dilemmas characteristic of the 1960s and 1970s. There is reason to believe that a new social order will emerge from the prevailing value system and that individuals will need additional strategies for successful living, strategies reflecting the 1980s and 1990s. Supplementary beliefs to those formulated by Rational-Emotive Theory will then be required by individuals in order to resist pathological disturbances. The following beliefs will assist individuals in seeking emotional stability in the future and, as such, are especially relevant to leaders. These beliefs are stated in their rational form rather than their irrational form, and they differ from the theoretical model in that respect.

A fundamental rational belief for leaders, depicting the necessity of developing a future consciousness, is stated as follows:

> The idea that a connectedness with the future is possible and is essential for human survival.

The literature on educational leadership clearly indicates the need for the development of the leader's future consciousness. A marked shift in individual and social values is presently changing the contemporary view of human behavior. The "I-ism" of the past, with emphasis on narcissism and self-centeredness,[35] is rapidly evolving into "We-ism" in the future, with a focus on cooperation and togetherness.[36] Emerging new views of the individual are resulting in the delineation of new alternatives in educational theory and practice.[37] The consequence of these new approaches for educational practice is an emphasis on students' future awareness as schools attempt to prepare them for the 1980s and 1990s.[38]

As the twenty-first century draws closer, survival of the human species is becoming a central theme in education.[39] Numerous skills, techniques, and strategies are being proposed as means of accomplishing this task.[40] Theoretical positions dealing with the concept of change,[41] the development of conscious awareness,[42] and a focus on cooperative tendencies, among nations as well as individuals,[43] are other avenues suggested for enhancing human survival. If, indeed, education is responsible for providing individuals with mechanisms of survival, then leaders must be aware of the preferred, probable, and possible futures.

Ellis strongly contends that leaders who develop rational thinking and a future consciousness will be adequately equipped to deal with the stress that accompanies social transformation.[44] A logical approach to thinking and an awareness of transitional contingencies reduce the likelihood of pathological resistance to change and result in an orientation that increases the tolerance of stress. New attitudes toward the future are a likely outcome, with a degree of "connectedness" resulting between the leader and tomorrow.

Another rational belief that emphasizes the concept of change is the following:

> The idea that rapid socio-politico-economic change will continue and that stability is attained in change.

According to Platt, scientific and technological advancement is more rapid today than at any previous time in the history of the human species.[45] Within the past century, for instance, a movement from an agricultural to post-industrial society has characterized Western civilization.[46] These developments have contributed to a lack of permanency among social structures and individuals and have resulted in a prevailing sense of instability. The constancy of the past is no longer evident, and the previous stability is no longer attainable. Today, a new perception of the concept of stability is necessary to restore that sense of security experienced by our ancestors.

Changing human values in the past, due perhaps to infrequent occurrence, often created unsuspected social upheaval. Today, however, change is commonplace in all sectors of society and repeatedly alters human life. Living in a world of change is the only possibility available to individuals, and a new sense of stability must be established within this milieu. In this manner, the concept of stability is equated with the permanency of change. If societal change is continual, then permanency is maintained and stability is attained. In other words, stability exists in change itself. Individuals adopting this position regarding our modern technocratic-industrial society will recapture the concept of permanency of the past by establishing a perception of stability consistent with the future.

The belief of "stability in change" as an underlying operating principle of human behavior in the future enhances the likelihood of psychological health. The anxiety that traditionally accompanies social transformation and alteration of human values will decrease as new perceptions increase the individual's tolerance of stress. The role of the leader is, in part, to introduce others to this perception so that all members of the organization develop constructive and responsible attitudes toward change. The role of leadership will be more gratifying when group members possess this, as it promotes emotional stability and reciprocally nurtures an inner calmness in the leader. In both instances, all individuals will be better equipped to pursue rational thinking.

The following rational belief deals with the openendedness of society in a time of constant change:

> The idea that one should not become upset over failure to obtain closure but, rather, function effectively with unclosure.

Historically, societies are never static but, instead, are continually in process of development with shifting fads and fashions that become embedded in the social structure. The ceaseless invasion of society by new and differing variables alters the foundations of social structures. The resulting change, in turn, promotes still further variations with a seemingly never-ending completeness. The outcome of this process is the emergence and responsible-emergence of new values, morals, customs, and habits. Repeated transformations of society, as the century draws to a close, will ensure the continuation of this openendedness, with a sense of "unclosure" persisting.

The contemporary view of human behavior in the future will reflect the accepted orientation of society.[47] Socially approved patterns of human functioning and mechanisms for inhibiting neurotic tendencies may differ from those approaches advocated today. For instance, the present aim is to reduce pathological anxiety according to most models of psychotherapy by helping individuals to seek and obtain closure to interactions with others, situations, and events. This approach, however, is based on psychotherapeutic principles that were derived when social structures maintained a degree of permanence. A predisposition toward the concept of a closure in a societal framework that lacks permanence is inconsistent and leads to emotional disturbance rather than productive behaviors in individuals.

The concept of "unclosure" is congruent with the nature of tomorrow's society, and new therapeutic structures are necessary in understanding human behavior. The assumption that compatibility between the individual and the environment is attainable through the concept of unclosure may be a strategy for successful living. In this context, the prevailing openendedness of social transitions are perceived positively and managed effectively. The leader, in particular, needs to see the value of this fundamental principle because it enhances the development of a future consciousness as well as personal growth.

The belief that follows is intended to assist the leader in developing strategies for coping with the uncertainty of the future.

The idea that since one cannot prepare for all impending change, one should instead prepare for the unanticipated.

Today, social and cultural transformation often occur without warning, and preparation for the resulting consequences is most difficult, if not impossible. The uncertainty permeating society is perplexing, and it prohibits accurate predictions. The unknown future cannot be predicted and, in many cases, cannot even be anticipated. Spontaneous and uncontrolled change is detrimental to individuals who consciously prepare for possible predicted alternatives. Preparing instead for unanticipated events is a strategy for the future.

The important underlying aspect of this principle is the individual's state of readiness to accept and react to unforeseen change. In this way, the emphasis is placed upon the process rather than the content. The process includes the many events that surround and lead to the change, while the content is the outcome of this process. Since unknown and unpredicted change is unknown and unpredictable, it is irrational to anticipate the actual change itself. A more productive approach is to establish a state of readiness, and this can be accomplished when individuals prepare for the unanticipated.

The above belief is a major principle of living for individuals facing the uncertainty of modern society. Everyday instances, however, are situationally specific and require approaches that are applicable and pertinent to the individual's personal environment. In the case of the leader, the personal environment is defined in terms of those elements and variables directly related to educational matters. For this reason, corollaries are presented in further articulating the concept of the unanticipated.

The corollary that *one cannot plan for everything* is used by the leader in dealing with immediate-situational interactions. The many variables influencing change will, at any given point in time, spontaneously alter the situation, institution, or actions by members of the organization. Unanticipated change may create significant effects for the leader, resulting in new concerns and unforeseen decision making. It is perhaps unrealistic for the leader to prepare for each and every incident influencing each and every situation. Accordingly, the likelihood of completely planning for everything is an impossibility. Functioning from this corollary will assist the leader in developing a state of readiness for unplanned events.

Another related corollary for leaders in dealing with everyday concerns is the following: *expect the unexpected.* This belief suggests that daily and even long-range plans can vary and change significantly from one moment to another. Such plans may need to be altered on short notice. The leader's aims, goals, and aspirations are drastically affected by policymakers, new information, and financial matters. In a similar fashion, the behavior of individuals can change surprisingly from that which is normally expected. The rescheduling of plans and activities, and the reassessing of individual motives, will be common tasks for the leader in the future. Learning to function effectively in the face of unexpected change will aid the leader in adjusting quickly to new contingencies. This major belief and its related corollaries will develop in the leader a degree of resiliency to unanticipated change, both in the immediate and distant futures.

The leader's degree of self reliance is expressed in the following belief:

The idea that one should not rely completely on the views of others but, rather, on one's own sense of inner knowledge.

In any social organization, leaders obtain advice and opinion regarding important decisions from other members of the group. In some instances, certain problems are resolved by individuals in positions of lesser authority, and frequently, the leader is obliged to defend the correctness of such solutions. Nonetheless, in the final analysis, the leader ultimately must accept responsibility for all decisions affecting the institution. The leader's ability to make the appropriate or right decision is enhanced by a sense of inner knowledge.

The quality of inner knowledge or personal spirit releases the leader from the traditional patterns of organization and structure. This internal strength enables the leader to go beyond established customs in finding new perspectives on solutions to problematic situations. The leader participates as a change agent without the fear of criticism, retribution, and rejection. Furthermore, the leader's inner confidence is the basis for informing others about organizational matters that they should know about, while remaining adamantly opposed to the traditional approach of telling others what they want to hear. Such an open-door policy to institutional concerns is not feared by the leader but is, instead, expected. This sense of self assurance in the leader is observable, since it is proportionately related to the progressiveness of the institution.

The leader's reliance on inner knowledge is interpreted as a sixth sense or psychic recognition. The role of the leader is that of directing and guiding the institution and others to agreed upon goals. This capacity of internally knowing the appropriate manner for accomplishing group goals further separates the leader from other members of the group. Intuitively, the effective leader may believe that since "I think, therefore, I know." In a sense, such a statement portrays the leader as narcissistic and elitist; however, the opposite is true. Inner knowledge is attained as the leader is actualizing self and possesses a conscious awareness of possible future alternatives. In accordance with this notion, the leader is more capable than others in making decisions for the group. Nevertheless, the sociocentric needs of the group are the primary focus of this unique trait of the leader, not self aggrandizement.

A related belief to inner knowledge involves development of the leader's self and transcending self:

> The idea that to be effective one should always be in the process of being and becoming.

The individual belief in being and becoming is perhaps the cornerstone of leadership. This belief fosters the process of integration of the individual and futures thinking components of leadership. The being component characterizes the leader's own search for personal growth and self enhancement. Being is enhanced when the individual is aware of potentials, recognizes capacities, and acknowledges resources—all facets of the self-actualizing person.[48] The following traits describe such a leader: inner directed, spontaneous, pragmatic, self-accepting, integrated, rational, and intimate. These qualities enable the leader to function in the here and now, with a personal need to be real, genuine, empathetic, and understanding toward others. This fully functioning nature of the leader is manifested in everyday interactions with individuals.

The becoming component, which is existential in nature, implies the leader's ability to transcend self and society. Unrestricted by the boundaries controlling reality, which, for the most part, confine others, the individual extends beyond the limits imposed by society in seeing an awareness of future alternatives. The future takes on meaning as new perspectives create a positive attitude toward the rapidly advancing society—an attitude that leaders must foster. Existentially, the leader goes beyond-the-world in the pursuit of visions and ideas and, thus, finds appropriate solutions to existing dilemmas. The leader's task is to inform others of impending situations and foster a positive attitude toward the future.

The process of being and becoming creates new characteristics in the individual. These traits are observable by examining behavioral outcomes resulting from an integration of the individual's pursuit of a higher level of personal functioning and the restructuring of the individual's cognitive dimension. The leader's self-actualizing tendency and future consciousness establish a new orientation to life and leadership.

BEHAVIORAL OUTCOMES

The previous sections of this article suggest the importance of the leader's emotional stability and future awareness. Through the integration of these dimensions, new leadership behaviors emerge. The behavioral outcomes component represents an attempt to delineate likely characteristics and traits of leaders evolving from this process. There is reason to believe that leaders who develop the kind of logical thinking advocated by Rational-Emotive Theory and adopt the supplementary rational beliefs for improved human functioning in the future will, in all probability, manifest unique leadership attributes.

Those attributes that are likely to evolve suggest that the leader is fully functioning and possesses a conscious awareness of the influence of social transformation on education. The leader develops new perceptions of the future and functions from rational mechanisms necessary for successful living in a world of rapid advancement. In addition, the leader has personal strength and courage to adduce new alternatives to existing frameworks and is equipped with a readiness to meet unexpected change. Newly acquired behavior will result in a differing orientation to life, and this will be reflected in the structural and dynamic qualities of the leader.

A number of traits associated with the structural qualities of the leader include the following: the scientific, rational, empirical, objective, observant, analytical, intellectual, cognitive, and realistic orientations toward action. These properties are the foundation on which leaders will base decisions and solutions to problems—in other words, on all human interactions. For example, institutional or personal decisions will be based on available information, data, facts, and evidence, not on false assumptions, hopes, prejudices, and fears. Typically, the leader will attempt to remove and demystify half-truths, preconceived notions, and current beliefs that are unfounded, unscientific, and irrational in nature. The leader's cognitive and intellectual components will be available to deduce analytically the validity of opinions, judgments, and contributions of others. For the leader, goal-directed behavior will be inductive-hypothetico-deductive in nature.

A dynamic property will unfold in the leader's ability to operate successfully within a subjective-objective continuum. This quality is closely related to being and becoming, but it differs insofar as the former deals exclusively with the leader's interaction with individuals and matters in the institution. For instance, subjective involvement arises due to the leader's understanding, empathy, respect, and caring for others and related issues concerning these individuals. Objectively, however, decisions are made about the issues, as well as the individuals themselves, without prejudice and bias. The ability to assess individual concerns and institutional needs without emotional involvement will characterize the decision-making process employed by the leader in all matters affecting the organization. This capacity to deal with individuals and institutional concerns subjectively and objectively will reflect the leader's integrity and independence.

There may be still other attributes of the leader that will arise from the convergence of emotional health and futures thinking. These attributes combined are perhaps best defined in terms of that "certain something." This aspect of the leader is difficult to articulate because it represents the totality of the individual. Heilbroner describes it by suggesting that, in times of crises and unrest, individuals seek leaders who are ordered, structured, and directive and, therefore, effective in reducing existential fears.[49] There is a natural tendency in individuals to strive for security and safety and, hence, to align themselves with strong parental-like figures. If this is the case, then tomorrow's leaders will, perhaps more than ever, need to possess those facets of human functioning described in this article.

IMPLICATIONS

In education, more so than any other area, definitional problems and conflicts arise when referring to the term, leader. For instance, certain individuals in education are perceived to be leaders of leaders. Educational leadership is often provided by philosophers, theoreticians, academics, and government officials, all of whom are far removed from the immediate school setting. Endorsing and implementing the ideas of these leaders is the educational administrator who operates at the grass roots level. Nevertheless, the school administrator is generally considered a leader in the educational community, although the role differs from other leader types.

The literature strongly suggests that the educational administrator is responsible for school policy, curricula, and program. Furthermore, the administrator is involved in crisis resolution, maintains the status quo, and assumes a reactive rather than proactive stance with respect to educational innovations. In short, the primary role of the school administrator is seen as calming the waters within the institution and among individuals. Perhaps it is these tasks that led Sergiovanni to conclude that educational administrators may, in fact, not be leaders at all; they essentially carry out the ideas of leaders.[50] This view creates added conflict in defining administrators and leaders. For the purposes of leadership training in education, however, there is general agreement that such programs are designed to produce leaders, not administrators.

Educational administrators today are, for the most part, trained for their eventual leadership positions. Educational leaders attend colleges of education and typically receive their specialized or advanced training in departments of educational administration. Students attending these institutions learn about theories of administration, school structure, policy formation, government involvement, legal jurisdiction, and analyze the required skills for dealing with personnel. The qualities and characteristics associated with good leaders are also evaluated and reviewed, but the student experiences these qualities in a theoretical and objective manner.

Those qualities advanced to be necessary for leadership effectiveness can be subjectively experienced and fostered by introducing psychotherapeutic models into leadership training programs. Incorporating therapeutic approaches into the training of educational leaders implies, according to Spady et al., "the new definition of the administration process which views leaders as part of the helping professions."[51] A closer working relationship between departments of educational administration and established counselling programs would assist in accomplishing this end. Implementing aspects of the Rational-Emotive approach in leadership training is a natural point of departure.

Another critical variable in the training of educational leaders is the development of a future consciousness. Commenting on this facet of the leader, Babin suggests that: "They must be 'futures-oriented' in their approach. They must have tomorrow in mind in all of their deliberations."[52] Courses in futures studies would indeed aid in establishing a futures orientation in the potential leader. New alternatives, choices, and solutions to educational issues would become available to the student. An understanding of the nature of the advancing society and a conscious awareness of its influence on the human being would provide a basis for educational change. The educational leader, prepared for change, would in turn implement those "basics" that are necessary for successful living in the future.

The selection of future leaders may well be based on criteria differing from those that are generally accepted today. The major criteria could indeed be the leader's degree of emotional stability and future consciousness. Leadership training programs need to incorporate these aspects of human functioning in preparing potential educational leaders for tomorrow. By changing the basic requirements for completion of leadership training programs, training institutions could contribute to the development of the new future leader.

SUMMARY AND CONCLUSION

A review of the literature on the concept of leadership, specifically in the field of education, clearly reveals the desired traits, behaviors, and approaches considered necessary for effectiveness. These descriptors of successful management, for the most part, can be considered in terms of recipes, formulas, and prescriptions. In other words, the determining qualities of leadership are merely a series of "dos and do nots" and "bes and be nots." According to theory, adhering to the related guidelines ensures leadership success.

A fundamental limitation appears, however, when using a prescriptive approach to leadership. This limitation involves the assumption that there is a defined congruency between the personality or nature of the leader and the stated formula. In the recipe approach, congruency is vital but not always attainable. It is often the case, however, that desired leadership behaviors lie outside the natural predisposition of the individual. The characteristics and procedures considered essential for effectiveness, in many instances, are foreign to the leader and, for all intents and purposes, lack relevance, specificity, and significance.

The position presented in this article, in contrast, stresses the leader's orientation to life. The inside nature of the leader is perceived to be of primary importance. A restructuring of the cognitive dimension of the individual helps in developing principles and guidelines leading to emotional health and psychological growth. A productive method of human functioning then emerges that is consistent with the leader's personal disposition. In this sense, a congruency does exist between the approach prescribed and the inner nature of the leader. In fact, in this manner of conceptualizing leadership, a congruency must result, otherwise the position taken is untenable.

If the inside nature is of merit to the study of leadership, then a new significance arises when examining this concept from a cognitive perspective. Determining the leader's degree of illogical thinking and identifying specific irrational beliefs provide a focus for research and investigation. The establishment of levels of or criteria for psychological health for successful leaders is another possible outcome. Moreover, a likely outgrowth is the development of standards for the selection of leaders based on the inner nature of the individual. In addition to the above, and of increasing importance, are the effects of this cognitive perspective on leadership training programs in education. If the inner nature of the individual is a viable subject of study, then future leader types will differ from their previous counterparts.

Historically, the contemporary principles underlying leadership closely corresponded to major movements in the socio-politico-economic framework. Continued societal change will tend to influence conceptualizations of leadership. According to Lasch, leaders have evolved from the Organization Man of the past to the present Bureaucratic Man.[53] In this view, the Organization Man improves social institutions whereas the Bureaucratic Man appeases political hierarchies. An appreciation of the leader's responsibility to anticipate and prepare for alternative futures will characterize tomorrow's effective leader. Ferguson believes that such an awareness is occurring more rapidly today in education than in any other area.[54] Perhaps in the advancing decades the educational leader will be described as the Anticipatory Man. New conceptualizations of leadership may further contribute to this end.

POSTSCRIPT

The development of new orientations and conceptualizations will further crystallize the concept of leadership. Educators can become leaders in the search for new perspectives. If new perceptions of leadership fail to materialize, prevailing circumstances may create an undesirable rational belief among individuals. It would be unfortunate for educators if individuals did in fact believe the following to be the case:

> The idea that, since good leaders are scarce, individuals should follow themselves.

The conceptualization of leadership presented in this article is intended to provide a framework for research and study. If the leadership concept is an issue for the 1980s and 1990s, and there is reason to believe that it is, then the challenge for educators is clear.

NOTES

1. J. M. Lipham, "Leadership and Administration," in *Behavioral Science and Educational Administration: The Sixty-Third Yearbook of the National Society for the Study of Education*, D. Griffiths, ed. (Chicago: The Society, 1964), p. 122.

2. L. L. Cunningham, "Educational Leadership: The Curious Blend," *Educational Leadership* 2 (91976): 324.

3. T. J. Sergiovanni, *Handbook for Effective Department Leadership: Concepts and Practices in Today's Secondary Schools* (Boston: Allyn & Bacon, 1977), p. 140.

4. J. M. Burns, "True Leadership," *Psychology Today* 12 (1978): 46-54.

5. A. W. Halpin, *Theory and Research in Administration* (New York: Macmillan, 1966), p. 81.

6. F. E. Fiedler, *A Theory of Leadership Effectiveness* (New York: McGraw-Hill, 1967); J. K. Hemphill, "Administration as Problem Solving," in *Administrative Theory in Education*, A. W. Halpin, ed. (Chicago: Midwest Administration Center, 1958); and A. Saville, "Conflict: New Emphasis in Leadership," *Clearing House* 46 (1971): 52-55.

7. J. G. Scott, E. S. Hickcox, and D. W. Ryan, "Education Management in an Era of Decline," *OCLEA* (June 1978): 3-7.

8. F. Spikes, "Choosing a Personal Leadership Style," *Lifelong Learning: The Adult Years* 3 (1979): 3-9.

9. J. M. Lipham, "Leadership: General Theory and Research," in *Leadership: The Art and Science Today*, L. L. Cunningham and W. J. Gephart, eds. (Itasca, IL: Peacock Press, 1973).

10. M. Weber, *The Theory of Social and Economic Organizations* (New York: Oxford University Press, 1947).

11. R. J. Havighurst, "Educational Leadership for the Seventies," *Phi Delta Kappan* 53 (1972): 403-406.

12. A. W. Halpin, *The Leadership Behavior of School Superintendents* (Chicago: Midwest Administration Center, 1959).

13. R. Likert, "The Nature of Highly Effective Groups," in *Organizations and Human Behavior*, F. D. Carver and T. J. Sergiovanni, eds. (New York: McGraw-Hill, 1969).

14. R. L. Abrell, "Educational Leadership without Carrot and Club," *Clearing House* 52 (1979): 280-285.

15. S. Marshall, "Leadership and Sensitivity Training," *Journal of Education* 153 (1970): 6-37; D. Cartwright and A. Zander, eds., *Group Dynamics: Research and Theory* (Evanston, IL: Rowe, Perterson, 1960); and W. E. Halal, "Toward a General Theory of Leadership," *Human Relations* 72 (1974): 401-446.

16. I. A. Taylor, "Characteristics of Creative Leaders," *The Journal of Creative Behavior* 12 (1978): 221-222.

17. R. M. Stogdill, *Handbook of Leadership: A Survey of Theory and Research* (New York: Free Press, 1974).

18. B. C. Jentz and J. W. Woford, *Leadership and Learning: Personal Changes in a Professional Setting* (New York: McGraw-Hill, 1979).

19. K. A. Berg, "Educational Leadership," *Clearing House* 50 (1977): 212-214.

20. P. Hersey and K. Blanchard, *Management of Organizational Behavior*, 3rd ed. (Englewood Cliffs, NJ: Prentice-Hall, 1977); and W. J. Reddin, *Managerial Effectiveness* (New York: McGraw-Hill, 1970).

21. Saville, "Conflict," p. 53.

22. T. J. Sergiovanni and F. D. Carver, *The New School Executive: A Theory of Administration* (New York: Harper & Row, 1980).

23. J. I. Goodlad, "Educational Leadership: Toward the Third Era," *Educational Leadership* 35 (1978): 322-331.

24. R. J. Spady, C. H. Bell, and G. A. D'Angelo, *A New View of Authority and the Administrative Process* (Bellevue, WA: Forum Foundation, 1979).

25. R. J. Duhamel and K. D. Johnson, "Leadership Skills of the Future," *Education Canada* 19 (1979): 42-47; R. L. Abrell, "Educational Leadership"; and C. A. Grant, M. B. Ridgway, and C. E. Sleeter, "Charles Cheng's Thoughts on Leadership in Education," *Educational Leadership* 37 (1979): 69-71.

26. S. Goldman, "Educational Leadership and the Emergent Future," *Education Research Quarterly* 1 (1977): 70-78.

27. R. C. Wenrich, "Leadership Development Ten Years Later," *American Vocational Journal* 51 (1976): 42-44.

28. D. van Avery, "Futuristics and Education," *Educational Leadership* 37 (1980): 441-442.

29. F. E. Fiedler, *Theory of Leadership*.

30. R. B. Kimbrough, "The Behavioral Characteristics of Effective Educational Administrators," in *Selected Readings on General Supervision*, J. E. Hearld, L. G. Romano, and N. P. Georgiady, eds. (Toronto: Collier-Macmillan, 1970); S. Fogel, "Hypnosis as an Aid in Education," *The Saskatchewan Administrator* 10 (1978): 14-20; and R. H. Farquhar, "The Nature of Leadership" (Paper presented at Phi Delta Kappa, Regina, Saskatchewan, April 1977).

31. D. J. Thom, "Administrating without Ulcers: A Key Challenge for the 1980s," *Ontario Education* 12 (1980): 11-15.

32. E. M. Bridges in *Educational Administration: The Developing Decades* (Berkeley, CA: McCutchan, 1977); and J. Dyer, "A Philosophy of Nonchalance as an Effective Deterrent to Physical and Mental Disorders in Educational Administration," *OCLEA* 9 (1977): 12-13.

33. A. W. Combs, "What the Future Demands of Education," *Phi Delta Kappan* 62 (1981): 369-372.

34. A. Ellis, *Reason and Emotion in Psychotherapy* (New York: Lyle Stuart, 1969); Idem, *Humanistic Psychotherapy: The Rational-Emotive Approach* (New York: Julian Press, 1973); and Idem, "The Human Connection" (Paper presented at Mosaic '80, Edmonton, Alberta, May 1980).

35. C. Lasch, *The Culture of Narcissism* (New York: Norton, 1979).

36. M. Ferguson, *The Aquarian Conspiracy: Personal and Social Transformation in the 1980s* (New York: St. Martin's Press, 1980).

37. H. G. Shane, "A Curriculum for the New Century," *Phi Delta Kappan* 62 (1981): 351-356.

38. H. Neibuhr, "Teaching and Learning in the Eighties: The Paradigm Shifts," *Phi Delta Kappan* 62 (1981): 367-368; C. Dede and D. Allen, "Education in the 21st Century: Scenarios as a Tool for Strategic Planning," *Phi Delta Kappan* 62 (1981): 362-366; and P. Wagschal, ed., *Learning Tomorrows: Commentaries on the Future of Education* (New York: Praeger, 1980).

39. J. D. Pulliam, "Toward a Futuristic Theory of Education," in *Educational Futures: Sourcebook I*, F. Kierstead, J. Bowman, and C. Dede, eds. (Washington, DC: World Future Society, 1979); R. Theobald, *Beyond Despair: Directions for America's Third Century* (Washington, DC: New Republic Book, 1976); and G. B.

Morris, "A Conceptualization of Education in the Future," *Canadian Journal of Education* (1984, in press).

40. C. J. Hurn, "The Prospects for Liberal Education: A Sociological Perspective," *Phi Delta Kappan* 60 (1979): 530-633; J. M. Becker, ed., *Schooling for a Global Age* (New York: McGraw-Hill, 1979); and N. Postman, *Teaching as a Conserving Activity* (New York: Delacorte Press, 1979).

41. H. G. Shane, "America's Educational Futures of 1976-2001: The Views of 50 Distinguished World Citizens and Educators," *The Futurist* 10 (1976): 252-257; and H. Kahn, "Prospects for Mankind" (Paper presented at Mosaic '80, Edmonton, Alberta, May, 1980).

42. T. Roszak, *Person / Planet* (Garden City, NY: Doubleday, 1978); and W. W. Harman, *An Incomplete Guide to the Future* (San Francisco: The Portable Stanford, 1976).

43. A. Peccei, "Mankind at the Crossroads," *The Futurist* 12 (1978): 374-378; and G. L. Kincaid, "Learning to Live in a Global Village," in *Educational Futures: Sourcebook I*, F. Kierstead, J. Bowman, and C. Dede, eds. (Washington, DC: World Future Society, 1979), pp. 107-120.

44. A. Ellis, "The Human Connection."

45. J. Platt, *Human Needs, New Societies, Supportive Technologies* (Rome: Trades, 1974).

46. D. Bell, *The Coming of Post-Industrial Society* (New York: Basic Books, 1973); and A. Toffler, *The Third Wave* (New York: William Morrow, 1980).

47. G. B. Morris, "Human Behavior in an Emerging Totalitarian Society," *Canadian Counsellor* 11 (1976): 15-19.

48. A. H. Maslow, *Toward a Psychology of Being* (Princeton, NJ: D. Van Nostrand, 1962).

49. R. L. Heilbroner, *An Inquiry into the Human Prospect* (New York: Norton, 1974).

50. Sergiovanni, *Effective Department Leadership.*

51. Spady, Bell, and D'Angelo, *A New View*, p. 7.

52. P. Babin, "Education in the Next Twenty Years: A Challenge to Principals and Teachers," *Teacher Education* (October 1980): 56-64.

53. C. Lasch, *The Culture of Narcissism.*

54. M. Ferguson, *The Aquarian Conspiracy.*

CHAPTER TWENTY

Educational Futures: Six Scenarios

JOHN D. HAAS

This article deals with the 80-90% of their lives that children will spend "in the future." It also addresses the question of why schools are so resistant to change, a resistance which results from both internal and external forces. Eleven key factors that are likely to affect future alternatives are identified and analyzed. Six possible scenarios are presented. They demonstrate the continuum of possible futures.

Knowledge seekers are time travelers, in the sense that learning is a process, a "continuous reconstruction of experience" to use John Dewey's famous phrase. Learning is an integration of past experience with one's present condition—in light of future expectations. For educators of children and youth, the future is that broad realm where their clients will spend 80 or 90% of their lives. What will education in America be like for young persons in the twenty-first century, less than 15 years from now?

Curiously, when comparing proposed or probable social and economic futures with educational futures, one is struck by the lack of bold, imaginative, exciting futures for education. Why this is the case is explained more fully later; for now, suffice it to say that public schools in America are amazingly resistant to change. Even so, the American public still considers "developing the best educational system in the world" as "very important," according to 84% of respondents in a 1982 Gallup poll.

The forces for change and those for little or no change can be found both within and without the educational establishment. These internal and external pressures seldom coincide. Usually, a precarious balance of power prevails between competing conceptions of what schooling should be, ensuring the status quo or a few incremental but insubstantial changes.

It is within these realities that the education futurist operates. In deriving images of educational futures, these forecasters employ at least four approaches: to seek the implications for education from general social indicators such as population projections; to pursue discrete develop-

SOURCE: John D. Haas, "Educational Futures: Six Scenarios," *Futures Research Quarterly*, Vol. 2, No. 2, pp. 15-30. Copyright © by The World Future Society. Reprinted with permission, from *Futures Research Quarterly* (Vol. 2, No. 2, Summer, 1986), published by the World Future Society, 4916 St. Elmo Avenue, Bethesda, Maryland 20814.

ments or events that may determine trends, such as the personal computer or a Supreme Court case; to combine several developments and events into a scenario, or comprehensive portrait of education in a particular time and place; finally, one can develop several scenarios, even a continuum of alternative futures, extending from most likely to least likely, and including key factors that may either hinder or enhance the likelihood of any one scenario coming to fruition. It is this last approach that was used here. Six scenarios were generated, with 11 impinging factors. For ease of presentation, these were collectively arrayed in a 6 × 11 matrix of educational futures.

THE MATRIX

The six scenarios are respectively labeled: (1) Contemporary Traditional, (2) Humanistic Traditional, (3) Partial Technological Deschooling, (4) Multiple Options (with three variants), (5) Experimental and/or Communal Schools, and (6) Total Deschooling. These extend from left to right across the top of the matrix (see Figure 20.1) and are ordered as a continuum from "Most Probable" on the left to "Least Probable" on the right. Down the left-hand margin are the 11 factors that it is postulated will crucially impinge on each scenario, hindering or enhancing its likelihood of becoming a dominant mode in the future. Each scenario is based on selected current trends and/or positions advocated by several contemporary leaders. It is readily acknowledged that the two "least probable" scenarios—experimental and/or communal schools and total deschooling—would require dramatic shifts in American socio-cultural values for either one to become a dominant reality.

The 11 key factors represent categories of events, developments or trends that are likely to affect the scenarios positively or negatively. These are: (1) public policy, (2) court decisions, (3) education leadership, (4) economic constraints, (5) school organization patterns, (6) curriculum framework, (7) education technology, (8) education demographics, (9) ideology and social values, (10) state of knowledge, and (11) surprises, crises, or catastrophes.

DYNAMICS OF THE MATRIX

In order to illustrate the ways in which the factors impinge on the scenarios, two examples are provided. Each example shows the effects of a single factor on the range of scenarios.

Factors Affecting the Six Scenarios	Contemporary Traditional	Humanistic Traditional	Partial Technological Deschooling	Multiple Options			Experimental/ Communal Schools	Total Deschooling
				Within A Single District	State Voucher Plan	Tuition Tax Credits		
1. Public Policy								
2. Court Decisions								
3. Education Leadership								
4. Economic Constraints								
5. School Organization Patterns								
6. Curriculum Framework								
7. Education Technology								
8. Education Demographics								
9. Ideology and Social Values								
10. State of Knowledge								
11. Surprises, Crises or Catastrophes								

Figure 20.1: Six Educational Scenarios

Factors Affecting the Six Scenarios	Contemporary Traditional	Humanistic Traditional	Partial Technological Deschooling	Multiple Options			Experimental/ Communal Schools	Total Deschooling
				Within A Single District	State Voucher Plan	Tuition Tax Credits		
1. Public Policy	- - -	- -	+	+ +	+/-	+/-	+ +	+

Figure 20.2: Example Relating to Public Policy

Factors Affecting the Six Scenarios	Contemporary Traditional	Humanistic Traditional	Partial Technological Deschooling	Multiple Options			Experimental/ Communal Schools	Total Deschooling
				Within A Single District	State Voucher Plan	Tuition Tax Credits		
2. Court Decisions	+	-	- -	-	- - -	- -	- -	- - -

Figure 20.3: Example Relating to Court Decisions

Example #1. Imagine that, over the next 15 years, state after state abolishes its compulsory attendance law until by 2001 a majority of states have eliminated such laws. Such a development would have an impact on all six scenarios: for some it would be "positive" (i.e., supporting the emergence of those scenarios); for others, it would be "negative" (i.e., hindering their occurrence). Degrees of negative or positive impact are possible, as is a neutral influence. These are indicated in appropriate cells of the matrix by the following symbols: "+ + +" ("strongly positive"), "+ +" ("generally positive"), "+" ("somewhat positive"), "+/–" ("neutral"), "–" ("somewhat negative"), "– –" ("generally negative"), "– – –" ("strongly negative"). Thus, in the case of the elimination of state compulsory attendance laws, the appropriate row of cells in the matrix (i.e., Row #1, Public Policy) might look like those in Figure 20.2.

Example #2. Let's assume that a court case concerning a lack of equal expenditures for public education between states reaches the U.S. Supreme Court, and that the Court decides "equal protection of the laws" demands greater equality of expenditures (per student) between and among the 50 states than currently exists. Clearly such a decision would call for greater federal and state control over the financing of public education. The impact of this decision on the six scenarios might be depicted as in Figure 20.3 (Row #2, Court Decisions).

Scenario #1—Contemporary Traditional

In education, more so than elsewhere, the more things change the more they remain the same. Tradition's heavy hand holds archaic practices in place. Schools do change, but inevitably they are constantly behind the times. Thus, if one is looking at a short-term future, say no further ahead than the year 2000, the best bet is to forecast that schools will be very much like those of the present. One can expect some tinkering, alignments with the economy, and updating of textbooks and equipment, but no deep structural or curricular changes will be evident.

Why take the conservative, or some would say negative, viewpoint on change in public education? There are several compelling reasons, one almost self-evident, one historical, another structural, and finally one pertaining to the social functions of schooling. These four reasons are actually constraints within which public schools operate.

The Age of Clients. The public schools serve a nonadult clientele, students ranging in age from about 5 to 18 years. As "minors," society compels this age group to attend school, and while they are in school their parents, as well as citizens in general, hold school officials almost totally responsible for their welfare. Thus, to suggest experimentation (i.e., innovations or alternatives to the status quo) with the lives of children and youth is tantamount to risking their present welfare and future prospects. A tyranny of tradition prevails among all decision makers involved in administering the public schools: local principals and superintendents, local and state school boards, the federal Department of Education.

As an example, imagine how long an elementary school principal would last as a school administrator if he insisted that any instruction in reading be delayed until children reach the age of 10—even if he could provide a rationale and some research evidence for such a practice? When one challenges convention in public education, the challenger invariably is defeated, because one of the more persuasive arguments against innovation (there are generally many) is that one should never change a practice until its alternative has been demonstrated to be overwhelmingly superior—a criterion almost impossible to meet. This is one reason most observers of public schools point to their "sameness," the uniformity of practices across schools, school districts and states—despite the "decentralization" of local and state control. Put another way, schools of today resemble the schools parents of today's students attended because the majority (not all by any means) of parents want and understand such schools. (Of course, these same parents would also like to see "a return to" the three Rs, strict rules of discipline strictly enforced, and some form of voluntary prayer in the classroom.)

The History of Reform Movements. During the past hundred years, there have been a dozen or so major and minor reform movements aimed at altering public education in the United States. The proposed reforms cover a range of school policies and practices: the physical environment of classrooms and schools, the junior high school, the comprehensive high school, the middle school, team teaching/flexible scheduling, the core curriculum, progressive education, life adjustment education, district/area vocational schools, updating the curriculum (e.g., the "new" math, science, social studies) followed by "downdating" the curriculum (e.g., back-to-the-basics), and a plethora of current proposals from the voucher plan to computer-assisted-instruction to "magnet" schools. There is also one major movement that extends over the entire 100 years—school desegregation.

How have these proposed reforms fared? Clearly it is difficult to generalize about dozens of proffered changes over a century of time, yet a few conclusions seem warranted by the historical evidence. First, the changes that have occurred did not challenge the basic infrastructure of schooling: group instruction, age/grade level assignment of students, reliance on expository instruction—telling and textbooks, hierarchical administration, testing and letter grades, and academic disciplines (subjects) as the structure of the curriculum. Furthermore, almost all the major changes came during the first two decades of the twentieth century: the form of the high school curriculum, the appearance of junior high schools, standardized tests, and several others.

A second conclusion is that, since the nineteenth century, American schools have become more and more alike. Given a lack of federal authority over public education, coupled with 50 state constitutions and education laws, and delegated responsibilities to over 1,600 local school districts, it is incredible that uniformity should pervade such a system. Yet such is the case, as recently observed by a former dean of the Harvard Graduate School of Education:

> This big country contains numerous educational jurisdictions, with authority decentralized. Nonetheless, as one visits communities, one is gradually struck by how similar the structure and articulated purpose of American high schools are. Rural schools, city schools; rich schools, poor schools, little schools: the framework of grades, schedules, calendar, courses of study, even rituals is astonishingly uniform and has been so for at least forty years. In most schools, I visited biology and social studies classes, and I could soon predict the particular topics under study during a given month in Bio I or US History, whatever the school. While the texts had different covers and authors, their commonness was stunning. Given the extraordinary changes in American society and scholarship over the last decades and the remarkable diversity of American communities, the similarities among American high schools' purposes, structures, and procedures are fascinating. High school is a kind of secular church, a place of national rituals that mark stages of a young citizen's life. The value of its rites appears to depend on national consistency.[1]

Third, the cost of suggested innovations generally has not been the decisive factor in decisions on adoption. Witness new vocational schools, school cafeterias and swimming pools, school athletic facilities, fields and equipment, and microcomputers. Still, school boards are not generous with teacher salaries or the costs of reducing class size.

Finally, one must conclude that American public schools are relatively stable, slow-changing institutions. When one considers that the famous Brown desegregation case was decided over 30 years ago, and today segregated public schools still exist, one can appreciate how difficult it is to alter public schooling in America. *Fundamental* change is difficult if not impossible to achieve, but *incremental* changes occur regularly. In the past 20 years, schools have rejected curricular innovations such as inquiry teaching and team teaching, but accepted educational games/ simulations and microcomputers.

The Structure of Schools. By the early decades of this century, the ways public schools today are organized and administered were well established. "Disorder terrified the late-nineteenth-century middle-class American, who thought he saw his stable life ruptured by newly populated cities, industrialization, and hordes of immigrants. In response, and in a quest for social order, progressive reformers placed great faith in 'scientific management.' ... Not surprisingly, this model of reform profoundly affected education and resulted in systems of schools ... organizations arranged in pyramidal tiers, with governing boards and administrators at the peaks and classrooms at the base."[2] To state a truism, we still have these top-down, hierarchical bureaucracies, and they are distinct impediments to change, exquisitely designed to perpetuate themselves and the status quo.

Bureaucratic structures tend to become more and more complex, adding layers that further separate the top of the pyramid from the bottom. "Bureaucracies lumber. Once regulations, collective bargaining agreements, and licensure get installed, change comes hard. Every regulation, agreement, and license spawns a lobby dedicated to keeping it in place."[3] This then leads to an interlocking directorate within a state, an oligopoly that exercises almost complete control over public education in that state. For example, in one Western state, two schools of education in major public universities claim as graduates (i.e., undergraduate and/or graduate degrees) all but a few of that state's public education leaders: the commissioner of education, a majority on the elected state board of education, the heads of the state's NEA and AFT affiliates, the executive directors of the state's school board members association and school executives organization, the head of the state's North Central Association accreditation bureau, a majority of the professional staff in the state's department of education, a majority of the superintendents of schools and secondary school principals. Rarely if ever, of course, do these leaders speak as a single voice on any public education issue, but they can be counted on to thwart attempts to force any major overhaul of the state's system of public education. What they do allow, and even support, are some small, adequately funded incremental changes.

The Social Functions of Schools. It is readily recognized that schools perform *educational* functions, but vocal critics and eager reformers often overlook the *social* functions of schools, which collectively tend to be constraints on proposals for change. Although there are probably a half dozen or more of these social functions, three of the more significant ones (as inhibitors of change) are: (1) custodial care, (2) indoctrination (or socialization), and (3) community activity.

By "custodial care" is meant what is popularly called "babysitting" or "keeping the kids off the street." Since children and youth are compelled by state laws to attend school (generally from age 5 or 6 to 16), the public schools have assumed the responsibilities of their general welfare by providing bus transportation, cafeteria lunches (in some cases breakfast also), study halls (to supervise and account for students when they aren't in scheduled classes), parental approval forms for field trips or other out-of-school activities, hall passes to account for students who are not in classroom or study hall, and many trivial ploys to maintain constant surveillance of students. Such inflexible constraints on "time and place" often are obstacles to the implementation of innovations, especially when the proposed changes involve out-of-classroom/school programs in the community or activities that call for greater student responsibility and independence.

"Indoctrination" is the uncongenial though accurate term for the process of socializing the young to the values, norms, and mores of the community and of the larger society. In this realm schools serve a conserving function by promoting traditional values as distinguished from newer or emerging values. Public schools tend to foster uncritical patriotism but not reflective thinking; to encourage competition but not cooperation; to support capitalism but not socialism; to promote analysis but not synthesis, cognition not affect, consensus not controversy, docility not initiative, the conventional not the creative, and conformity not independence. This institutional ethos is most inhospitable to virtually any controversial proposal for reform and serves mainly to perpetuate stability and the status quo.

Especially in small towns and small cities, the local public schools are a center for "community activities." Many of these events focus on public performances by students: basketball and football games, vocal and instrumental music concerts, plays and musical comedies, gymnastic displays, and fairs of all types. Preparations for such public performances occur during the school day and in after-school times, sponsored and scheduled by school officials. Understandably, school leaders expect unusual quality if not perfection in these highly visible public events. Thus, too often, the preparations for such spectacles take precedence over the rest of the school curriculum, and not infrequently the high school master schedule is designed around those subjects that are "performance-oriented." The priority of community spectaculars frequently frustrates educational reformers who usually focus on the academic program in the schools. To meddle with the typical schedule of an elementary or secondary school is to invite lively resistance from many quarters.

Scenario #2—Humanistic Traditional

Beginning just before the USSR launched Sputnik I (in 1957) and extending through the early 1970s, an educational reform movement, with several separate strands, attempted to change schooling in America. The several strands included efforts to change (1) school organization (differentiated staffing patterns and flexible scheduling of secondary school students), (2) classroom organization ("open classroom" and team teaching), and (3) curriculum (content, materials, textbooks, and simulations). Hundreds of millions of federal and foundation dollars were spent over the 20-year span. The results of this multidimensional enterprise were generally disappointing to all parties. A few schools, mainly in relatively wealthy suburban districts, did change by adopting or adapting one or more of the organizational innovations and/or by buying or using some of the new textbooks, curriculum materials packages, simulations, and audio-visual products. But overall the reformers and their sponsors were frustrated and disillusioned. To many, the public schools were seen as impenetrable bastions of rigidity that could readily deflect any and all incursions of innovation.

Against this background, some educators within the public school ranks who recognized the need for improvement, yet who also had seen the failure of frontal assaults, began in the 1970s to focus their change efforts on the "climate" of individual schools. By "climate" they meant the health of the organization, the degree to which interpersonal relations of every type contributed to group purpose, cohesiveness, amicability, and comfort. They believed that school climate improvement would directly and indirectly contribute to improved instruction and to greater student learning, both occurring within a more humanistic educational setting.

The general factors which contribute to a comfortable, satisfying, and productive school climate are trust, respect, high morale, continuous personal and social growth, cohesiveness, caring, and processes for organizational renewal. There are three clusters of determinants that affect the degree to which the climate factors are present in a school. These are: (1) program determinants, (2) process determinants, and (3) material determinants.[3]

The program determinants include opportunities for active learning, expectations of individualized performance, varied learning environments, flexible curricular and extra-curricular activities, a support structure appropriate to the learner's maturity, cooperatively determined policies, rules and recommendations, and a varied reward system. The process determinants are problem solving ability, a process for improving school goals, involvement and skill in making decisions, autonomy with accountability, effective learning-teaching strategies, and skills in planning for the future. Finally, the material determinants are all those aspects of the school that are physical resources which support the human activities, such as the building, furniture, equipment, esthetic features, and learning materials.[4]

This movement—school climate improvement—has gained momentum in the past decade, and may become a promising and pervasive school reform effort for the remainder of the century.

Scenario #3—Partial Technological Deschooling

In the past 20 years three developments have occurred in what is sometimes termed the Information or Communications Revolution which may, in combination, cause dramatic changes in the nature of public education by as early as the 1990s. The first of these is the combination of information technology companies and publishing houses in single conglomerate corporations. For example, IBM and SRA (a publisher of mainly school curriculum materials), or Xerox and Ginn, or CBS and Holt, Rinehart and Winston. This effectively links the communications industry with trade and textbook publishers. The second development is the emergence of powerful television, motion picture, newspaper, publishing conglomerates such as Warner Communications. The third is the beginning of widespread use of two technologies—cable television systems and the microcomputer. Taken as a whole, these three developments combine to create the power and potential to alter almost every element of schooling the the United States.

The potential application of multiple communications media to public education is here referred to as "Partial Technological Deschooling." What could happen in this scenario is that some school functions might be decentralized to a number of places in the community, away from the schools. The "new" locations could be businesses, public agencies, students' homes, and school annexes. At the local businesses and public agencies, students would be engaged in apprenticeship internships. At their homes, students would spend part of the school day in the communications center, where a master console would integrate several media technologies: over-the-air educational television, selected cable television channels, videotape (or videodisc) recordings, computer tapes and diskettes—all under control of a microcomputer. The home communications center would handle the teaching of specific knowledge and cognitive skills as called for in individual learning modules prescribed by teachers at the school's Home Learning Curriculum Communications Center.

School annexes, located in neighborhood education cottages or storefront education arcades, would provide consoles for students without home communications centers, and would also handle remediation programs. These annexes would coordinate with other social service agencies in the neighborhood and in the community at large. School buildings similar to those of today would still exist to serve some of the group-oriented educational and social functions. These would probably include limited custodial care including breakfasts, lunches and recreation; community-oriented activities such as plays, musicals, interscholastic athletic events, and science-technology fairs; "real-world" simulations for learning interpersonal and group process skills; and a lengthy sequence of one-student-to-one-counselor career guidance and planning sessions. A major activity in the school would involve teachers in the library-media-communications center preparing new curricula and prescribing and collating individual learning modules for students' home learning.

Scenario #4—Multiple Options

Gradually, over the past century, American schools have become more and more alike, while during the same period Americans have become more dissimilar and diverse. There are numerous causes of these two trends, but two that have been particularly significant for education are: (1) new immigrant groups and (2) school laws and policies that promote uniformity. The old immigrant groups were mainly from Western and Central Europe. The new immigrants come from the Caribbean area (e.g., Cuba, Haiti, and Puerto Rico), from Mexico and Central America, and from Asia, especially Southeast Asia. These groups, combined with the heightened ethnic awareness of Blacks and Native Americans, have created the appearance of a multi-racial, multicultural society. Meanwhile, in public education the following policies and practices, among others, have moved schools toward uniformity: (1) assigning students to grade levels according to the single criterion of age, (2) compulsory attendance laws, (3) the national textbook industry, (4) the concept of the comprehensive high school (one type for all), (5) legal requirements for equality of treatment, (6) the national testing industry, and (7) state and regional school accrediting organizations.

In the last two decades, there have been numerous calls for the creation of alternatives to and options within the public school system. Although the motives of most advocates for specific schemes are honest, legitimate, and benign, a few are pernicious, thinly disguised moves to perpetuate bigotry, sexism, and racism. There appear to be three variants of the Multiple Options scenario that have some potential for becoming major educational movements. These are:

1. Within-a-School-District Options. Many parents and students who are believers in and supporters of the public schools would like to have available to them more educational options, more involvement in key decisions, more choices from an array of alternatives. Some school districts have responded to these requests for change with various organizational and curricular innovations. One of the easiest changes school leaders can implement is to allow students (and/or their parents) to choose the school within their own district that they would like to attend. Where feasible, this option could be extended to include choice of teacher. Though easier than other possible changes, giving students choices of school and teacher creates logistical and morale problems for school administrators, especially at the elementary school level.

Another plan calls for the creation of special-purpose alternative schools—K-12, K-6, K-8, 7-9, 9-12, or 10-12. Often this means establishing one, two or more new schools, each with a distinct focus and milieu. For example, one large suburban school district founded two new K-12 schools, one called "The Fundamentals School" and the other "The Open Living School." These schools can be placed at appropriate points on a continuum extending from "free" to "open" to "modified" to "standard"—a freedom-to-prescription range. In the cases of the "Fundamentals" and "Open Living" schools, the former would be located at the "standard" point on the "prescription" end of the continuum, while the latter would be placed between "free" and "open" on the "freedom" side. In this particular school district, the attendance area for the two alternative schools is coterminous with the district boundary, while each of the other "regular" elementary and secondary schools has a specific, restricted attendance area, encompassing one or more neighborhoods in relatively close proximity to each school.

A final model in the "within-a-district" category allows for open enrollment in any public school in a school district. This could amount to no choice, however, if all the elementary and secondary schools are virtually alike and interchangeable. What is called for in this model is distinctive schools, reflecting differing educational philosophies and different curricula and organizational patterns. Since the school district does not assign any student to a school on the basis of geographical proximity, this has the effect of forcing students and their parents to choose from among several options.

The number of options available at each combination of grade levels (e.g., K-3, 4-6, 7-9, or 10-12) is somewhere in the range of three to five. Each school (i.e., set or cluster of grade levels, or "non-graded" arrangement) has a unique focus such as any one of the following:

- Open Living/Freedom/Street Academy
- Fundamentals/Basics/Structured Skills
- Multicultural
- Community

- School of Science/of Performing Arts/of Commerce
- Montessori/Steiner/Academic Leadership
- Humanistic

2. Voucher Plans. When a state wishes to allow the use of tax revenues (within state and federal legal constraints) to pay for education in public, private, and parochial schools, one scheme for making such options available is called a "voucher plan." A "voucher" here is an entitlement or education stamp that can be redeemed (by students or their parents) in any school licensed by the state. The school accepting the voucher then submits it to the state for reimbursement according to a funding formula (e.g., $3,000 per student).

There are many versions of voucher plans and many crucial problems and issues involved with all the plans. For example, there is the problem of undermining the public schools, the issues of racism, sexism, and elitism, the church/state issue, and the problems of propaganda and false or fraudulent advertising. But there is little doubt that the voucher plan would enhance competition and promote innovation by making education into a limited market economy.

3. Tuition Tax Credits. Although formulated and promoted earlier, this means of providing public support for options in schooling is most associated with the Reagan administration. Here, also, there are many versions of the basic idea, including both federal and state schemes. The main elements of all tuition tax credit plans are: (1) prior payment of tuition to a private or parochial school and (2) a tax credit (like solar energy credits) on state or federal tax forms—in effect, an amount subtracted from gross income or from taxable income or from taxes owed to the government. Clearly, tax deductions and credits tend to favor those taxpayers with the largest amounts of disposable income—the middle and upper classes. Nevertheless, this plan would place the support of the government behind diverse approaches to public education. Among the numerous criticisms of tuition tax credit proposals, probably the most serious is that these plans would condemn the poor to having no effective choice other than the tuition-free public schools, which would result in resegregation.

Scenario #5—Experimental and/or Communal School

It isn't too probable that this type of educational future will become a widespread phenomenon. What is more likely is that it will be an alternative for some students and their parents. As its name implies, there are two variants of this type of future, experimental schools and communal education.

Over the years there have been numerous instances of educational and religious ideologies founding schools, some of which remain vigorous institutions for decades and others that collapse in a year or two. In its early years, for example, the federal Head Start program provided funds to establish at the local level new schools (i.e., pre-schools) for the children of poverty households. The basic ideas behind Head Start schools, then (the late 1960s) and still today, are: community and parent involvement; care and concern for the growth of the whole child—physical, psychological, social, experiential, and intellectual growth, including regular medical and dental checkups; experiences, via walks and field trips, that expose the child to all facets of the local community; provision of parenting education at the Head Start center and in the homes of participating families; and inclusion of special needs persons and programs such as bilingual-bicultural teachers and aides or teachers and equipment for the handicapped.

In today's educational climate, the focus of many relatively new schools is on the education of gifted and academically talented youth. These are usually private schools with substantial tuitions, which tend to emphasize intellectual development and/or skills in the visual and performing arts. It is difficult to forecast what ideas will undergird the experimental schools of the future. Some possible organizing themes are: travel/extended trips (weeks or months); multicultural/cross-cultural living and learning; high technology-based schools and camps; multiple psychotechnologies (e.g., meditation, psychosynthesis, ESP); and nonschools based on integrated networks of home microcomputer users.

Communal education is an old idea that was revived during the 1960s and early 70s. The motivation to create "intentional communities" (i.e., communities founded on exclusive religious or secular ideologies) grows out of dissatisfaction with modern societies, especially the impersonality and lack of group cohesiveness in cities and their suburbs. Thus, communal social experiments attempt to reestablish a "sense of community," by which is usually meant the cohesive character of small, closely knit, extended-familylike urban or rural communes. The German language contains two contrasting words that describe two different types of communities: *"gesellschaft"* and *"gemeinschaft."* A typical small suburb of any large American city manifests *gesellschaft,* while an Amish community in Pennsylvania would embody *gemeinschaft.* The following lists characterize these two concepts:

Gemeinschaft	*Gesellschaft*
Private life	Public life
Exclusive membership	Arbitrary, unplanned membership

Face-to-face interactions	Very loose cohesiveness
Natural, unforced association	Emphasis on contracts and rights
"Family" attitude	Lack of communal atmosphere
Intentional collective	Relatively impersonal interactions
Group ends/means are inextricable	Carefully specified means and ends
"Small" number of members	"Large" membership
Sympathetic identification of member with member	Interactions based on rationality
Resistant to change	Change is valued; sign of progress
Members possess general knowledge and skills (non-specialized)	Specialization of work
Differential status for members	Equality of treatment within statuses

Those who seek *gemeinschaft* in community life also generally have in mind definite ideas about education for communal living. For one thing, advocates of communal education place greater reliance on the community meeting as instructor rather than the teacher in the classroom. This is similar to life in an Israeli kibbutz where lines distinguishing school and community, teacher and student, work and play, and age cohorts are blurred in the unity of organic existence. In communal education everyone, regardless of age or status, is sometimes teacher and sometimes learner.

In the future, there will continue to be new, planned, intentional communities being built, each possessing its own version of communal education, and some even substituting educational networks for what today we call schools. The prototypes of these "new towns" and rural communities already exist in such places as Auroville, a cross-cultural agrarian community in India; Columbia, a planned urban "new town" in Maryland; Findhorn, a religious agrarian community on the North Sea shore of Scotland; and Arcosanti, a high-density, urban-rural town being constructed in the desert 70 miles north of Phoenix, Arizona.

Scenario #6—Total Deschooling

This highly improbable educational scenario calls for the complete elimination of schools from postindustrial societies like the United States, Japan, and Western European nations. It's a romantic proposal because of its naive and excessive idealism. Most forcefully advocated by Ivan Illich in his book *Deschooling Society,* this position draws heavily on anarchist and Marxist traditions, and exemplifies the extreme of a revolutionary future perspective.[5]

Illich develops his argument along the lines of a critique of modern society (and its schools) followed by proposed radical changes. The modern society, the United States, for example, has created social institutions that are evil to the core and that cannot adequately be modified or reformed. The evils, says Illich, are bureaucracy, specialization and division of labor, professionalization of occupations (e.g., doctors and teachers), technification of work, and alienation of workers from their work and from each other.

Like every institution in these "sick" societies, schools manifest the same array of "diseases." Schools are highly bureaucratized institutions in which specialization has led to over 100 new job classifications over the past 30 years. Yet, Illich points out, costs continue to rise while enrollments and overall student achievement decline. Schools also perpetuate the false meritocracy where job entry levels are geared to levels of school completed regardless of skills needed for the job or skills possessed by applicants.

Illich considers schools to be an unwarranted public monopoly. Schooling is an age-specific, teacher-related process requiring full-time attendance to an obligatory curriculum. Furthermore, students are made subject to a hidden curriculum that socializes them to conventional norms and values and to their assigned roles and occupations. Schools also teach the young to confuse process and substance, teaching and learning, grades and education, and diplomas and competence. Finally, because membership in this institution is mandatory, schools are "nonconvivial" institutions.

The solutions to these problems, says Illich, are to eliminate schools and to establish in their place four kinds of convivial networks or "learning webs." These are:

1. Reference Services to Educational Objects. This is a directory (a special version of the Yellow Pages) which provides learners "access to things or processes used for formal learning. Some of these things can be reserved for this purpose, stored in libraries, rental agencies, laboratories, and showrooms like museums and theaters; other can be in daily use in factories, airports, or on farms, but made available to students as apprentices or on off-hours."[6]

2. Skill Exchanges. These are like classified advertising sections of newspapers "which permit persons to list their skills, the conditions under which they are willing to serve as models for others who want to learn these skills, and the addresses at which they can be reached."[7]

Presumably, this exchange of "valuables" would occur in a barter economy.

3. Peer-Matching. This process requires an extensive "communications network which permits persons to describe the learning activity in which they wish to engage, in the hope of finding a partner for the inquiry."[8] Here the goal is to assemble a mini-class of learners who can then use the group's bargaining power to secure appropriate instruction.

4. Reference Services to Educators-at-Large. This is another form of Yellow Pages where self-appointed teacher experts "can be listed in a directory giving the address and self-descriptions of professionals, para-professionals, and freelancers, along with conditions of access to their services."[9]

CONCLUSION

Although there is every reason to expect that either Scenario #1 (Contemporary Traditional) or Scenario #2 (Humanistic Traditional) will be the prevailing mode in the next century, some surprising events along the way could enhance the likelihood of one of the other four scenarios becoming more probable. For example, if more funds were to be available to public education and more and better educational software for personal computers were also available, then Scenario #3 (Partial Technological Deschooling) might come into existence in a decade or so. Or, if some alternative to state and local funding of only public schools were to gain public endorsement, along with acceptance of the concept of "alternative schools," then Scenario #4 (in some form) would have a chance to emerge.

Scenario #5 (Experimental and/or Communal Schools) may become the case here and there, in one small community or another, but its widespread adoption is highly improbable. As for Scenario #6, short of social and cultural revolution, it will remain the romantic dream of an idealist.

NOTES

1. T. Sizer, *Horace's Compromise: The Dilemma of the American High School* (Boston: Houghton-Mifflin, 1984), pp. 5-6.

2. Sizer, op. cit., pp. 205-206.

3. R. Fox, et al., *School Climate Improvement* (Bloomington, IN: Phi Delta Kappa, 1974), pp. 7-12.

4. *Ibid.*, pp. 13-17.
5. I. Illich, *Deschooling Society* (New York: Harper & Row, 1970).
6. *Ibid.*, p. 78.
7. *Ibid.*, p. 79.
8. *Ibid.*
9. *Ibid.*

About the Editor

Joel L. Burdin brought to the planning of this book diverse perspectives and experiences. His graduate-level academic preparation was educational administration, heavily infused with curriculum. Sociology was his cognate area. He has taught on elementary and secondary, undergraduate and graduate levels, and has held administrative posts on those levels as well. His work has been in large and small, private and public institutions. On the national level he headed national association offices and federally funded projects.

As a writer, editor, and association official, Burdin has been exposed to the knowledge and thoughts of hundreds of key educators. He has sought to keep abreast of changing developments and conditions and has published analyses of those changes. As an alternative futurist, he has created images of likely conditions and developments which are likely to be important to educators. Without claiming success, he has committed himself to being a lifelong learner relative to past, present, and future and to ageless concepts of administration as well as current pressing social issues such as educational opportunity for all.

He earned an M.A. and Ed.D. from Michigan State University and has been a teacher, principal, and curriculum coordinator; professor of educational administration and program head; journal editor and ERIC clearinghouse director; associate director and executive secretary of national professional organizations. Until recently, he was professor of educational administration, City University of New York. In the past year he has been a UCEA visiting professor and has studied administrative practices in nontraditional settings.

NOTES

NOTES

NOTES